CONTINGENT FACULTY and the REMAKING of HIGHER EDUCATION

THE WORKING CLASS IN AMERICAN HISTORY

Editorial Advisors
James R. Barrett, Thavolia Glymph, Julie Greene,
William P. Jones, and Nelson Lichtenstein

A list of books in the series appears at the end of this book.

CONTINGENT FACULTY and the REMAKING of HIGHER EDUCATION

A Labor History

edited by
ERIC FURE-SLOCUM
& CLAIRE GOLDSTENE

UNIVERSITY OF ILLINOIS PRESS
Urbana, Chicago, and Springfield

Library of Congress Cataloging-in-Publication Data
Names: Fure-Slocum, Eric Jon, editor. | Goldstene, Claire, editor.
Title: Contingent faculty and the remaking of higher education : a
    labor history / edited by Eric Fure-Slocum & Claire Goldstene.
Description: Urbana : University of Illinois Press, 2024. | Series: The
    working class in American history | Includes bibliographical
    references and index.
Identifiers: LCCN 2023022310 (print) | LCCN 2023022311 (ebook) |
    ISBN 9780252045547 (cloth) | ISBN 9780252087653 (paperback)
    | ISBN 9780252055201 (ebook)
Subjects: LCSH: College teachers—Salaries, etc.—United States.
    | College teachers, Part-time—Salaries, etc.—United States.
    | College personnel management—United States. | College
    teachers' unions—United States. | Collective bargaining—College
    teachers—United States.
Classification: LCC LB2334 .C84 2024 (print) | LCC LB2334 (ebook) |
    DDC 378.1/20973—dc23/eng/20230606
LC record available at https://lccn.loc.gov/2023022310
LC ebook record available at https://lccn.loc.gov/2023022311

To our contingent faculty colleagues,
in appreciation of your commitment
to teaching, scholarship, and justice

CONTENTS

ACKNOWLEDGMENTS

The editors of this book first worked together during the founding of the Labor and Working-Class History Association (LAWCHA) contingent faculty committee. We are grateful to the members of this committee who continue to advocate for contingent faculty within the profession. Nancy MacLean, the president of LAWCHA who helped get the committee up and running, provided unwavering support, as have subsequent presidents and board members.

The contributors to this volume deserve our most hearty thanks, tolerating many requests and reminders amid the challenges of the COVID-19 pandemic, as they composed a set of significant and timely essays. In addition to those who appear in the table of contents, we thank other colleagues who participated at earlier stages of the project, especially A. Ricardo López-Pedreros, Julie Schmid, and Robin Sowards.

The initial idea for this book was hatched during conversations with James Engelhardt, then editor for the University of Illinois Press's "The Working Class in American History" series. Thanks for that initial spark. Since then, Alison Syring took on the role of series editor, offering her enthusiasm and superb guidance along the way. We are grateful, indeed, for the labors of skilled editors and others at the press who have helped produce this book, especially Megan Donnan, as well as the work of our copyeditor Marilyn Campbell and our indexer Sheila Hill. The anonymous reviewers and James Barrett read the manuscript with care and expertise, making this a stronger and more integrated volume. We also appreciated opportunities to present portions of this work to audiences at meetings of the

United Association for Labor Education, the Organization of American Historians (OAH), and LAWCHA.

Eric thanks the extraordinary group of non-tenure-track colleagues at St. Olaf College, including Diane Angell, Marc David, and Jeanne Willcoxon. Colin Wells, associate dean for the humanities and valued American Conversations coteacher, helped secure funds for the index. Chris Elias, Tim Howe, Linda K. Kerber, and Shelton Stromquist provided ongoing encouragement for this project. I also am grateful to have worked with the dedicated members of the OAH's contingent faculty committee. Finally, I am blessed to be part of a family that supports this work and, most importantly, with whom my ties are as far from contingent as imaginable. I am boundlessly grateful for Carolyn, for Anna, Eddie, and Zayah, for Jacob, Sid, and Georgia, and for the rest of our family.

Claire acknowledges her contingent faculty activist colleagues who have taught her so much, especially those with whom she served on the board of New Faculty Majority and the LAWCHA Contingent Faculty Committee. Paul N. Goldstene, Kate Keane, and Vicki Pearson-Rounds proved, as always, to be careful and thoughtful readers of various drafts of what ultimately became the final chapter of the book. James, Jami, Lily, and Beth have helped sustain me in all ways, as family does. My mother, Pat, continues to leave no doubt that she's on my side, for which I'm profoundly grateful, and, though my father, Paul, is unable to celebrate the culmination of this endeavor, he was a champion of this book and its cause.

FRAMING CONTINGENCY IN HIGHER EDUCATION

A LABOR HISTORY
OF CONTINGENT FACULTY

ERIC FURE-SLOCUM

Contingent Faculty in Higher Education

Contingent faculty are a fixture on the landscape of higher education today. Almost three-quarters of the people teaching in all two- and four-year colleges and universities in the United States are employed as contingent faculty, a reversal from the period just before the economic turmoil of the 1970s when three-quarters of the faculty held tenured or tenure-track positions. These tenure-stream positions came with a promise of job security as well as assurances of academic freedom for teachers and scholars. But today, precarious academic workers—ranging from course-by-course adjuncts to long-term contingent faculty to graduate student workers—fill the classrooms of universities, liberal arts colleges, community colleges, and for-profit institutions. Contingent faculty share worries and uncertainties that plague other workers in today's gig economy, including little to no job security, few if any healthcare benefits, insufficient retirement savings, and diminished professional status. Many adjuncts juggle multi-campus gigs, often without adequate teaching resources or support to remain active as scholars. Even basic tools for teaching and scholarship, including library access and offices in which to meet students or prepare classes, are unavailable to some contingent faculty members.

Contingent faculty, according to the US Government Accountability Office, are found throughout the higher education ecosystem. They make up "about 61.4 percent of the instructional positions at 4-year institutions, 83.5 percent at 2-year institutions, and 99.7 percent at for-profit institutions." In its survey of *nonprofit* colleges and universities, the American Association of University Professors (AAUP) reports that tenured faculty count for 26 percent and tenure-track faculty just over 10 percent of total positions. Part-time non-tenure-track (NTT) faculty constitute about 43 percent of the total and were the fastest growing sector during the first half of the 2010s. The full-time NTT group, now about 20 percent of the faculty, grew even faster in the years leading up to 2020. Graduate student workers, another part of the expanding contingent workforce that should be added to these statistics, amount to 13 percent of the faculty.[1]

This reliance on a "flexible" academic workforce means that low pay and instability—including tangible and intangible forms of professional loss—are ever-present in the daily lives of teachers and scholars. Pay ranges vary widely and are difficult to pin down, but inadequate compensation is a constant. Contingent faculty wages average slightly over $20,000 per year, falling below the federal poverty guidelines for a three-person household. Likewise, the average of $3,000 per course means that many adjuncts who teach course-by-course barely scrape by. Contingent faculty earn considerably less than their tenure-track and tenured colleagues. Wages are depressed even further by unethical schemes to redefine adjunct positions as internships, with no financial compensation at all. The disparities between adjuncts and high-paid college presidents or higher-level administrators are glaring, mirroring the inequities evident in corporate America and society more generally. As late as the end of the twentieth century, course-by-course contracts or one-year contracts had been viewed as steppingstones to permanent academic positions, or as apprenticeships. Now, just a few years on the non-tenure track can turn a scholar into "spoiled goods," no longer seen as competitive for tenure-track positions. After years of frustration on a deteriorating job market, growing numbers of scholars resign themselves to NTT careers.[2]

The reversal in the ratio of tenure stream to contingent faculty—coinciding with diminished government funding for education, the corporatization of higher education, and an explosion of student debt—represents a dramatic change in the structure of higher education, upending daily work lives in colleges and universities. Along with the ill effects on contingent faculty, this neoliberal transformation in higher education puts increased pressure on tenure-track and tenured faculty. These colleagues frequently carry increased administrative and service duties, as many adjuncts are shut out of shared governance and lack any real voice at the department or institutional level. As the number of precarious faculty rise, some tenure-stream faculty, especially those in universities facing funding crises and austerity measures, discover that professional privileges and even their presumed employment stability are threatened. Most importantly perhaps, especially for higher education's educational and intellectual missions, is the erosion of faculty autonomy and academic freedom—unattainable for NTTs who lack job security, which in turn weakens academic freedom for all. This occurs at a time when higher education faces increasing political scrutiny and cultural scorn. In attacks on public institutions, conservative legislators mount assaults against tenure and faculty autonomy.[3]

Despite adjuncts' devotion to their work as educators, students also are ill-served by these changes in higher education. The quality of teaching offered by contingent faculty members is often equal to, if not better, than that of their tenure-stream peers. Nevertheless, faculty instability discourages pedagogical innovation, undermines continuity in learning, hampers student-teacher relationships, and subverts the possibility of longer-term mentoring. Without adequate public funding, colleges and universities of all types have raised tuition and increased fees, while also turning to corporate dollars. Heavy student debt-loads and the infusion of market values have shifted what it means to be a student, as well as what it means to be a teacher-scholar. Education is measured by questionable return-on-investment (ROI) calculations, with students and their parents understandably shopping for a deal or buying into perceived status, rather than valuing education itself. Cost-cutting measures aimed at the heart of schools' educational work degrade faculty working conditions and tarnish the quality of a college degree. As students become consumers in this world of education retail, faculty become shop clerks, with adjuncts as the frontline discount store workers.[4]

The uncertainties inherent to contingent employment, as well as the false hopes and disappointments that accompany such unpredictability, have a palpable human cost. The immediate impact of this uncertainty is evident in the burgeoning "quit lit"—or more appropriately "driven-out lit"—authored by frustrated contingent faculty deciding to abandon academic careers, despite their significant investment of time in graduate training, forgone income, geographic relocation, and years devoted to teaching. For NTTs still inside the academy, their relations with administrators, colleagues, and students are shaped by the instability of contingency. Concerns about future teaching assignments hang over almost every interaction. And any interruption in work due to illness or a family emergency means not only lost pay but also the likelihood of lost employment. Like most private-sector workers in the United States, contingent faculty job insecurities are rooted in the doctrine of at-will employment, giving employers the power to dismiss workers without reason—except for provable discrimination—or without warning. For adjuncts, the grind of course-by-course renewals or one-year contracts serve to keep such job insecurity front and center.[5]

Along with employment and economic hardships, contingent faculty bear the daily burden and wear-and-tear of professional and personal disrespect—slights by tenure-stream colleagues, exclusion from decision-making, or the adjective "visiting" attached permanently to a job title, to name just a few. These are compounded by worries about academic failure, an insecurity perpetuated by the "meritocracy myth." Despite ample evidence that hardworking and talented scholar-teachers fill the contingent faculty ranks, the culture of higher education maintains that merit is rewarded, ignoring the skewed market for academic jobs that ensures that most candidates will be consigned to non-tenure-track jobs. The line between contingency and the tenure stream is drawn, in most cases, simply by luck and timing. But this boundary defines workplace interactions and professional opportunities that, in turn, reinforce the divergent paths. In the grip of this myth of meritocracy, adjuncts fall into self-blame, questioning their worthiness as academics and educators. Many other precarious workers who do low-paid manual labor or service jobs, of course, suffer far greater hardships and assaults on their dignity. Despite these differences, contingent faculty have much to learn from collective actions undertaken by these and other workers.[6]

Contingent faculty have responded to precarity with a range of actions—raising their voices to influence departmental and campus practices, urging professional organizations to recognize their plight, and organizing faculty unions to bargain collectively. At many colleges and universities, NTTs gather with their colleagues to petition faculty committees and campus decision makers, directing resources to support contingent faculty as teachers and scholars. These NTT groups also press for timely renewals that would allow adjuncts adequate time to plan courses or seek alternative employment and lobby for longer-term NTT contracts, policies now found in a growing number of faculty manuals. But because NTT leverage is limited without formal organization, progress against administrators' embrace of "flexibility" is stymied.

Contingent faculty call increasingly on professional associations to act in the face of an altered academic landscape. Priorities include reducing membership costs, opening conferences to greater contingent faculty participation, and reconfiguring organizational cultures to welcome contingent faculty and independent scholars. Some associations have created standing committees dedicated to these issues, surveyed their contingent faculty members to better understand needs, and outlined "best practices," promoting the use of these standards by departments in their disciplines. Others have dedicated board positions for contingent faculty and independent scholars, recognizing the salience of these members' concerns for the organization's structure and priorities and opening the door to wider participation. Progress is slow, but a wide range of disciplines are represented in these efforts, including the Modern Languages Association (MLA), Organization of American Historians (OAH), Labor and Working-Class History Association (LAWCHA), American Sociological Association, American Musicological Society, Society of Christian Ethics, and American Psychological Association.[7]

Most significant for adjuncts' immediate concerns and longer-term benefits are formal organizing campaigns to establish collective bargaining units on campus, notable especially at a time when union density in many industries has sharply dropped. This is the most effective response for those without the protection of tenure, facing the volatility of at-will employment. For public university workers, unions serve the purpose of both collective bargaining and developing a public voice. Labor unions active in organizing adjuncts in the United States include the AAUP, the Service Employees International Union (SEIU) and their Faculty Forward campaign, the United Auto Workers (UAW), the United Steelworkers (USW), the Communications Workers of America (CWA), the American Federation of Teachers (AFT), and the National Education Association (NEA). Advocacy organizations and initiatives such as the Coalition of Contingent Academic Labor, New Faculty Majority, Higher Education Labor United, and New Deal for Higher Education provide important resources in this movement. Contingent faculty have worked with labor unions to build metro-area organizing campaigns, to form collective bargaining units on campuses throughout the country, and to experiment with "one union" strategies that bring tenured and contingent faculty into a single bargaining unit. Labor scholar William A. Herbert documents a notable increase in the number of contingent faculty covered by collective bargaining agreements, especially during periods with a receptive National Labor Relations Board (NLRB).[8]

Organizing begins, of course, at the grassroots, with contingent faculty talking and acting together. But the legal and administrative landscape configures faculty collective bargaining options. In the United States, the NLRB has jurisdiction over labor organizing at private nonprofit colleges and universities. The Supreme Court's 1980 decision in *NLRB v. Yeshiva University* ruled that tenure-stream faculty were exempt from National Labor Relations Act protections because of the managerial roles they play, stalling faculty unions in these private institutions. The *NLRB v. Catholic Bishop of Chicago* (1979) decision, deeming NLRB oversight as religious interference, hindered faculty organizing at religiously affiliated institutions. Together, these decisions provided the background for the NLRB's 2014 ruling when administrators at Pacific Lutheran University tried to prevent adjuncts from unionizing. In that case, the NLRB determined that neither the management nor the religious exemptions applied to the college's contingent faculty. As the NLRB membership shifted under the Trump administration and as college and university leaders tried to counter growing contingent faculty organizing, this ruling was revisited and narrowed with stricter tests about faculty managerial roles. With a shift back to a Democratic-majority NLRB during the Biden administration, the space for adjunct and faculty organizing has again opened. The legal terrain for graduate worker organizing at private, nonprofit universities has also shifted back and forth, largely over whether graduate assistants' work can be distinguished from their role as students, determining if they are employees with the right to organize.[9]

Contingent faculty, tenure stream faculty, and graduate worker organizing has been most successful at public universities and colleges, both two- and four-year institutions. For public institutions, state laws govern organizing and collective bargaining, shaping what is possible. State laws regarding public employees, however, vary widely. In many states—especially in the Northeast, areas of the Midwest, and West Coast—laws are based on the NLRA and protect the right to form unions and bargain collectively. However, organizing and sustaining a union is more difficult in the growing number of "right to work" states, in which individual employees can opt out of union membership. Other states restrict the scope of collective bargaining or prohibit specific labor activities (e.g., strikes) by public employees. Nevertheless, contingent faculty and graduate worker unions—along with informal campus groups and professional association committees—have helped to build power and raised public awareness about the alarming growth of contingency in higher education. Precarity persists, but the costs of "flexibility" and the two-tiered system in higher education are becoming increasingly evident.[10]

Collecting a Labor History of Contingent Faculty

Contingent Faculty and the Remaking of Higher Education uses the tools of labor history to examine how structural changes have heightened contingency in colleges and universities and how this precarity has shaped day-to-day faculty experiences in the academic workplace. The book also asks what contingent faculty have done, especially through collective action, to resist these changes, improve working conditions, and reform higher education. The variety of contributors' experiences drives home the complexity of these histories, making clear that not only institutional differences but the dynamics of gender, race, class, ability, and generation shape the possibilities and the constraints in these accounts. As an interdisciplinary endeavor that invites scholars of varying ranks and positions (from contingent faculty to tenure-stream faculty to organizers and activists) and a range of types of institutions (from research universities to small colleges), this collection of essays investigates precarious academic labor and efforts to improve contingent faculty work, as well as the workplaces that serve students and society.

Writing about contingent faculty has flourished in recent years. Articles chronicling the adjunct's plight appear in newspapers and popular magazines such as the *Atlantic* and the *New Yorker*, as well as widely circulated higher education publications such as the *Chronicle of Higher Education* and *Inside Higher Ed*.[11] In more specialized academic journals, scholars analyze the impact of contingency on institutional structure, teaching, and scholarly life.[12] The past two decades have also seen a stream of book-length accounts and studies. A handful of these address contingency in higher education broadly, but most focus on specific aspects of this phenomenon, including union organizing, labor management, and pedagogy.[13] Even novelists, some of whom are adjuncts plying a new craft, find grist for their fiction in contingent faculty tales.[14]

This volume builds on the work of writers and activists who study precarity in higher education while recognizing that contingency is neither confined to academia nor harshest for those who are privileged to engage in academic work. Scholars and activists who attend to contingency in other sectors of the economy and precarious work around the globe provide a broader perspective for understanding changes in academia. Historian Louis Hyman and sociologist Erin Hatton chart the development of "temp" work in the United States, exploring how it became a catalyst for a wide-spread decay of job stability that corresponded to employers' insistence on flexibility in the later twentieth century and early twenty-first century. According to Hyman, women who filled postwar temp jobs and migrant workers—two groups of "people who were left out of the good postwar jobs"—were on the front lines of the trend toward outsourcing and employment precarity.[15] This, in turn, is one part of the explanation for declining union membership in the United States. Historians and social scientists also research the work and lives of migrant workers, gig workers, temps, and other precarious laborers globally, many of whom face difficult conditions. In the Global South, but also within the borders of the United States, the most precarious workers face especially brutal working conditions and violent consequences when they resist, either individually or collectively. Although these studies feature struggles of a different magnitude than those faced by academic adjuncts and other white-collar contingent workers, they provide models for analyzing the management and control of labor and underscore the ongoing changes in higher education that stem from transformations in the global political economy. They also suggest that contingent faculty should pay close attention to the collective actions undertaken by precarious workers in various sectors of the economy and build bridges to other workers to launch broader demands for employment security and better compensation.[16]

Scholars and activists contributing to *Contingent Faculty and the Remaking of Higher Education* examine the causes and consequences of increasingly precarious employment for faculty, along with the robust resistance to these trends. By bringing together historical inquiries of higher education, structural analyses of employment patterns, meditations on adjuncts' everyday experiences, and essays documenting resistance and organizing, this volume illuminates manifold dimensions of the historic shift to a contingent faculty majority. The book considers how contingency marginalizes teachers and scholars, degrades academic work, impinges on students' education, and threatens even tenured faculty members' security—all in the name of flexibility, austerity, and innovation. These essays grapple as well with the gender, racial, and class inequities that permeate this history and contemporary challenges. Contingent faculty efforts to organize and improve their conditions, while up against daunting odds, hold the potential to address job grievances, bolster academic workers' security, contest the relentless corporatization of the university, and bolster the proposition that education ought to be designed and funded to serve a broad public purpose.

As the title indicates, this volume turns to labor history to study contingent faculty. Individual contributors deploy a range of disciplinary approaches to examine the history and contemporary scenes of contingency, casting a critical gaze at higher education institutions as contested sites of labor. Taken together as a labor history, these essays advance our understanding of contingent work, workers, and workplaces: first, by attending to the historical context and political economy of contingency; second, by recounting the experiences of contingent workers in higher education workplaces; and third, by investigating collective actions undertaken to challenge precarity and build power. Following two essays that frame the collection, arguing that contingency is no longer peripheral but central to higher education, the collection is divided into three main sections, distinct yet overlapping. Each of these sections begins with a brief story that emphasizes paying attention to both the fine-grained details of individual contingent faculty experiences and the larger patterns of these histories.

Part I focuses on "The Making of a Contingent Faculty Majority," with essays that probe the political economy of higher education, the industry's role in modern capitalism, and shifting employment patterns. Grounded in historical and sociological analysis, as well as institutional data about higher education faculty, these essays provide an essential basis for the chapters that follow. This section, informed by histories of capitalism and the social construction of labor, includes chapters on the business of higher education and the management of academic labor; the relationship between the rise of contingency and formation of neoliberal academic capitalism; the correspondence between increasing rates of contingency and a more diverse faculty; and the rising rates of contingency at different types of institutions (public, private, community college). These historical accounts differ in timing and interpretations of how market values shaped higher education. Some emphasize continuity in higher education since colonial times in the United States, with institutions built by business-driven calculations, unstable faculty employment, persistent student debt, and inadequate public support defining this history. Others see a decisive shift beginning in the last quarter of the twentieth century to a neoliberal university, marked by contracting public support, rising percentages of contingent faculty, widespread use of austerity policies, and a cultural shift in which market values redefined education's purpose.[17] Despite differing interpretations, essays in this and other sections of the volume make clear that the contemporary academic labor force, although always in flux, is molded by the politics of austerity and deliberate budgetary choices, not pedagogical imperatives.

Part II, built around the theme "Contingency at Work and in the Workplace," delves into the everyday frictions experienced by contingent faculty in the class-rooms and hallways of colleges and universities. These essays provide both indi-vidual and group accounts about the experience of being precariously employed and marginalized in the academic workplace, while also assessing the ramifica-tions of this precarity in both the humanities and STEM fields. Chapters also ex-amine the intersection of multiple identities (including gender, race, generation, and ability) embedded in the contingent experience; the coercion of graduate student labor in the sciences; actions by administrators and, too often, tenure-stream faculty that prop up a multitiered system of faculty labor; and the effect of contingency on students and educational quality.

Part III, "Challenging Precarity and Contingency in Higher Education," charts efforts by contingent faculty and their allies to respond collectively to the griev-ances and injustices of contingency through advocacy and union organizing. Con-tributors outline the larger patterns of collective action, while also asking about the successes and shortcomings of specific organizing campaigns. This section includes essays that explore faculty union composition (i.e., separate or combined units of contingent and tenure-stream faculty); organizing strategies and collective bargaining outcomes in a range of settings; appraisals of union effectiveness in blunting the decline of tenure-track jobs; graduate student organizing campaigns; and international dimensions of contingency and organizing, with a UK case. The collection concludes with two essays that offer "Paths Forward for Academic Labor and Higher Education"—calling for faculty solidarity, with tenured faculty supporting non-tenure-track colleagues' efforts, and recognition that the isola-tion of contingency harms all faculty, threatens academic freedom, and endangers education's public purpose. Throughout the volume, authors share in the endeavor of scholar activism.

As a collection, *Contingent Faculty and the Remaking of Higher Education* directs at-tention to a form of academic labor that now has become prevalent in college and university classrooms and yet continues to be defined as aberrant. We feature the term "contingent faculty" in the book's title and many of the essays. "Contingency" points directly to the instability of these positions; "faculty" makes clear that this work is central to higher education's teaching and scholarly mission. "Contingent faculty" also signifies a broad category of academic workers outside the tenure stream, similar to the frequently used term non-tenure-track faculty, or NTTs, which stresses, however, the absence of an employment status. Another com-mon term, "adjunct," refers especially to shorter-term appointments, but often is applied broadly. While favoring "contingent faculty," we do not use this exclusively in the volume, for both practical and strategic reasons. Labels given to the academic workers who are the subject of and contributors to this book vary from campus to campus and even within campuses. For individual faculty members, these labels can shift from semester to semester or from job to job as they commute between campuses. Whereas tenure-stream faculty have a comprehensible set of titles (i.e., assistant, associate, and full professor), the proliferation of labels for contingent faculty is staggering. One study cataloged two dozen different titles—from adjuncts to lecturers to instructors to professors of practice to acting faculty.[18] And that list does not even include the ubiquitous tag attached to course offerings: "staff." This variety creates confusion and obfuscation, complicating the counting of contingent faculty. Nevertheless, each label speaks to the precarity of employment for a growing cohort of academic workers.[19]

So, while readers will encounter a range of labels for contingent faculty, the project of bringing these varied essays under one cover is part of the larger endeavor to comprehend the challenges of contingency in higher education. The contributions to this volume situate the increasing reliance on contingent faculty in a broad framework of precarious work, with academics as workers at the center.

COVID-19 and Contingency

This book was planned before the pandemic of 2020–2022 emerged, but our emails requesting essays landed in contributors' inboxes just as COVID-19 spread rapidly and nonessential workplaces shut down. The impact of the pandemic has been profound, of course, killing millions worldwide, exhausting frontline workers, and wreaking havoc in the economy. The pandemic also touched this book, directly and indirectly. Contributors wrote under the strain of worry, as family members or colleagues fell ill. Others juggled writing and the unexpected burden of teaching online. Others lost their jobs, saw prospects of stable employment fade even further, or waited nervously for delayed contracts, as colleges and universities slashed classes. Heavier teaching loads, intensified uncertainty, and job losses defined a new low for contingent faculty. While as historians we refrain from predicting the extent of the pandemic's impact on higher education, the effects of illness, economic turmoil, and institutional restructuring widened existing inequities along racial, class, and gender lines on campuses, in communities, and globally, compounding longer-standing trends that the Great Recession already had accelerated. We have little doubt that the instability characterizing the contingent faculty experience will become even more entrenched in higher education in the future.[20] The need for this book—along with other efforts to understand and push against contingency in contemporary work and life—is even more urgent.

Notes

1. US Government Accountability Office, *Contingent Workforce: Size, Characteristics, Compensation, and Work Experiences of Adjunct and Other Non-Tenure-Track Faculty* (October 2017), 10–11; Colleen Flaherty, "A Non-Tenure Track Profession?," *Inside Higher Ed* [hereafter *IHE*], October 12, 2018, https://www.insidehighered.com/news/2018/10/12/about-three -quarters-all-faculty-positions-are-tenure-track-according-new-aaup; Kathryn Q. Thirolf and Rebekah S. Woods, "Contingent Faculty at Community Colleges: The Too-Often Overlooked and Under-Engaged Faculty Majority," *New Directions in Institutional Research* 176 (2018): 55–66; American Association of University Professors (AAUP), *The Annual Report on the Economic Status of the Profession, 2020–21* (July 2021), 13–15; A. J. Angulo, "From Golden Era to Gig Economy: Changing Contexts for Academic Labor in America," in *Professors in the Gig Economy: Unionizing Adjunct Faculty in America*, ed. Kim Tolley (Baltimore: Johns Hopkins University Press, 2018), 3–26; Adrianna Kezar, Tom DePaola, and Daniel T. Scott, *The Gig Academy: Mapping Labor in the Neoliberal University* (Baltimore: Johns Hopkins University Press, 2019); TIAA Institute, "Adjunct Faculty: Who They Are and What Is Their Experience?," *Trends and Issues*, November 2018, https:// www.tiaainstitute.org/sites/default/files/presentations/2018-10/TIAA%20Institute _2018%20Adjunct%20Faculty%20Survey_November%202018.pdf; National Center for Education Statistics, "Characteristics of Postsecondary Faculty," updated May 2020, https://nces.ed.gov/programs/coe/indicator_csc.asp; Doug Lederman, "Federal Data Show the Proportion of Instructors Who Work Full-Time Is Rising," *IHE*, November 27, 2019, https://www.insidehighered.com/news/2019/11/27/federal-data-show-proportion -instructors-who-work-full-time-rising. As seen throughout this volume, tallies of contingent faculty vary, depending on period and institutions covered. All agree, however, that they now constitute a supermajority of the faculty.

2. American Federation of Teachers, *An Army of Temps: AFT 2020 Adjunct Faculty Quality of Work/Life Report* (2020); Carolyn Betensky, "Exclusion of NTT Faculty from Scholarly Research and Funding," *AAUP Academe Blog*, October 23, 2019, https://academeblog.org/ 2019/10/23/exclusion-of-ntt-faculty-from-scholarly-research-and-travel-funding/; Herb Childress, *The Adjunct Underclass: How America's Colleges Betrayed Their Faculty, Their Students, and Their Mission* (Chicago: University of Chicago Press, 2019); Daniel Davis, "Contingent Faculty Compromise," *IHE*, August 28, 2019, https://www.insidehighered.com/ views/2019/08/28/we-need-new-approach-contingent-faculty-pay-opinion; Joanna R. Frye, "Organizational Pressures Driving the Growth of Contingent Faculty," *New Directions for Institutional Research* 176 (2018): 27–39; Anemona Hartocollis, "Help Wanted: Adjunct Professor, Must Have Doctorate. Salary: $0," *New York Times*, April 6, 2022; Laura McKenna, "The College President-to-Adjunct Pay Ratio," *Atlantic*, September 24, 2015, https://www.theatlantic.com/education/archive/2015/09/income-inequality-in-higher -education-the-college-president-to-adjunct-pay-ratio/407029/.

3. Claire Goldstene, "The Politics of Contingent Academic Labor," *Thought and Action: The NEA Higher Education Journal* (Fall 2012): 7–15; Aaron Hanlon, "The University Is a Ticking Time Bomb," *Chronicle of Higher Education* [hereafter *CHE*], 65:13 (April 2019): B4–B5; Nicole Monnier, "'One Faculty' and Academic Governance," *Academe* (May-June 2017): 25–28;

Henry Reichman, "Do Adjuncts Have Academic Freedom? Or Why Tenure Matters," *Academe* (Winter 2021): 32–40; Henry Reichman, "Statement on the Iowa Legislature's Threats to Academic Freedom and Tenure," *AAUP Updates*, March 4, 2021, https://www.aaup.org/news/statement-iowa-legislatures-threats-academic-freedom-and-tenure#.YEpQkZ1Kg2x; Eva Swidler, "Can the Adjunct Speak?," *Academe* (September-October 2016): 34–37.

4. Dan Berrett, "Adjuncts Are Better Teachers Than Tenured Professors, Study Finds," *CHE*, September 9, 2013, https://www.chronicle.com/article/ad-juncts-are-bet-ter-teachers-than-tenured-professors-study-finds/; Adrianna Kezar and Daniel Maxey, "Student Outcomes Assessment among the New Non-Tenure-Track Faculty Majority," Occasional Paper #21, National Institute for Learning Outcomes Assessment (July 2014), www.learningoutcomesassessment.org/wp-content/uploads/2019/02/OccasionalPaper21.pdf; Lance Thurner, "Adjuncts and Excellence in Teaching," *The American Historian* (September 2021): 12–15; Rachel Bonaparte, "Investing in Part-Time Faculty Success Supports Student Success," *IHE*, April 1, 2022, https://www.insidehighered.com/advice/2022/04/01/colleges-must-support-adjuncts-order-support-students-opinion; Elizabeth Tandy Shermer, *Indentured Students: How Government-Guaranteed Loans Left Generations Drowning in College Debt* (Cambridge, MA: Harvard University Press, 2021).

5. Erin Bartram, "The Sublimated Grief of the Left Behind," *Doomed to Distraction* blog, February 11, 2018, http://erinbartram.com/uncategorized/the-sublimated-grief-of-the-left-behind/; Colleen Flaherty, "Historians' 'Quit Lit' Essay Rejects Notion That Leaving Higher Ed Equals Personal Failure," *IHE*, February 13, 2018, https://www.insidehighered.com/news/2018/02/13/historians-quit-lit-essay-rejects-notion-leaving-higher-ed-equals-personal-failure; Linda K. Kerber, "We Must Make the Academic Workplace More Humane and Equitable," *CHE*, March 18, 2005, B6–9; Diane Mendoza Nevárez, "UC Churns Through a Quarter of Its Lecturers a Year," *Los Angeles Times*, November 9, 2021; Catherine M. Young, "Netflix Announces New Series 'The Adjunct,' as Follow-up to 'The Chair,'" *Academe Blog*, September 17, 2021, https://academeblog.org/2021/09/17/netflix-announces-new-series-the-adjunct-as-follow-up-to-the-chair/. On private-sector at-will employment, see Nelson Lichtenstein, *State of the Union: A Century of American Labor*, rev. ed. (Princeton, NJ: Princeton University Press, 2002), 2–3.

6. On meritocracy and steppingstone mythology, see Part II of this collection; Matthew J. Gaudet, "Toward an Inclusive Faculty Community," *Journal of Moral Theology* 8:1 (2019): 147–153; Michael J. Sandel, *The Tyranny of Merit* (New York: Farrar, Straus and Giroux, 2020), 17–29.

7. Committee on Contingent Labor in the Profession, MLA, https://www.mla.org/About-Us/Governance/Committees/Committee-Listings/Professional-Issues/Committee-on-Contingent-Labor-in-the-Profession; Committee on Part-Time, Adjunct, and Contingent Employment, OAH, https://www.oah.org/insights/archive/standards-for-part-time-adjunct-and-contingent-faculty/; Contingent Faculty Committee, LAWCHA, https://www.lawcha.org/committee-portal/contingent-faculty/.

8. William A. Herbert, Jacob Apkarian, and Joseph van der Naald, *2020 Supplementary Directory of New Bargaining Agents and Contracts in Institutions of Higher Education, 2013–2019* (New York: National Center for the Study of Collective Bargaining in Higher Education and the Professions, 2020); William A. Herbert, "The Winds of Changes Shift: An Analysis

of Recent Growth in Bargaining Units and Representation Efforts in Higher Education," *Journal of Collective Bargaining in the Academy* 8 (December 2016), https://thekeep.eiu.edu/cgi/viewcontent.cgi?article=1647&context=jcba; Mia McIver and Trevor Griffey, "A New Deal for College Teachers and Teaching," *Academe* (Spring 2021): 48–52; Christian A. I. Schlaerth, "Adjuncts Unite! The Struggle to Unionize, Administrative Response, and Building a Bigger Movement," *Labor Studies Journal* 47:1 (2022): 5–27. On Canada and the UK see: Frank Cosco, "Building Job Security in Community College Faculty Work: Experiences in British Columbia," *LAWCHA LaborOnline*, November 6, 2017, https://www.lawcha.org/2017/11/06/building-job-security-community-college-faculty-work-experiences-british-columbia/; Steven Parfitt, "Academic Casualization in the UK," *International Labor and Working-Class History* 93 (Spring 2018): 221–227; and Parfitt's essay in this collection.

9. Gregory Saltzman, "Union Organizing and the Law: Contingent Faculty and Graduate Student Assistants," in *Professors in the Gig Economy*, ed. Tolley, 69–84; William A. Herbert, "A New Morning in Higher Education Collective Bargaining, 2013–2019," *CUNY Academic Works* (2021), https://academicworks.cuny.edu/hc_pubs/688/; Joseph A. McCartin, "Confronting the Labor Problem in Catholic Higher Education: Applying Catholic Social Teaching in an Age of Increasing Inequality," *Journal of Catholic Higher Education* 37:1 (2018): 71–88; Colleen Flaherty, "'Tweaking' Which Adjuncts Can Form Unions," *IHE*, February 25, 2021, https://www.insidehighered.com/news/2021/02/25/nlrb-ruling-potentially-limits-which-adjuncts-can-form-unions; Risa Lieberwitz and Nancy Long, "The Status of Graduate Assistant Organizing," *Academe* (Winter 2020): 64.

10. Joe Berry and Helena Worthen, *Power Despite Precarity: Strategies for the Contingent Faculty Movement in Higher Education* (London: Pluto Press, 2021), 198–209; Bob Hutton, "One Big Orange Union: Faculty-Staff Organizing in a Right to Work State," *LAWCHA LaborOnline*, October 19, 2017, https://www.lawcha.org/2017/10/19/one-big-orange-union-faculty-staff-organizing-right-work-state/.

11. Adam Harris, "The Death of an Adjunct," *Atlantic*, April 8, 2018, https://www.theatlantic.com/education/archive/2019/04/adjunct-professors-higher-education-thea-hunter/586168/; Hua Hsu, "The Professor and the Adjunct," *New Yorker,* April 10, 2019, https://www.newyorker.com/books/under-review/the-professor-and-the-adjunct; James Rushing Daniel, "The Cruelty of Faculty Churn," *CHE* 69:7 (November 2022): 11; Adrianna Kezar, "Hope for Faculty Off the Tenure Track?" *IHE*, May 27, 2019, https://www.insidehighered.com/views/2019/05/28/institutions-should-learn-some-good-examples-how-support-adjunct-faculty-opinion.

12. *New Directions in Institutional Research* 176 (2018); *Journal of Moral Theology* 8:1 (2019); *Working USA (Journal of Labor & Society)* 18:3 (2015); George Towers, "The Precarious Plight of American Working-Class Faculty: Causes and Consequences," *Journal of Working-Class Studies* 4:1 (2019): 98–115; Robin Zheng, "Precarity as a Feminist Issue: Gender and Contingent Labor in the Academy," *Hypatia* 33:2 (2018): 235–255; and Alexandra Bradner, "The Cruelty of the Adjunct System," *Issues in Philosophy*, April 13, 2022, https://blog.apaonline.org/2022/04/13/the-cruelty-of-the-adjunct-system/.

13. Joe Berry, *Reclaiming the Ivory Tower: Organizing Adjuncts to Change Higher Education* (New York: Monthly Review Press, 2005); Marc Bousquet, *How the University Works: Higher Education and the Low-Wage Worker* (New York: New York University Press, 2008); Childress, *The*

Adjunct Underclass; Natalie M. Dorfeld, ed., *The Invisible Professor: The Precarious Lives of the New Faculty Majority* (Fort Collins: WAC Clearinghouse and University Press of Colorado, 2022); Kezar, DePaola, and Scott, *The Gig Academy*; Ishmael I. Munene, ed., *Contextualizing and Organizing Contingent Faculty: Reclaiming Academic Labor in Universities* (Lanham, MD: Lexington Books, 2018); Tolley, ed., *Professors in the Gig Economy*. For an overview, see Charles Peterson, "Serfs of Academe," *New York Review of Books*, March 12, 2020, 42–45.

14. James Hynes, *The Lecturer's Tale* (New York: Picador, USA, 2001); Alex Kudera, *Fight for Your Long Day* (New York: Hard Ball Press, 2016); Christine Smallwood, *The Life of the Mind* (New York: Hogarth, 2021).

15. Louis Hyman, *Temp: How American Work, American Business, and the American Dream Became Temporary* (New York: Viking, 2018), 13; Erin Hatton, *The Temp Economy: From Kelly Girls to Permatemps in Postwar America* (Philadelphia: Temple University Press, 2011); Juliet B. Schor et al., *After the Gig: How the Sharing Economy Got Hijacked and How to Win It Back* (Oakland: University of California Press, 2020); Guy Standing, *The Precariat: The New Dangerous Class* (London: Bloomsbury, 2011).

16. On precarious labor in the Global South and North—from manual laborers, to call center workers, to Uber drivers, see Marcel van der Linden, "San Precario: A New Inspiration for Labor Historians," *Labor: Studies in Working-Class History of the Americas* 11:1 (Spring 2014): 9–21; Cindy Hahamovitch, *No Man's Land: Jamaican Guestworkers in America and the Global History of Deportable Labor* (Princeton, NJ: Princeton University Press, 2011); Sarah Mosoetsa, Joel Stillerman, and Chris Tilly, eds., "Special Issue on Precarious Labor in Global Perspectives," *International Labor and Working-Class History* 89 (Spring 2016): 5–152.

17. See essays in this collection and Elizabeth Tandy Shermer, "What's Really New about the Neoliberal University? The Business of American Education Has Always Been Business," *Labor* 18:4 (December 2021): 62–86 (with responses). See also Gary Gerstle, *The Rise and Fall of the Neoliberal Order: America and the World in the Free Market Era* (New York: Oxford University Press, 2022).

18. John G. Cross and Edie N. Goldberg, *Off-Track Profs: Nontenured Teachers in Higher Education* (Cambridge, MA: MIT Press, 2009), 19–25; Thomas A. Discenna, *Discourses of Denial: The Rhetoric of American Academic Labor* (New York: Routledge, 2018), 109–113.

19. On "staff," see Steve Street, Maria Maisto, Esther Merves, and Gary Rhoades, "Who Is Professor 'Staff': And How Can This Person Teach So Many Classes," Center for the Future of Higher Education Policy Report #2, August 2012, https://www.insidehighered.com/sites/default/server_files/files/profstaff(2).pdf.

20. Molly Ball, "Contingency in an Expanded Crisis: Lessons from the Past to Build a Better Future," *The American Historian* (December 2021) 8–10; Colleen Flaherty, "From Bad to Worse," *IHE*, February 24, 2022, https://www.insidehighered.com/news/2022/02/24/survey-adjuncts-finds-pandemic-made-their-situation-worse; Julie Greene, "Rethinking the Boundaries of Class: Labor History and Theories of Class and Capitalism," *Labor* 18:2 (2021): 92–112; Trevor Griffey, "Lecturer Organizing and COVID-19," *LAWCHA LaborOnline*, July 21, 2020, https://www.lawcha.org/2020/07/21/lecturer-organizing-and-covid-19/; Annelise Orleck, "And the Virus Rages On: 'Contingent' and 'Essential' Workers in the Time of COVID-19," *International Labor and Working-Class History* 99 (Spring 2021): 1–14.

CHAPTER 1

FROM THE MARGINS
TO THE CENTER

Negotiating a New Academy

GARY RHOADES

Speaking at a November 2013 Faculty Forward launch in Los Angeles of a metro campaign to organize adjunct and (full-time) contingent faculty, I offered three observations. First, invoking the term "adjunct," which part-time faculty have taken ownership of, I asserted that although part-time faculty members are treated as "adjunct" (i.e., auxiliary) by management and (too often) by tenure-track faculty, "You are not 'adjunct' to your students and to their education; you are central to them." Second, noting the "new faculty majority" of part- and full-time contingent faculty in higher education, now roughly two-thirds of the instructional workforce, I quoted Thomas Paine's *Common Sense*: "There is something very absurd in supposing a continent to be perpetually governed by an island. In no instance hath nature made the satellite larger than its primary planet."[1] Finally, I stated that these low-wage members of the instructional workforce were in the academic labor movement's vanguard. Each of these observations remains true a decade later.

Contingent faculty have not always been central players in either the academy or in academic unionization. Quite the opposite has been true. Some sustained contingent faculty organizing around collective bargaining dates back to the 1960s and early 1970s, and even in non-CB locals prior to enabling state legislation for collective bargaining going back to short-lived and intermittent organizing of locals in the 1910s, 1920s, 1930s, and 1940s.[2] But contingent faculty organizing in their own bargaining units has proliferated in the 2000s, as it has with graduate student and postdoc employees. And these marginalized academic employees are now at the center of negotiating a new academy.

In this chapter, I review the past half century of growth in contingent faculty, as well as of graduate student and postdoctoral workers, relating these trends to the surge of academic organizing in the 2000s. The storyline is of a systematic increase of employees who were previously on the margins numerically and percentage-wise, and who in the twenty-first century have moved to the center of the academic labor movement. Part of the plotline speaks to how contingent employment has grown both in broader society and as part of ascendant neoliberal policies and organizational logics in higher education, called "academic capitalism."[3] This has meant fewer tenure-stream faculty positions available for growing numbers of contingent faculty, graduate student employees, and postdocs who desire them. The narrative weaves together personal accounts borne of my connections to the academic labor movement alongside (my and others') scholarly work.

A further fleshing out of the narrative embodies these long-term, large-scale trend lines in employees' identities. Declining opportunities for tenure-stream positions at the top of the academic ladder and the growth of contingent positions at the bottom have been taking place at the same time as (slightly) increasing percentages of women, Black, Indigenous, and people of color (BIPOC) and international students have gained the certification necessary to become tenure-track faculty. The structural disjuncture between credentials, aspirations, and more secure tenure-track positions, then, is part of a classed, racialized, and gendered occupational restructuring and reduction of opportunity.[4] This disjuncture and restructuring is also shaped by national origin.[5]

The above patterns lay the foundation for understanding how contingent (and graduate and postdoc) academic employees have in the 2000s creatively and aggressively negotiated a new academy. They are organizing new bargaining units and in these, as well as organizing contract campaigns, they have foregrounded negotiations that address the pressing demands of the labor movement and of other social movements of the day. These include just employment and common good concerns—public interest issues that resonate broadly with members and that impact local and wider communities. They also include issues featured in identity-based movements driven by marginalized populations. More than simply an increase in numbers, the growing activism of contingent academic employees has triggered creative organizing and shifted those who are marginalized by their employment status and demographics to the center of reshaping higher education, offering possible paths to a more transformative academy. There are, then, embodied, embedded layers to both the marginalization and the "centering" of contingent faculty in organizing.

Setting the Stage for a Surge in Organizing: The Growth of Academic Contingent Labor

From the end of the 1970s to the second decade of the 2000s, contingent faculty steadily shifted from the margins to the center of the academic workforce. Indeed, the proportions have reversed. In 1979, roughly one-third of instructional faculty were part-time, and nearly two-thirds tenure stream. By 2013, less than one-third of faculty were tenure stream, and the percentage of part-time faculty had increased to roughly one-half, with the remaining being full-time contingent faculty.[6] If we look back to the early 1970s, the shift was even more dramatic, as part-time faculty then accounted for one-quarter of the instructional workforce.[7]

In every institutional type of not-for-profit higher education there were major increases in part-time faculty percentages. By 2013, part-time faculty were central players in the instructional workforce of all private and public institutional types—at 68.5 and 70.1 percent in private and public two-year institutions respectively, 57.2 and 44.9 percent of "other four-year institutions," and 45.3 and 29.1 percent of private and public research universities.[8]

Factoring in the steady and substantial growth of full-time non-tenure-track faculty makes the pattern even more stark. The proportions of these faculty rose by roughly 50 percent from 1970 to 2013. Moreover, in public and private universities, which have the lowest proportions of part-time faculty, the proportions of full-time contingent faculty increased the most, to roughly one-fifth of all faculty. That brought the total percentage of non-tenure-track faculty to just over one-half in public and to roughly two-thirds in private universities. Indeed, by 2013, 56 percent of new full-time hires were full-time, non-tenure-track faculty.

The demographics underlying these employment patterns are important indicators of stratification of access to tenure-track positions for women and faculty of color. There have been gains in the representation of female-identified faculty in every institutional type, except four-year for-profit institutions.[9] Yet, most female-identified faculty are in part-time positions (56.1 percent in 2013, versus 48.2 percent in 1993). Among female-identified full-time faculty, the largest proportion (44.3 percent) are non-tenure-track, up from 35.5 percent in 1993.[10]

Similar social stratification exists for underserved minority faculty. There has been some increased representation of these faculty over time, though percentages remain quite small. In 2013, 12.7 percent of all faculty were from "underrepresented" racial minorities, plus 6.4 percent Asian or Pacific Islander, up from 8.6 and 3.9 percent two decades earlier.[11] The greatest growth and representation has been among part-time faculty—of all underrepresented racial minority faculty, 58 percent are in part-time positions (another 17 percent are in full-time contingent positions).[12]

During this time, as a share of the instructional workforce, graduate assistants remained steady. But the demographics of graduate students broadened substantially from the 1970s to 2010. That included significant growth in the proportions of women among graduate students, and at least a doubling of the percentage shares of each underserved minority group.

A key consideration here is the relative decline in the proportion of full-time tenure-track faculty positions at just the time the numbers of women and graduate students of color were increasing. Even in better-resourced science, technology, engineering, and mathematics (STEM) fields, relatively few women and graduate students of color have secured tenure-track positions—by one count only one in four obtain such a position.[13] All of this translates into greater percentages of women and people of color in postdoc, adjunct, and full-time non-tenure-track faculty positions.

One of the outlets for this supply of graduate students seeking faculty positions was postdocs. In the early 1980s, when such positions emerged, particularly in STEM fields, as another step on the academic ladder, 18.6 percent of the graduating PhD cohort took postdocs.[14] By 2000, that figure was almost one-third.[15] Such positions proliferated in the 2000s, and postdocs became a key predictor of external research monies.[16] The demographic diversity of postdocs diverged from that of graduate student employees, however, as larger proportions of postdocs were international students, and smaller proportions were women.

Academic Capitalism—Beyond Disembodied Labor and Management

The employment restructuring described above is connected to centralized managerial power and higher education corporatization known as "academic capitalism."[17] It parallels patterns in the broad economy of increasingly casualized, at-will, precarious (professional) labor and concentrated managerial power.[18] Such patterns are playing out amid profound changes in women's participation in the paid workforce, and in demographic changes in higher education's student population. Recognizing this connection helps explain why current, progressive counter-mobilization in the management-labor struggle against what could be termed "disaster academic capitalism" also addresses aspects of contemporary social justice movements.

Ascendant since the 1980s, "academic capitalism" is most often understood as a move by not-for-profit higher education institutions toward intersections with private sector markets through new "circuits of production" of research (e.g., technology transfer) and instruction (e.g., technology-mediated instruction). That is central to this knowledge/learning regime, with internally embedded private sector marketplace logics driving decision-making in the academy.

However, academic capitalism is far more than entrepreneurial colleges/universities chasing new revenue streams. It necessitates rebalancing power between management and labor; it involves organizational restructuring; and it is grounded in restructuring the academic workforce and the terms and conditions of academic employment.

At its core, academic capitalism entails extended managerial capacity, enhancing management's capability to oversee, manage, and control academic work in offices staffed by administrators and managerial professionals. The emergence and growth of these boundary-spanning organizational structures in colleges/universities' interstices to leverage market position and revenues shift capacity and power from academics to administrators. As Sheila Slaughter and Gary Rhoades state: "In our view, the ascendance of the academic capitalist knowledge/learning regime requires us to rethink the centrality and dominance of the academic profession."[19]

Such developments are grounded in a fundamental restructuring of higher education's workforce and academic employment. As institutions seek to capitalize on the fruits of faculty labor, they invest in hiring more non-academic positions of "entrepreneurial managerial professionals"—for example, in distance and technology mediated education.[20] At the same time, institutions have been disinvesting from tenure-track positions in favor of part- and full-time non-tenure-track ones, decreasing faculty labor costs, and increasing managerial control. The result is that course production and provision are no longer the sole or primary domain of faculty.[21] In short, academic capitalism's rise involves a systematic political and economic change that drives the increased casualization of academic labor.

This same pattern has also played out in the private sector economy. There, too, the structure of employment has become precarious. Starting in the mid-1970s, managers sought greater "flexibility" in employing workers, which meant more unpredictability and risk for workers' employment.[22] Moreover, such changes were taking place just as "the labor force became more diverse, with marked increases in the number of women, nonwhite and immigrant workers, and older workers."[23] Further, these shifts have been tied to a changing political economy, where economic and institutional transformations are the products of conscious choices imposed by political and corporate leaders (and to a lesser extent made by workers).[24]

The irony of these transformations in the larger economy is captured by the seeming paradox between, on the one hand, the increased emphasis on "productivity" and, on the other, the declining investment in "production workers" and the growth of managerial personnel. Terming this pattern the "revenge of the managers," sociologist Adam Goldstein traced the disproportionate growth of managerial positions and managerial salaries as a share of institutional expenditures in fifty-nine industries from 1984 to 2001, even as companies reduced, in relative terms, labor costs for production workers through various processes. Counterintuitively, heightened emphasis on productivity, and public discourse about companies becoming "lean and mean," has translated into something quite different: "fat and mean," according to David Gordon.[25] The push to increase productivity has led to the development of control and monitoring strategies, which, along with other strategies, have fostered managerial growth. In Adam Goldstein's words: "By this logic, Gordon argues that aggressive efforts to reduce labor costs during the 1980s contributed to managerial growth by increasing supervisory requirements over increasingly squeezed and de-skilled workers. In other words, strategies nominally oriented toward making firms lean and streamlined had the effect of making them fatter at the top."[26] Moreover, the process involved various "mean" strategies: layoffs, de-unionization, and computerization—all contributing to reduced job security and diminished rights for production workers and increased at-will employment.

The parallels to academic capitalism and the ongoing trend lines in academic and professional employment in higher education are clear. Adjunct and full-time contingent faculty are far easier to downsize than are tenure stream faculty. As I previously wrote: "There are more subtle ways of reorganizing the academic workforce, of reallocating and reducing faculty resources, than by retrenching [tenure-stream] faculty. There are more efficient and less politically problematic ways. . . . Hire more part-time faculty. They are cheaper. They make it easier to shift faculty resources from one unit to another, for they are easier to hire and to release."[27] Contingent faculty can be non-renewed (laid off) with little to no due process, and with no recall rights. In addition, up until 2000, adjunct faculty were considerably less likely to be represented by collective bargaining units (the same situation held for graduate and postdoctoral employees). Moreover, their work is more likely to be outsourced in distance education to third-party providers (the higher education equivalent of computerization). Further, as they came to comprise a substantially increased proportion of the academic workforce, faculty salaries' share of institutional expenditures has declined. And all the while, the proportion of full-time senior administrators has increased marginally, and for support professionals it has increased substantially.

Such patterns are not color blind. The relative reduction in tenure-stream opportunities weighs heavily on women and people of color who are graduating with the appropriate credentials in growing numbers. Further, in the postdoc market "neo-racism" can operate to undermine the faculty aspirations of postdocs from non-European nations.[28] Moreover, a variation of "racial capitalism" is playing out—commodifying diversity to a minimal threshold but then cutting back in hard economic times.[29] As economic crises have hit higher education, in the 2008–2010 recession and amid the COVID pandemic and recession, colleges and universities have doubled down on "mean" employment practices, delimiting expanded access to tenure-stream positions for marginalized populations. That has led to academic employees' countermobilization.

Contingent Faculty Organizing in the 2000s

The 2000s have seen a proliferation of adjunct and contingent faculty organizing. This has been particularly manifest after 2008, with the formation of new part-time only (PTO) bargaining units in private universities, including several elite private institutions, and largely in non-academic unions. But adjunct and contingent faculty organizing has grown significantly in public sector institutions as well, with the establishment of new part-time only and lecturer units, and in the folding of non-tenure-track faculty into existing bargaining units of tenure-stream faculty. Indeed, it has taken root within the three major academic unions—the American Association of University Professors (AAUP), the American Federation of Teachers (AFT), and the National Education Association (NEA).

The growing significance of contingent faculty in the academic labor movement was augured quite dramatically by the increased strength of these faculty in two of the most prominent, now progressive bargaining units in the country, the Professional Staff Congress (PSC) in New York City and the California Faculty Association (CFA). It continues through the present in the foregrounding of contingent faculty issues in the academic labor movement amid COVID-19 and is further paralleled in graduate and postdoc employee organizing.

In April 2003, I delivered the Irwin Polishook lecture in Atlanta to the American Federation of Teachers' Higher Education conference. I was introduced by Barbara Bowen, PSC president. The irony was not lost on me. Bowen was head of the progressive "New Caucus" slate that had been elected in 2000, replacing the slate supported by retiring Irwin Polishook, who had been PSC president since 1976. Part of the New Caucus's focus was on adjunct faculty issues, which became central in their contract campaigns.[30] That centering was linked to a critique of corporatization in higher education, a theme of my lecture on "academic capitalism."[31]

Another progressive takeover of a union occurred around the same time, within the California Faculty Association. In 1999, Susan Meisenhelder, who had been a lecturer prior to obtaining a tenure-track position, was elected as part of a leadership team that at the time and subsequently centered "lecturer" (their term for part- and full-time non-tenure-track faculty) interests. Their project reflected and built on the work of California's Part-time Faculty Association, which included leaders from five unions.[32] Moreover, the CFA restructured its internal governance and bargaining team membership to ensure and increase lecturers' representation,[33] such that some tenured faculty suggest the union is "only for lecturers."[34] As with the PSC, the CFA leadership articulated a broad critique of corporatization in the academy that they linked to sexism and racism. Then and since, the CFA has been defined by a diverse leadership profile and pursuit of social justice visions of the California State University system's future.[35] As with the later Polishook lecture, I knew this recent history and trajectory when I spoke in November of 1999 to the CFA's state assembly. My talk mapped out "the restructuring of academic labor," placing it in a national perspective and offered thoughts about "rethinking campus union strategies" that centered lecturers and combatted corporatization.[36]

Just five years after my Polishook lecture, the first of many Service Employees International Union (SEIU) campaigns to organize adjunct-only bargaining units (and some combined part- and full-time faculty units) succeeded at George Washington University (GW). The first contract was signed in January of 2008.[37] That same year, adjunct faculty affiliated with SEIU Local 500 also signed a contract with Montgomery Community College. The success at GW triggered similar victories in the ensuing decade at other private universities in the DC metro area, including Georgetown University and American University, followed by Howard University. It also modeled a key element of a "metro strategy," the formation of an additional organization beyond individual campus bargaining units (and in DC, beyond SEIU Local 500); in the case of the Coalition of Contingent Academic Labor that extended beyond metro areas and now even national boundaries.[38] The DC "metro campaign" success helped foster "Faculty Forward," organizing launches in large metro areas across the country, primarily in private universities, but also in some cases, as in Miami, at public universities and community colleges as well.

Thus, "metro strategies" emerged across the nation.[39] The second such SEIU campaign success was in Boston (in contrast to an earlier unsuccessful effort by another union there in 1998). These strategies entailed organizing across a metro region through coordination among organizing committees and bargaining units of different campuses as part of an effort to organize a majority of adjunct faculty into one local, sometimes with the aspirational goal of a metro-wide contract. Such a strategy was pursued by other unions too, including the United Steelworkers (USW) in Pittsburgh and the AFT in Philadelphia, with the United Academics of Philadelphia, where, in 2015, adjunct faculty voted to become part of the established full-time faculty unit, the Temple Association of University Professionals. AFT has also organized in non-metro campaigns—for example, at Eastern Michigan University in 2010 and 2011 full-time and part-time lecturers formed separate AFT bargaining units (tenure-track faculty had an AAUP-affiliated unit).

However, the metro work has been animated and dominated by SEIU. From 2013 through 2015, SEIU affiliates accounted for thirty-eight of the sixty-six new bargaining units.[40] And, in the first three quarters of 2016, SEIU organized 90 percent of the new bargaining units of contingent faculty in private institutions (the organizing in private universities has been complicated by the stance of some religiously affiliated universities, like Duquesne and Pacific Lutheran, to claim exemption from the National Labor Relations Act).[41]

Contributing to the increased organizing and dynamism of adjunct and contingent faculty at this time, including in the three academic unions, was the formation in 2009 of an advocacy group—the New Faculty Majority (NFM).[42] NFM's leadership included members and prominent players in the major unions involved in organizing contingent faculty—the AAUP, AFT, NEA, SEIU, and USW. As an independent group, NFM has had an outsized influence in the media, speaking on behalf of contingent faculty concerns. It has effectively highlighted adjunct faculty working conditions as deeply problematic, connecting them to students' learning conditions. Moreover, within their respective unions, NFM leaders worked to advance the interests of contingent faculty. An example of an "inside/outside strategy," NFM substantially improved "the chances of getting contingent faculty issues prioritized inside unions."[43] NFM's push heightened academic unions' focus on contingent faculty.

During my tenure as AAUP's general secretary, from January 2009 through mid-June 2011, I witnessed and experienced the effects of such pressure in each of the academic unions. That pressure was articulated by and contributed to strengthening the unions' contingent faculty caucuses. It played out in annual conferences (e.g., in programs, conference sessions, and decision-making), policy statements, and data gathering. It also played out in dynamics among leaders, the rank and file, and advocacy groups, as unions' higher education national directors and leaders were called out by contingent faculty members or NFM activists for not doing enough. It played out as well in the growth of contingent faculty organizing in unions such as SEIU, United Auto Workers (UAW), and USW, where contingent faculty (and graduate and postdoc employees) received more support. It played out further in the internal politics of the academic unions over whether and how to organize contingent academic employees.

Not least of all, such top/bottom and inside/outside pressures stimulated important coalitional action in data-gathering about contingent faculty. The best example was the Coalition on the Academic Workforce survey, distributed in 2010 by a group that included academic unions (e.g., AAUP and AFT), as well as disciplinary associations (e.g., the Modern Languages Association).[44] It was the largest survey of contingent faculty ever conducted, with 10,331 adjunct faculty and 9,519 full-time contingent faculty respondents.

The pressure to address contingent faculty concerns was reflected also in academic unions' organizing campaigns, especially in defining bargaining units. The particular form varied by state, as decisions about whether full- and part-time faculty could be in the same bargaining unit and what faculty share a "community of interest" are shaped by employees, state law, and employment boards.[45] Thus, in Ohio, part-time faculty do not have collective bargaining rights. By contrast, although they do in Illinois, some employment board rulings held that full- and part-time faculty do not share a "community of interest" required to be in the same unit. But in Oregon and New Mexico (and other states) boards have ruled that they do.

One key development in each of these settings was the greater proclivity for tenure-stream faculty to form common cause with full- and part-time contingent faculty. Thus, Bowling Green State University's successful campaign in 2010 included all full-time faculty. Similarly, subsequent successes in AAUP/AFT joint campaigns were characterized by solidarity among tenure-stream and contingent faculty. Relatedly, at the University of Illinois, Chicago (UIC), although the initial efforts of full-time faculty to organize a single bargaining unit of tenure-stream and contingent faculty were obstructed by administrative intransigence and court filings, the two bargaining units that eventually formed work closely and cooperatively. At the University of Oregon, United Academics includes tenure-stream, contingent and adjunct faculty, and postdocs (graduate employees already had a union). And the University of New Mexico's United Academics includes full- and part-time, tenure-stream, and contingent faculty.

The common cause, activism, and agitation about contingent faculty's vulnerability continued amid COVID. Common cause among tenure-stream and contingent faculty extended beyond bargaining unit configuration in 2020 COVID negotiations that centered contingent faculty's concerns. United Academics University of Oregon successfully advanced proposals to protect "career track" (contingent) faculty. The pay reduction burden was disproportionately carried by tenure-stream faculty.[46] So, too, at UIC, the tenure-stream faculty unit pushed to reappoint non-tenure-track faculty "let go prematurely due to fear of decreased enrollments,"[47] and in August 2020, it filed an unfair labor practice charge against the administration for not bargaining in good faith on this and other matters. The solidarity and activism extended beyond contingent faculty concerns to support access to PPE (personal protective equipment) and disinfectant for unionized custodial workers.[48]

For all the collective struggle and success, though, the attacks on adjunct (and full-time contingent) faculty continue amid the pandemic and recession. For example, adjunct faculty at Eastern Michigan University fought an administrative proposal, introduced at the last minute in summer 2020 negotiations, that would prevent them from receiving full-time employment.[49] Almost unbelievable in a pandemic.

Also unbelievable at the time were the national levels of unemployment, in conjunction with the federal administration's failure in spring/summer 2020 to continue with the $600/week unemployment adjustment. Among higher educa-tion faculty, the hardest hit segment, by far, were "non-renewed" (effectively laid off) adjunct and full-time contingent faculty. The advocacy and organizing that has foregrounded faculty's casualization has also focused on mobilizing resources to support these faculty in gaining access to unemployment benefits. The New Faculty Majority has led a national initiative to expand contingent faculty access to unemployment, and SEIU Local 500 provides an important local example of a bargaining unit addressing these needs.[50] Similarly, the Temple Association of University Professionals has "Welcome Back" and "FAQs" pages for adjunct faculty, with information about unemployment compensation workshops, class cancella-tion fees, health insurance, and more. The AFT Adjunct Contingent Caucus (ACC) has issued eleven demands, including training for remote teaching, technological tools for teaching online, and ensuring eligibility for unemployment compensation. The ongoing push has been to advance contingent workers' rights and to enhance their working conditions to the benefit of students' learning.

Perhaps ironically, in this challenging recession context, while employment and online/remote teaching are harder, the organizing may be easier. The politi-cal context is clarifying—from ongoing attacks on labor and collective bargain-ing rights to the #MeToo and #BLM social movements.[51] The new organizing of contingent academic employees (and in existing units, too) includes issues from broader social movements.

One development in organizing is the emergence of "wall-to-wall" locals that include staff, student employees, and contingent and tenure-stream faculty. The national leader in this regard is the Communications Workers of America's (CWA) "United Campus Worker" locals. Some locals have been around for years (e.g., UCW-Tennessee and UCW-Georgia). A few, as with UCW-Colorado and UCW-Arizona, were organized during the pandemic. In all cases, justice issues embedded in larger social movements were at the core of the campaigns, whether phrased in terms of diversity, economic justice, and democracy, or "dismantling structural racism and other forms of oppression."[52]

A social justice focus linked to broader social movements is found as well among graduate and postdoc employees. In the former, a number of new bargaining units in elite private universities—American, Brown, Georgetown, and Harvard—have achieved voluntary recognition.[53] Issues of racial justice, heightened protections against harassment, and support of international students are key elements of the unions' campaigns, as at Brown where the union "Stand Up for Graduate Student Employees" centers in one of its campaigns on racial justice to protect Black lives. The Georgetown Alliance of Graduate Employees highlighted among its contract gains social justice provisions regarding sexual harassment (providing additional reporting options) and protecting undocumented graduate student employees from prosecution. Similarly, in postdoc organizing, Sayil Camacho and Robert A. Rhoads point out how the vulnerability of employees, especially of international postdocs, played out in organizing.[54]

Conclusion

Adjunct and contingent faculty have long done the core academic work of higher education. Over time, systematically propelled by patterns of academic capitalism that mirror developments in the broader economy, their proportional share of the academic workforce has moved them from academia's margins to its center. They now far outnumber tenure-stream faculty, even more so if graduate and postdoc employees are included. Yet, the numerical change alone, driven by shifting managerial practices, was not sufficient to challenge the political economy of academic employment. Organizing was needed.

The 2000s have witnessed the collective mobilization of adjunct and full-time contingent faculty, reenergized graduate employee organizing, and seen emergent postdoc employee unionizing. Well after their numerical rise, the political emergence of part- and full-time contingent faculty has arrived. These once marginal academic employees have taken a leadership role in the academic labor movement. They are organizing with new unions—including SEIU, USW, UAW, and CWA—whose influence in the academy is growing; they have reenergized the three once-dominant education unions, AAUP, AFT, and NEA; and they have organized in new spaces, such as private universities and union-hostile states.

Moreover, the public discourse and membership of adjunct and full-time contingent faculty organizing and contract campaigns, and those of graduate and postdoc employees, are also reshaping the academic labor movement. The changing configuration of contingent academic employees embodies larger proportions of people with marginalized identities and working-class backgrounds, people with deeper ties to marginalized communities than tenure-stream faculty. This reality is expressed in organizing campaigns that center the concerns, discourse, and activism of contemporary broader social movements. And it expands the possibility of collectively negotiating a new academy grounded in these justice-oriented realities.

Notes

1. Thomas Paine, *Common Sense* (1776; reprint, New York: Fall River Press, 2013), 37. On the "new faculty majority," see Maria Maisto, "Taking Heart, Taking Part: New Faculty Majority and the Praxis of Contingent Faculty Activism," in *Embracing Non-Tenure Track*

Faculty: Changing Campuses for the New Faculty Majority, ed. Adrianna Kezar (New York: Routledge, 2012), 190–204.

2. For earlier examples, see Timothy Reese Cain, "A Long History of Activism and Organizing: Contingent Faculty, Graduate Students, and Unionization," in *Professors in the Gig Economy: Unionizing Adjunct Faculty in America*, ed. Kim Tolley (Baltimore: Johns Hopkins University Press, 2018), 46–68.

3. Sheila Slaughter and Gary Rhoades, *Academic Capitalism and the New Economy: Markets, State, and Higher Education* (Baltimore: Johns Hopkins University Press, 2004).

4. Joan Acker, "Hierarchies, Jobs, Bodies: A Theory of Gendered Organizations," *Gender & Society* 4:2 (1990): 139–158; Joan Acker, "Inequality Regimes, Gender, Class, and Race in Organizations," *Gender and Society* 20:4 (2006): 441–464; Victor Ray, "A Theory of Racialized Organizations," *American Sociological Review* 84:1 (2019): 26–53.

5. Brendan Cantwell and Jenny Lee, "Unseen Workers in the Academic Factory: Perceptions of Neo-Racism among International Postdocs in the United States and the United Kingdom," *Harvard Educational Review* 80:4 (2010): 490–517.

6. Martin J. Finkelstein, Valerie M. Conley, and Jack C. Schuster, *The Faculty Factor: The American Academy in a Turbulent Era* (Baltimore: Johns Hopkins University Press, 2016), figure 3.1.

7. Gary Rhoades, "Disruptive Innovations for Adjunct Faculty: Common Sense for the Common Good," *Thought & Action* 29 (Fall, 2013): 71–86.

8. Finkelstein, Conley, and Schuster, *The Faculty Factor*, figures 3.4 and 3.5.

9. Ibid., table 3.4.

10. Ibid., table 3.3.

11. Ibid., table 3.5. The "underrepresented" terminology is from ibid.

12. Ibid., table 3.5.

13. Gary Rhoades and Blanca M. Torres-Olave, "Academic Capitalism and (Secondary) Academic Labor Markets: Negotiating a New Academy and Research Agenda," in *Higher Education: Handbook of Theory and Research*, vol. 30, ed. Michael P. Paulsen (New York: Springer, 2015), 283–430. On postdoc tenure-track position attainment, see Paula E. Stephan, *How Economics Shapes Science* (Cambridge, MA: Harvard University Press, 2012).

14. William M. Zumeta, *Extending the Educational Ladder: The Changing Quality and Value of Postdoctoral Study* (Boston: Lexington Books, 1985). Also see Erin Hatton's and Diane Angell's chapters in this volume.

15. Brendan Cantwell and Barrett J. Taylor, "Rise of the Science and Engineering Postdoctorate and the Restructuring of Academic Research," *Journal of Higher Education* 86:5 (2015): 667–696.

16. Ibid.

17. Slaughter and Rhoades, *Academic Capitalism*.

18. Adam Goldstein, "Revenge of the Managers: Labor Cost-Cutting and the Paradoxical Resurgence of Managerialism in the Shareholder Value Era, 1984 to 2001," *American Sociological Review* 77:2 (2014): 268–294; David Gordon, *Fat and Mean: The Corporate Squeeze of Working Americans and the Myth of Managerial Downsizing* (New York: Free Press,

1996); Arne L. Kalleberg, "Precarious Work, Insecure Workers: Employment Relations in Transition," *American Sociological Review* 74:1 (2009): 1–22; Vicki Smith, "You Get the Economy You Choose: The Political and Social Construction of the New Economy," *Work and Occupations* 39:2 (2012): 148–156.

19. Slaughter and Rhoades, *Academic Capitalism*, 10.

20. Gary Rhoades and Barbara Sporn, "New Models of Management and Shifting Modes and Costs of Production: Europe and the United States," *Tertiary Education and Management* 8:1 (2002): 3–28.

21. Gary Rhoades, "Whose Educational Space?: Negotiating Professional Jurisdiction in the High-Tech Academy," in *The American Academic Profession: Transformation in Contemporary Higher Education*, ed. Joseph C. Hermanowicz (Baltimore: Johns Hopkins University Press, 2011), 92–110; and Vernon C. Smith and Gary Rhoades, "Community College Faculty and Web-Based Classes," *Thought & Action* 22 (Fall 2006): 97–110.

22. Kalleberg, "Precarious Work."

23. Ibid., 3.

24. Smith, "The Economy You Choose," 148.

25. Gordon, *Fat and Mean*.

26. Goldstein, "Revenge of the Managers," 277.

27. Gary Rhoades, *Managed Professionals: Unionized Faculty and Restructuring Academic Labor* (Albany: State University of New York Press, 1998), 131.

28. Cantwell and Lee, "Unseen Workers."

29. Nancy Leong, "Racial Capitalism," *Harvard Law Review* 126:8 (2013): 2152–2226.

30. Luke Elliott Negri, "Wall to Wall: Industrial Unionism at the City University of New York, 1972–2017," in *Professors in the Gig Economy*, ed. Tolley, 153–171.

31. Slaughter and Rhoades, *Academic Capitalism*.

32. Joe Berry and Helena Worthen, "The Metro Strategy: A Workforce-Appropriate, Geography-Based Approach to Organizing Contingent Faculty," in *Contextualizing and Organizing Contingent Faculty*, ed. Ishmael I. Munene (New York: Lexington Books, 2018), 35–60.

33. Elizabeth Hoffman and John Hess, "Organizing for Equality within the Two-Tier System: The Experience of the California Faculty Association," in *Equality for Contingent Faculty: Overcoming the Two-Tier System*, ed. Keith Hoeller (Nashville: Vanderbilt University Press, 2014), 9–27.

34. Kim Geron and Gretchen M. Reevy, "California State University, East Bay: Alignment of Contingent and Tenure-Track Faculty Interests and Goals," in *Professors in the Gig Economy*, ed. Tolley, 174.

35. CFA, *Equity Interrupted: How California Is Cheating Its Future* (Sacramento: California Faculty Association, 2017); Charles Toombs, "Antiracism, Social Justice, and the California Faculty Association," *Academe* (Winter 2022).

36. Rhoades, *Managed Professionals*.

37. See Anne McLeer's essay in this volume.

38. Berry and Worthen, "The Metro Strategy."

39. Joe Berry, *Reclaiming the Ivory Tower: Organizing Adjuncts to Change Higher Education* (New York: Monthly Review Press, 2005); and Berry and Worthen, "The Metro Strategy."

40. William A. Herbert, "The Winds of Changes Shift: An Analysis of Recent Growth in Bargaining Units and Representation Efforts in Higher Education," *Journal of Collective Bargaining in the Academy* 8 (2016), https://thekeep.eiu.edu/jcba/vol8/iss1/1/.

41. William A. Herbert, "The Future of Tenure: Implications for University Operations and Finance" (Paper presented at the Higher Education Advanced Seminar of the National Federation of Municipal Analysts, Phoenix, AZ, January 14, 2016).

42. Maisto, "Taking Heart."

43. Berry and Worthen, "The Metro Strategy," 54.

44. CAW, *A Portrait of Part-Time Faculty Members* (Washington, DC: Coalition on the Academic Workforce, 2012).

45. See William A. Herbert and Joseph van der Naald's essay in this volume.

46. UAUO, "United Academics University of Oregon Frequently Asked Questions for Spring, the COVID Crisis, and Summer Bargaining," http://uauoregon.org/faq-spring-2020/.

47. UICUF, "University of Illinois Chicago United Faculty Press Releases," http://uicunitedfaculty.org/news/2020/.

48. Ibid.

49. Steve Marowski, "Eastern Michigan University Still Negotiating Contract with Lecturers Union," *Mlive.com*, July 9, 2020, https://www.mlive.com/news/ann-arbor/2020/07/eastern-michigan-university-still-negotiating-new-contract-with-lecturers-union.html.

50. SEIU, "Service Employees International Union, Unemployment Assistance," 2020, https://www.seiu500.org/covid19-resources.

51. Anne McLeer, "Presentation" (National Inter-Union Academic Labor webinar, National Center for the Study of Collective Bargaining in Higher Education and the Professions, July 24, 2020).

52. UCW-Arizona, "What Do We Do as a Union?," United Campus Workers, Arizona, Local 7065, 2020, https://www.cajuarizona.com/union.

53. Jon Marcus, "Amid Pandemic, Graduate Student Workers Are Winning Long-Sought Contracts," *Washington Post,* July 19, 2020, https://www.washingtonpost.com/education/2020/07/19/grad-student-unions-pandemic/.

54. Sayil Camacho and Robert A. Rhoads, "Breaking the Silence: The Unionization of Postdoctoral Workers at the University of California," *Journal of Higher Education* 86:2 (2015): 295–325.

THE MAKING OF A CONTINGENT FACULTY MAJORITY

CHAPTER 2

FRAMING PART I

R-E-S-P-E-C-T

ELIZABETH HOHL

When I was hired as an adjunct professor at a Jesuit university in 1984, I was unaware of the sea change underway in academic life. My first clue should have been the form letters "inviting" me to teach every semester, as if new to the job.[1] Gradually, I learned I did not fit the criteria for adjunct status in the "Redbook" of the American Association of University Professors. I had plenty of company.[2] Essays throughout this volume illustrate our steady growth into the contingent faculty majority. We worked primarily not *outside of* but *inside* higher education. On campus a few of us found one another, but ascertaining the size of the larger group proved daunting. No grand list circulated; rarely did departments feature the names of part-time faculty nor did college catalogs include us.[3] At the root of these haphazard employment practices was a fundamental lack of respect.

Our official invisibility corresponded to the hostility and disregard we frequently encountered as professionals beyond the pale.[4] It was not unusual for the classics program chair to loudly rail against the audacity of an adjunct faculty professor's request for office space to meet students. Others were dismissive; a tenured business professor concluded a new course design demonstration by announcing his plan not to teach the class but "to hand it off to an adjunct." Even as a dean expressed enthusiasm for the best employment practices standards issued by the Organization of American Historians (OAH), she balked at allocating funds for contingent faculty research or conference presentations. Such resources, she intoned, were reserved for tenured and tenure-track faculty, thus reinforcing the segregated spaces faculty occupy.[5]

Given the environment, we sought incremental change on my campus. Four initiatives with different coalitions over nearly fifteen years produced campaigns for university email addresses, mailboxes that did not vanish, shared office space, and expanded library privileges. Countless meetings, at least two contingent faculty surveys, and months of negotiation yielded a standing committee in the faculty governance structure devoted to non-tenure-track faculty policy and issues. Other recommendations for a faculty solidarity statement, contingent faculty career ladder, and dedicated resources were rejected, a sure sign of our limited efficacy.[6]

While official invisibility and disrespect for contingent faculty seemed to permeate higher education, the opportunity for me to serve on a joint committee of the OAH and the American Historical Association (AHA) looked promising. Still, the note confirming my appointment described the charge as addressing "the *problem* of the growing reliance of colleges and universities on low-paid and adjunct faculty to teach history courses."[7] Shortly after I joined the OAH Committee on Part-Time, Adjunct, and Contingent Employment (CPACE), the AHA inexplicably ceased appointing new members.[8] We urged the OAH Executive Board to continue our work. The rationale we crafted pivoted to the importance of contingent faculty and the necessity of improved working conditions. As a permanent committee of the OAH, we updated the *Standards for Part-Time, Adjunct, and Contingent Faculty*, made recommendations, endorsed a collective bargaining statement, and added advocacy to our purpose.[9]

Raising awareness inside and outside of the OAH necessitated different strategies. We issued periodic press releases and news of CPACE business within OAH outlets; at annual meetings we organized panels and workshops. Despite the energetic support of vocal allies, however, we struggled to make our agenda resonate with some of the leadership. We understood the OAH, like every other professional association, faced the larger, long-term problem of recruiting and retaining the ever-expanding number of contingent professors. Few faculty off the tenure track could afford the cost of membership dues or conference travel. Over time, the board endorsed travel stipends and reduced membership fees; they also acted on our recommendation to designate a non-tenure-track board slot and agreed to encourage the inclusion of contingent faculty on all OAH committees. The OAH mission to "encourage . . . the equitable treatment of all practitioners of history" is ongoing.[10] Professional associations across disciplines have yet to commit collectively to this struggle.

The kind of comprehensive change essential to ending the exploitation of non-tenure-track faculty labor remains elusive. Contingent faculty may be ubiquitous in the classroom but largely absent in governance structures and in decision-making positions on campuses and in professional associations. The narrative problematizing contingent faculty persists despite concerted efforts to retire it. Economic trends indicate increasing precarity in higher education. Yet, if I learned anything over the last few decades, it is that collective action is the way forward. With the knowledge that we are vital to student learning, scholarship, and university life we need to organize one step at a time, demanding and cultivating respect for the work we do.

Notes

1. The current three-page Adjunct Appointment Agreement still fails to acknowledge years of employment.

2. Earlier definitions of adjunct faculty status meant full-time employment outside of academia.

3. The 1999 Fairfield University *Fact Book* listed full-time, tenured/tenure-track faculty at 187 and part-time faculty at 138, for a total of 325. Another 65 were in the Schools of Engineering and Continuing Education, many of whom were tenured faculty teaching an overload. "Fairfield University History Online," Fairfield University, accessed August 6, 2020, https://digital.fairfield.edu/cdm/pageflip/collection/FUHDnew/id/37/type/singleitem/pf.type/pdf. For a headcount, we crunched the numbers by department.

4. Claire Raymond describes it conceptually in this volume.

5. Claire Goldstene explores this in this volume.

6. The 2013 Task Force summarized the issues as "lack of voice, absence of respect and unstable employment." We analyzed "A Portrait of Part-Time Faculty Workers," Coalition on the Academic Workforce, June 2012, accessed February 20, 2022, http://www.academicworkforce.org/survey.html. We consulted "One Faculty," American Association of University Professors, accessed August 6, 2020, https://www.aaup.org/chapter-resources/one-faculty.

7. The December 14, 2005, invitation to serve described the charge; my initial term (2006–2010) was renewed three times. The committee name underwent changes; it is now called CPACE.

8. CPACE reached out to the AHA. Jointly, we convened a meeting of representatives from many disciplinary associations and hosted three forums on "Non-Tenure Track Faculty: Dialogue and Cooperation across Disciplines." With the pandemic, a fourth gathering was cancelled in April 2020.

9. We selected the term non-tenure-track faculty as all-encompassing. "Standards for Part-Time Adjunct, and Contingent Faculty," Organization of American Historians, accessed February 20, 2022, https://www.oah.org/insights/archive/standards-for-part-time-adjunct-and-contingent-faculty/.

10. For the full statement on historical questions and the equitable treatment of all practitioners of history see "About Us," Organization of American Historians, accessed February 20, 2022, https://www.oah.org.

CHAPTER 3

"THOSE WHO DON'T ACCEPT THIS DON'T LAST LONG"

Two Centuries of Cost Cutting and Laboring
in the US Higher Education Industry

ELIZABETH TANDY SHERMER

"College presidents are having to face up to the fact," higher education expert Donald Buttenheim warned in 1969, "that higher education is an industry as well as a social and academic institution; and those who don't accept this don't last long." Reporters admitted that Buttenheim's bluntness would catch many Americans off guard. "We don't commonly think of the nation's almost 2,500 colleges and universities as comprising an industry because they aren't run for profit." That "huge industry" nevertheless "opens two plants a week—new colleges—on the average" and "creates jobs rapidly," for both faculty and staff. Universities had become the preeminent industry and employer in both college towns and sizeable cities. Buttenheim doubted this educational enterprise would change anytime soon. He predicted its impact would be as revolutionary as the automobile industry had been in the early twentieth century.[1]

That comparison sounds crude decades later, when a handful of campuses close annually and academics increasingly bemoan the rise of the "neoliberal university." That catchall label damns college administrators for hiking fees, seeking private donations, profiting from patents, limiting tenure lines, hiring adjuncts, and fighting unionization efforts (as recounted in several of this volume's essays). From the perspective of outspoken faculty, staff, students, and parents, those practices have steadily made colleges and universities seem more like businesses than nonprofit institutions dedicated to research, service, and teaching.[2]

Labeling campuses neoliberal does not capture the complexity of the growing turn-of-the-millennium reliance on contingent faculty. Campus managerial norms have shifted since the 1970s. Those changes reveal how the country's business and workplace standards have always shaped the structure, culture, and labor practices of US colleges and universities. Many now insist that "neoliberal universities" have replaced far more progressive, inclusive, and affordable institutions solely dedicated to and able to robustly support the life of the mind for students and faculty. But most campuses' finances have historically been precarious and have constrained these institutions' ability to fully serve the public. Campuses often needed to focus on serving business donors' research and workforce training needs. Moreover, working and studying conditions only improved as faculty, staff, and students began organizing for them in times when Americans laboring off campuses made similar demands for secure jobs and more democratic workplaces.

The ways in which campus finances and labor practices have intersected and changed over time reflect how the country's educational enterprise has continually adapted to and shaped the nation's evolving, contested political, economic, and social norms. The academy's pre-1970 transformation looks different than the one Joe Berry and Helena Worthen lay out early in their essay for this volume. Such descriptions of meteoric growth in the first two-thirds of the twentieth century, particularly after World War II, are common but ignore the historic complexity of university finances and labor practices. Slavery and seizing native lands helped fund and build the first postsecondary schools founded to train the Republic's gentry. Gilded Age entrepreneurs also donated money to push campuses to offer the research, development, and workforce training needed for an industrial overhaul of the country's economy. That emergent corporate elite used their philanthropies to force administrators to embrace their preferred business and labor practices, which included then-novel employee benefits but not the job security that tenure provided decades later as workforce labor standards evolved during the broad 1930s and 1940s search for economic stability. Union drives nationwide inspired staff and faculty to demand the security and power on the job that helped transform research, service, and teaching. Yet, even at the height of post–World War II government support for postsecondary schools, public and private nonprofit institutions all depended on grants, government earmarks, donors, and student fees increasingly financed through student loans. Citizens, CEOs, and lawmakers did not pressure campuses to improve job quality. They wanted rapid growth to offer equal opportunities to pursue the degrees that had already become a prerequisite for being able to compete for well-paying work.

What now seems to many like a golden age began to unravel when 1970s stagnation ushered in a new era of austerity that undermined work standards, labor rights, and social welfare guarantees across the country. Stable middle-class and professional jobs disappeared in decades when inequality widened, individual debt increased, and finance became even more interwoven in American life. Historically cash-strapped campuses were hardly immune to societal shifts that many academics now consider synonymous with neoliberalism's rise. Most colleges and universities continued to rely on tuition for which a growing number of students and parents had to borrow. Many undergraduates still struggled to stay in schools that relied on contingent faculty to reduce labor costs as those essential campus workers, like so many Americans, scrambled to do more with less on and off campuses.

Precarious Prologue

Uncertain finances, fiscal catastrophes, and unseemly labor practices have been a longstanding characteristic of US higher education, which never received consistent, robust "financial aid." Before World War II, that term described direct funding from legislators or donors to underwrite the costs of running any type of postsecondary school, many of which, as historians have noted, bear little resemblance to what present-day Americans (including academics) recognize as a college or university. Experts have emphasized that US campuses "stand alone in the world in terms of their abundant numbers, the variety of their forms, and the extent to which they derive their sustenance from numerous sources." They have competed for numerous revenue streams since the colonial era, which belies the sharp distinctions between public, private, and for-profit institutions increasingly made since the Gilded Age. "Financial aid" evolved to include "student aid" during the Cold War and only at the end of the twentieth century did it come to mean, at least colloquially, tuition assistance. That linguistic shift reflected how enrollees' and their families' real financial sacrifice had historically been time, not money. Hours devoted to studying instead of work came at the expense of a household's income, especially in decades when a job in a factory or a field was so much easier to find than white-collar or professional work.[3]

Precarious campus finances and jobs have always, as political scientist Virginia Sapiro has stressed, been a part of the complex, evolving business of US higher education. Postsecondary institutions generally charged students less than the full cost of instruction. As such, most nonprofit campuses "spent significant parts of their institutional existence teetering on the brink of ruin, deeply vulnerable to having to close." Trustees, presidents, professors, students, and surrounding communities "usually do everything they can to keep them alive, even when their enrollment numbers are falling and they are in increasing debt." Cutting salaries or not paying faculty at all was a common strategy. Instructors and students also regularly handled the daily tasks and maintenance work before the Civil War even outside the South, where schools forced enslaved people to do such vital labor. Yet the astounding range of strategies to cut costs, entice donors, and attract students, which often included drastic curriculum changes, failed to protect many campuses from economic downturns, wars, pandemics, population changes, and environmental disasters.[4]

Unsteady collegiate finances reflected how the slave and cotton economy, as well as aggressive, lucrative territorial expansion, shaped the business of education. Historian Craig Wilder has highlighted how much the so-called peculiar institution financed the North's Ivy League institutions. Unfree labor also helped build what became the South's preeminent schools, including the University of North Carolina. Tar Heels had pushed for the "funding and endowing of a Public School" since 1754. That desire became urgent after the Revolution, when prominent citizens hesitated to keep sending promising young men to Europe or other states to study. Revolutionary war hero Benjamin Smith bequeathed a portion of the 20,000 acres of Chickasaw land awarded to him for service. Donating an area known as New Hope Chapel Hill enabled the forty trustees (thirty-one of them slaveholders) to cover the expense of constructing a two-story brick building, a wooden house for a presiding president, and begin work on a chapel and other buildings, all of which a local contractor likely accomplished by renting enslaved people and hiring white laborers. Trustees auctioned off surrounding lots to wealthy residents (most of them slavers) to establish the actual Town of Chapel Hill but still lacked the money to appoint a president to oversee the first state university to admit students.[5]

Laying a literal and figurative cornerstone hardly assured solvency or the use of paid labor in the Early Republic. Political, religious, and class differences running throughout the country and individual states also divided UNC trustees, whose slaveholding gentry and western farmers vehemently disagreed on the best course of action for the school, North Carolina, and the Republic. Trustees especially fought over what subjects to offer and ultimately decided, as one explained, to place "the 'bourgeois' sciences on an equal plane with the 'aristocratic' classics." Bad roads and storms did more to deter students than degree options and fees. The school charged $15 a year for the sciences, $12.50 for languages and history, and just $8 for bookkeeping, math, reading, and writing. That revenue supplemented the salary of both the presiding professor and the steward, who oversaw the enslaved people providing the meals and housing needs of men (and only men) trickling in from across the state.[6]

The so-called land grants also reflected how intertwined nineteenth-century financing and labor concerns were. Vermont Republican Justin Morrill promised the Land-Grant Agricultural and Mechanical College Act of 1862, better known as the Morrill Act, would bolster the country's vital industries. He dedicated that storied legislation, not to those schools' administrators or faculty, but to the "sons of toil" in need of both a liberal arts education and practical training in agriculture, military science, and engineering (then called the mechanical arts). Twenty-first-century investigative reporters and historians have described this law as a "massive transfer of wealth" that "turn[ed] land expropriated from tribal nationals into seed money for higher education." The government paid far less than the reported $400,000 for the 11 million acres of western land sold. Many of the 80,000 parcels were either violently seized or taken through unratified treaties. Some of the original land-grants were not institutions that Americans would now consider state schools, like the Massachusetts Institute of Technology. Legislators used the law to help founders open this now expensive, prestigious private school in 1865, which had been discussed as vital to businesses' labor and research needs since the 1840s but only chartered in 1861.[7]

That delayed start epitomized how the Morrill Act offered a tenuous lifeline, not the robust, continuous support that many still assume that law provided. Congressional delegation size determined how many acres a state received. Sales provided an individual legislature with money for an endowment that only five southern states split between white and Black institutions. Most legislatures got far less than they hoped (the average across the country was $1.65 an acre). That money also trickled in over time; by 1900, the University of California Regents still held unsold parcels. Profits sustained endowments but did not cover operating costs (like staff salaries). The principal had to be conserved and invested, though lawmakers sometimes transferred that endowment to other schools (both Brown's and Yale's grants were reassigned to state institutions in the 1890s). Nothing in the law dictated that legislators generously fund land-grant institutions. Interest income did establish new colleges, reopened shuttered institutions (like the preparatory school that became the University of Minnesota), and even helped the Michigan Agricultural College (today's Michigan State University), when legislators assumed the agricultural college could sustain itself on the 667 acres and handful of buildings for which the legislature paid.[8]

Financing shaped the quality of campus jobs on land-grants, many of which, as Sapiro noted, relied on paid and unpaid student labor to expand. Michigan Agricultural College's inaugural class of sixty-three men, for example, had a fieldwork requirement that they fulfilled by clearing land to enlarge the campus beyond the few buildings already erected in East Lansing. They were compensated so that they could afford remedial instruction to eventually study the still ill-defined agricultural sciences.[9]

Industrialized Academy

The Morrill Act did little to guarantee that colleges and universities would survive the Civil War or end their reliance on the poorly paid labor common in the Gilded Age and Progressive Era. Enrollments plummeted everywhere. Campuses subsequently closed on either side of the Mason-Dixon Line. A larger number did not reopen until 1870 or ever again, particularly those in the South. That sectional conflict subsequently left intact regional differences in higher education. The Northeast largely had private institutions of varying size, the South and Midwest held a mixture of state and private institutions, whereas public campuses were predominant in the Far West.[10]

Those disparities persisted in the Gilded Age and Progressive Era, when major philanthropists provided uneven, targeted support that reflected how industrialization transformed the entire country. Some business and political powerbrokers considered overhauling education to be a part of the rapid, corporate transformation of farms, transportation networks, communications, factories, and cities. Magnates like John D. Rockefeller and Andrew Carnegie invested some of their fortunes in colleges and universities, whose faculty and administrators had become far more willing to accept donations and earmarks to underwrite scientific instruction and job training after Reconstruction. Tycoons and their foundations generally targeted programs of study that interested them, started new schools (like Johns Hopkins and Stanford), or rescued cash-strapped campuses (including the University of Chicago and Duke University). Their charitable foundations also offered much-needed aid to schools willing to improve their finances, standardize their course offerings, embrace what these foundations considered to be practical programs of study, and, in general, operate in a more professional, businesslike manner.[11]

Carnegie stood out for devoting money toward better compensation for faculty, who increasingly hoped, like so many in the Progressive Era, for power and security on the job. He established the Carnegie Teachers Pension Fund in 1905 to provide college and university instructors with free pensions, a benefit that reflected the insurance products then becoming more common to mitigate risk. That fund eventually spawned the Carnegie Foundation for the Advancement of Teaching and today's TIAA (Teachers Insurance and Annuity Association of America). That perk ignored the professors who had already begun to express increasing anxiety about their academic freedom and to ask for tenure, then more common at German research universities. The American Association of University Professors (AAUP) issued a Declaration on Academic Freedom in 1915, when membership included just 6 percent of faculty. It demanded that professors, not administrators, determine who was hired, fired, or given tenure after ten years, ultimatums that also reflected a desire to give faculty more power and authority on campuses.[12]

Job security and financial stability, however, continued to be rare. Philanthropies spent far more on wealthy Northeastern campuses, which only exacerbated the geographic inequities in American postsecondary education, even as donors, lawmakers, and citizens started to draw distinctions between public, private, and for-profit institutions. Only a handful of legislatures spent the money to create outstanding public universities before World War I. Even University of California administrators relied on donors to fund Berkeley's rapid turn-of-the-century expansion.[13]

Limited federal aid continued to reflect how intertwined the academy was with the business of America and its labor needs. Congressional aid primarily bolstered campus operations that supported the engines of the turn-of-the-century economy. The 1887 Hatch Act, for example, targeted experiment stations and programs that bolstered agricultural production and manufacturing. Those industries also benefitted from the so-called Second Morrill Act of 1890, which earmarked money for separate land-grant institutions for African Americans. By 1910, funds tied to those laws accounted for more than a third of the income of most land-grant colleges, which reflected how little most state legislatures spent.[14]

Limited earmarks were one reason the growing number of aspiring students found more seats in proprietary schools, which also served the needs of a country emerging as the world's preeminent supplier of raw materials and manufactured goods. Historian Cristina Groeger shows that ordinary people aspiring for better jobs created the demand for these forebearers to today's for-profits. Proprietary institutions were responsible for much of the academy's growth in the Gilded Age, Progressive Era, and Roaring Twenties. Older colleges and universities, often remote, cultivated a "Culture of Aspiration" that scholar David Levine characterized as lily-white and overwhelmingly masculine. New, relatively inexpensive for-profits in cities across the country catered to white middle-class Americans, who wanted business or commercial training but did not have the social connections to matriculate in more established nonprofit public and private colleges. Jews, Catholics, immigrants, African Americans, and other residents of color soon flocked to evening classes that taught skills needed for better-paying, white-collar jobs. Women especially embraced institutions that enabled them to earn the credentials to teach, take shorthand, type, and bookkeep. Although some enrollees complained about the expense and the quality of these for-profits, many alumni offered glowing praise for alma maters that helped move them from the factory floor to the front office.[15]

Those for-profits unintentionally pushed revered campuses to serve industry's workforce needs more and heightened the scramble for the revenue needed to cover operating costs, like faculty salaries. Groeger stresses that some for-profits were undoubtedly rackets. Yet Harvard University president Charles Eliot and other elites, who denounced these schools, seemed even more disdainful of the men and women these institutions dared train. Competition and prejudice spurred Eliot and other Ivy League administrators to demand that public high schools offer business training. High-brow university leaders also started new schools for education, law, and business that provided the kind of premier academic credentials that would, in effect and practice, be unavailable to the many immigrants and citizens who had few options but proprietary programs. That kind of exclusivity not only kept top private universities overwhelmingly white and male but also ensured that those at the helm of the country's business and politics would be so as well.[16]

Matriculation nevertheless doubled in the Roaring Twenties. More citizens and immigrants risked the expense of enrolling in order to have the chance to enter the growing managerial and professional classes. Demand did little, however, to shore up the academy's finances. Donations increased, business and federal funding for scientific research grew, and legislatures earmarked more in the 1920s. But all postsecondary schools, not just for-profits, still needed students and their tuition. Public institutions relied on fees for 22.5 percent of revenue, whereas private institutions used tuition to cover 54.2 percent of expenses. Most campuses continued to charge less than administrators spent educating students. Tuition only had to cover roughly half of the University of Michigan's payroll. But that revenue paid for 63 percent of Columbia's operating expenses and almost 90 percent of those costs at the University of Pennsylvania and MIT. Campuses, philanthropies, business associations, churches, and individual donors increased tuition assistance options, including the risky student loans that reflected the spirit of the highly speculative decade just before the Great Depression. Yet elite, private institutions refused to substantially increase student bodies to meet demand. Administrators limited enrollments. They also created quotas that limited the number of Jews and Catholics admitted and generally excluded African Americans to maintain an atmosphere attractive to the country's white, Protestant elite. That pervasive campus culture helped ensure that the higher education training and credentials needed for well-paid work remained largely a white privilege, not a right for all.[17]

Federally Financing Higher Education's Expansion

Organizing did a lot to improve educational opportunities, labor rights, and work standards on and off college campuses during the academy's storied mid-twentieth-century expansion. But that growth was not as robustly funded as Worthen and Berry suggest at the start of their essay. Even though most of the nation's colleges and universities teetered on the brink of bankruptcy during the Depression, New Dealers never considered a bailout. The Roosevelt administration prioritized economic stability and security epitomized in landmark legislation like the 1935 Social Security Act, the 1935 Wagner Act, and the 1934 Federal Housing Act. The last captured how many New Deal experiments significantly improved the lives of the white working-class and revived American capitalism. The federal mortgage program, for instance, gave more white men the chance to buy a home, increased the need for construction workers, and created a government-guaranteed financial product for bankers. Federal aid for higher education seemed less cost-effective to New Dealers and would have been an unprecedented break with federalism. Many elite academics, including Harvard President James Conant, still openly opposed the direct federal aid that the Roosevelt administration never considered. They were among the president's most outspoken critics and insisted a bailout would threaten their cherished institutional autonomy and academic freedom.[18]

But ordinary Americans across the country, whom many campuses still had no interest in admitting, demanded opportunities to learn, which stunned both retrograde college faculty and the Roosevelt administration. FDR and his advisors steadily wove higher education into then-controversial, now iconic 1930s and 1940s initiatives, including the Civilian Conservation Corps, Tennessee Valley Authority, Works Progress Administration (WPA), National Youth Administration (NYA), wartime campus programs, and the 1944 Servicemen's Readjustment Act, better known as the GI Bill of Rights.[19]

Citizen demand and national defense were as important to FDR and his advisors as business and labor market considerations. For example, New Dealers considered matching WPA grants and loans to repair or expand campuses as a source of jobs for small college towns that were willing to apply and raise the rest of the money needed. The president likewise approved of NYA's work-study experiment, which was designed to keep young people from applying for work and welfare by enabling them to earn some money to study. Their degrees seemed to assure their ability to find decently paid work in the future, especially in a country that likely needed a more skilled labor force after the Depression ended. That program continued during the war to prepare young people to serve as nurses, doctors, engineers, and officers. Many returned from overseas with unprecedented guarantees to seek additional learning through a GI Bill, crafted in large part to improve the new superpower's workforce and avoid the unemployment crisis that had followed World War I's end.[20]

Yet the Roosevelt administration never prioritized improving the quality of jobs in public or private universities that chose to take part in the federal programs that provided additional revenue, not robust financing. Federal assistance for improving public campuses and the work-study available to any nonprofit institution had not covered increasing campus operating costs. Tuition continued rising and college finances remained uncertain throughout the 1930s and 1940s. Training programs, correspondence courses, and other efforts helping soldiers to study in foxholes were instances of targeted spending that had begun to dwindle before the GI Bill's passage. Those initiatives did not include rules about or oversight of campus managerial practices nor generate the revenue necessary to expand or staff campuses for an unexpected deluge of veterans.[21]

Activism was vital to changing academic labor practices so that they reflected the country's shifting workplace norms and labor standards. National faculty organizations had pushed for job security and academic freedom throughout the 1920s and 1930s, when recent PhDs, particularly Catholics and Jews, found themselves relegated to poorly paid, temporary positions. Historian Ronald Story credits nationwide, Depression-era union activism for inspiring professors to join the AAUP. Some faculty also tried to unionize. Instructors even organized in states that refused to recognize locals, which were not protected by the 1935 Wagner Act because that legislation excluded public employees (like the teachers and staff toiling in state colleges and universities). Professors also demanded faculty grievance committees, which first took hold at the elite research universities that smaller institutions often sought to emulate. That activism made the AAUP's 1940 statement on tenure far more consequential than previous demands. Likewise, the credit that university scientists received for the Allied Powers' victory abroad helped faculty make the case for continuing to improve jobs as campuses scrambled to hire instructors to teach GIs. Higher education groups and postsecondary institutions across the country subsequently endorsed the AAUP's insistence on a seven- to ten-year probationary period, faculty involvement in awarding tenure, and reliance on due process for dismissal. Those standards giving faculty a voice in the business of education nevertheless recognized that this unprecedented job security was contingent on a campus's finances.[22]

Even as faculty job security generally improved, budgets remained uncertain despite robust government and private support throughout the early Cold War. As such, public, private, and for-profit campuses remained in a competitive market for donors and students as faculty expectations for the job quality and security found in the largely white middle and professional classes increased. More Americans wanted to enroll after World War II when allocating time to study for degrees seemed to guarantee well-paying, white-collar work. Yet few could easily afford fees, books, and living expenses. Few legislatures allocated money for much-needed expansions, much less to keep fees down. Some states, most notably New York and Massachusetts, did experiment with tuition assistance programs, including helping students and parents secure loans from banks experimenting with new consumer financial products. That method did little to contain education costs, a key concern of the businesses and philanthropies that desperately tried to secure donations for private schools in order to sustain them without additional revenue from students who might be attracted to less-expensive public options. The relatively modest funding available through government defense contracts and grants for health or scientific research hardly helped. That money went to specific projects, labs, and departments at well-established state and private universities able to compete for support. That revenue, however, could never have paid for an entire university's expansion, ensured affordability, nor guaranteed faculty and staff decent jobs on campus.[23]

Laggard, conditional support worried a growing number of lawmakers. They regularly introduced various bills to federally underwrite colleges and universities in the House and Senate education subcommittees, tellingly part of those bodies' labor committees. Senators and representatives found more faculty and administrators open to the national support that many had opposed in the 1930s in the name of federalism, institutional autonomy, and academic freedom. Bills nevertheless died over disagreements about government support for private, religious, or segregated schools in the 1950s and early 1960s.[24]

Those concerns, not campus labor practices, almost scuttled the 1958 National Defense Education Act (NDEA), which did little to free the higher education enterprise's reliance on fees. That hard-fought, much-celebrated law promised limited, temporary assistance to college students after a year of fighting between and within Congress, the White House, and the Department of Health, Education, and Welfare. Money went only to science, engineering, math, and foreign-language programs with obvious importance for defense. These new resources could neither cover the collegiate growth needed, nor force more equitable admission practices, nor dictate the job quality and security for everyone working on campuses. Student assistance also went to applicants promising to study something related to defense. Only graduate students were eligible for small scholarships that lawmakers hoped would encourage more young people to pursue advanced studies that would prepare them to work in vital industries and teach on campuses that needed to expand to meet growing demand for bachelors' degrees. But lawmakers created a complicated loan program for undergraduates, which gave schools discretion over who received aid and the administration of this supposedly self-perpetuating loan program. Financial-aid officers had tremendous difficulty managing these ten-year, low-interest loans since federal deferments delayed how quickly an individual school's loan fund was replenished.[25]

The celebrated 1965 Higher Education Act (HEA) created an even more complicated financial product that foretold how important finance would become to Americans' ability to afford basic needs as the quality of American jobs began to simultaneously decline. HEA's eight titles did not explicitly address the quality of campus jobs but seemed to offer substantial general and direct support for colleges, universities, and their libraries to keep campuses open and fees down, something a handful of Democrats had been seeking since the late 1940s. Higher-education spending jumped from $1.4 billion to $3.7 billion between 1963 and 1966, but never challenged American higher education's historic reliance on a range of revenue sources. Neither the Johnson administration nor Congress entertained fully funding any components of HEA amid escalating US involvement in Vietnam, wrangling over other expensive aspects of the Great Society, pressures to avoid sizeable tax increases, and struggles to enforce the Civil Rights Act's historic guarantees. Federal spending approached the percentage of higher education revenue that local and state governments provided but private donations remained an important funding source.[26]

Lawmakers allocated the most money for the Guaranteed Student Loan Program, one of the Title IV tuition-assistance offerings that reified the importance of fees as a longstanding revenue source for colleges and universities. That section included funding for the War on Poverty's work-study program, national defense loans, and undergraduate fellowships. The recently passed 1964 Civil Rights Act seemed to offer some assurance that campus financial-aid officers would equitably allocate this federal assistance, including the loans that LBJ and other Great Society liberals hoped would spawn a new student-loan industry. That plan reflected the seeming success of the New Deal's mortgage program to enable the white working-class to buy homes. Lawmakers, in fact, modeled key aspects of the guaranteed-student loan program on that 1930s experiment because enabling Americans to borrow the money for the fees, upon which most campuses still depended, seemed a relatively inexpensive way of expanding access to higher education.[27]

"As Characteristic an Institution"

College closures and mergers nevertheless spiked in the mid-1960s. Buttenheim noted the seemingly remarkable increase in the number of campuses started in the mid-twentieth century, when growing federal support between 1954 and 1974 helped multiply the number of community colleges, enabled almost every state to develop at least one new public research university, and tripled the country's student body, which included a growing number of women, students of color, and graduate students. But federal earmarks largely went to tuition assistance. In retrospect, HEA's passage marked the zenith of direct federal support for campuses, which foretold what education experts proclaimed to be a "New Depression in Higher Education." Those early 1970s proclamations coincided with growing public awareness of the declining auto industry, whose early twentieth-century potency Buttenheim daringly compared to the seemingly new business of education in 1969.

Uncertainty about the finances, quality of jobs, and power of employees plagued both American manufacturing and higher education. Administrators at nonprofit institutions continued to charge less than the cost of instruction and did not receive enough direct support from state or federal officials to end the financial problems that had long plagued many colleges and universities. Almost half of US campuses seemed headed for trouble in the early 1970s, when another 19 percent already faced financial difficulties. Campus shutdowns, like plant closures, had a devastating impact on students, professors, and surrounding communities. Small towns and city neighborhoods often relied on campuses to serve the many functions that University of California President Clark Kerr described in his 1963 *Uses of the University*. Employment was especially important in the 1970s, when researchers noted that universities had "become as characteristic an institution in America as the church was three hundred years ago."[28]

Campus job quality worsened in a country whose economic fortunes became more closely linked to deregulated finance than to unionized manufacturing. Only 78 percent of faculty were tenured or tenure-track faculty three decades after the AAUP's 1940 tenure statement. That figure reflected how, as labor historians have shown, many Americans, especially those of color, had also been left out of postwar American prosperity. Experts have emphasized that only a third of the postwar labor force was organized. Scholars of race and gender, like Gwendolyn Alker who offers a feminist rethinking of contingent labor in this volume, have highlighted that those unionized workers were predominantly white men, a fact that has also helped illuminate why New Deal experiments exacerbated longstanding inequalities over time. Job quality and security remained far less certain for non-union workers, particularly women of color who disproportionately struggled to pursue the advanced degrees needed to just compete for well-paying work. Parallels between the academic and national labor market only continued in the late twentieth and early twenty-first centuries. Berry and Worthen note in their essay how much has changed. Recent studies focusing on the academic labor market also underscore that the percentage of tenured and tenure-track faculty has steadily declined since the early 1970s. Some reports now indicate that roughly 75 percent of faculty have no possibility of tenure. That shifting reality, evident in the declining availability and quality of academic jobs (discussed throughout this volume), was hardly unique to the American higher education enterprise. Labor historians have emphasized for years that the decent, secure white- and blue-collar jobs that bolstered the largely white middle-class's postwar prosperity have steadily disappeared.[29]

Lawmakers, parents, and students have been far more focused on rising fees and student debts than overhauling higher education's business model and labor practices since the 1970s. Taxpayers revolted as the economy stagnated, inflation soared, and inequality increased. These uprisings left local and state officials with far less revenue to cover critical services, including education, and often empowered politicians eager to further cut taxes and spending. DC Democrats and Republicans also prioritized the student loan industry. They made for-profit schools eligible for federal student assistance programs, enabled parents to borrow, made discharging student debt during bankruptcy proceedings almost impossible, and used Fannie Mae as a model for Sallie Mae, a government-sponsored enterprise that made profiting off student debt easier for banks.[30]

Those reforms did little to help the millions drowning in debt, colleges struggling to remain open, and staff and faculty decrying the loss of job security. Since the early 1990s, lawmakers have battled over replacing guaranteed loans with direct loans from the government, tax breaks, public service forgiveness programs, and repayment options, which often leave parents and students, particularly borrowers of color (especially women), paying more over a longer period of time. Such reforms did little to shore up the academy's finances. Administrators have resorted to devising ways to profit from patents, international students, transnational partnerships, foreign degree programs, and online options. Those experiments, cutting costs, and hiring more adjuncts led many to label these institutions as neoliberal, which did little to stop a handful of campuses from closing or merging annually before COVID-19 upended many schools' already-precarious finances.[31]

Congress and the Trump administration did not offer much more during the pandemic. Lawmakers expanded access to federal tuition assistance options that have been linked to federal aid for colleges and universities since the early 1970s. The $14 billion allocated for campuses in the March 2020 CARES Act included $6 billion for emergency grants for students as well as funds to cover costs connected to COVID-19. Americans paying off certain kinds of federal student loans also received several months of suspended payments and interest charges.[32]

Much more would have been needed to change higher education's business model. Even President Joe Biden's push to make community college tuition-free would not have been enough. Campuses have relied historically on a mix of revenue sources that included philanthropy, government support, and student tuition financed increasingly through complicated loan programs. Finance's longstanding and increasing importance to the business of education epitomizes how colleges and universities have continuously reflected, shaped, and sustained the prevailing political, economic, cultural, social, and workplace standards. Those norms have largely kept postsecondary schooling a private luxury instead of a public good, which campuses have only come close to being after sustained organizing from those working on, studying on, or aspiring to enroll in campuses. As such, everyone has a role to play in securing the funding for and ensuring it is used to make colleges and universities model employers, schools, and research centers.

Notes

1. This essay draws on work first published in Elizabeth Tandy Shermer, "What's Really New about the Neoliberal University? The Business of American Education Has Always Been Business," *Labor* 18:4 (December 2021): 62–86. "Donald Buttenheim, 91, Magazine Publisher," *Berkshire Eagle*, December 12, 2006, https://www.berkshireeagle.com/stories/donald-buttenheim-91-magazine-publisher,483654; UPI, "Best Growth Industry in U.S. Today: Schools," *Chicago Tribune*, January 4, 1969, D7.

2. Elizabeth Tandy Shermer, "The Ongoing Crisis in American Colleges," *European Journal of American Culture* 37:1 (April 2018): 90–94; Shermer, "What's Really New about the Neoliberal University?" For recent examples of uses of the "neoliberal university phrase," see Tom Hansberger and Sarah Kizuk, "The Neoliberal University Is Failing on Coronavirus," *Jacobin*, August 19, 2020, https://www.jacobinmag.com/2020/08/marquette-university-reopening-covid-coronavirus; Todd Wolfson and Astra Taylor, "Beyond the Neoliberal University," *Boston Review*, August 4, 2020, http://bostonreview.net/class-inequality/todd-wolfson-astra-taylor-beyond-neoliberal-university.

3. Elizabeth Tandy Shermer, "From Educator to Creditor in Chief: The American Presidency, Higher Education, and the Student Loan Industry," in *The President and American Capitalism since 1945*, ed. Mark Rose and Roger Biles (Gainesville: University of Florida Press, 2017), 123–150; Shermer, "What's Really New about the Neoliberal University?"; Elizabeth Tandy Shermer, "Financing Security and Opportunity: The New Deal and the Origins of the Millennial Student Debt Crisis," in *Capitalism Contested: The New Deal and Its Legacies*, ed. Romain Huret, Nelson Lichtenstein, and Jean-Christian Vinel (Philadelphia: University of Pennsylvania Press, 2020); Elizabeth Tandy Shermer, *Indentured Students: How Government-Guaranteed Loans Left Generations Drowning in College Debt* (Cambridge, MA: Harvard University Press, 2021), 15–32; Roger Geiger, *To Advance Knowledge: The Growth of American Research Universities, 1900–1940* (New York: Oxford University Press, 1986), 12–14, 107–110; Roger Geiger, *Research and Relevant Knowledge: American Research Universities since World War II* (New York: Oxford University Press, 1993), quoted vii.

4. Shermer, *Indentured Students*, 15–32; Shermer, "What's Really New about the Neoliberal University?"; Virginia Sapiro, "The Life Course of Higher Education Institutions: When the End Comes," working paper, 2019, 5–9, quoted 5, http://blogs.bu.edu/vsapiro/files/2019/02/SapiroWhentheEndComes2019-1.pdf; Virginia Sapiro, "When the End Comes to Higher Education Institutions, 1890–2019," *PEGS: The Blog*, February 28, 2019, http://blogs.bu.edu/vsapiro/2019/02/28/when-the-end-comes-to-higher-education-institutions-1890–2019/.

5. Craig Wilder, *Ebony and Ivory: Race, Slavery, and the Troubled History of America's Universities* (New York: Bloomsbury Press, 2013); William Snider, *Light on the Hill: A History of the University of North Carolina* (Chapel Hill: University of North Carolina Press, 1992), 3–38, quoted 5; John Chapman, "Black Freedom and the University of North Carolina, 1793–1960" (PhD diss., University of North Carolina, Chapel Hill, 2006), 7–72.

6. Snider, *Light on the Hill*, 3–38; Chapman, "Black Freedom and the University of North Carolina," 7–72.

7. Shermer, *Indentured Students*, 15–32; Shermer, "What's Really New about the Neoliberal University?"; Robert Lee and Tristan Ahtone, "Land-Grab Universities," *High Country News*, March 30, 2020, https://www.hcn.org/issues/52.4/indigenous-affairs-education-land-grab-universities?utm_source=pocket-newtab; Tristan Ahtone and Robert Lee, "Ask Who Paid for America's Universities," *New York Times*, May 7, 2020, https://www.nytimes.com/2020/05/07/opinion/land-grant-universities-native-americans.html?referringSource=articleShare; Admissions, "A Brief History of MIT," accessed September 10, 2020, https://mitadmissions.org/discover/about-mit/a-brief-history-of-mit/.

8. Shermer, *Indentured Students*, 15–32; Lee and Ahtone, "Land-Grab Universities"; Paul Dressel, *College to University: The Hannah Year at Michigan State, 1935–1969* (East Lansing: Michigan State University Publications, 1987), 17–96; Lyle Blair and Madison Kuhn, *A Short History of Michigan State* (East Lansing: Michigan State College Press, 1955), 5–13; Verne Stadtman, *The University of California, 1868–1968* (New York: McGraw-Hill, 1970), 45–47.

9. Sapiro, "Life Course of Higher Education Institutions"; Dressel, *College to University*, 17–96; Blair and Kuhn, *Short History of Michigan State*, 5–13.

10. Shapiro, "When the End Comes."

11. Shermer, *Indentured Students*, 15–32; Shermer, "What's Really New about the Neoliberal University?"; Roger Geiger, "Ten Generations of American Higher Education," in *American Higher Education in the Twenty-First Century: Social, Political, and Economic Challenges*, ed. Michael N. Bastedo, Philip G. Altbach, Patricia J. Gumport (Baltimore: Johns Hopkins University Press, 1999), 38–69; Laurence Veysey, *Emergence of the American University* (Chicago: University of Chicago Press, 1970), 1–20; Merle Curti and Roderick Nash, *Philanthropy in the Shaping of American Higher Education* (New Brunswick: Rutgers University Press, 1965), 111–132; David Levine, *American College and the Culture of Aspiration, 1915–1940* (Ithaca, NY: Cornell University Press, 1986), 13–22; Ernest Hollis, *Philanthropic Foundations and Higher Education* (New York: Columbia University Press, 1938), 1–6, 268–281; Trevor Arnett, *College and University Finance* (New York: General Education Board, 1922), 3–14.

12. Curti and Nash, *Philanthropy*, 212–237; Ronald Story, "New Deal and Higher Education," in *New Deal and the Triumph of Liberalism*, ed. Sidney Milkis and Jerome Mileur (Amherst: University of Massachusetts Press, 2002), 272–296; Shermer, "What's Really New about the Neoliberal University?"

13. Shermer, *Indentured Students*, 15–32; Shermer, "What's Really New about the Neoliberal University?"

14. Ibid.

15. Ibid.; Veysey, *Emergence of the American University*, 1–20, 110–113; Levine, *American College and the Culture of Aspiration*, 13–22; Cristina Groeger, *Education Trap: Schools and the Remaking of Inequality in Boston* (Cambridge, MA: Harvard University Press, 2021), 139–181.

16. Shermer, *Indentured Students*, 15–32; Shermer, "What's Really New about the Neoliberal University?"; Groeger, *Education Trap*, 221–229, 242–248.

17. Geiger, *To Advance Knowledge*, 12–13, 94–139; Levine, *American College and the Culture of Aspiration*, 113–135; Shermer, *Indentured Students*, 15–32; Shermer, "What's Really New about the Neoliberal University?"

18. The material in this and the following paragraphs is drawn from: Shermer, "From Educator to Creditor in Chief"; Shermer, "What's Really New about the Neoliberal University?"; Shermer, "Financing Security and Opportunity"; Shermer, *Indentured Students*, 15–75.

19. Ibid.

20. Ibid.

21. Ibid.

22. Shermer, "What's Really New about the Neoliberal University?"; Story, "New Deal and Higher Education." See also the essay by William A. Herbert and Joseph van der Naald in this collection.

23. Shermer, "From Educator to Creditor in Chief"; Shermer, "What's Really New about the Neoliberal University?"; Shermer, "Financing Security and Opportunity"; Shermer, *Indentured Students*, 117–202.

24. Shermer, "From Educator to Creditor in Chief"; Shermer, "What's Really New about the Neoliberal University?"; Shermer, "Financing Security and Opportunity"; Shermer, *Indentured Students*, 117–202.

25. Ibid.

26. Ibid.

27. Ibid.

28. Ibid.; Sapiro, "When the End Comes"; Earl Cheit, *New Depression in Higher Education: A Study of Financial Conditions at 41 Colleges and Universities* (New York: McGraw-Hill, 1971), table 1 in unpaginated foreword; Clark Kerr, *Uses of the University* (Cambridge, MA: Harvard University Press, 2001); quoted Veysey, *Emergence of the American University*, ix.

29. Adrianna Kezar and Daniel Maxey, "Changing Academic Workforce," *Association of Governing Boards of Universities and Colleges* 21:3 (May/June 2013), https://agb.org/trusteeship-article/the-changing-academic-workforce/; Todd Wallis, "Rise of Adjunct Faculty: A Brief History," *Inside Scholar*, April 11, 2018, https://insidescholar.org/the-rise-of-adjunct-faculty/; Shermer, "What's Really New about the Neoliberal University?" On the changing nature of the twentieth-century labor market see: Nelson Lichtenstein, *State of the Union: A Century of American Labor* (Princeton, NJ: Princeton University Press, 2002).

30. Shermer, "From Educator to Creditor in Chief"; Shermer, "What's Really New about the Neoliberal University?"; Shermer, "Financing Security and Opportunity"; Shermer, *Indentured Students*, 202–302.

31. Shermer, *Indentured Students*, 288–302; Stephen Mihm, "Coronavirus Pushes Higher Education to the Brink," *Bloomberg*, April 4, 2020; https://www.bloomberg.com/opinion/articles/2020-04-04/coronavirus-u-s-colleges-and-universities-reach-breaking-point#xj4y7vzkg.

32. Shermer, "What's Really New about the Neoliberal University?"; Shermer, *Indentured Students*, 288–302; Danielle Douglas-Gabriel, "Stimulus Deal Delivers Billions in Pandemic Aid to Colleges," *Washington Post*, December 21, 2020, https://www.washingtonpost.com/education/2020/12/21/stimulus-colleges-relief/.

CHAPTER 4

WHY FACULTY CASUALIZATION?

Its Origins and the Present Challenges
of the Contingent Faculty Movement

JOE BERRY AND HELENA WORTHEN

Casualization, today's prevailing workforce management strategy, has transformed employment relations in the industry of higher education. Within a single lifetime, an overwhelming majority of faculty jobs in higher education have gone from being permanent positions with employment security, benefits, good wages, and academic freedom to being precarious low-wage jobs with few benefits and little control in the workplace. In the late 1960s, 70 to 75 percent of faculty positions were tenure-stream and full-time. Today, the percentage is reversed, making for a casualized workforce that, from management's view, is flexible and manageable.

College and university administrators, the local-level managers of higher education, turned to casualization in the later twentieth and early twenty-first centuries, a period of neoliberal contraction, as they faced a set of interlocking challenges connected to changes in the political economy and to other societal shifts. These challenges—or "problems" from the perspective of local-level mangers—revolved around a financial crisis leading to cutbacks, uncertainty about enrollment due to a changing student body, a rising threat of academic faculty unionization, and an increasingly diversified academic labor pool that did not resemble the white male professorate of the past. Following a brief overview of transitions in higher education since the later nineteenth century, each prompted by changes in American capitalism and society, we then examine these more recent challenges, discussing how they emerged and how managers responded.

Each transition marked a distinctive phase in the history of higher education. Entire institutions reinvented themselves at least four times, entailing struggles over governance, financing, its student body, and—our focus here—its faculty. As local-level managers grappled with the implications of large-scale changes, they sought to reconfigure labor relations and the profile of the faculty. In each period, answers to questions about who was to be hired, what should be taught, and the conditions of faculty work were adapted to solve immediate problems. Each solution was a response not to pedagogical demands or needs, but to actions by powerful actors who controlled crucial resources in society. We concentrate on the fourth transition, the neoliberal contraction in which the dynamic driving faculty employment in higher education is characterized by casualization, the sharp increase in the use of contingent faculty, and the general undermining of job security. By locating casualization within this history of transformations, we also argue that this need not be the end of the story; the wheel will turn again, and organized campaigns for stability and justice can help to move it.

Higher Education and Capitalism
since the Late Nineteenth Century

Elizabeth Tandy Shermer, in her chapter in this volume, portrays the macro financial history of the delivery of higher education in the United States as a relentless push and pull among legislation, student tuition, and philanthropy. However, beneath this macro level, managers in institutions of higher education have had to respond to these pressures as they were handed down from above. How they did so in the past and under what conditions provides context for the more recent changes that we experience today.

The demands of industrialization in the late nineteenth and first part of the twentieth centuries created a new segment of the middle class—corporate managers, accountants, and communications experts—which, in turn, generated the need for a more educated workforce. But educational standards varied from state to state in form, character, purpose, and quality. In response, many saw a need to standardize teaching and learning. In 1905, the Carnegie Foundation for the Advancement of Teaching issued a report that laid out the basis for the future standardization of education in the United States, parallel to the simultaneous process of rationalization in industrial workplaces.[1] The "Carnegie credit unit," which assumed one hour of classroom lecture and two hours of study outside the class spread over a fifteen-week semester, became the foundation on which most three-credit college courses are built today. In addition, this period saw the formation of many academic professional associations, such as the American Historical Association, the American Anthropological Association, and the American Economic Association, which further regularized standards within disciplines.

This standardization of higher education helped make possible its expansion in the years immediately following World War II. The Servicemen's Readjustment Act, or GI Bill, of 1944, sought to provide military-trained veterans recognizable qualifications through access to higher education as they pursued a better standard of living after fifteen years of economic depression.[2] As a result, the college student population drastically increased. The 1947 Truman Report, *Higher Education for American Democracy*, proposed the establishment of a community college within sixty miles of every American, equipped to offer postsecondary, as well as vocational training for "all youth who can profit."[3] The *1960 California Masterplan for Higher Education* reflected similar goals.[4] At one point in the United States, a new community college was opened each week, totaling over 1,000 in the 1970s.[5] This increased demand for higher education meant an increased demand for a higher education workforce.

In this hungry labor market, the possibility of tenure for faculty, as laid out in the American Association of University Professors (AAUP) *1940 Statement of Principles of Academic Freedom and Tenure*, became the ideological standard.[6] However, amid the charged atmosphere of the Cold War, neither tenure nor academic freedom was universal. Nonetheless, under the AAUP standard, the professional life expectancy of an academic could reasonably be thirty or forty years in a single job.

Notably, both the student population and faculty were predominantly white, male, and able-bodied in the decades immediately following World War II, as quota systems limiting entry for Black and Jewish students prevailed, as female students were often restricted to particular programs, and as wounded veterans often found these institutions literally inaccessible. In retrospect, while the adaptation of higher education to the needs of the mass of returning veterans led to a vast expansion in enrollments and programs, it did not try to break down the barriers of race, gender, or disability. This would be the work of students in the 1960s and beyond.

Struggles in higher education during the 1960s erupted from within and without. Outside of higher education this arose first among participants in the civil rights movement and later among other racial and ethnic groups, LGBTQ activists, women, people with disabilities, and working-class women and men, as seen in campaigns for voting rights, labor rights, and social rights. Inside higher education, the initial goals of these struggles were to increase access and support followed by efforts to transform the curriculum, which had been structured around the experiences of an overwhelmingly white, male professoriate. These struggles led to modifications of admission requirements in previously selective and restrictive institutions alongside a change in who would be hired to teach these classes. This resulted in a more diverse student body and the establishment of new academic fields, such as ethnic studies, Black studies, women's studies, peace and conflict studies, and expanded labor education programs. But these social and political movements, what the Trilateral Commission, tasked with investigating the student activism of the 1960s, labeled an "excess of democracy," converged with the economic crisis of the 1970s.[7] Economic stagflation and a falling rate of profit in the business sector, combined with a broad loss of faith in government following Watergate, the resignation of President Richard Nixon, and defeat in Vietnam, created a context in which market-based solutions became dominant. Higher education was not immune from this transformation.

The Neoliberal Contraction (1970–the Present)

The higher education industry that contingent faculty work in today reflects the widespread application of neoliberal policies to education finance, governance, and workforce management. An overarching set of social and political priorities, neoliberalism operates through privatization, deregulation, and market supremacy. Like classical liberalism, it prefers limited government. Neoliberalism diverges, however, from the classical liberalism of Adam Smith; the government that he envisioned in 1776 in *The Wealth of Nations* was in its infancy as a creator of a public sector and a positive force in the economy.[8] Today's neoliberalism, a return on new terrain to liberalism after the excursion into Keynesianism and social democracy of the first three quarters of the twentieth century, confronts a government that has developed a public sector large enough to play a significant role in equalizing and moderating the impacts of the capitalist business cycle. But in the ideal neoliberal state, government should do no more than enforce property rights and private contracts and protect capital accumulation and profits domestically and abroad. Government supports for public goods are labeled a monopoly. In the neoliberal regime, governmental regulation, labor and environmental protections, services such as public schools and public health are all cast as suspect, as impediments to unfettered trade and to the primacy of capital.[9]

The economic contraction of the 1970s precipitated the long-term decline in public funding for all sorts of programs. The 1973 oil shock raised the price of oil and thus increased the costs of doing business, private and public, in a carbon-dependent economy and society. The hardships of 1970s stagflation and the anxiety that this economic turmoil prompted undercut earlier support for Keynesian policies and public spending. These trends accelerated with the rise of finance capitalism, growing demands at home and abroad for "belt-tightening" measures, and intensifying globalization (due to a combination of technological innovations, such as computer-based information systems, and international arrangements favoring low-cost trade). In the wake of these and other social upheavals, including the debacle of the US war in Vietnam, the priorities and extent of public spending shifted. While spending for Medicare, Medicaid, and even some areas of education continued to grow, a greater portion of public spending went to policing, incarceration, and defense, accompanied by state- and federal-level tax cuts.[10]

The neoliberal contraction of the late twentieth and early twenty-first centuries shaped the economic context in which policymakers, managers, workers, and consumers operated, as well as constraining the range of policy options or daily practices that were defined as "realistic" or possible. In short, material life and ideas during this period have reflected the neoliberal contraction. This includes, of course, how the higher education system and specific institutions have transformed during this time, affecting administrators, faculty, and students. Especially revealing are the ways in which local-level managers in higher education, or administrators at a range of levels (i.e., from presidents, to financial officers, to associate deans, and to department chairs), have perceived and responded to challenges, or problems. To apply the neoliberal agenda to higher education, local-level managers dealt with four interlocking problems: declining funding, a "just-in-time" student body, faculty solidarity, and increasing diversity in a time of austerity. While other people involved in higher education, such as faculty and students, certainly acted and helped to reshape individual institutions and, to a lesser degree, the system of higher education, local-level managers have had a disproportionate role in both defining problems and putting into place procedures and expectations that recast higher education to fit the neoliberal regime.[11]

PROBLEM 1: DECLINING FUNDING

One goal of the neoliberal agenda is to make large cutbacks in the public sector and other public goods. In addition to austerity measures, privatization initiatives are used to transform or shrink public, or nonmarket, institutions. Parks, K–12 schools, public health, communication networks, transportation systems, prisons, and even major portions of the military have been brought under "market discipline" by being sapped of public funding, run according to market values, and privatized.

Higher education has also been a target for austerity and privatization. For-profit entities, such as the University of Phoenix, DeVry University, and Kaplan University, have edged their way into the mainstream (along with the now-defunct Trump University), growing well past their roots in trade and commercial schools to grant college and postgraduate degrees and receive top-level accreditation. The people who teach in these for-profit institutions are almost all contingent faculty, often with the lowest pay and least amount of control in their work as educators.[12]

For the larger system of public and nonprofit colleges and universities, the impetus for austerity and privatization means running these institutions like businesses, assessing institutional practices and educational outcomes by the values of the marketplace. For instance, program-based budgeting and, therefore, the implementation of program-based discipline and performance metrics to replicate those used in the private sector, reach now into every corner of higher education. Every economic unit within a university is expected to become a profit-center or justify its continuation by pricing out costs and benefits. This calculus undermines the global mission of the institution, placing every one of its units in competition, at some level, with the others. At Harvard, the term employed was "every tub on its own bottom."[13] Small units (like a foreign language institute or a labor studies program) may find that they are being charged rent for the use of classrooms or computer labs.[14] Students are understood to be "customers" or "products" prepared for and delivered to employers. Or students are generators of debt, connected to lending institutions by way of their school.[15] Tuition has risen steeply in recent decades, representing a cost-shifting to students and parents. Education is promoted increasingly for its return on investment (ROI), with ROI claims and analytics found on college websites and in reports to grantors. This perspective on education converts what was previously considered a social good, supported by taxation and public investment, into a private commodity, purchased by individual families.

The immediate roots of these shifts in education are found in the decline in public funding for higher education and other public programs, prompted initially by the national economic contraction of the 1970s. Even though demand for higher education remained high, public funding on a per-student basis plummeted. In the private nonprofit higher education sector, 1970s stagflation and the cost of progressive reforms led to declining revenues; charitable donations and the investment revenue from endowment funds shrank, or at least stagnated in purchasing power. In earlier decades, these had supported private higher education and kept its tuition manageable. Now, in both the public and private nonprofit sectors of higher education, chancellors, administrators, department chairs, and other local-level managers had strong incentives to tighten budgets and reduce labor costs.

Higher education administrators implemented these cuts in the face of a seemingly intractable tenure-stream workforce that had job security, academic freedom, decent pay, benefits, and, often, a significant role in institutional governance. One path toward reduced labor costs in colleges and universities lay in expanding the once-small group of contingent faculty, separating their pay rate and status from those of tenured faculty, and institutionalizing a permanent second tier. So, while hiring contingents started, or at least accelerated, as a short-term response to a national economic crisis, it soon became standard operating procedure.

PROBLEM 2: A JUST-IN-TIME STUDENT BODY

In the post-1970 period, non-elite higher education saw an increasing percentage of "nontraditional" students coming through the door, many of whom were working adults, often with years of experience in the labor market. In this large, non-elite sector of higher education, which includes community colleges, some state universities, and for-profit institutions, people tend to return to school when finding a decent job is difficult, if layoffs increase, or if existing skills are becoming obsolete. People aspired to retrain, add new skills, or to pursue a new path in life. Many of these students looked for classes in vocational and professional training with an emphasis on science, technology, engineering, and math courses (STEM), as well as finance, insurance, and real estate (FIRE). This marked a shift from the humanities, social sciences, and the arts as core elements in undergraduate education.

Reflecting other domestic and global changes, the student body became more diverse in composition and in educational needs. New or expanding groups of students included veterans from the Vietnam War and subsequent conflicts; immigrants and refugees, many needing English-language-learner classes; "displaced homemakers" and other recently divorced women seeking economic independence; women and men pursuing personal growth; and students of color attracted by a newfound accessibility to higher education and a more representative curriculum won by the civil rights struggles of the 1960s and 1970s. Many of these students could not afford to attend school full-time or consistently, facing both economic barriers and other commitments as adults. Their continued attendance depended on financial aid, low tuition rates, work schedules, childcare, healthcare, and accommodations for physical or psychological disabilities. Crucial, of course, was the availability of needed classes, in time slots and locations that made enrollment feasible.

Many "nontraditional" students lacked what were dubbed "basic skills" for college success. In California, for instance, cutbacks resulting from Proposition 13 in 1978 and the general antitax movement undermined the K–12 system. Remediation, which previously had been available at the high school level, moved upward to community colleges and four-year institutions.[16] Remedial reading and writing programs burgeoned in colleges and universities, serving students who had not been supported sufficiently in grade school or high school. Administrators sought to regularize and lower costs in remedial programs by creating computerized learning labs staffed not by faculty but by work-study students or low-paid technicians whose main expertise was software. Companies selling educational hardware and software for these labs encouraged administrators' efforts in this direction.

Overall, these changes and the unpredictability of enrollments, the composition of the student body, and educational needs created complications for lower-level managers. In the past, they could plan budgets and staffing based on how many students graduated from high school the previous year. With this new demographic, managers had to be able to set up classes quickly, adding more if needed, or canceling them if they did not fill. The solution that administrators embraced, first for the short term and then in the longer term, was a flexible contingent faculty that could be hired on a per-class basis and laid off ("descheduled" or "nonrenewed") when not needed. This faculty, which had no job security, would be in no position to complain about increasing class sizes, lack of preparation time, or loss of control over what and how they were expected to teach. Somewhat ironically, a just-in-time faculty, often part-time, served just-in-time students, also mostly part-time.

PROBLEM 3: FACULTY SOLIDARITY

Administrators' efforts to deal with funding cuts and a changing student body have led in the direction of a fragmented faculty with diminished workplace control. The previously secure tenured faculty find themselves with increasing demands on already full schedules and, in many cases, anxiety about their financial security and voice in the university. At the same time, the growing cohort of contingent faculty is characterized most starkly by the adjunct professor who becomes a "freeway flyer," driving from campus to campus for a series of low-paid gigs. The pressures on academic workers and fragmentation of the workforce have sparked moves toward solidarity and stirred up administrators' worries about faculty organizing.[17]

Although overall rates of union membership have declined in the United States since peaking in the mid-twentieth century, public sector unionism, spurred on especially by the civil rights movement, had been on the rise throughout much of this period. Likewise, union organizing among faculty, graduate assistants, and other campus workers took hold in the era of neoliberal contraction, driven by both the social movements of the 1960s and 1970s and the increasing pressures in higher education. Faculty unionization was cut short, however, in private nonprofit colleges and universities by the 1980 US Supreme Court *Yeshiva* decision that defined full-time tenure-track and tenured faculty members in private institutions as managers, therefore outside the protections of the National Labor Relations Act.[18]

The United States lacks a national public sector collective bargaining law, leaving collective bargaining for teachers and campus workers up to the states. Beginning in the 1960s and 1970s and continuing today, political pressure has forced the passage of laws in thirty-nine states to allow for collective bargaining. The specter of collective bargaining for public sector workers is fearsome enough to employers and managers, however, that a few states prohibit teachers' collective bargaining—North Carolina, Mississippi, Texas, and Virginia, which not long ago loosened its ban. Despite the obstacles in these and other states, teachers recently have used direct action to force state authorities or local school districts to the bargaining table.[19] These actions, along with those undertaken to organize faculty and other campus workers at community colleges, four-year colleges, and state universities, seek to improve employment conditions and to alter the balance of power in education.

One of the key demands in most union drives has been for transparency and equity in compensation. This includes setting clear salary schedules and pay rates, pushing for pay equalization across categories by bringing up the bottom, demanding fairer treatment, and implementing grievance procedures. Tenure-track and non-tenure-track faculty, clerical and support staff, graduate assistants, and students often support these efforts. Faculty also call for a meaningful voice in crucial decisions about curriculum and the use of institutional resources, through shared governance and other means. When these demands are won, they have the capacity to frustrate managers' plans, constraining the range of their discretion.

While faculty unionization threatened to limit management's power to casualize part of the faculty, the creation of a permanent two-tier system within the faculty presents an obstacle to solidarity. Not only does a two-tier system divide the faculty, but it forces tenure-stream faculty to confront questions such as: Who should be in the union? Are contingent faculty our brothers and sisters, or are they scabbing? It similarly forces contingents to ask: Can tenure-stream faculty be our brothers and sisters? Or are they, with semi-supervisory and quasi-managerial roles, part of the opposition? These questions suggest that contingents must choose between fighting over pieces of a management-set budget pie or waging a combined struggle to force an expansion of the pie. At the very least, a two-tier system distracted from unified struggle against the employer. At the worst, it resulted in hamstrung and often aborted union drives. Even today, the two-tier system has produced unions incapable of either representing their emerging contingent majority or exercising the strength and authority needed vis-à-vis the employer.

Most managers did not explicitly plan this divide-and-conquer approach when they first hired adjuncts in greater numbers. Nor did most of them intentionally casualize and fragment their own faculty to gain greater control (although, certainly, some did). But once the benefits of this tactic became apparent, administrators accepted it as an effective strategy to thwart unionization, contain costs, and retain power.[20] This strategy is now almost universally supported by management, as made evident by numerous legal challenges against attempts to create combined tenure-stream and contingent bargaining units.

The expansion of contingent faculty, and consequent loss of job security for the majority of faculty, has disempowered the faculty as a whole. We agree with historian and activist Richard Moser's claim that the neoliberal agenda took hold in higher education only after its main internal opponent, the faculty, had been weakened by casualization.[21] The faculty of the 1960s and 1970s was a workforce that still could have waged, if sufficiently organized, effective resistance in the face of management. But by the time the neoliberal agenda had become not just an imminent but a present threat in the 1980s, the typical faculty member did not have the resources, the time, the organization, the incentives, or the academic freedom to take risks and oppose it. As Moser argues, the casualization of the faculty was the "camel's nose under the tent of academia."[22] Despite a later upsurge in faculty organizing, once the nose was under the canvas, the rest of the camel walked in and virtually filled up the tent with neoliberal "reforms."

PROBLEM 4: DIVERSITY, INCLUSION, AND AUSTERITY

The social and political ferment of the 1960s and 1970s, overlapping with the early phases of neoliberal contraction, recast higher education. Civil rights and freedom movements, the women's movement and second-wave feminism, and the antiwar and youth movements reshaped the curriculum, the student body, and the faculty, while also briefly challenging administrators' power. As more students of color began attending colleges and universities, as more faculty of color were hired, and as more women entered the academy, tools of casualization accompanied those of racism and sexism to make the presence of marginalized people insecure. While women and people of color continued to be underrepresented in higher education, especially in positions of power, their entry in greater numbers coincided—not accidentally—with the undermining of stable faculty jobs. The growth of lower-paid, lower-status positions formed in this process of casualization accompanied a change in the applicant pool for academic labor, as more women and previously underrepresented groups sought to enter the profession. Casualization and inclusion joined together as higher education became more diverse, although still predominantly white and male, and contingent.

By the 1980s, a more diverse cohort—along the lines of race, gender, and class—was entering the market for faculty jobs. Women and people of color attended graduate schools as the doors for admission slowly opened, and now with credentials in hand (completed MAs or PhDs) began applying for faculty positions. Affirmative action policies, although under attack in courts and the public arena, aided a gradual shift in hiring practices. Some aspiring faculty members also were veterans of social movements, bringing commitments to equity and social justice to their scholarship and teaching. Along with other social movement allies, this younger cohort began to challenge existing curricular and disciplinary boundaries, bringing concerns about race and gender into new programs—for example, Black studies and gender studies programs—as well as to stalwarts of the academy—for example, biology or history courses that attended to race or gender as a social construction. Likewise, the faculty emerging from social movements challenged the distribution of power on the campus, confronting administrators and forming faculty unions. Many students, also drawn from an increasingly diverse pool of potential applicants, were attracted to these teachers and eager to benefit from innovations in pedagogy and subject matter. Opposition to these new approaches coalesced within the academy and from outside, especially as political conservatives sought to score points, creating further turmoil in reaction to these changes.

As a part of this diversification of the faculty, administrators began hiring more contingent faculty to teach courses for an increasingly diverse student body. Many faculty jobs were stripped of resources, security, or the professional status previously enjoyed. Some teachers in the growing population of adjuncts were part-timers with experience in newly expanding fields of study, including business, finance, and real estate. Others staffed the new interdisciplinary programs, such as race and ethnic studies and gender studies. Viewed by administrators as temporary or supplementary, these positions did not come with the traditional perquisites of a faculty job that had accrued to previous generations of white, male professors. These jobs now lacked security, a livable salary, respect, academic freedom, or authority within the institution. In other words, diversity and casualization shaped administrators' hiring and employment practices during this era of neoliberal contraction. (See Gwendolyn Alker's chapter in this volume for how academic work, as it became feminized, became more exploitable.) In turn, an increasing percentage of the students taught by this now "lower-class" professorate could themselves be described as nontraditional, working-class, people of color, and women.

What Next?

Amid all the changes in higher education over the last decades there remains a constant: both a popular demand and a societal need for what institutions of higher education offer. Neither the demand nor the need disappears. Today, despite neoliberal privatization and corporatization, higher education remains alive and significant. It also remains publicly subsidized. Although significantly weakened, it still functions and is viewed by many as a public good. When we look ahead to the inevitable next transition in higher education, we must ask: What will be its key mission?

The four problems, to which higher education administrators responded by increasing faculty casualization, can be turned inside out. Why call them problems? For example, for whom is diversity a problem? Diversity is a desired goal and not a hurdle in a society that has long privileged white men. For whom is unionization a problem? Not for faculty or for other workers in higher education who need adequate compensation, job security, and control over their work. Nor should it be for higher education managers, who ought to support a stable, accountable partner in governance that represents the priorities and capacities of the faculty. On the contrary, unionization is a solution. For whom are budget cuts a problem? Here the question should be, instead, why is higher education underfunded? There is plenty of money to fund colleges and universities. The problem lies with decisions about budgets and taxes. What are society's priorities and who pays? That is a different kind of problem, one that casualization will not solve. Recalibrating this question can, in turn, provide a different solution for the challenge of the just-in-time-student body. Commitments to fund higher education offer students a dependable path, without the unreasonable burden of debt. Once again, casualization is no longer the solution.

Flexibility should continue to be a concern for higher education administrators. The need for higher education will not go away: however, where it is needed, when, and by whom will continue to change as an increasingly diverse student body includes greater numbers of older and part-time students alongside recent high school graduates who are full-time students. So, while the need for flexibility will continue, it can be better planned for and designed to serve students while simultaneously treating faculty fairly. Flexibility can be achieved without degrading academic work, crushing academic freedom, and destroying the proper role of faculty in teaching, research, and service. To do so, planning for flexibility must come from those who do the central work of higher education, who know best how the work should be done.

The outrage that most contingent faculty feel about their current working conditions is not fundamentally personal or individual, although that is important. Instead, it is directed toward the obstacles that make it impossible to carry out our professional responsibilities. This outrage can be mobilized to envision and make real an approach that neither degrades teaching and scholarship nor destroys the value of higher education to society. A better approach would be a unionized faculty with a guaranteed wage, job security, democratic power in governance, and a robust right to academic freedom, all supported by a society that ensures access to healthcare and education. This would eliminate the problem, as it exists, of providing flexible staffing for a flexible student body. A reset for higher education, then, is part of a reset for society.

The higher education industry is racing to take advantage of the COVID-19 pandemic to transfer more academic work onto internet platforms, eliminate tenure, close or consolidate small unprofitable colleges and universities, and focus on short-term vocational and "professional" programs designed to credential graduates and match them to employers. As faculty begin to realize that they are all potentially contingent, an alternative vision and strategy for higher education is imperative. The fundamental question should be: What reduces inequality? This means addressing inequalities not only in the academic workforce but among current and potential students, as well as nearby communities and the endangered planet. Flexibility as now practiced—rooted in the casualized work force of low-wage, just-in-time gig faculty with no job security or benefits—is neither inevitable nor permanent. Nor is it sustainable.

Notes

An earlier version of this essay was published in Joe Berry and Helena Worthen, *Power Despite Precarity: Strategies for the Contingent Faculty Movement in Higher Education* (London: Pluto Press, 2021).

1. Carnegie Foundation for the Advancement of Teaching, "Foundation History: The Early Years," accessed December 30, 2020, https://www.carnegiefoundation.org/about-us/foundation-history/. On industrial workplaces, see David Montgomery, *Workers' Control in America* (New York: Cambridge University Press, 1979).

2. "The GI Bill of Rights: An Analysis of the Serviceman's Readjustment Act of 1944," *Social Security Bulletin*, July 1944, accessed December 30, 2020, https://www.ssa.gov/policy/docs/ssb/v7n7/v7n7p3.pdf.

3. George P. Zook, *Higher Education for American Democracy: A Report on the President's Commission on Higher Education*, Vols. 1–6 (Washington, DC: US Government Printing Office, 1947).

4. "The History and Future of the 1960 California Masterplan for Higher Education," accessed December 30, 2020, https://www.lib.berkeley.edu/uchistory//archives_exhibits/masterplan/heartmp.html.

5. Claire Gilbert and Donald E. Heller, "The Truman Commission and Its Impact on Federal Higher Education Policy from 1947–2010," Report from Penn State University, 2010.

6. American Association of University Professors, "1940 Statement of Principles on Academic Freedom and Tenure, with 1970 Interpretive Comments," accessed December 30, 2020, https://www.aaup.org/file/1940%20Statement.pdf.

7. See Michael Crozier, Samuel P. Huntington, and Joji Watanuki, *The Crisis of Democracy: A Report on the Governability of Democracies to the Trilateral Commission* (New York: New York University Press, 1975).

8. Adam Smith, *An Inquiry into the Nature and Causes of the Wealth of Nations,* 5th ed. (1776; reprint, London: Methuen, 1904).

9. See Wendy Brown, *Undoing the Demos: Neoliberalism's Stealth Revolution* (New York: Zone Books, 2015); and David Harvey, *A Brief History of Neoliberalism* (New York: Oxford University Press, 2005).

10. On economic, social, and political shifts in the 1970s and 1980s, see Meg Jacobs, *Panic at the Pumps: The Energy Crisis and the Transformation of American Politics in the 1970s* (New York: Hill and Wang, 2016); Judith Stein, *The Pivotal Decade: How the United States Traded Factories for Finance in the Seventies* (New Haven, CT: Yale University Press, 2010); and Julilly Kohler-Hausmann, *Getting Tough: Welfare and Imprisonment in 1970s America* (Princeton, NJ: Princeton University Press, 2017).

11. A. J. Angulo, "From Golden Era to the Gig Economy: Changing Contexts for Academic Labor in America," in *Professors in the Gig Economy: Unionizing Adjunct Faculty in America*, ed. Kim Tolley (Baltimore: Johns Hopkins University Press, 2018), 3–26.

12. See the essay by Sue Doe and Steven Shulman in this collection.

13. For another example, Vanderbilt University says its ETOB (every tub on its own bottom) budgeting policy began in the 1980s. Vanderbilt University, "University Budgeting

System Evolves to Support Strategic Priorities," accessed December 30, 2020, https://news.vanderbilt.edu/2016/09/19/university-budgeting-system-evolves-to-support-strategic-priorities/.

14. Helena Worthen, "The Status of Labor Education in Higher Education in the U.S.," United Association for Labor Education, 2015, accessed March 16, 2021, https://uale.org/resources/links/.

15. See Elizabeth Tandy Shermer's essay in this collection.

16. Public Policy Institute of California, "Proposition 13," accessed December 30, 2020, https://www.ppic.org/blog/tag/proposition-13/.

17. For a labor history that underscores this dynamic of fragmentation and solidarity, see Richard Jules Oestreicher, *Solidarity and Fragmentation: Working People and Class Consciousness in Detroit, 1875–1900* (Urbana: University of Illinois Press, 1986).

18. American Association of University Professors, "Yeshiva Ruling," accessed December 30, 2020, https://www.aaup.org/import-tags/yeshiva-ruling.

19. On West Virginia, Oklahoma, and Arizona in 2018, see Eric Blanc, *Red State Revolt: The Teachers' Strike Wave and Working-Class Politics* (London: Verso, 2019).

20. Keith Hoeller, ed., *Equality for Contingent Faculty: Overcoming the Two-Tier System* (Nashville: Vanderbilt University Press, 2014).

21. Richard Moser, "Campus Democracy, Community, and Academic Citizenship" (Paper presented at the Conference on Contingent Academic Labor VI, Chicago, August 2004).

22. Ibid.

CHAPTER 5

WOMEN'S WORK

A Feminist Rethinking of Contingent Labor in the Academy

GWENDOLYN ALKER

A few years back, I was invited to speak about labor, from my perspective as a long-time contract faculty member, at the Women and Theatre Program's annual conference.[1] Viewing this as a good opportunity to formally research an area of personal interest, I began a deep dive into the history of tenure and unionization, the rise of adjunct labor, and the emergence of a "silent majority" of non-tenure-track faculty. I brought to this research my experiences as a contract faculty member, as an activist in the early adjunct unionization campaigns, and as a feminist. I found that a feminist lens is not only one of the best ways to understand the basic facts of contingent faculty on the ground, it also helps build a foundation to move forward collectively and respectfully. As I continue to work in this area, I have become convinced that we cannot repair the inequality of contingent labor in academia unless we acknowledge the issue of women's work more generally; these two issues feed off each other symbiotically. And the murky mix that they create is one reason why contract labor has become so intractable. The recent global pandemic has further revealed the labor inequities for women and people of color, and how they are baked into our global economies, including the economy of academic labor. The time for change has arrived.

Let's Get Personal

The old adage of the feminist movement—"the personal is the political"—is still a useful place to begin. In 2003, I earned my doctorate from New York University's

(NYU) Department of Performance Studies. By that point, I had already taught as an adjunct at various institutions around New York City. Here I am defining the term "adjunct" as referring to part-time teachers who usually earn less than $5,000 per class on a per-term basis with no benefits. That same year I was hired as a contract faculty member at the Tisch School of the Arts—this meant I graduated to full-time employment (with benefits) but worked on a short-term contract with no long-term job security or room for promotion. To this day, I hold a variant of that position, albeit with better pay and a longer contract. I feel fortunate that I am a full-time, non-tenure-track member of the faculty. As a colleague who holds a similar position at the University of Pennsylvania once said, we occupy nebulous positions in the research university, commanding "neither carrot nor stick." My position, and I suspect others like it, is complex rather than untenable: I continue to have a robust scholarly life; I have gained the respect of my students and many colleagues; I am currently the director of a large program with about thirty full- and part-time faculty members; and I have (on a good day) managed to find work-life balance.

During my years shifting from graduate student to full-time teacher, I was an organizer in the ACT-UAW (United Auto Workers) Local 7902 campaign, which led to the formation of NYU's adjunct union in 2002. It is one of the largest examples of a successful collective bargaining unit at a private university. One of my pertinent memories was having conversations with colleagues who were concerned about joining the UAW, worries that suggested a class bias against a blue-collar (and stereotypically male) workforce from adjuncts who were earning approximately $3,000 per class at a Research-1 University. Such interactions revealed to me how class and gender biases are often infused within people's perception of the academy in ways that do not reflect the on-the-ground economic realities.

Women's Work

The central frame that will guide this chapter is the notion of "women's work." Here I understand such work to mean both the labor done by cisgender women (those whose biological bodies match their gender identifications), such as birthing and nursing, and stereotypically "feminine" endeavors which can be done by bodies of all sorts, such as domestic work and caretaking. The feminization of labor was used to describe the lower-paying jobs that women held, including the period during and after World War II. Globally, it also refers to the ways in which a neoliberal economy has increasingly funneled undervalued labor, usually done by women, to third-world regions. As Gloria Steinem notes in "Revaluing Economics," the term also applies to the way labor once done by women becomes economically devalued in all geographic regions.[2] Women's work supposedly comes "naturally" to cis-women and therefore functions outside of an economic marketplace. Women's work is indeed a broad category—that is part of its potential strength for collective organizing and its weakness as it encompasses a vague and undefined web of labor practices, roles, and social perceptions.

Within an educational setting, concerns surrounding women's work have been more clearly recognized within K–12 education than within higher education. One could point to the recent rise of labor activism among K–12 teachers as a specific response to society's devaluation of the labor of teachers. Jane McAlevey, an organizer and historian at the Labor Center at University of California at Berkeley, notes that most of the labor of K–12 teaching, as well as the movements to gain better working conditions for these workers, is done by women, specifically women of color, and many continue despite or in direct reaction to undermining by state and federal officials.[3] She notes, for example, the successful revamping of leadership in Los Angeles' Unified School District in 2014, after years of Democratic leadership dismantling of teachers' unions and privatizing public schools.

The movement for labor fairness in educational settings can be traced back to John Dewey and early twentieth-century pragmatism, including intriguing ties between the pragmatists and the early suffragist movement. Such initiatives for labor fairness occurred more often than not in secondary schools—another area that is feminized and therefore devalued among academics. This history has added to the larger perception of labor activism by and for women in educational settings as somehow foreign to labor fairness in higher education. Standard histories of labor in higher education tie the idea of labor equality instead to academic freedom and the institution of tenure, not to labor activism, as will be discussed below.

K–12 teaching and caregiving are two areas that are clearly definable as "women's work." Research in these areas reveals the complexities and challenges of this type of labor. In *The Age of Dignity*, Ai-Jen Poo describes how the present realities of caregiving are connected to histories of institutional racism and sexism in the United States: "Domestic workers have always been treated as a 'special class' of workers; they have been 'specially' undervalued as workers and excluded from labor laws since the New Deal."[4] She links this perception of class to the legally binding labor laws of the 1930s that began to standardize definitions of labor. When such laws were being debated in Congress, southern states, as part of the ongoing legacy of unpaid labor emerging from slavery and domestic servitude, blocked legislation that would provide protections for farmworkers and domestic workers. It was only after the exclusion of these workers from New Deal protections that these labor laws passed—setting a legal precedent for labor stratification in the United States that lasts to this day.[5]

The Feminization of Academic Labor

In our neoliberal context, the intransigent and longstanding histories of women's work mix with the current contingent labor crisis in the academy in a toxic way.[6] Despite its verbal commitment to egalitarianism, the US academy has participated in the so-called feminization of labor as much as any other workforce in the nation.

The work of teaching and advising, which are undervalued and done increasingly by members of the contingent faculty, should be understood as feminine labor. At research universities especially, teaching and advising constitute less significant parts of tenure and promotion portfolios than scholarly publications. As a result of this and other factors, the bulk of teaching and student contact hours are increasingly relegated to the domain of adjuncts. In departments and schools that highlight teaching—such as educational programs and teaching colleges— faculty are more likely to be women. Teaching and scholarship have themselves become binaries: increasingly, those on tenure-track appointments are pushed to focus primarily on the monograph (or the peer-reviewed article, especially in certain social science fields), while those on non-tenure-track appointments have heavy course loads and are usually unable to conduct research that could rip them out of the tangled web of adjunctification. As Herb Childress notes in *The Adjunct Underclass*, "we see the highly paid, highly respected male professors who proclaim from the podiums, supplanted by lower paid, less respected female faculty who do more of the hands-on work of student support."[7]

With the advent of the corporate university—institutions wherein economic success is prioritized over educational goals—service and committee work has proliferated.[8] Service is a complicated subject, but committee work that is often repetitive or goes unnoticed must also be understood as feminine labor. Studies show that women are more likely than men to commit to service that is less prestigious, while high-profile service jobs, such as department chair or director of a graduate studies program, are more likely to be filled by men. A 2009 study at the University of Massachusetts found that three-quarters of female associate professors take on time-consuming service roles, compared with only half of their male counterparts.[9] Audrey Williams June of the *Chronicle of Higher Education* has written about the service load for faculty of color who mentor more students of color and who may feel alienated from their white faculty.[10] Not surprisingly, these "feminine" areas of teaching and service map onto the well-worn Cartesian dualisms of mind and body, where the stereotypical researcher—a white man—remains concerned with the pursuits of the mind, while the stereotypical woman—often of color—is left to take care of the children and their messes.

Moving from a discursive argument, we turn to evidence of inequity for women in an increasingly stratified labor economy. The most complete book-length study on women in academia is Maureen Baker's *Academic Careers and the Gender Gap*, published in 2012. Her study hinges primarily on two data sets—both qualitative and quantitative—gathered in the United Kingdom, New Zealand, Canada, and Australia from the 1970s to the time of the book's writing. These locations allow her to highlight and analyze the neoliberal policies of these countries' governments over the last four-plus decades. According to Baker, at what we often think of as the "beginning" of one's career (a false teleology in today's marketplace), "many of the part-time and temporary positions in universities are occupied by doctoral students, partnered women, and mothers."[11] As they struggle to move up the job ladder, women are more likely to move (or not move) to accommodate a partner's career.[12] While the proportion of women as tenure-track hires is improving, it remains below that of men.[13] Women are less likely to find mentors to guide them through the difficult process of professionalization, thus increasing attrition rates for those on the tenure track.[14] Women are less likely to be promoted to full professor, and when they are, it takes them, on average, two more years to do so.[15] Marc Bousquet, in his influential book *How the University Works*, concurs: "poorly paid adjunct, or contingent faculty . . . are women by substantial majorities."[16] Female academics are more likely to start out—and remain—as contingent faculty, at almost every stage of professional development.[17]

The most consistent data on academic labor in the United States comes from the American Association of University Professors (AAUP), which has tracked faculty salaries by gender since 1975, but only began tracking data on part-time faculty in 2015. Their *2018–19 Annual Report on the Economic Status of the Profession* includes an in-depth analysis of gender disparities in US academia over the last decade. AAUP's findings corroborate Baker's conclusion, stating "the progress towards equity has been exceedingly slow."[18] This report points to important reasons for the continued inequity: women are more likely to be hired in fields that are lower paying; women are more likely to be hired into better positions (i.e., tenured professorships) at community colleges that have fewer full-time faculty and have a heavier reliance on contingent labor; women are less likely to be hired in the more prestigious doctoral programs. AAUP also notes that while the overall rate of hiring women has improved, it has been commensurate with the overall decline of tenure-track and full-time positions. Within contingent positions, the report notes that more women are hired than men. Thus, "women remain underrepresented at the most senior and highest-paying posts, and their aggregate position has barely budged in ten years."[19] While this report is useful, supporting the larger argument of this chapter, a few oversights merit analysis.

At present, the AAUP annual survey does not include data based on race, which makes an intersectional analysis, central to any feminist methodology, impossible.[20] Furthermore, the authors of this report do not take the final step to suggest that a relevant factor for a gendered analysis of all of these factors is gender itself: contingent labor, more poorly paid disciplines (particularly the feminized humanities), and two-year and community colleges all serve more women and people of color. They are interstitial with women's work. As Childress notes, "as women have entered the professoriate, we have diminished the standing and security and the unified role of the faculty . . . if a woman can do it, it must not be very important, and we shouldn't have to pay much for it."[21]

Research is building on the related conversations about motherhood within an academic context.[22] In 2016, economists Heather Antecol, Kelly Bedard, and Jenna Stearns published a study of gender-neutral policies to stop the tenure clock at the top fifty economics departments in the United States.[23] Their findings were sobering: whereas women used their maternity leave to have a child, more men in their study used their paternity leave to engage in research and publishing. The result heightened the competitive nature of the culture of "publish or perish" in these departments. Women who went up for tenure after utilizing a leave found themselves at a disadvantage compared with men who had received the same benefits. Add onto such studies the larger problem of mothers hired as adjuncts or contract faculty with no benefits, and the scale of the problem balloons. Such concerns follow in the footsteps of early feminists like Tillie Olsen, who, in the 1970s, warned of the incompatibility of child rearing and writing.[24] Because the entire economy of higher education relies increasingly on tenured and tenure-track faculty to do the writing and the rest of us to do the teaching, the split that has evolved has contributed to an unacknowledged dependence on a feminization of labor.

How Did We Get Here?

I have been surprised by faculty members' lack of knowledge of their own labor conditions and histories. Perhaps our increased specialization and white-collar attitudes toward issues of labor have facilitated the emergence of the current system—academic institutions in which a diminishing tenure pool and a sea of adjuncts are intertwined yet largely remain separate. These histories point to the ways that labor equity in the US academy were tied to the institution of tenure. And as tenure was created in the mid-twentieth century when most faculty were white men, I argue that this system has unwittingly tied labor equity to sexist and racist structures. A feminist analysis suggests that we should not focus on the death of tenure as much as we should fear the death of an academic middle class.

The idea of tenure as a way to secure academic rights against the whims of administrations, boards, and donors had its origins in the case of Edward A. Ross, who was dismissed from Stanford University in 1900. Ross, who repeatedly spoke out against privately owned railroads and Chinese immigration, was fired when the widow of the former president of the university complained about his views. This case and others contributed to the founding of the AAUP in 1915, and the subsequent creation of its *Statement of Principles on Academic Freedom and Tenure*, first published in 1940.[25] At the time of its writing, tenure became irrevocably tied to the concept of academic freedom. The AAUP became the main national group advocating for economic security in higher education. At this time, almost all the professors who had tenure in 1940 were white and male. This created a structure where if a professor had a family, a considerable amount of domestic work had to be done by an unpaid wife or low-wage caregiver, and such workers were not acknowledged within this system. If an academic followed the traditional time-line—from college, to graduate school, to work—childbearing and the most labor-intensive years of child raising would occur while a faculty member was building a portfolio for tenure review.

Tenure as a system that ensured faculty security and stability reached its height in the post–World War II era when demand for higher education flooded the university system and resulted in bountiful academic job opportunities. It was not until the 1970s, a decade that witnessed continued growth of the civil rights and second-wave feminist movements, that major changes began to occur in faculty personnel patterns and in student enrollment; ever-greater numbers of female students and students of color enrolled in college. These students, who often maintained other jobs and family responsibilities, were more likely to attend part-time and often less able to afford full tuition. This financial shift was compounded by that decade's economic turmoil. With the advent of neoliberal policies especially in the 1980s under Ronald Reagan—emphasizing privatization, labor union busting, and decreased funding for public education—the financial stability of the educational marketplace worsened. Colleges and universities began to hire adjuncts in larger numbers, a trend that steadily increased, and that will no doubt worsen with the present economic challenges of the global pandemic, if schools manage to keep their doors open at all. Thus, while the feminist and civil rights movements allowed for the entrance of women and people of color into academic institutions, they did not fully transform institutions that were created for and by white middle- and upper-class men.

As the main organization in higher education supporting academic freedom and tenure, the AAUP operates largely as a professional association rather than a union, although some AAUP chapters do engage in collective bargaining. Their historic focus on pairing academic freedom with tenure means an emphasis on controlling curriculum and the ability to speak one's mind freely—all admirable qualities. But in an educational institution, this also means that faculty as the arbiters of the curriculum are ideally in charge of the educational institutions in which they are employed. This gives them employment status as "managers" that, within settled union law of the last fifty years, excludes them from possible participation in collective bargaining.

A foundational fracturing of the idea of a unified faculty resulted from the 1980 Supreme Court *Yeshiva* ruling, which stated that full-time, tenure-track faculty in private colleges and universities were "managerial," and thus ineligible to organize under the National Labor Relations Act (NLRA). Notably, the language from this ruling did not apply to part-time faculty, while employees at public universities form a different legal class under previous legislation. Thus, legal rifts were created between public and private institutions and between tenured and tenure-track faculty and the adjuncts at these same institutions, and between higher education and K–12 teachers. Tenured faculty members at private universities who were in-eligible for collective bargaining were less likely to educate themselves about their own labor histories—or even see the work that they do as labor. This perspective is baked into critiques of unionization by some tenured faculty and administrators, who see faculty unions as antithetical to the preservation of tenure.[26] An impor-tant coda to *Yeshiva* occurred in December of 2014 with the ruling against Pacific Lutheran University. This more liberal version of the National Labor Rights Board (NLRB) "rejected the claims of Pacific Lutheran University that its full-time, non-tenure track faculty members are managerial employees and thus are not entitled to collective bargaining."[27] The legal precedents of such cases are still evolving.

Too often, discussions of contingent faculty are simplified into an "us-versus-them" dichotomy, with "us" being the last of those fighting against the death of tenure and "them" being non-tenure-track faculty who face imminent financial dangers. This must be seen as a profound heritage of the *Yeshiva* ruling. And this is another insight that a feminist methodology can give us: in many discussions of the labor crisis in the academy, what emerges is the application of a tight binary frame. But binary thinking leads to an inability to acknowledge economic and social complexities among contingent faculty. It also obscures the disconnection between the more privileged class of faculty and their part-time colleagues. Furthermore, such thinking has facilitated the growth of a complex, poorly understood web of adjunct and contract jobs without much oversight of faculty governance structures. The AAUP's "one faculty" campaign,[28] launched in 2014, is one important response to such binary legacies.

Full-time contract faculty occupy a nebulous place within the *Yeshiva* ruling. We are usually not classified as "managerial," and thus may be eligible to union-ize. That being said, the various titles that we are given become an effective cor-porate strategy, preventing camaraderie even among ourselves. And the lack of cohesive data makes it almost impossible for organizers to find us. We are a small middle class within a widening gulf that threatens to destroy the larger whole, as in many industries in this country and other neoliberal economies. Nonetheless, our numbers are growing: the AAUP notes that full-time, non-tenure-track appointments grew from approximately 10 percent of all full-time positions at the end of the last decade to just over 26 percent by the end of 2019.

A Feminist Critique of Tenure

I was raised by two well-known academics.[29] One was tenured at Yale at a young age; the other, a British-born woman, received a graduate degree in 1960, when few women were in higher education. I first learned about tenure from my family, and only later as a member of the academy. In hindsight, I believe that my parents leveraged tenure the way it was meant to be used. Once they procured job security, they committed to new ways of thinking that challenged disciplinary boundaries. Both situated in the field of international relations, my father brought new and controversial interdisciplinary methodologies to this offshoot of political science, while my mother introduced gender to a highly masculinized field. They capitalized on their positions to enter into a global community of intellectual thought. They used tenure to bolster their Quaker values of speaking truth to power, becoming a voice for those who were academically, politically, and economically less secure.

What I see from looking at my parents' history is that the culture of tenure is different now, as are the rules for attaining and retaining it. In contrast to a few decades ago, there is an increase in the basic components of the tenure portfolio. Now, faculty must publish numerous peer-reviewed articles and demonstrate good progress on a second book. Academia, for all its egalitarian theorizing, remains hierarchical, predicated on the maintenance of institutional prestige. And this hierarchy filters down to the production of new PhDs. According to a study from 2015, "25% of institutions produce 71 to 86% of all tenure-track faculty." In the field of history, "the top 10 schools produce *three times* as many future professors as those ranked 11 through 20."[30]

One of the most surprising finds in my research was the way in which tenure-track faculty have fully participated in the growing divide between the working and upper middle class in the United States. For the 1976–77 academic school year, the PSC (the City University of New York's faculty union), listed faculty salary averages for full-time teaching faculty for three New York City–based institutions: CUNY (a public university) at $21,841; NYU (a private university) at $21,964; and Columbia (a private Ivy League school) at $24,454 per annum. All these salaries (for what were mostly tenure and tenure-track positions at that time) were well below the cost of living in New York City, which was, according to this same source, $29,677 per annum. Yet the differences between the three salary averages were minimal.

Compare such figures to data from NYU in 2012, when the mean salary for tenured and tenure-track (TTT) faculty was $145,977, while the mean salary for full-time contract faculty (FTCF), was $60,987. If one factors in the labor costs of such salaries, the differences between these numbers become even more startling. That same year, TTT faculty taught an average of 2.34 courses and 59.94 students annually, whereas FTCF taught an average of 4.74 courses and 102.04 students. In other words, TTT faculty cost $62,383 per course and $2,435 per student, whereas FTCF cost $12,866 per course and $598 per student.[31] Using a common formula for accessing cost of living (fair market rental cost for a two-bedroom apartment in New York City, multiplied by three), a rough estimate for 2012 comes to $50,400.[32] Notably, this is just under the median salary for full-time contract faculty for this same year, but far below the median salary for tenured faculty. In this comparison, NYU full-time contract faculty of this decade make as much, proportionately, as tenured faculty of a few decades ago, but those with tenure are compensated at levels well above those in an earlier phase that was drawing to close by the end of the 1970s. And while I do not have exact numbers for adjunct pay at NYU for these years, a rough estimate would be $4,000 per class. With a teaching load of three courses, (the maximum amount most adjuncts have been allowed to teach at NYU), they would be paid $12,000 annually, with sparse benefits through their union contracts. To this day, adjuncts teach a majority of classes at NYU.

Despite these changes and the pressing realities of contingent labor, tenure is still held up as the best answer. Tenure as an institution, I would argue, is more than a political strategy aimed at rectifying the undervalued professoriate; it is a mythology that is tied to the cultural imaginary of the American academy. This idea is unpacked most fruitfully by labor historian Frank Donoghue in *The Last Professors*. I was intrigued by his question of "why the idea of tenure remains central to all discussions of higher education, even as the practice itself becomes increasingly rare."[33] The answer seems to lie somewhere between tenure as a timeless institution with ties to the moral imperative of academic freedom, and tenure as a discourse written, and still frozen, in the culture of mid-twentieth-century America. Applying a feminist lens, we must acknowledge that this image of twentieth-century America includes a domestic scene where white men go to work, white women stay at home, and people of color—whose labor is and has always been central to the nation's prosperity—are disappeared entirely.

A pamphlet published in 1979 by the American Association for Higher Education captures the way in which tenure is implicitly but subtly built upon patriarchal norms. This pamphlet staged a debate between the AAUP historian Walter Metzger and James O'Toole, at that time a professor who renounced his tenure at the University of Southern California. Metzger gives an impassioned defense of tenure, linking it to academic freedom, as is customary, and situating his history of tenure alongside the "history of the academic enterprise."[34] O'Toole's counterargument hinges upon a parallel between a typical patriarchal defense of male superiority and Metzger's defense of tenure. O'Toole states, "This man might well conclude by warning that any attempt to alter the 'natural scheme of things' would lead to (a) an increase in homosexuality; (b) the failure to properly care for children; and (c) the demise of civilization as we know it."[35] He then acknowledges both the sexism and the foolishness of this argument but notes that it contains the same logic that Metzger has used in his defense of tenure—which is to say that O'Toole uses an explicitly feminist argument to critique Metzger's emphasis on preserving tenure as "what has always been"[36] rather than looking at the current context of the professoriate.

Such an argument has only increased in relevance in the decades since the pamphlet was published. O'Toole stumbled upon the foundations of the feminization of labor in the academy. The rules of tenure were designed for, and still apply to, the bodies of white men. Tenure was created in this country in a moment when white men taught other white men, while the hidden forces of female labor were, more often than not, sequestered in the privacy of the domestic sphere. The fact that the erosion of tenure began when women and people of color began to enter the academy in large numbers is not happenstance. It fits a pattern that enables the feminization of labor.[37] Furthermore, the continued push to preserve tenure, and the very inability to question its efficacy, is not about academic freedom at all. Especially at research universities like mine, it is about maintaining a divided class and feminized structure within the marketplace of the university. If we continue to divide the work of academics between a less valued system of teaching and an increasingly cutthroat publication system, the seams of our patriarchal beginnings will show themselves. And the split down the middle will erode our ability to maintain a collegial community of teachers and scholars.

Some Small Steps

As Donoghue notes in *The Last Professors*, there is no wider disparity in income and day-to-day experience than that between adjuncts and their tenured colleagues. Yet these two groups engage in labor that is, at least on paper, very similar. My position as neither an adjunct nor a tenure-track faculty member has helped me see the pros and cons of tenure as one strategy for labor equality within a larger toolbox. We cannot send the majority of our adjunct colleagues down with a sinking ship and not end up in the water ourselves. We must rise collectively, and we must treat everyone fairly.

In closing, then, I recommend a few ways that we can behave as feminists and take action in academe and beyond:

1. *Remember that faculty are interconnected.* Understand that all of our labor in the academy is interconnected. If you are fortunate enough to receive research

leave, note that your classes are probably being taught by an adjunct. If a union drive is percolating, focus less on your perks and more about the faculty who are at the bottom of the ladder. Practice your Marxist theory and advocate for those faculty who make your job possible.

2. *Think beyond the binary.* There is not the "real faculty" and everyone else. Administrators in the increasingly corporate environment of higher education thrive on the simplicity of "everyone else." Contingent faculty are not all the same. Some colleagues in these positions need advocacy, and some have thriving academic careers. Such structural differences need to be analyzed using our strongest critical skills.

3. *When thinking about academic labor, ask what we mean by "labor."* If we are a community responsible for creating new knowledge, then teaching, advising, and service are integral to that work. Leaving the teaching and advising to a lower class of citizens creates class stratification that contributes to the death of an egalitarian community.

4. *Be collegial.* This seems obvious, but I say this most emphatically: do not be paternalistic, do not be sympathetic; be respectful of adjuncts and contract faculty alike. Advocate for structures where contingent faculty are consulted about issues of curriculum and governance. Assume we should be included.

5. *Be aware of our current context.* Neoliberalism functions best while swimming in the mythologies of individualism, independence, and meritocracy. Feminism and collective bargaining depend on prioritizing collectivity, a recognition of interdependency, and attention to reciprocity. Note the points of connection between the work of your field and related work outside of academia, whether in K–12 education or in sectors employing more contingent workers.

6. *Broaden the frame.* As teachers, we are part of a large community that extends well beyond higher education. That reach gives us strength in numbers. Next time someone asks you what you do for a living, reply "I'm a teacher," and see what ensues. Yes, tenured faculty at research universities are the most privileged group within this cohort, but they are part of it, nonetheless. Such colleagues must wield their privilege for the greater good of the many.

Notes

1. A condensed version of this keynote presentation was published by the AAUP under the title, "From a Contract Faculty Member to Her Colleagues: It's a Feminist Issue," *Academe: Magazine of the American Association of University Professors* (November–December 2017), https://www.aaup.org/article/contract-faculty-member-her-colleagues-its-feminist -issue#.Xxt6ny2ZOt8. This chapter is an extended version of this piece.

2. Gloria Steinem, "Revaluing Economics," in *Moving Beyond Words* (New York: Simon and Schuster, 1994), 199–246.

3. Jane McAlevey, *A Collective Bargain: Unions, Organizing, and the Fight for Democracy* (New York: HarperCollins, 2020).

4. Ai-Jen Poo, *The Age of Dignity: Preparing for the Elder Boom in a Changing America*, (New York: New Press, 2015), 88.

5. Ibid., 89. On the topic of racial discrimination in the New Deal, also see Ira Katznelson, *When Affirmative Action Was White: The Untold History of Racial Inequality in Twentieth-Century America* (New York: W. W. Norton, 2005).

6. For a further discussion of the "casualization" of labor in a neoliberal context, see Berry and Worthen's essay in this volume.

7. Herb Childress, *The Adjunct Underclass: How American's Colleges Betrayed Their Faculty, Their Students, and Their Mission* (Chicago: University of Chicago Press, 2019), 127.

8. For an in-depth analysis of the shift of universities toward market power and away from educational goals, see James H. Mittelman, *Implausible Dream: The World-Class University and Repurposing Higher Education* (Princeton, NJ: Princeton University Press, 2018). For more on the corporatization of universities, see Frank Donoghue, *The Last Professors: The Corporate University and the Fate of the Humanities* (New York: Fordham University Press, 2008).

9. Joya Misra, Jennifer Hickes Lundquist, Elissa Holmes, and Stephanie Agiomavritis, "The Ivory Ceiling of Service Work," *Academe* (January–February 2011), https://www.aaup.org/article/ivory-ceiling-service-work#.X-yrPi2cafV.

10. Audrey Williams June, "The Invisible Labor of Minority Professors," *Chronicle of Higher Education,* November 8, 2015.

11. Maureen Baker, *Academic Careers and the Gender Gap* (Vancouver: UBC Press, 2012), 18.

12. Ibid., 38, 80–83.

13. Ibid., 40. On this point, also see Jack Schuster and Martin J. Finkelstein, *The American Faculty: The Restructuring of Academic Work and Careers* (Baltimore: Johns Hopkins University Press, 2006); and American Association of University Professors (AAUP), "*2018–19 Annual Report on the Economic Status of the Profession*" (May 2019).

14. Baker, *Academic Careers and the Gender Gap*, 41.

15. Ibid., 129–134.

16. Marc Bousquet, *How the University Works: Higher Education and the Low-Wage Nation* (New York: New York University Press, 2008), 3.

17. For further data see Donoghue, *The Last Professors*; and Schuster and Finkelstein, *The American Faculty*.

18. AAUP, "2018–19 Annual Report," 6.

19. Ibid., 9.

20. Kimberlé Crenshaw originally coined the term "intersectional" to describe the incompatibility of Black women's identities with legal protections under US case law; it is now used more commonly to acknowledge how and when political agency is complicated by the multiple factors of race, class, gender, sexuality, dis/ability, and other identity markers. See Crenshaw, "Demarginalizing the Intersection of Race and Sex: A Black Feminist Critique of Antidiscrimination Doctrine, Feminist Theory, and Antiracist Politics," *University of Chicago Legal Forum* (1989): 139–167.

21. Childress, *The Adjunct Underclass*, 129.

22. See, for example, D. Lynn O'Brien Hallstein and Andrea O'Reilly, eds., *Academic Motherhood in a Post–Second Wave Context: Challenges, Strategies, and Possibilities* (Bradford, ON: Demeter Press, 2012); Kelly Ward and Lisa Wolf-Wendell, *Academic Motherhood: How Faculty Manage Work and Family* (New Brunswick, NJ: Rutgers University Press, 2012).

23. Heather Antecol, Kelly Bedard, and Jenna Stearns, "Equal but Inequitable: Who Benefits from Gender-Neutral Tenure Clock Stopping Policies?," *American Economic Review* 108:9 (2018): 2420–2441.

24. Tillie Olsen, *Silences* (New York: Feminist Press, 2003).

25. A link to a PDF of this document, as well as a brief history of their formation, can be found in "1940 Statement on Principles on Academic Freedom and Tenure" available through AAUP's website at: https://www.aaup.org/report/1940-statement-principles -academic-freedom-and-tenure.

26. See Richard Chait, "Faculty Unions and Academic Tenure: On a Collision Course" (Paper presented at the Third Annual Conference of the National Center for the Study of Collective Bargaining in Higher Education, April 29, 1975, Tamiment Archive, NYU), 9.

27. Scott Jaschik, "Big Union Win: NLRB Ruling Could Clear Way for More Collective Bargaining—of Adjuncts and Other Faculty Members—at Private Colleges and Universities," *Insidehighered.com,* January 2, 2015.

28. The drive includes a list of principles, information on bargaining agreements and other resources, available to AAUP members at their website at: https://www.aaup.org/ chapter-resources/one-faculty.

29. My father, Hayward R. Alker, passed away in 2007. My mother, J. Ann Tickner, is professor emerita at the University of Southern California.

30. Aaron Clauset, Samuel Arbesman, and Daniel B. Larremore, "Systematic Inequality and Hierarchy in Faculty Hiring Networks," *Science Advances* 12:1 (February 2015):1.

31. Rebecca Karl, personal email to NYU Faculty Democracy Group, November 5, 2014.

32. In the absence of data for the cost of living (COL) from 2012, I used the US Department of Housing and Urban Development's rate for a two-bedroom rental at fair market value in New York City, and multiplied by three, which is a common formula for accessing COL. Source: https://www.huduser.gov/portal/datasets/fmr/fmrs/FY2012_code/ 2012summary.odn.

33. Donoghue, *The Last Professors*, xvii.

34. Walter Metzger, James O'Toole, and Penina M. Glazer, *Current Issues in Higher Education: Tenure, #6* (Washington DC, AAUP, 1979).

35. Ibid.

36. Ibid.

37. Gary Rhoades expands upon this argument in this volume.

CHAPTER 6

CONTINGENCY ACROSS HIGHER EDUCATION

SUE DOE AND STEVEN SHULMAN

Since the 1970s, colleges and universities of all types have increasingly relied upon contingent instructors, including non-tenure-track faculty, instructors without faculty appointments, and graduate student instructors and teaching assistants, to teach their undergraduates.[1] According to the American Association of University Professors (AAUP), 70% of all faculty positions were contingent in 2015, up from 66% in 1995 and 55% in 1975.[2]

This chapter provides new quantitative and qualitative evidence about these trends and explores some of the explanations for them. Our focus is on showing how contingency varies across different types of colleges and universities. These cross-tabulations use federal data on higher education from the Integrated Post-secondary Education Data System (IPEDS), the major federal database on higher education.[3] We supplement this data-driven approach with reporting on the experiences of contingency across institutional types as described in the published literature and on-the-ground eyewitness sources. While contingency roles vary across institutional type, the challenges faced by contingent faculty generally do not. Finally, we assess the most common reason given for contingent hiring—that it is a budgetary necessity—and examine practices that yield better outcomes.

IPEDS provides the only consistently collected data about contingency in the academy. Previous efforts to describe contingency on a national scale included the 2003 National Study of Postsecondary Faculty and the 2010 survey of instructional faculty by the Coalition on the Academic Workforce. When the latter was published, it cited the scarcity of data on contingency as a major obstacle to understanding the phenomenon: "Despite the majority status of the contingent academic workforce, the systematic information available on the working conditions of these employees is minimal. . . . As a result, the large and growing majority employed in contingent positions is rendered largely invisible, both as individuals on the campuses where they work and collectively in the ongoing policy discussions of higher education."[4]

We seek to address this problem by offering a snapshot of contingency across institutional types, drawing on IPEDS data, published literature on the needs of contingent faculty, and firsthand sources. Contingency has been a surprisingly consistent phenomenon, whether in research-intensive universities or baccalaureate colleges. Consequently, we believe that the remediations of contingency are fairly consistent across institutional types. What contingent faculty most need is precisely what, by definition, they don't have: job security, better pay, and benefits that enable them to participate fully in faculty work. Here lies the paradox of contingency in higher education: although contingent instructors are treated as though they have little value as individuals, their collective labor is the bedrock of the educational enterprise. The financial model of higher education depends upon contingent academic labor on the one hand, and relentless tuition increases on the other. Tuition increases drive up revenues while contingent academic labor drives down costs; the resulting surpluses are often diverted to non-educational spending on administration, sports, student support services, student amenities, and other luxury and status goods. Contingent academic labor is often described as "casualized," even as it has become a seemingly permanent fixture on which academic budgets and administrative priorities depend.

A few clarifications are in order before we begin. First, most contingent instructor positions are part-time, especially at two-year colleges. For example, *Inside Higher Ed* reported in 2009 that 70% of community college faculty were hired on a part-time basis. They taught 58% of the classes and 53% of the students; 55% of them did advising and 33% of those hired had more than ten years' experience.[5] However, full-time non-tenure-track positions have grown as well. According to the AAUP document cited above, part-time faculty positions grew from 24% to 40% of all faculty positions (including graduate student employees) from 1975 to 2015. Over the same period, full-time non-tenure-track faculty positions grew from 10% to 17%. Correspondingly, tenure-line positions fell from 45% to 30%.

In the research described below, we count all contingent instructors equally, without distinguishing between part-time and full-time. While that distinction is important for some purposes (for example, salary and benefits are much better for full-time contingent instructors than part-time contingent instructors), it is not immediately relevant to our concern with the overall growth of contingent academic labor.

Second, the AAUP's terminology is confusing, as is probably apparent in the preceding paragraphs. Graduate student employees are not "faculty." Among graduate student employees, those hired to teach should be distinguished from those hired to conduct research, as is possible with the IPEDS data. These graduate students may teach their own courses like any other instructor, or they may assist in large lecture classes where they usually teach recitation sections. Other instructors without faculty status should also be included, such as employees categorized as administrative professionals or research scientists who sometimes teach in addition to their other responsibilities. For this reason, we use the phrase "contingent instructors" to refer to all of these groups taken together.

Third, contingent instructors have become the dominant delivery system for undergraduate education. Many undergraduates rarely meet with or have classes taught by tenure-stream professors, who are frequently diverted from undergraduate programs in order to teach graduate students, conduct research, and attend to administrative responsibilities. Thus, the concerns about contingency in higher education—including low pay, lack of resources, exclusion from departmental governance, and job insecurity—are central to the concerns about the future of undergraduate education. Higher education is going through an institutional shakeup for many reasons that have been exacerbated by the pandemic. This shakeup calls into question the traditional model of undergraduate programs, which unconscionably combines excessive costs for students with low wages and bad working conditions for their instructors. None of this is ethical or sustainable.

Finally, the IPEDS data is based on institutions. We include only those institutions categorized as associate's, bachelor's, master's, or doctoral degree colleges and universities by the Carnegie Commission on Higher Education. We exclude special focus institutions and those institutions that do not provide all the relevant information in the IPEDS files we use to generate the data in this paper. These exclusions limit our sample to the traditional landscape of higher education, that is, academic institutions that offer an accredited degree.

Patterns of Contingency

College and university use of contingent instructors differs by *institutional types*, which can be defined along two dimensions: *level* (associate's degree colleges, baccalaureate colleges, master's degree universities, and doctoral universities) and *sector* (public, private nonprofit, and private for-profit). Table 6.1 shows the number of colleges and universities in our sample, distributed by institutional type. It serves as the database for the figures reported in the remainder of this chapter.

Table 6.1. Number of Colleges and Universities by Institutional Type, 2019

	Public	Private Nonprofit	Private For-Profit	ALL SECTORS
Associate's degree colleges	843	14	27	884
Bachelor's degree colleges	119	391	38	548
Master's degree universities	245	355	30	630
Doctoral degree universities	206	185	9	400
ALL LEVELS	1,413	945	104	2,462

We measure contingency across these twelve institutional types with an index called the "contingency rate," defined as the fraction of all instructors who are non-tenure-track. The numerator of the contingency rate—non-tenure-track instructors—is the sum of non-tenure-track faculty (both full-time and part-time), instructors without faculty appointments, plus graduate student instructors and teaching assistants. The denominator of the contingency rate is all instructors, including tenured and tenure-track faculty as well as non-tenure-track instructors. This measurement of contingency shows the overall dependence of undergraduate programs on contingent instructors.

The AAUP has conducted similar research using the IPEDS data. In a 2018 report, the AAUP defines the "instructional faculty workforce" as the sum of full-time faculty on and off the tenure track, part-time faculty (almost all of whom are off the tenure track), and graduate student employees.[6] The report shows the distribution by institutional level but not sector; furthermore, it breaks doctoral universities into R1, R2, and R3. Thus, it shows a different set of categories than ours with more detail by level but less detail by sector.

We seek to improve upon the AAUP analysis in two ways. First, as noted above, we include only graduate student employees who teach, as opposed to all graduate student employees, since our concern is with undergraduate education. We also include instructors other than graduate student employees who lack faculty appointments, a group that the AAUP report ignores.

Second, the AAUP report shows more detail among doctoral universities, but it ignores sector. Yet sector is important: public institutions may have different mandates and should be held to different standards than private institutions. The same could be said for private nonprofit institutions in comparison to private for-profit institutions. Conversely, the distinction between R1, R2, and R3 doctoral universities seems to serve little purpose in this context. To maintain a manageable number of institutional types, we combined these into a single category of doctoral universities.

Table 6.2 shows contingency rates by institutional type in 2019, the most recent year with final IPEDS data. Across higher education as a whole, the contingency

Table 6.2. Average Contingency Rates by Institutional Type, 2019

	Public	Private Nonprofit	Private For-Profit	ALL SECTORS
Associate's degree colleges	81.5%	93.7%	100.0%	82.2%
Bachelor's degree colleges	61.9%	61.6%	100.0%	64.3%
Master's degree universities	56.8%	77.6%	99.4%	70.5%
Doctoral degree universities	63.5%	70.1%	100.0%	67.4%
ALL LEVELS	72.9%	69.7%	99.8%	72.8%

rate is 73%. Although we define contingency somewhat differently than the AAUP, as discussed above, we agree that it has continued to grow since 2015.

Contingency rates are lower in the public sector than the private nonprofit sector among associate's degree colleges, master's degree universities, and doctoral degree universities. This is not what one would expect if contingency rates were driven by cuts in state support to the public sector. Among baccalaureate colleges, contingency rates are almost equal in the public and private nonprofit sectors. But because bachelor's degree colleges are much more prevalent in the private nonprofit sector than in the public sector (41% versus 8% of all institutions according to table 6.1), the contingency rate overall in the public sector is slightly higher than in the private nonprofit sector. Private for-profit institutions are completely contingent, as is explicit in their business model. These institutions make no pretense about their concern for the protection of academic freedom provided by tenure. Of course, almost the same could be said about public and private nonprofit institutions, given their high rates of contingency.

The Instructional Budget

Now that we have described the patterns of contingency, we turn to its most common explanation: the instructional budget. Colleges and universities often claim that their increased employment of contingent instructors has been forced on them as a cost-savings measure to offset drops in instructional revenue, particularly at public institutions that have faced cuts in state support. Do the patterns of instructional costs and revenues back this claim?[7]

Our method is to cross-tabulate instructional costs and revenues by institutional type and compare them to the patterns of contingency shown in table 6.2. This is admittedly an informal approach, with findings that are suggestive rather than conclusive. It would be better to use a more sophisticated procedure (such as a multiple regression) that could control for other influences on instructional budgets. Then the relationship between instructional budgets and contingency could be established with "all else held constant." But we lack the data to do so in a meaningful way. We also believe that the figures shown below on instructional costs and revenues are novel, and we want them to be accessible to a general audience.

IPEDS provides data that can be used to calculate instructional costs and revenues as totals for each institution. We present these figures on a per student basis by dividing the totals by each institution's full-time equivalent (FTE) student enrollment, measured as full-time fall enrollment plus half of part-time fall enrollment (i.e., two part-time students are considered equivalent to one full-time student). This adjustment is an approximation that makes part-time students comparable to full-time students when we add them up to calculate total fall enrollments.

There are two reasons for presenting the budgetary data on a per-student basis. First is a simple measurement issue. Because large institutions have greater costs and revenues than small institutions, considering them on a per-student basis makes large and small institutions comparable, as well as making institutional types with different numbers of institutions comparable.

Second is a more conceptual issue. Instructional costs are the amount of spending that institutions undertake on each student's education, summed up over all students. The same is true for instructional revenues. The per-student figures focus our attention on the budgetary impact of each student with respect to the educational mission of these institutions.

We begin on the cost side. IPEDS provides data on the total instructional spending of each institution, defined as "the sum of all operating expenses associated with the colleges, schools, departments, and other instructional divisions of the institution, and for departmental research and public service that are not separately budgeted." Note that the instructional expenditure figures may overstate actual instructional expenditures to the extent that they include full salaries for faculty and administrators who have responsibilities other than teaching (unless the research and service they perform are separately budgeted). The data presented in table 6.3 should be viewed with this caveat in mind. However, this type of caveat is common in quantitative research since the available data are often an imperfect fit for the research question they are applied to.

If the budgetary rationale for contingency is correct, institutional types with higher contingency rates would show lower instructional spending per student. However, table 6.3 shows that this is generally not the case.

For example, private nonprofit colleges and universities spend almost twice as much on each student's education than public colleges and universities spend. Yet, overall, contingency rates in these two sectors are similar. Among doctoral universities, the contingency rate is higher in the private nonprofit sector, yet this sector spends much more on each student's education than the public sector. Public and private nonprofit master's degree universities are similar with respect to instructional spending per student, yet the contingency rate is much higher in the

Table 6.3. Instructional Costs: Instructional Expenditures per FTE Student by Institutional Type, 2019

	Public	Private Nonprofit	Private For-Profit	ALL SECTORS
Associate's degree colleges	$5,872	$7,502	$5,555	$5,874
Bachelor's degree colleges	$6,687	$13,688	$5,097	$10,315
Master's degree universities	$8,144	$8,671	$3,927	$8,115
Doctoral degree universities	$13,723	$27,428	$3,226	$17,053
ALL LEVELS	$9,594	$19,131	$3,822	$11,592

latter. Among baccalaureate colleges, contingency rates are similar in the public sector and the private nonprofit sector, yet instructional spending per student is much higher in the latter. The only sector that is consistent with the expectation that greater contingency should reduce instructional spending is the for-profit sector. These comparisons underscore that contingency is not correlated with instructional spending per student in any obvious way in the public and private nonprofit sectors despite claims that contingent instructors are employed in such large numbers precisely to lower instructional costs. The private for-profit sector could be considered the single example of contingency clearly reducing instructional expenditures, though in associate's and bachelor's degree colleges the effect seems smaller than one would expect.

This finding may seem surprising. One can imagine reasons for it, although without more data these reasons must remain speculative. For example, instructional costs are calculated over a variety of academic programs (sciences versus humanities, for example), so they will vary with the distribution of these programs. Instructional costs also depend upon the salaries of tenure-track faculty. And perhaps the availability of cheap contingent instructors creates an incentive for institutions to hire larger numbers of them to teach more classes, raising total instructional costs for the same number of students. Whatever the reason, these figures show that there is no clear relationship between contingency rates and instructional spending on each student that would support the budgetary rationale for contingency.

On the revenue side, the budgetary rationale for contingency implies that institutions with greater instructional revenues per student would face less pressure to cut costs by hiring contingent instructors. If that is true, we should observe a negative correlation between instructional revenue per student and the contingency rate.

The instructional revenue generated by each student can come from two sources: tuition/fees and government subsidies. The figures on instructional revenue shown in table 6.4 are the sum of these two sources, calculated per FTE student and averaged by institutional type. Note that government subsidies (federal, state, and

Table 6.4. Instructional Revenues: Tuition/Fees Plus Government Subsidies per FTE Student by Institutional Type, 2019

	Public	Private Nonprofit	Private For-Profit	ALL SECTORS
Associate's degree colleges	$9,370	$16,398	$14,726	$9,409
Bachelor's degree colleges	$10,527	$17,897	$19,026	$14,762
Master's degree universities	$13,087	$16,511	$14,896	$14,290
Doctoral universities	$20,475	$27,050	$15,743	$22,080
ALL LEVELS	$14,727	$22,150	$15,724	$16,425

local appropriations, with state appropriations by far the largest) do not include contracts and grants. These appropriations are meant to subsidize students and cover operating costs, and typically are calculated on a per student basis. To the extent that they fund programs other than classroom education (e.g., extension programs) they will overstate instructional revenues. Contingency in public institutions is often rationalized as a response to cuts in state support that lower instructional revenues. The figures in table 6.4 should allow us to evaluate that claim.

Again, the expected correlation is not observable in the figures shown in table 6.4. Instructional revenue per student is higher at every level (as one would expect) in the private nonprofit sector than in the public sector, yet the contingency rates are generally higher in the private nonprofit sector. The for-profit sector has higher instructional revenues per student than the public sector at every level except at doctoral universities. Yet this is the sector that is completely contingent! Clearly, there is little evidence to suggest that contingency goes up when instructional revenues go down.

Although the evidence on instructional costs and revenues does not clearly support the budgetary rationale for contingency, the conclusion should not be that this is irrelevant. Budget considerations are relevant, but not because they force administrators to hire contingent instructors. Rather, they are relevant because administrators choose to hire contingent instructors in order to maximize the surplus generated by instruction, which they can then put toward other purposes.

Let us first get a sense of the size of this surplus. A comparison of tables 6.3 and 6.4 shows that instructional revenues consistently exceed instructional salary costs for each student. Table 6.5 shows the difference between the two, which we call the *instructional surplus*. (Note that the possible overstatement biases in the measurements of both instructional costs and instructional revenues tend to cancel out in the calculation of the instructional surplus.) Perhaps not surprisingly, the instructional surplus is greatest in the private for-profit sector. One could interpret this finding as showing that this sector exploits its students in the sense that it spends the least on their education relative to the revenues they generate.

Table 6.5. Instructional Surplus per FTE Student, 2019

	Public	Private Nonprofit	Private For-Profit	ALL SECTORS
Associate's degree colleges	$3,498	$8,896	$9,170	$3,535
Bachelor's degree colleges	$3,840	$4,209	$13,928	$4,447
Master's degree universities	$4,943	$7,840	$10,968	$6,176
Doctoral universities	$6,751	-$379	$12,517	$5,027
ALL LEVELS	$5,133	$3,019	$11,902	$4,834

It should also be noted that the instructional surplus generated by each student is greater in the private nonprofit sector than in the public sector at every level except doctoral universities, where it is actually negative in the private nonprofit sector. Private nonprofit doctoral universities are the only institutional type that can claim to spend "too much" on each student's education. However, this finding is driven by a few universities—especially Washington University, Columbia University, Stanford University, and Johns Hopkins University—that claim to spend over $100,000 per year on each student's education. It is hard to say why they would spend so much in comparison to, say, Harvard University, which spends less than half that amount. Looking at this institutional type as a whole, 22 institutions out of 185 have a negative instructional surplus. Aside from these outliers, the instructional surplus is consistently positive across higher education. Colleges and universities clearly make money on their educational mission. The question is what they do with it.

Table 6.6 provides a more aggregated view by showing the total instructional surplus by institutional type. In 2019, the total instructional surplus across all of higher education was more than $67 billion. The size of the instructional surplus in each sector depends upon the number of students as well as the surplus per student. Consequently, the public sector generates the largest total instructional surplus, especially at doctoral universities. But all three sectors generate significant surpluses from instructing their students.

The sheer size of the instructional surplus makes it hard to believe that higher education is facing a budgetary crisis due to its educational mission. Instead, it is the choices made by administrators to spend the instructional surplus on other

Table 6.6. Total Instructional Surplus by Institutional Type, 2019

	Public	Private Nonprofit	Private For-Profit	ALL ALL SECTORS
Associate's degree colleges	$13,146,583,196	$72,919,727	$153,814,545	$13,373,317,468
Bachelor's degree colleges	$1,655,825,775	$2,217,841,534	$568,957,410	$4,442,624,719
Master's degree universities	$9,476,246,691	$7,834,415,090	$1,603,577,715	$18,914,239,496
Doctoral universities	$29,464,703,436	-$612,142,621	$2,028,915,221	$30,881,476,036
ALL LEVELS	$53,743,359,098	$9,513,033,730	$4,355,264,891	$67,611,657,719

priorities—sports, student amenities, the expansion of administration itself—that create a budgetary crisis. These non-academic priorities are not just diversions from the educational mission of colleges and universities. They also increase spending without generating corresponding revenues (or, in the case of sports at most institutions, without generating revenues large enough to cover costs). That is why so many colleges and universities face financial problems. Many observers feel that colleges and universities have an ethical and social obligation to concentrate their spending on their primary educational mission. The same could be said from a budgetary perspective. The instructional surplus is the reason higher education has any financial strength at all. Colleges and universities should be investing more in instruction and less in status goods like sports and administrative bloat. To the extent colleges and universities refuse to do so, the budgetary problems that they face are problems of their own making. In the pages that follow, we consider the human costs of the fiscal choices that are widely being made.

The Persistent Experience of Contingency across Institutional Type

Having debunked the myth of higher education costs being driven by rising educational expenses, we now consider the experience of contingency through recent firsthand accounts of contingent instructors. We asked, what are the costs of contingency to individual instructors and how do they vary across sector and level? The accounts demonstrate that the experiences of contingency are remarkably similar across institutional type. Our eyewitness accounts, which were collected from 2019 to 2021, were initiated through a call on the "Con Job: Stories from Adjunct and Contingent Faculty" Facebook group. These testimonies show that contingent instructors have successfully negotiated improvements but too often continue to be denied the traditional rights and expectations of faculty. Where gains have been made, contingent instructors are largely responsible, having effectively advocated for themselves.[8]

So, what are those needs? The 2010 Coalition on the Academic Workforce (CAW) survey, which brought in 20,000 responses from NTT (non-tenure-track) faculty, and another 10,000 from tenure-track faculty, found that NTT faculty generally face poor compensation, employment instability, the absence of career ladder, few opportunities for involvement in shared governance, and a dearth of material support for professional development.

Inadequate Compensation

The AAUP's report "The Status of Non-Tenure-Track Faculty" posits that "the key factor in the growth of part-time faculty is the economic advantage for institutions that pay them substantially less than the prorated equivalent paid for comparable work by full-time faculty."[9] Yet two studies from the Delta Cost Project and the American Institutes for Research challenge the notion that contingency results in savings.[10] These studies, consistent with our own data, found that any savings associated with contingent hiring tends to be redirected toward non-instructional expenditures such as administration, maintenance, and employee benefits.[11]

Our eyewitnesses flesh out the implications of low pay. NTT faculty member Jessica Ennis earns less teaching than is needed to meet her childcare expenses. Still, she has successfully argued for better compensation over her years at Augsburg University, a private nonprofit baccalaureate institution where she teaches physics. There, she reports, administrators increasingly understand that they cannot ask her to do work for which she is not compensated. Due in large part to her own self-advocacy, when she is asked to help with special projects, administrators today ask, "How much should we pay you for this work?"

Joe Schicke, who currently teaches full-time at a public doctoral university, previously taught at three community colleges, sometimes in full-time and other times in part-time positions. He says that the work was not sufficiently different across the two roles to justify the substantial pay increase deriving from full-time status. Schicke's case sheds light on the way in which many, if not most, community college systems remain solidly committed to a two-tier system by maintaining a largely low-paid workforce overseen by a few well-paid administrative faculty. This economy often leads to community college faculty working at several locations to make ends meet, which brings us to a second challenge facing contingent faculty as named by the CAW report, unstable employment.

Unstable Employment

As Schicke observes: "In community colleges, faculty are as transient as students. In fact, the two are often indistinguishable. As they fly in and out of the parking lot together, they seem made for each other." Contingency allows administrators to expand and contract the teaching workforce as enrollment dictates. Adrianna Kezar, Tom DePaola, and Daniel T. Scott, higher education scholars associated with the University of Southern California's Delphi Project, note that such unstable gig labor exacts financial and emotional strain.[12] Juggling multiple gigs at separate institutions accentuates the professional isolation, costs, and risks endemic to contingency. Further, as the AAUP has reported, "the growth of part-time faculty has often come at the cost of stable employment."[13]

Institutions have historically absolved themselves of responsibility for such practices, claiming that contingent instructors are hobbyists who teach for fulfillment. M. J. Sharp, who started teaching at Duke University in 2012, states, "There is a feeling that you're just doing this for the love of it, so you don't need to be treated like a real employee. . . . It keeps you nice and disposable."[14] This idea of the "psychic income" associated with teaching as "a labor of love" has been thoroughly discredited by Eileen Schell and others.[15] Women, in particular, have often been told "they would be more satisfied with a lower-achieving teaching track that might offer more flexible hours to accommodate a family."[16] Yet the CAW survey reported that 75% of all NTT faculty would take a full-time position if one were offered.

Substandard Working Conditions

Contingent labor has historically been characterized by substandard working conditions due to low institutional investment. Julie Shayne, teaching professor and faculty coordinator of Gender, Women & Sexuality Studies at the University of Washington–Bothell, suggests that one consistent material difference is office space.[17] On nearly all campuses, space is at a premium and contingent faculty generally pay the price. Shayne points out that NTT faculty are often required to share space much as they did as graduate students, even as contingent faculty often have "more visits from students and greater need for an unshared office."[18] Karen Kendrick a fourteen-year veteran of Albertus Magnus College, a private nonprofit college, states that faculty off the tenure track, even those who are full-time, carry rank of full professor, and have yearly contracts, as Kendrick does, often seek the same, elusive things over a career—professional development funds, better pay, office space.

Hiring, Evaluation Processes, and Career Ladders

Informal hiring practices, inadequate or absent evaluation processes, and little opportunity for advancement are traditionally linked facets of contingent employment. Traditionally, while tenure-track faculty are hired after competitive, time-intensive national searches that demand much of employer and applicant alike, contingent instructors are too often hired largely because they are readily available. Tenure-track hiring processes thus cultivate reciprocal loyalty between institution and faculty in ways that casual hiring does not. Yet given reductions in tenure lines, competition for non-tenure-track jobs has intensified over at least the last twenty years. And when tenure-track positions do emerge, local non-tenure-track faculty, even if highly qualified, generally are not considered due to both the glut in qualified applicants and to misperceptions of NTT faculty as second-tier, stalled academics, their teaching experience "evidence of failed promise" rather than high qualification.[19] Faculty eyewitnesses who contributed to this study reported *across all institutional types* that they would not be considered for tenure-track positions at their institutions.

Evaluation of contingent instructors is often problematic as well. As Adrianna Kezar and Daniel Maxey suggest, evaluation processes for contingent instructors are often either entirely absent or highly dependent on student evaluations.[20] Without good evaluation processes, they do not receive the formative feedback that is routinely part of tenure processes, nor do they have opportunity to compete for recognitions of good work. Portfolio assessment, peer observations, and outcomes assessments could be used to evaluate contingent faculty performance, but generally these approaches are not taken because they involve a significant investment of time and energy.[21] In contrast, tenure-track faculty work is meticulously documented, perhaps as much to construct the tenure case as for accountability purposes.

The circumstances vary. An early-career contingent faculty informant for this study, who asked to not be named, teaches entirely online for two public doctoral universities that approach evaluation matters completely differently. At one location there is no evaluation process, and contingent faculty are simply invited back each time a particular course is offered; the other institution undertakes meaningful annual evaluation with an expectation that professional development will be substantially integrated into the year's activities. The professional development requirements at the second institution, this faculty member points out, have provided opportunity to learn about better approaches for online instruction, collaborative approaches with university libraries, and participation in faculty learning communities focused on a variety of topics. Vastly differing institutional investments are made in this contingent faculty member's two universities.

We argue that the professional development offered at the one location is a fair tradeoff: the institution gets an individual who can deliver continuously improved instruction and the faculty member derives lasting professional growth. We also note that this new contingent faculty member is encountering some of the core devaluing myths that sustain contingency, such as the idea that abbreviating or avoiding professional development and annual review is a desirable simplification for the faculty member. As an early-career professional, this faculty member values instead the opportunity to develop teaching experience, as well as to understand institutional structures. Comparisons between the two institutions also underscore the choices that universities make when establishing relationships with contingent faculty. Some campuses see professional development and strong evaluation processes as time-consuming and expensive nuisances, while others see them as matters of institutional responsibility.

Disenfranchisement from Shared Governance

While the number of contingent instructors has steadily grown over the past forty or more years, most remain disenfranchised, prohibited from influencing curriculum or contributing to policy and decision-making. According to the AAUP's report

"The Inclusion in Governance of Faculty Members Holding Contingent Appointments," "when half or more of the faculty at an institution may not participate in meetings of the faculty senate . . . something is amiss."[22]

Some institutions have enacted policies that more fully enfranchise NTT faculty. At Indiana University Bloomington, for instance, full-time NTT faculty have voting rights on their faculty senate, even though tenure-track faculty maintain control of governance through a 60:40 rule.[23] At the University of Missouri–Columbia, voting rights were extended to the council's four NTT faculty representatives, who are elected by their non-tenure-track peers.[24] A 2017 study reported that 85% of doctoral universities, 88% of public institutions, and 76% of private institutions made full-time NTT faculty eligible to serve on their faculty senate/council, while only 11%, 12%, and 8% of doctoral, public, and private institutions, respectively, extended governance participation to part-time NTT faculty.[25]

Full participation in shared governance remains elusive for many. At Augsburg University, Ennis is warmly welcomed to both department and faculty senate meetings, but she is not allowed to vote at either. At Albertus Magnus, Kendrick reports that full-time NTT faculty can vote but are often hesitant to do so, or at least are reluctant to vote their conscience, due to their one-year contracts and the presence of administrators at faculty senate meetings. Perhaps administrators are unaware of the subtle "governance threat" they represent to contingent faculty in such circumstances.

Weak Material Support

Contingent instructors are often deprofessionalized through the inequitable distribution of material resources for daily work and career development. Professionalizing opportunities, such as conference travel and course releases for scholarship, are relatively rare for contingent faculty. Yet material support can occur in simple, less costly ways as well. Ennis of Augsburg University suggests that contingent faculty, if they are given opportunity to know a campus well and to spend time there, will exceed expectations for supporting students. She prides herself for staying up to date on the Augsburg campus's student resources—where they are located, what they offer, who to contact. In contrast, when she takes short-term gigs at community colleges, she does not know the offices or the people who could assist students. As she puts it, "This gets at contingency's potential impact on students."

Contingency's implications for students have less to do with the individual instructor than with the opportunities provided by institutions to develop knowledge through a reciprocally committed relationship, faculty member to institution and vice-versa. This point is made even clearer through Ennis's work in the for-profit sector where she occasionally teaches to supplement her income.

Ennis explains: "Rasmussen has specific and stringent requirements for adjunct instructors, including being visibly active in courses for five non-consecutive days per week, using students' given names in all feedback, and providing feedback on student work within seven days of assignment submission, with consequences if deadlines are not met." While Ennis believes that Rasmussen's expectations have held some value for her teaching, the surveillance at this for-profit is high. As such, Ennis's conundrum is clear: Augsburg, which values her expertise and experience and benefits from her knowledge of the campus, is unable or unwilling to make a formalized commitment to her despite years of service. To supplement her income, Ennis takes on heavily surveilled work at a for-profit, and tries to make the most of it.

Better Contingent Approaches

Better NTT faculty policies exist, even if they mostly only approximate tenure and often feature significant internal contradictions. Lacey Wootton, of American University, a private nonprofit research university, works off the tenure track as the writing program administrator for a program with no tenure-line faculty. Her institution has three tiers of faculty—tenure-track, term (which carries some parity with the tenure-track), and adjunct—the last of which are unionized yet remain precarious and weakly supported. Wootton describes her own situation as "superb," suggesting that the presence of tenure is not necessary for establishing good conditions. She enjoys a high level of influence and visibility on her campus and has even served as chair of American University's faculty senate. These opportunities were not granted by a benevolent administration but came due to the hard work of contingent faculty like herself. As a result, "Administrators do not wield power against us. Contingency is not used as a weapon to silence people." Her circumstances suggest what is possible when NTT faculty successfully argue for renewable multiyear contracts, active participation in governance, and advancement opportunities. In contrast, Wootton reports, noncontracted instructors (adjuncts) at American have gained little ground through their unionized status.

Chris Dean of the University of California, Santa Barbara (UCSB) describes a mature union context in which the union has achieved "tenure-lite." The UCSB system features pre- and post-six-year continuing appointment review processes and a tenuous form of sabbatical for NTT faculty, although this "sabbatical" is underwritten entirely by a senior faculty member, a situation that is probably unsustainable. Dean also notes of the tenure-lite system, "the problem is getting there." The "pre-six cohort," as he calls it, has special needs, and while there is a commitment to mentoring faculty through the process, faculty assurances during this period are tenuous. Dean highlights that there are also significant differences in the professionalizing opportunities available to full-time and part-time contingent faculty members, again noting an improved but tiered system.

Alexis Moore, who recently retired from Pasadena City College, worked also as an organizer for the California State University system, a period that she describes as "a very rewarding time to work on the inside of an excellent union." She also held union leadership positions at community colleges. Yet unionization has not solved all problems and has created some of its own. As Moore describes it, there are 73 districts and 116 colleges in the California Community College system, which makes up the largest higher education system in the nation. Moore worked at seven colleges in five districts in this community college system and experienced a dizzying array of contract manifestations. "Herein, lies the problem," Moore states. "We have three main union affiliates, CTA/CCA, AFT/CFT, and an independent union called California Community College Independents (CCCI)." Moore and colleagues successfully argued for the Pasadena City College to become part of the CCCI in 2006 after arguing before the Public Employment Relations Board (PERB) that CTA/CCA be decertified as having exclusive rights for full-time and adjunct representation. During this period Moore was driving to three different colleges a semester, earning a meager living, and paying dues to three different union locals. The situation's difficulties were exacerbated by tenured faculty domination of the unions. These tenure-track faculty rarely shared leadership with contingents even though contingent instructors outnumbered tenure-track faculty two to one. Tenure-track faculty also moved between management jobs and teaching positions, utilizing "retreat rights" to take on overloads and increase their salaries, thus displacing contingent faculty in the process and stripping them of sections. "The key to an effectively unionized campus," Moore states, "is parity between those who are full-time and those who are part-time." This is why she appreciates Vancouver Community College's Program for Change, which makes "regularization" a key objective.[26]

When we step back from these better situations, it becomes clear that it is the provisions of tenure itself that are being approximated. Faculty across institutional type seek participation in shared governance, steady and stable work, recognition and reward for good teaching, evaluation approaches that include a career ladder, and parity in compensation. In the absence of tenure, the very hard work of constructing reasonable conditions tends to fall to contingent faculty themselves.

Challenging Commonplace Explanations

We now return to the most common explanations for why contingent hiring and the conditions associated with such hiring have become normalized. Based on our research, we challenge those explanations and suggest the implications of contingent hiring practices for faculty, students and families, and the broader culture.

The casualization of the academic workforce has been explained by shifts in state funding and vacillating enrollment. The National Bureau of Economic Research, for instance, has documented the long-term effects of declining state funding for public institutions, suggesting that "the decrease has had, and will continue to have, damaging repercussions, suggesting reason to be concerned about the future of public higher education."[27] University of Michigan economist John Bound, one of the report's authors, asserts that "public universities are privatizing, depending more on tuition, depending more on private contribution."[28] Sarah Turner, another author of the study and an economist from the University of Virginia, states that "declines in appropriations make it difficult for institutions to fund investments to increase the pool of low-income students, and . . . for universities to provide the resources to make college affordable for 'near poor' and 'middle-income' families."[29]

There are other factors, however. After the 2009 recession's sharp cuts to higher education, some states started reinvesting when the economy picked up, but others did not.[30] Those that did not relied more and more on raising tuition, which in turn resulted in enrollment dips among low- and middle-income students and increased competition for students who could pay. This led to "colleges . . . becoming more likely to spend scarce resources on marketing, amenities, . . . and sports programs."[31]

New cuts resulting from the pandemic spell further trouble for higher education in the years ahead. State tax revenues are expected to fall by 20% or more in the postpandemic period, and significant budget cuts to higher education are likely to follow. Even before the pandemic, in the summer of 2019, downward enrollments were driven by a "declining number of high school students, families' increasing sensitivity to tuition and other costs, questions about the overall value of a college degree, and the ease with which students can apply to and consider multiple colleges."[32] The pandemic amplified these trends.

Finally, while the prepandemic narrative around public disinvestment and downward enrollment has had explanatory appeal, it is not a satisfactory justification for the increasing dependence on contingent faculty. As table 6.3 shows, instructional spending per student is actually greater than tuition revenue per student in the public sector, while the inverse is true in the private sector. The private nonprofit sector generally has a higher contingency rate than the public sector even though the public sector has experienced cutbacks in state appropriations. Recent analysis by the *Chronicle of Higher Education*, using US Department of Education data, shows a startling relationship between revenue from tuition and fees and spending on instruction for a certain subset of campuses across the public-private divide.[33] Since revenue from tuition far outstrips investment in instruction in many locations, where is the money going? Why aren't colleges and universities being called to account for the human toll of contingency, seen in all sectors and levels, as described in this chapter?

We urge further investigation into additional implications of broad contingent hiring, such as its impact on the development of teaching expertise. Contingency sets up an endless loop of onboarding, as faculty must be reidentified and rehired, then fired or "nonrenewed," over and over. This approach leads to many inefficiencies, such as the repetition of novice training rather than the development of increasingly sophisticated college teachers. Contingency therefore works against stated commitments to student success and institutional objectives for student retention and persistence. The Engaging Adjunct Faculty in the Student Success Movement, which focuses on community colleges, holds that if we are serious about student success, we must be serious about faculty appointments, status, and working conditions.[34] Similarly, the Delphi Project on the Changing Faculty and Student Success extends this concern to four-year colleges and universities.[35] Both of these initiatives suggest that contingency poses significant risks to student outcomes. They remind us that at least since the 1970s, labor theorists have argued that teachers' working conditions are students' learning conditions. It is not inferior qualifications of NTT faculty that explain the deficits but the dearth in institutional support.[36] According to the Delta Cost Project, NTT faculty, as teachers who are disproportionately responsible for lower-division courses, likely educate "higher shares of students at risk of noncompletion."[37] College teaching so conceived works at cross-purposes to supporting high-impact practices or closing achievement gaps. If we are serious about student success, we must address contingency as a critical rupture in the promise of higher education.

Conclusions

We believe that change is possible. The Delphi Project on the Changing Faculty and Student Success offers $15,000 annual awards to colleges and universities that make strong improvements to policies pertaining to contingent instructors. Recent recipients have focused on many of the factors outlined in this article: compensation, job stability and security, career ladder and sound evaluation processes, material support, participation in governance, and professional opportunities.[38] Such examples suggest a world in which contingent instructors are treated as valued colleagues.

Colleges and universities can no longer maintain the tired narrative that they cannot afford better treatment of their contingent instructors. These instructors generate far more revenue than they cost in salaries, so much so that the financial model for higher education has come to depend upon them. They have become responsible for most undergraduate education. It is time to stop acting as though these essential professionals are an afterthought. The pervasive and predictable refrain of institutional helplessness in the face of contingency must end. Further, as Kezar has argued, fair treatment of contingent instructors pays for itself over the long run.[39]

Ultimately, contingency says far more about the priorities of higher education than about public priorities around disinvestment in higher education. Contingency not only disenfranchises the contingent instructors, removing a majority of faculty from governance, but it also taints the entire educational mission, calling into question the value of a higher education. Contingent instruction needs to be at the center of a long-overdue reform of higher education.

Notes

1. Judith M. Gappa and David W. Leslie, *The Invisible Faculty: Improving the Status of Part-Timers in Higher Education* (San Francisco: Jossey-Bass, 1993); Martin J. Finkelstein, Robert K Seal, and Jack H. Schuster, *The New Academic Generation: A Profession in Transformation* (Baltimore, MD: Johns Hopkins University Press, 1998); Jack H. Schuster and Martin J. Finkelstein, *American Faculty: The Restructuring of Academic Work and Careers* (Baltimore, MD: Johns Hopkins University Press, 2006); US Government Accountability Office, "Contingent Workforce: Size, Characteristics, Compensation, and Work Experiences of Adjunct and Other Non-Tenure-Track Faculty," October 19, 2017.

2. American Association of University Professors, "Data Snapshot: Contingent Faculty in US Higher Ed," October 18, 2018, https://www.aaup.org/sites/default/files/Academic_Labor_Force_Trends_1975–2015_0.pdf.

3. Integrated Postsecondary Education Data System (IPEDS), National Center for Education Statistics, https://nces.ed.gov/ipeds/.

4. Coalition on the Academic Workforce, "A Portrait of Part-Time Faculty Members: A Summary of Findings on Part-Time Faculty Respondents to the Coalition on the Academic Workforce Survey of Contingent Faculty Members and Instructors," June 2012, http://www.academicworkforce.org/CAW_portrait_2012.pdf.

5. "Part-Timers Leading Class," *Inside Higher Ed,* 2009, infographic, https://www.insidehighered.com/sites/default/server_files/media/IHE-pt-comm-college-faculty.png?width=500&height=500.

6. AAUP, "Data Snapshot."

7. On higher education finances, see also Elizabeth Shermer's essay in this collection.

8. On the experiences of contingent faculty and collective actions to improve conditions, see also the essays in Parts II and III of this collection.

9. American Association of University Professors, "The Status of Non-Tenure-Track Faculty," June 1993, https://www.aaup.org/report/status-non-tenure-track-faculty.

10. Danielle Douglas-Gabriel, "'It Keeps You Nice and Disposable': The Plight of Adjunct Professors," *Washington Post,* February 15, 2019, https://www.washingtonpost.com/local/education/it-keeps-you-nice-and-disposable-the-plight-of-adjunct-professors/2019/02/14/6cd5cbe4–024d-11e9-b5df-5d3874f1ac36_story.html.

11. Steven Hurlburt and Michael McGarrah, "Cost Savings or Cost Shifting? The Relationship between Part-Time Contingent Faculty and Institutional Spending," Delta

Cost Project, November 2016, https://deltacostproject.org/sites/default/files/products/Cost-Savings-or-Cost-Shifting-Contingent-Faculty-November-2016_0.pdf.

12. Adrianna Kezar, Tom DePaola, and Daniel T. Scott, *The Gig Academy: Mapping Labor in the Neoliberal University* (Baltimore, MD: Johns Hopkins University Press, 2019). On the Delphi Project, see https://pullias.usc.edu/delphi/.

13. AAUP, "The Status of Non-Tenure-Track Faculty." On the costs and varied experiences of contingent faculty who teach at multiple institutions, see Miguel Juárez's essay in this collection.

14. Douglas-Gabriel, "'It Keeps You Nice and Disposable.'"

15. Eileen Schell, "The Feminization of Composition: Questioning Metaphors That Bind Women Teachers," *Composition Studies* 20:4 (1992): 55–61, https://www.uc.edu/content/dam/uc/journals/composition-studies/docs/backissues/20–1/Eileen%20E.%20Schell-The%20Feminization%20of%20Composition.pdf.

16. Kay Steiger, "The Pink Collar Workforce of Academia," *Nation,* July 2013, https://www.thenation.com/article/archive/academias-pink-collar-workforce/.

17. Julie Shayne, "Senior on the Lecturer Track?," *Inside Higher Ed,* September 28, 2018, https://www.insidehighered.com/advice/2018/09/28/colleges-need-make-concrete-changes-improve-working-conditions-senior-non-tenure.

18. Ibid.

19. AAUP, "The Status of Non-Tenure-Track Faculty."

20. Adrianna Kezar and Daniel Maxey, "Student Outcomes Assessment among the New Non-Tenure-Track Faculty Majority," Occasional Paper #21, National Institute for Learning Outcomes Assessment (July 2014), 10, https://www.learningoutcomesassessment.org/wp-content/uploads/2019/02/OccasionalPaper21.pdf.

21. Ibid.

22. American Association of University Professors, "The Inclusion in Governance of Faculty Members Holding Contingent Appointments," November 2012, 79, last modified 2014, https://www.aaup.org/report/inclusion-governance-faculty-members-holding-contingent-appointments.

23. Bloomington Faculty Council, "Resolution Concerning Voting Rights of Full-Time Non-Tenure Track Faculty," Indiana University Bloomington, accessed July 28, 2020, https://bfc.indiana.edu/policies/statements-resolutions/policy-resolutions/ntt-voting-rights.html.

24. Colleen Flaherty, "Voting Rights for Adjuncts," *Inside Higher Ed,* November 21, 2012, https://www.insidehighered.com/news/2012/11/21/u-missouri-moves-toward-giving-adjuncts-voting-rights-faculty-governance.

25. Willis A. Jones, Neal H. Hutchens, Azalea Hulbert, Wayne D. Lewis, and David M. Brown, "Shared Governance among the New Majority: Non-Tenure Track Faculty Eligibility for Election to University Faculty Senates," *Innovative Higher Education* 42:5 (2017): 513.

26. Jack Longmate and Frank Cosco, "Program for Change," Vancouver Community College Faculty Association, 2016, http://vccfa.ca/program-for-change/. https://cpfa.org/wp-content/uploads/2020/11/ProgramForChange_07–20–2016_006.pdf.

27. Liam Knox, "These Cuts Have Real Consequences," *Chronicle of Higher Education*, June 18, 2019, http://www.chronicle.com/article/these-cuts-have-real-consequences-a-new-study-surveys-the-damage-of-state-disinvestment-in-public-universities.

28. Ibid.

29. Ibid.

30. Kevin Carey, "The 'Public' in Public College Could Be Endangered," *New York Times,* May 5, 2020, http://www.nytimes.com/2020/05/05/upshot/public-colleges-endangered-pandemic.html.

31. Ibid.

32. Eric Kelderman, "Enrollment Shortfalls Spread to More Colleges," *Chronicle of Higher Education,* May 20, 2019, https://www.chronicle.com/article/enrollment-shortfalls-spread-to-more-colleges/.

33. "Colleges That Spent Far Less or More on Instruction Than They Brought in in Tuition and Fees, 2016–17," *Chronicle of Higher Education,* July 14, 2019, https://www.chronicle.com/article/colleges-that-spent-far-less-or-more-on-instruction-than-they-brought-in-in-tuition-and-fees-2016–17/.

34. "Engaging Adjunct Faculty in the Student Success Movement," *Achieving the Dream,* accessed July 20, 2020, https://eric.ed.gov/?id=ED606158. Just as we argued for more research on the implications of contingency, we call for more investigation into where higher education revenue goes and how contingency affects those contingent instructors who are not faculty.

35. "Colleges Increasingly Use Contingent Faculty to Cut Costs, but Savings Are Modest When Accounting for Compensation of All Employees," American Institutes for Research, January 2017, https://www.air.org/news/press-release/colleges-increasingly-use-contingent-faculty-cut-costs-savings-are-modest-when. See also Maria Maisto's essay in the collection.

36. Audrey J. Jaeger and Kevin M. Eagan Jr., "Unintended Consequences: Examining the Effect of Part-Time Faculty Members on Associate's Degree Completion," *Community College Review* 36:4 (2009): 167–194, https://escholarship.org/uc/item/2h55c9t1.

37. Steven Hurlburt and Michael McGarrah, "The Shifting Academic Workforce: Where Are the Contingent Faculty?," Delta Cost Project, November 2016, 4, https://deltacostproject.org/sites/default/files/products/Shifting-Academic-Workforce-November-2016_0.pdf.

38. Adrianna Kezar, "Hope for Those Off the Tenure Track," *Inside Higher Ed,* May 28, 2019, https://www.insidehighered.com/views/2019/05/28/institutions-should-learn-some-good-examples-how-support-adjunct-faculty-opinion.

39. Adrianna J. Kezar, *Embracing Non-Tenure Track Faculty: Changing Campuses for the New Faculty Majority* (New York: Routledge, 2012).

CONTINGENCY AT WORK AND IN THE WORKPLACE

CHAPTER 7

FRAMING PART II

Multiple Contingencies

AIMEE LOISELLE

In May 2018, I composed a resignation email to the chair of the Critical Cultural Studies Department (CCS), which houses several areas of study at the community college where I was teaching as an adjunct history professor. I had recently received a 2018–2019 dissertation fellowship and would need a full-time position with benefits upon completing my PhD. I wrote an appropriate message expressing my authentic appreciation for the students and experiences. In my mind, however, I had an image of myself as Trinity in the opening scene of *The Matrix*, springing in slow motion into a high-speed kick. I was the woman in smooth black leather vaulting from a city rooftop.

When I took my first adjunct contract for Fall 2011, I could not have imagined this outcome. The dean of social sciences, who oversees CCS, tracked me down on the campus where I worked as the transition-to-college instructor. A man she had hired for History of the Caribbean unexpectedly withdrew from his contract, but it was August and students had filled the course because it had not been taught for ten years in a small city with a substantial Puerto Rican population. In addition, the mortgage recession was hitting bottom, so enrollment was increasing. The dean required a professor, and I had a master's degree in history. That October, the adjunct for World Cultures to 1500 was called to reserve military duty, and I took that contract too.[1] When I chatted with the history professor serving as CCS chair, she mentioned the department was submitting a proposal for a tenure-track history line. As I fulfilled these two contracts, I felt optimistic.

I knew adjuncts existed and did not have the highest status, but like most people who have not been immersed in an academic department, I thought it was a choice due to life circumstances or a viable avenue to a permanent position. I was not naïve—I asked about pay per credit, opportunities for rate increases, and benefits. But I was ignorant. I did not realize the loaded connotations attached to different types of faculty and the stigma tied to serving as an adjunct. So, I could not imagine their persistence despite the realities of budget austerity, financialization, and declining tenure-track hires.

From Fall 2011 to Fall 2015, as my sections increased to two every semester and one or two for the short summer session, I threw myself into designing syllabi, teaching, and advising. With the encouragement of the economics professor who now served as CCS chair, I proposed a course on hip-hop and an independent study in US foreign policy. I attended professional development workshops and division meetings, despite the lack of welcome from most administrators and tenured faculty.[2] The work rekindled my enthusiasm for scholarly history, and I left the transition-to-college job to start a PhD program. I had no idea this decision would make me less appealing as an adjunct.

At the same time, regional high-school graduation numbers dropped due to demographic change while the economy recovered and employment rates improved, all of which caused enrollment to plummet. Sections stopped filling, administrators rejected the proposed tenure-track history position in 2012 and again in 2015, and the CCS chair did not greet me with the same smile when we passed in the beige halls. Without notice, the number of sections in my email offers declined, and when the hip-hop course was supposed to run a third time in Spring 2016, it was not scheduled. I tracked down the chair, who said they could not offer courses that only an adjunct could teach. I imagined it also involved making sure the tenured faculty's specialty courses were filled.

When my offer for Fall 2016 listed only one section, I again went to the chair. She said they knew I was getting close to finishing my PhD and seeking a full-time job—and they had to cut sections anyway. The cold calculation and brittle statement knocked me into silence. These faculty taught about economic justice, women's activism, social movements, and communist revolutions. They advocated for low-income and undocumented students. The chair and a few others had behaved, at one point, as colleagues. Yet they refused to address precarity or adjunctification in their own labor hierarchy. They grumbled but tolerated institutional budgets as their tenure privileges endured behind a shrinking perimeter. I increasingly felt confused because the chair and senior history professor seemed concerned when they saw me, yet also acted like I was an embarrassment. I eventually realized it was possibly guilt, but not camaraderie.[3]

I pushed back as much as I could. I hung bright posters to attract students to my courses and explained to them the differences between tenured and adjunct.[4] I researched community college funding in Massachusetts and realized that tenured faculty not only had no pragmatic incentive to demand permanent positions, they had disincentives. Statewide, tuition for sections taught by adjuncts stayed with campuses, while tuition for tenured faculty sections went to the state budget. I voted for adjunct candidates when they ran for key leadership with the state union in 2017. But their overly simple contract demand for higher pay could not even unify most adjuncts, who had different goals based on their circumstances. Vocational professionals with full-time jobs wanted pay equity and limited benefits but were content with contingency; retirees from other careers were interested in better pay but not enough to get active; and academic scholars like me wanted to fight for a path to permanent employment based on years of service.

By May 2018, my annual income from contracts had dropped from $17,000 to $6,800. I scanned the online system to see which history adjuncts were still teaching two sections a semester: the retirees with pensions, usually from public school administration or the military. They were not necessarily better professors and did not have more teacher training or research, but they were readily available any semester for the foreseeable future, without needing full employment or benefits. For departments aiming to maximize both class size and flexibility in their contract offers and cancellations, retirees are more compliant workers.

I enjoy the classroom and students' explorations. One of my career missions is access, retention, and completion for first-generation and underrepresented students. This was the type of institution where I had envisioned teaching. Walking the campus halls, however, had become an exercise in disillusion and alienation. When I received the fellowship, I had to leave. So, I mentally leapt into the air with my black boots, kicked that sternum, and bolted. Like Trinity, I launched into another unpredictable situation that was not necessarily better. But I could not stay where I was.

Notes

1. See Diane Angell's chapter in this volume on the challenges that adjunct faculty face when teaching as generalists, not specialists.

2. Claire Goldstene's essay examines the lack of collegiality or interaction for adjuncts.

3. See Claire Raymond on the discomfort that contingent faculty, as outcasts, evoke for tenured faculty.

4. Maria Maisto analyzes the vital if tenuous role of adjuncts as teachers and mentors.

CHAPTER 8

SOCIAL DIRT, LIMINALITY, AND THE ADJUNCT PREDICAMENT

CLAIRE RAYMOND

> All margins are dangerous. If they are pulled this way
> or that the shape of fundamental experience is altered.
> Any structure of ideas is vulnerable at its margins.
>
> —Mary Douglas

In this chapter, I combine personal exposition and social theory to analyze parameters of my experience teaching, from Fall 2007 to Spring 2020, in a non-tenure-track position. After the events described in this chapter, I accepted a research collaboration fellowship at another university, an act that led to my being summarily "off-boarded" from my already tenuous teaching position at the university described here. Drawing from Mary Douglas's theory of social concepts of purity and danger, I will develop here the concept of *social dirt*, moving through thick description of experience to illumination through social theory. Aligned with feminist standpoint theory, I theorize the personal.

A Confusion of Categories

As I'm preparing to give my afternoon lecture, there comes a knock on the office door. It's not during my office hours, but we're nearing final exams and I guess there may be an anxious and needful student standing outside. I open the door to find our departmental administrative assistant carrying a stack of library books. "Professor X ordered these to be put in her office," she informs me.[1] She comes into the tiny, well-appointed office and proceeds to carefully arrange the books on the shelves. This is not my office. It belongs to a tenure-track faculty member on leave, living abroad for a year. She is, generously, allowing me to use the space, while I labor as an adjunct faculty member, teaching at the tier-one research university in the southeastern United States where I have taught for the past twelve years.

This kind of interruption of my labor is par for the course. Though the administrative assistant is friendly, I cannot tell her (1) that the books should not be placed in the office because I need the space for my own books and (2) that she should not interrupt me when I'm working. It's understood that I inhabit this office through the largesse of the tenure-track colleague on leave and the departmental chair. Because I'm not tenure-track faculty, the university does not owe me an office. So, the space is not actually mine. I am an intellectual migrant, shifting each year to a different office, depending on who is on leave. And each year I sign a contract that grants me one additional year of teaching employment and that specifies that no matter how many consecutive years I teach for this same university, I am given no ECE (expectation of continued employment).

None of this information is available to the many undergraduates whom I teach. Outside the office, my name is on the nameplate. On the departmental website, I am listed along with other faculty, albeit under the designation "Lecturer." But this small sign that something is different about my situation is unlikely to be meaningful to most undergraduate students, if they even read the faculty website. The university where I have taught since 2007 prides itself on combining teaching excellence with scholarly research. Students expect their professors to represent exemplary positions in the fields that they teach. And, during my twelve years of teaching as an adjunct for this university, I published seven scholarly books and seven books of poetry, as well as two edited volumes (at the time of the final edit of this chapter, I am the author and lead editor of eighteen books covering three fields—English literature, poetry, and art history). A student could be forgiven for thinking that I bring scholarly accomplishment to my role as "professor," a title students use when addressing me. I do not correct them.

But I am not a professor. Not in the sense of the word that we associate with the liberal project of sustaining a national and international scholarly community: professor as a scholar and teacher supported financially through a salary at or above the living wage and supported socially through some version of collegiality by the university where they teach. Instead, as a lecturer on a year-to-year contract, I inhabit a kind of shadow world, a social vista in which, as in a tilted holograph, I appear at times to be a professor—give lectures, teach classes, assign grades to students, mentor and write letters of recommendation for students, publish my work—and at other times do not appear to be a professor. I lack a stable commitment from the university and I am, within my annual contracts, specified to be working without benefits and at a less-than-living wage. Most years, depending on the number of courses I am able to shoulder, I make less than a manager at McDonalds.

How did this happen? I earned a doctorate from a high-ranking research university and was awarded departmental and university-wide honors for my dissertation. A deeply edited version of the dissertation was published as a book by a scholarly press a few years after I received my doctorate. From there, I went on to publish several more books. If *publish or perish* were the reality of academia today, I'd be just fine. Every adjunct's story is personal, and mine was inflected by a fateful third pregnancy, which co-occurred with the completion of my PhD. During this difficult time—I had experienced other pregnancy losses and was determined to carry my third pregnancy to term—my dissertation advisor and I had a falling out, and she refused to tender letters of support when I went on the job market. In my case, the problem may be that specific.

And yet, as sociologist C. Wright Mills argues, most events in our lives that feel personal, because they happen to us personally, exemplify broader generational and socioeconomic forces, and have been largely determined by those forces. According to Mills, the individual's sense of her own fate is mostly illusory: our individual fates are almost always determined by the larger social parameters and groups within which we happen to find ourselves.[2]

The adjunctification of universities is this kind of generational trend. Well over half of all American faculty in this second decade of the twenty-first century are non-tenure-track.[3] Although at times I regret passing up a position offered when I was completing my dissertation, and which also coincided with that high-risk third pregnancy, there is no guarantee that job would have held together. Statistically speaking, the odds are that I would have ended up adjuncting regardless. What is the social meaning of that fate?

To address this question, in this chapter I apply cultural theory to personal insight, sounding out the peculiar form of "social dirt" that is the adjunct predicament. What does it mean to be hired to appear as a teacher at a university yet to not have claim to inhabit that social space? To be hired to teach but not have a teacher's voice? Mary Douglas's theory of social concepts of purity and danger informs my approach to analyzing the subaltern quality of the adjunct's intellectual labor that takes place, almost invisibly, in the context of a prestigious university. I develop the concept of *social dirt* in this writing, drawing from Julia Kristeva's theory of abjection, Victor Turner's theory of liminality, Arnold van Gennep's notion of rites of passage, and Orlando Patterson's theory of social death and the *non né,* to deepen our understanding of the adjunct predicament. I draw from their work to analyze the shadowland of adjunct employment. I offer analysis rather than solution. Perhaps, though, within analysis are seeds of resolution. For with the academic precariat, the reasons we don't implement fairer systems have to do with "social dirt," the unspoken premise that adjuncts are outside the bounds of the university's proper social boundary, symbolically unclean, and therefore not a group whose difficulties can be mended. Here, I use the word "proper" in the sense that Didier Anzieu develops the term in *The Skin Ego*.[4]

Adjuncts are the abject of the professoriate. Julia Kristeva defines "abjection" as that which is socially determined to be outside the boundary of the proper self, that which must be rejected to maintain the feeling of social integrity that maintains the bounded social self.[5] Within the university social system, the proper social self manifests as either (1) a successful student or (2) a professor expert in her field.[6] But adjuncts' position within this university social system eludes properness. The adjunct is certainly not a student: her entire job is not to learn but to teach. Her knowledge is valued by the university only insofar as she is able to convey it to students. But she also is not a professor: her expertise is, curiously, believed to extend only to the classroom and not outside of it.

This distinction occurs partly because the adjunct is typically hired to teach specific courses. Many adjuncts survive by cobbling together a large array of courses taught at different universities. I have survived by presenting courses taught within one university for five different departments and programs: English Literature, Art History, Sociology, Media Studies, and Women, Gender, and Sexuality Studies. The force of the adjunct contract is clear: *you are hired to teach this course, and only within this specific domain does the university consider you qualified.* Hired thus to teach courses, rather than to be an expert in a field, you are not supported by the university in any publications you may write. In the social world of the university the adjunct is an incomplete professor, with expertise that is considered by the university *not* to extend beyond the contained act of teaching a specific course-for-hire.

The incomplete professor that is the adjunct is a source of the role's abjection. The adjunct's social position abrades the definition of the proper subject identity that tenure-track faculty occupy. And from this abjection stems unvoiced but clear social pressures against rectifying injustices that face adjuncts. Instead, as the abject in the text of the university social world, the impetus is—just as Kristeva states of all abject objects—to cast out the adjunct.[7] For Kristeva, the abject is that which the physical body must expel to remain proper, and she draws a parallel with her argument that the collective social body feels compelled to cast out that which it considers abject, as if its social survival might depend on this act of expulsion.[8] This casting out may take the form of creating a low-status social group that is at once acknowledged and simultaneously disavowed. In the context of American universities now, adjunct labor is essential to the functioning of the institution. More students are taught by non-tenure-track faculty than by tenured and tenure-track faculty; non-tenure-track instructors constitute a cheap labor source that allows universities to stay afloat.

Adjuncts, then, vulnerable to being literally cast out—being on temporary contracts, they can easily lose their employment—are also abject, in Kristeva's definition of the term: at once cast out of and retained within the social body of the university. This taint of that which is improper to the professor hovers around the adjunct, creating a system wherein the fact of adjuncts is kept behind closed doors, not mentioned or, if mentioned, then never extolled. In my experience with my tenure-track colleagues, the word "adjunct" is politely avoided, in the way one decorously avoids scatological language. A few older colleagues, whose experience of academia formed before the advent of adjunctification, discreetly took me aside to tell me that the university's treatment of me was "outrageous," and "scandalous," and to encourage me to stand up for myself. I deeply appreciated these words of kindness, but—as I hope I make clear in this essay—the problem of adjunct labor reaches far beyond any individual's capacity to stand up for herself. Collective action is the only path.

The adjunct's sense of stain coexists with her embodied nonexistence in the university context. In drawing on concepts originated in sociologist Orlando Patterson's lengthy and exhaustively researched *Slavery and Social Death,* I do *not* suggest that adjuncts experience conditions that approach the horrors of enslavement.[9] The differences between what it means to be an adjunct and what it meant to be enslaved are too numerous to list, but principally, one may note that adjuncts are always able, legally speaking, to quit their jobs and seek employment elsewhere. Likewise, adjuncts are not necessarily visible as abject persons once they leave the university. The moment I step on the train to leave Charlottesville and go into DC, for example, I join a privileged social class, a cisgendered, white woman. Moreover, my child—the son I bore in that third pregnancy—will not by law inherit my abject role in the academy.

Patterson yields a succinct yet capacious definition of "social death" different from and not related to physical death. The "socially dead" is the *non né*, the "never born."[10] Patterson is *not* referring to the fetus, the unborn. Rather, his term, the *non né*, indicates the one whose birth is not accorded social meaning as the birth of a person. The socially dead person is one who cannot publicly claim an inheritance from his parents and cannot publicly bequeath family name to his children. He cannot be situated, publicly, in a lineage either as scion or progenitor.[11]

What does this have to do with the adjunct faculty member? In the career of the university professor, one can see mentorships as parenting, and adjunct faculty members almost never have publicly acknowledged university "parents." The support afforded junior tenure-track faculty is notably missing for entering adjuncts: no one is responsible for their professional success because they are assumed to be temporary faculty.[12] This absence of formal mentoring by faculty who know the ropes is yet another impediment to the adjunct's realization of the role of professor.

Adjunctcy has become a permanent form of social invisibility and precarity, with adjuncts accepting the uncertain terms of their employment for years on end. During my early years of adjuncting, I was advised by a well-meaning dean to cozy up to my departmental chair, so as to be shifted to tenure track. The dean stated that it didn't matter what I published; it mattered that this chair *like me*. This dean was drawing on extensive knowledge of how things work at this university, trying to help. But I have an aversion to cozying up to those in power. As the editors of *Civic Labors* note, in regard to the narrow range of acceptable academic paths, there is a price to be paid for not scrupulously adhering to the social desires of one's supervisors.[13] Instead of seeking to become the pet of the departmental chair, I did my job and did it well: I taught classes, wrote books. Remaining "unparented" in the university system—lacking a senior faculty member who would allow me, as junior faculty, to draw from their status—I remained an adjunct. The sloppiness of "cozying up" to a chair as opposed to the clear patterns of mentoring offered to full-time junior faculty is stark. Does cozying up mean flirting? Does it mean becoming friends with someone you might otherwise not wish to befriend? As there are no parameters to protect adjuncts from exploitation, the risks are high. Adjuncts are orphaned within the university system, unprotected.

Just as the adjunct does not have "parents," he, she, or they do not produce "children" in the scholarly world. Given the supposed impermanence of each adjunct's contract, it is unusual for an adjunct to serve as a doctoral student's dissertation advisor and to see that student through the process of earning the doctorate. This structural impediment to the adjunct producing scholarly heirs seals the deal: the adjunct is, using Patterson's definition, the socially dead person in the context of the university community.

Adjuncts can have rich and full social lives outside the university. But within their workplace, the university community, they are the socially dead. Adjuncts are typically deprived of forms of agency available to tenured and tenure-track faculty such as the ability to choose their own courses and vote in departmental meetings. I was, for the record, allowed to develop my own original courses, an opportunity withheld from most adjuncts. However, I was never given vote nor voice in departmental meetings and yet was pressured to attend these meetings to show my support for the department (and thus hold onto precarious employment). During such meetings, I would sit silently against the wall, excluded from the inner circle of the "real" faculty, taking notes on the topics discussed, but not given a voice regarding those matters.

For many adjuncts lack of social power (and the agency it confers) carries over into their social lives, as poverty afflicts virtually all adjuncts who do not have other means of financial support.[14] Were we subsisting solely on my adjunct wages, my son and I would be living at the poverty line. As it is, our lives are constrained financially. And yet I teach at a university where I am surrounded by the physical manifestations of money: well-dressed students, beautifully maintained buildings, and well-paid senior professors and even more highly paid administrators. The classrooms in which I teach are elegant, with the university's architecture a sublime mix of Greek Revival and contemporary. In thirteen years of teaching in these lovely classrooms, I never received a raise.

Social Dirt

To clarify the link between social death and social dirt, I turn to Mary Douglas's definition of "dirt," extending the language of her fundamental argument by defining as "social dirt" that which has no stable physical property whatsoever, but instead is all that we associate with powerlessness: the indigestible taint of nonbeing, the object that confuses or sullies social categories. Douglas in *Purity and Danger* shapes a cartography of the fear of contamination through social connection.[15] Her definition of purity is to be distinguished from Max Weber's theory of status.[16] Purity stands in contrast to abjection, that which must be expelled, whereas caste incorporates notions of hierarchy. My point is not that adjuncts are low status (though obviously we are) but that the category of adjunct presents academia with a risk of impurity by contagion.[17] Douglas explores origins of notions of impurity in biological risk, but she discerns that what is considered socially dangerous is *not* correlated with this biological risk. Instead, the social danger emerges from a notion of nonbeing in relation to the boundary of the human. Dirt, then, is a concept that blurs categories—the living and the dead, the margin and the center. The margins of the body, Douglas argues, are the realm of social anxiety and variable social proscriptions and taboos.[18] The concept of "dirt" is the concept of risk. The concept of "social dirt" expresses a fear of social risk, fear of the margins of the social body.

Douglas's theory of "purity" extends Emile Durkheim's earlier work on the sacred.[19] However, Douglas brings to her analysis, as Durkheim does not, a sensitivity to how forms of social power are structured by, and imbricated with, culturally specific beliefs about contamination and danger. For her, the pure and the sullied are not eternal verities. Their ontology is frangible, fungible, and entirely structured through social process.

But how are adjuncts "dirty," even in the highly socialized sense that Douglas intends, in the social system of the university? Adjunct teaching does not differ performatively nor visually from tenure-track teaching. Adjuncts teach in the same classrooms as tenure-track faculty. The work of teaching itself—lecturing, grading—does not involve touching substances that we, in the United States, consider "dirty." Nor does it involve embodied physical activity assigned a position of being "dirty" in the wider culture. Adjuncts, in their role as adjunct professors, do not engage in sex for money, do not display themselves nude for financial gain. Not that these examples are intrinsically dirty, but they are categories of social dirt through communal development of such a perspective.

Instead, adjunct teaching occupies the realm of social dirt in the university because it inhabits the margins of the university social body—and these margins cohere with the locus of Douglas's theory of dirt.[20] A university professor, or faculty member, is generally regarded as holding a respected position. Regardless of the nuances of one's academic title, outside the university community the distinction between various faculty positions is not always understood. However, within the university system—not only in the institution where one teaches but also in one's interface with other universities—the status of adjunct is a mark of social dirt. The adjunct is proscribed as a visitor to the institution wherein they may well spend their entire teaching career. Every year that I taught at the same university I was considered a new hire, even though I taught consecutive, back-to-back years without gaps. As a perpetual new hire, I accrued no status or leverage within the university.

If this status as social dirt does not derive from the physical act of teaching while an adjunct, which is indistinguishable from the physical act of teaching while tenured, whence does it derive? Social dirt is marked by that which must be kept secret, sequestered, outside the boundary that wears the mask of "cleanliness."[21] Adjunct labor falls decidedly in this category of that which is set outside the boundary of propriety, as universities rarely advertise their adjunct faculty. Students are not lured to the tier-one university where I teach with the promise of being educated by adjunct faculty paid less than a living wage. No. The marketing of the university is achieved through suppression of this fact. Paradoxically, my department's success was also publicly proclaimed by displaying faculty publications, including mine, on its website.[22] But this website page did *not* note that I was paid less than a living wage and without a stable contract. Thus, the adjunctification of the university is kept quiet. This elision is a sign of the coded shamefulness of the condition.

One might imagine that scandal reflects the university's own shame at its exploitative practices. But that is not the case. The shame instead devolves onto adjuncts. As Claire Goldstene argues in this book, the myth that academia is a meritocracy fuels the shaming of the adjunct, who is seen as deserving of her fate. This is, of course, parallel to the larger myth of capitalism as a meritocracy and indicates the deepening and toxic fusion of academia and no-holds-barred late-stage capitalism. When, five years into my employ, I made a concerted effort to push against my situation by addressing the administration in an informal complaint, I was told that adjuncts are exchangeable—I could easily be "exchanged" for another adjunct. The condition for keeping my job, such as it was, was to accept my own "exchangeable" status.

Here is a second marker of social dirt: that one's identity in one's social world is aligned with that which is unbounded. Having no fixed identity is the definition of being interchangeable with another, a type of porous margins. The premise of adjunct labor *is* this interchangeability. The adjunct plays the role of a professor but is not imbued with the social reality of a professor. It is somewhat analogous to the way that actors, in traditional British culture, were considered profane: they played the role of another; they were not reliable selves but mimickers of others.[23]

As teachers, I know that most of us adjuncts give our students all we have. So, I am not implying that adjuncts are fake teachers in any deep ontological sense. On the contrary, in promoting the idea that the adjunct—whose sole role in the university is to teach—is socially dirty, the neoliberal university's mythology creates a belief in the *unimportance* of teaching. The sociality of the university world casts the adjunct in the role of false professor, one who mimics the actions of the professoriate yet does not carry the reality of the professor's role. While typically it is argued—and this designation holds at my university—that adjuncts and other non-tenure-track faculty are "teaching faculty" and tenure-track faculty are "research faculty," my own experience has been that even as I produced significantly more scholarship than same-age "research faculty" in my department, I continued to be called "teaching faculty." The use of euphemism indicates a terrain of social dirt. In truth, adjunct faculty should be called "minimal pay faculty."

Social dirt means hiding the obscene (literally, off-scene) within the putative "clean": bathrooms and brothels are kept out of sight, or to the side, in buildings and cities.[24] Adjunct labor, though it occurs in the same physical realm as tenure-track labor, is hidden by the language used to describe adjuncts, by the selective use of propaganda that forwards university goals without mentioning the substantial role played by adjuncts in achieving those goals. The obscene (off-scene) linguistic positioning of adjunct labor signifies its status as social dirt, and this haunts the margins of the social body of the university community. As a source of anxiety at the margins of the social body, adjunctcy is handled with secrecy, as with all formations placed in the socio-symbolic realm of dirt, pollution, taboo.

Adjuncting Race and Gender

Adjunct, non-tenure-track faculty are all genders and races.[25] And yet, women, including women of color, are more likely to be adjunct hires.[26] What role does gender play in this dynamic?[27] As a cisgender white woman who at times performs outside the boundary of traditional gender expectations, I have anecdotal insight into the gendered topology of adjuncting. In my experience, my inability to spontaneously produce some of the tropes of traditional femininity at times has worked against me as an adjunct. I am not often a person who lends a motherly ear to students' emotional turmoil. It's not that I don't care; it's that I don't feel qualified to act as a therapist. I have trained to write lectures, not to be a therapist. During my time adjuncting at the university discussed in this chapter, I noted that a handful of women who were hired, like me, as adjuncts became either tenure track or received steady, reliable, and well-remunerated long-term non-tenure-track contracts, because they performed traditional femininity in ways that pleased the administration. One such hire taught courses on the history of gender-based violence and, in the context of teaching those courses, encouraged countless students to share their stories of personal trauma, lending a maternal ear. On the one hand, that is admirable. On the other, it plays into constrictive gender expectations. Even as feminist pedagogy can—and should—be based on bringing human and caring interaction to the college classroom, to enforce essentialist notions of womanliness onto women faculty is a form of gender-based violence. During my years of adjuncting, I noted that another similarly placed hire was able to perform flirtatiousness in a way that seemed successful in securing a stable position. For me, flirting with men, however innocuously, is uncomfortable. I found that in my adjunctcy, my extreme reluctance to perform certain key tropes of traditional femininity counted heavily against me.[28] This may in part have been due to the traditionalist social framework of the university, in the American Southeast, where I was teaching.

Would I have faced these sanctions if teaching as a tenure-track hire? It is a complicated question, as tenured female faculty do face sexism. But adjuncting creates an especially vulnerable space for the crosscurrents of sexism and racism. As a female adjunct, one becomes a kind of walking Rorschach test of others' beliefs about women. As you have no institutional protection—your job defines you as vulnerable—you see firsthand how others (faculty, administrators, students) project their thoughts about women onto you. Kristeva, in her theory of abjection, argues that Western culture defines women as the abject. In particular, she contends that the female body is imagined as grotesque.[29] Simply having the outward appearance of a female body can register, in the deep regresses of the psyches of many, as a form of abjection. Coupled with being an adjunct, being female extends the depth of one's position as the "dirty" or unclaimable component of the academic body. While femininity itself is always already rendered under threat of abjection (and, no, Judith Butler's argument that it is performative does not alleviate that social censure), in the merging of women's oppressed status and the adjunct's structural powerlessness, one finds the very epitome of marginality.[30]

It is impossible to accurately interpret the problematic of femininity as dispossession in adjunct labor without noting how such oppressive definitions of the feminine cohere with coloniality's regime codified as "race," a pseudoscientific category. Inhabiting the implicitly silenced space of the adjunct, my silencing was simultaneously enforced and ironically *protected* by my visual status as a slender cisgender white woman. As a student noted, "You can get away with teaching radical stuff because you look like a cheerleader." Because, at first glance, I fit the look of the nonthreatening white woman and the aging cheerleader, the administration did not fear what I might do if they continued to exploit and structurally abuse me. But, also, I did not lose my job—for many years—because I looked like a nonthreatening aging white cheerleader. Judging by looks, I was an ideal babysitter, presumed incapable of rocking the boat. When I took the teaching of nonwhite scholarly texts too far (in the view of my employer), my employment was threatened in painful and debilitating ways. That process is described in a book I cowrote with former students, *Substance of Fire: Gender and Race in the College Classroom.*[31]

The point I make here is that the soft violence by which white cisgender women's oppression is enforced entwines with structures of socialized seeing that emerge from and hold in place coloniality's regime of racial oppression. As Fannie Lou Hamer rightly notes, "Nobody's free until everybody's free."[32] Adjunct labor as a system in the academy broadly serves to hold in place inherited structures of dispossession and silencing that are the hallmarks of coloniality and racism, creating a new way to silence and marginalize groups of people traditionally silenced and marginalized in coloniality's regime of resource extraction. This new class, however, is granted no fixed articulation because it is held in place by the false pretense of meritocracy, the pretense that adjuncts are given a fair chance to succeed in this system and are simply unable, due to personal limitations, to graduate through the prescribed levels of the academy. Academia's myth of meritocracy allows coloniality's violent impetus to extract resources free range in the university, creating through adjunctification a plunder of each adjunct's knowledge, skill, and energy.

Liminality, Interrupted

The adjunct structurally retains the place of the neophyte, the one in transition between completing a graduate degree and obtaining employment as a professor. Adjunct labor originally *was* intended as a stopgap, a between-times way for newly minted doctorates to teach while seeking tenure-track appointments. But it has become a way of life for a substantial segment of university faculty, while retaining the taint of liminality: the one who has earned a doctorate but has not yet secured a tenure-track appointment. Despite the glaring statistics indicating that the odds of moving into a tenure-track position are small, as the number of PhDs far exceeds tenured positions available in the new structure of academia, the question "why" hangs over the adjunct's apparent acceptance of marginality.

As a departmental chair once put it to me: adjuncts are failed PhDs. Caught in a rite of passage that has no ending in sight, the adjunct retains the position of the initiate—a position that renders one outside the bounds of the university's social world. Whereas true rites of passage render the initiate outside for a stretch of time, such time is self-limited.[33] The initiate is, say, an adolescent who becomes an adult or a catechumen who joins the religion. But adjunctcy has no self-limiting timeframe. The adjunct is a permanently liminal figure, no longer a graduate student and not a professor—not one who is in line to become a professor in the full sense of the social role. The adjunct has, instead, become a spectral figure, a figure that haunts the university—striking fear into the hearts of tenure-track hires who have not yet achieved tenure and, as well, in graduate students nearing completion of their doctorates, as Erin Hatton elucidates in this volume. If, following Patterson's theory of social death, the adjunct is the never-born professor, she is also in some ways the living dead. The adjunct is present in the university, often teaching a heavier course load than her tenure-track colleagues. But she is also *not* there: subject to abrupt dismissal, cancellation of employment, without recourse if employment is terminated. She is a figure on the margins, nearly invisible.

Invisibility and Its Discontents

During my time as an adjunct, while I have not mentored graduate students through their doctorates, I have mentored many undergraduate students in writing what the university calls distinguished major projects. These year-long projects result in lengthy written works of original research. Often, these research projects are funded by small university grants and the best of them are comparable to master's theses in depth and reach. It became a pattern that the students I mentored won departmental awards for excellence in their distinguished major projects. Once this pattern became apparent, tenure-track faculty flipped the script by proactively engaging me as a *second reader* on distinguished major projects. I became, in effect, a "closer," brought in at the end of the project to give it vision and clarity. The university found a way to use my gifts and simultaneously render me invisible. As second reader, I received scant credit for the students' success. Nor was I paid for my work. Although gratifying, mentoring students' honors theses was immensely time-consuming and uncompensated. This invisibility is endemic to adjuncting. Liminality, sustained, becomes social erasure.

A Dirty Deal

Most adjuncts, myself included, end up accepting non-tenure-track employment through a combination of desperation and hope. After staying home with my son for five years, I knew that my chance for teaching at a research university had narrowed. When I was offered a one-year, nonrenewable contract teaching full-time at a prestigious state university, I felt lucky. We decamped from rural Maine, my son started first grade at an excellent school, and I began teaching under a title (Visiting Assistant Professor) that obscured the terms of employment: teaching twice the load of tenure-track faculty for less than half the pay. That first year, unaware of this imbalance, I was enthralled by my bright students and my role as a faculty member at a prestigious university. Then, slowly, I became trapped. The next year, I continued to teach at the same university, same year-by-year contract, though at this point I accepted a different title: Lecturer. But it was early days, and as I was already writing my second book, an elder faculty member assured me that soon I would be shifted to tenure track. My second . . . third . . . fourth . . . and then fifth, sixth, and seventh, scholarly books were published, and yet, as the years went by, I was not shifted to tenure track. Hope waned, but desperation held. How else to give my son the privilege of living in a university town, attending its extraordinary schools? The social dirt of my position paid for my child's access to an education and social world I wanted for him.

Before becoming an adjunct, I lived through some tough times, experiences that taught me about being on the outside. Yet the years of social abjection that I have lived as an adjunct have proven more depressing than my earlier more dramatic encounters with outsider status. This is, I feel, because the social dirt of adjunctcy is so adroitly hidden by the university: only by attending to the hierarchies of power and the way they enforce terms of social dirt in academia will we find a solution to the adjunct predicament.

Notes

With deepest gratitude to Margaret Bendet and Hahna Cho, for their devotion, friendship, and support of this essay.

1. The challenge of combining theory, analysis, and personal testimony is protecting the privacy of others while being scrupulously accurate. I write about this university where I taught from 2007 to 2020 not to impugn anyone, but because it is the place I taught and therefore am able to address in granular detail, with thick description.

2. C. Wright Mills, *The Sociological Imagination* (New York: Oxford University Press, 1959), 5.

3. AAUP Data Snapshot, Mike Palmquist and Sue Doe, "Contingent Faculty: Introduction," *National Council of Teachers of English* (March 2011): 355.

4. Didier Anzieu, *The Skin-Ego* (New York and London: Routledge, 2016).

5. Julia Kristeva, *Powers of Horror: An Essay on Abjection* (New York: Columbia University Press, 1982), 6.

6. Anzieu, *The Skin-Ego*, 31.

7. Kristeva, *Powers of Horror*, 65.

8. Ibid., 6–8; see also René Girard, *The One by Whom Scandal Comes* (East Lansing, MI: Michigan State University, 2014), 13, 85.

9. I am not alone in drawing on Patterson's capacious theory of social death to explain social phenomena that are not slavery. For example, his work has been used to illuminate the situation of rape survivors. See Cathy Winkler, "Rape as Social Murder," *Anthropology Today* l.7:3 (June 1991): 12–14.

10. Orlando Patterson, *Slavery and Social Death: A Comparative Study* (Cambridge, MA: Harvard University Press, 1982), 38, 164–174.

11. Ibid., 26–40.

12. Jody Norton, "Reason, Responsibility, and Post-Tenure University: Theorizing the Role of the Adjunct Professor," *Journal of the Midwest Modern Language Association* 34 (April 2001): 17–19.

13. Dennis A. Deslippe, Eric Fure-Slocum, and John W. McKerley, eds., *Civic Labors: Scholar Activism and Working-Class Studies* (Urbana: University of Illinois Press, 2016), 4–5.

14. American Association of University Professors, "The Annual Report on the Economic Status of the Profession, 2018–2019," (May 2019); Ken Jacobs, Ian Perry, and Jennifer MacGillvary, "The High Public Cost of Low Wages," *UC Berkeley Center for Labor Research and Education* (April 2015): 3.

15. Mary Douglas, *Purity and Danger: An Analysis of Concepts of Pollution and Taboo* (New York and London: Routledge, 2001), 119.

16. Tony Waters and Dagmar Waters, "Are the Terms 'Socio-Economic Status' and 'Class Status' a Warped Form of Reasoning for Max Weber?," *Palgrave Communications* 2 (2016).

17. A version of this chapter was originally presented at the Southern Labor Studies Association conference, University of Georgia, Athens, in 2018. Perhaps fear of contagion is clearer in our present-day COVID-19 epidemic context.

18. Douglas, *Purity and Danger*, 122.

19. Ibid., 6–12.

20. Ibid., 53–78.

21. Ibid., 92.

22. I no longer teach at this university and am no longer represented on its websites.

23. Jane Wessel, "Mimicry, Property, and the Reproduction of Celebrity in Eighteenth-Century England," *Eighteenth Century* 60 (2019): 65.

24. Douglas, *Purity and Danger*, 158.

25. The American Federation for Teachers Higher Education Program and Policy Council, "Promoting Racial and Ethnic Diversity in the Faculty: What Higher Education Unions Can Do" (2010): 13.

26. Martin J. Finkelstein, Valerie Martin Conley, and Jack H. Schuster, "Taking the Measure of Faculty Diversity," *TIAA Institute* (April 2016); Social Sciences Network Interest, "The Burden of Invisible Work in Academia: Social Inequities and Time Use in Five University Departments," *Humboldt Journal of Social Relations* 39 (2017): 228–245.

27. For an analysis of the nexus of gender and precarity, please see Gwendolyn Alker's essay in this volume.

28. Barbara Mandleco, "Women in Academia: What Can Be Done to Help Women Achieve Tenure?," *Forum on Public Policy* 5 (2010): 4.

29. Kristeva, *Powers of Horror*, 4; Mary Russo, *The Female Grotesque* (New York and London: Routledge, 1994), 1–3; Elizabeth Grosz, *Volatile Bodies: Toward a Corporeal Feminism* (Bloomington: Indiana University Press, 1994), 13–14.

30. Combahee River Collective, "A Black Feminist Statement," in *This Bridge Called My Back*, ed. Cherríe L. Moraga and Gloria E. Anzaldúa (Berkeley, CA: Third Woman Press, 2002), 238.

31. Claire Millikin, ed., *Substance of Fire: Gender and Race in the College Class*room (New York: 2Leaf Press, 2018).

32. Fannie Lou Hamer, Speech Delivered at the Founding of the National Women's Political Caucus, Washington, DC, July 10, 1971.

33. Arnold van Gennep, *The Rites of Passage* (Chicago: University of Chicago Press, 1961), 10; see also Victor Turner, *The Ritual Process* (New York and London: Routledge, 1996), 48.

CHAPTER 9

THE GOOD, THE BAD, AND THE UGLY

Being Contingent and Female in STEM Fields

DIANE ANGELL

Between my college graduation and my first years teaching in the mid-1990s as a non-tenure-track (NTT) faculty member in the biology department of a small liberal arts college, the proportion of non-tenure-track faculty in the United States grew. During my more than twenty years as a contingent faculty member, that number has continued to swell. None of us seek NTT positions; for most of us they just happen. As I trace my experiences back through teaching and graduate school, I have come to understand that my non-tenure-track experience cannot be disentangled from my academic path as a female in a STEM (science, technology, engineering, and mathematics) field, since both experiences have positioned me as an outsider in a world where insiders make the rules, even when insiders might no longer be the majority.

As NTTs and women in the sciences, we often live and work within academic communities in which our membership is tenuous at best. We avoid calling attention to our positions, worrying that this will emphasize our outsider status and will lead to being viewed as a "problem." Our workplace colleagues—whether they are tenured, tenure-track, or male STEM faculty—are friendly, especially at small liberal arts colleges, but seldom serve as true allies. We struggle to share our lived experiences, since those conversations risk highlighting the power differential that exists between us and our peers who enjoy job security and privilege in gender relations. I and other NTT women in STEM fields struggle to claim agency in the workplace and legitimacy in our higher education careers. My path as a field biologist may not be typical for all STEM disciplines, but I ask all of us to question the academic structures we have created and to imagine building a more welcoming and fairer environment for all who enter. As I reflect on my path, I can tentatively celebrate the good experiences, keep helping others avoid the bad experiences, and continue to process and question the ugly experiences.

The Path

Like many women scientists, my undergraduate experience was almost completely dominated by male faculty and mentors, a fact I never questioned. Another fact I never questioned was my position as the only female field assistant in every research team I was a part of. Undergraduate students interested in going on to graduate school and teaching in biology, as well as many other science fields, are required to conduct research. That work often takes place well beyond the bustle of labs in big science buildings, remote from the institution. This is true of biology, where undergraduate student ecologists, wildlife biologists, and others must gain experience by collecting data as field research assistants, often working and living in isolated locations before applying to graduate programs. This is also true of other science and social science fields, including geology, anthropology, paleontology, and archaeology.

At the time I was an undergraduate, living in remote locations meant sharing housing and working all day in small groups, often as the only female member of a team. As a research assistant on a National Wildlife Refuge in northern North Dakota and in the Black Hills of South Dakota, days were long and breaks were few. While my experiences were positive, such work left me more vulnerable than my peers working in laboratories on campus. Recent surveys point out that women at field sites regularly experience inappropriate behavior from superiors and peers.[1] Even large, well-established field stations have recently been exposed as places where women regularly experience harassment.[2] Of particular concern are recent reports from BIPOC (Black, Indigenous, people of color) field biologists who have shared their experiences of completing research in out-of-the-way places.[3] While white male STEM faculty, field scientists, and teams of researchers often can be welcoming, racial and gender inequities, exclusions, and vulnerabilities have direct and subtle long-term effects.

My motivation to attend graduate school was prompted by both a bad economy and predictions of an impending shortage of faculty that only seemed to become more urgent as I continued in my program. While the predictions of faculty shortages are hard to believe now, at the time data-filled reports by respected scholars outlined the desperate labor shortage that colleges and universities would face in the 1990s.[4] As a female STEM student, my graduate study was funded by the Patricia Roberts Harris fellowship program, named after a member of President Jimmy Carter's cabinet. The program supported underrepresented groups and women in graduate, professional, and doctoral programs.[5] These fellowships were funded through Title IX of the Higher Education Act. While Title IX may be most familiar for its role driving colleges and universities to balance their men's and women's sports teams or establish structures to manage sexual harassment charges, it was also a key source of federal funding for women and minority graduate students.

Thus, my path through graduate school began with a small cohort of women, long before research on the value of academic cohorts emerged. Fellowship over food, small interdisciplinary research teams, and a committed group of welcoming faculty mentors helped to make graduate students feel supported. Although women were well represented among the graduate students due to our Title IX funding, faculty still were disproportionately male. It was immediately clear that our academic paths were likely to be different from theirs. Many male faculty had wives at home who cared for families, allowing them to focus on their careers. Two women faculty in the department played key roles in helping to normalize our experiences, demonstrating what it could look like to be an academic scientist. At the time, I was blissfully unaware that these two women had been hired following a landmark class action lawsuit brought against the university charging sex discrimination, a charge prompted in part by the denial of tenure to a qualified female candidate.[6]

As participation by women in biology graduate programs was encouraged, the percentage of all PhD degrees earned by women increased from roughly a third when I began my graduate program to over 40 percent a decade later.[7] However, while more women enrolled in graduate programs, the academic ground shifted underneath us. Previous reports warning of waves of faculty retirements and the need for more college and university faculty failed to materialize.[8] The reasons for these failed predictions are complex, but the advent of the Age Discrimination and Employment Act prohibiting compulsory retirement of tenured faculty after the age of seventy likely played a role. Faculty were permitted to continue teaching and doing research far longer than they had before, without stepping down to make room for replacements. Budget cuts that hit public universities and shifting spending priorities away from academics also reduced hiring. As the predicted demand for new college faculty evaporated, and as science PhDs started piling up or "log jamming," a new kind of position was created in the sciences and rapidly became the norm, the postdoc.[9]

While most of our male graduate school advisors probably had gone directly from graduate school to a faculty position, that practice changed in the sciences. These postdoc positions were described as a way to provide newly minted PhDs with additional training and lab experience. In practice, though, postdocs resembled intermediate positions, like planes in a holding pattern waiting to land. These positions were full of uncertainty as to when, how, and where that landing would take place. Like planes circling in the air, the low-paying positions came with little certainty or security of a safe landing. As I progressed through graduate school, it became clear that many PhDs found themselves moving from one postdoctoral position to another, every several years. This problem has not gone away; current ecology graduates spend an average of four years as postdocs.[10] Moreover only 17 percent of science postdocs "land" in a tenure-track position.[11] For field biologists already traveling regularly to conduct field research, this instability can feel overwhelming. The thought of picking up a family and moving several times across the country for relatively low-paying, short-term positions is deflating and almost impossible for an emerging scientist with limited financial resources.

My cohort of women had enthusiastically entered graduate school, but as we looked around us, we began to feel as if we had missed the message that being both a scientist and having a family was not a "thing." The reality of our situations started to sink in: two years of research before applying to graduate school, five to six years of graduate school, and then two to four years of postdoctoral experience. The women faculty in our program did not have children, so we had no one to ask about the challenges of having a family as an academic scientist. At professional meetings women faculty were scarce, and tenured or tenure-track women with children were especially scarce. When I cornered them, I found their comments raw and honest. They shared the conflict they felt between the all-consuming demands of young children and the demands of a position that required giving 150 percent. Many female tenure-track scientists appeared overwhelmed and unsupported, taking on enormous responsibilities while feeling powerless during their period of probation on the path to tenure. Even those who had gained a tenure-track position described a long, anxiety-filled, and unstable pretenure period. I heard and saw dissatisfaction, a lack of opportunity, and little flexibility for those that had a family. It was clear that our male graduate advisors would be unable to provide advice about the personal and professional dilemmas we were beginning to experience. As a result, they often were the last to be told that we were getting married or starting a family. I remember many hushed conversations in hallways.

As graduate students we were trained to follow the facts and were warned about clinging to hypotheses unsupported by the data in front of us. My informal research at the time on life after graduate school no longer supported my initial enthusiasm. Unfortunately, these challenges have mostly continued. I was recently reminded that my time in graduate school covered a period just before the passage of the Family and Medical Leave Act in 1993. This legislation required employers to provide job-protected, unpaid leave for up to twelve weeks after the birth or adoption of a child. Although the act may have empowered women to request and expect more flexibility from their academic institutions, almost thirty years later many women continue to feel pressure about family and reproduction, timing pregnancies to accommodate academic schedules. Women fear being "mommy tracked."[12] Children are born at the start of the summer or end of a semester so that women avoid inconveniencing their departments. These challenges have only been magnified by the pandemic.[13] Today, while more women are in the sciences in colleges and universities, including more who balance parenthood and professional responsibilities, the barriers are still very real and many new mothers leave fulltime STEM positions after the birth of their first child.[14]

Research has highlighted the precarious balancing act between parenting and full-time employment in the sciences, indicating that US science and engineering fields will continue to lose well-trained and experienced professionals.[15] Some women may have sought out smaller, teaching-intensive colleges, imagining that they offer a better work-life balance, but the reverse seems to be true.[16] These tensions are the very reason why women often end up in non-tenure-track positions or leave academics entirely. We have been asking where the women are in ecology for more than ten years.[17] Today, at a time when the portion of women graduating with a PhD in ecology has grown to over 50 percent, women remain overrepresented in non-tenure-track positions.[18] When I recently overheard a faculty member referencing the uneasy balance between home and work demands, trying to stay positive and pointing out that she could "make it work," I realized that such language illustrates the problem. Women should not have to "make it work."

All these forces—the dissatisfaction and isolation of women faculty, the added years of training as a postdoc, the diminishing number of academic positions, the pressure of fieldwork, and family responsibilities—created a headwind that exhausted me, and has likely exhausted many other women. A headwind makes some dig in and become even more determined to march onward. But instead, I braced myself uncertainly, ducked my head, and strategized ways to avoid the full impact of these forces. I considered leaving academics directly after graduate school, but invitations to teach kept me in the classroom. While short-term teaching positions sustained my interest, and while part-time work allowed me to spend time with my young children, this arrangement was not sustainable. I had serious reservations about participating in a system that showed little interest in accommodating the family and work pressures that women experience.

Teaching a course or two each semester was intellectually rewarding, but certainly not financially rewarding. A turning point almost came when I overheard my spouse lecturing a confused plumber that we had hired to do some repairs. My spouse was emphatic, "How could a plumber be making more than a professor?" He fully appreciated the skill required of plumbers since he had frequently taken on such work himself. Like many, he suffered from the misconception that more years of schooling and training translates into higher pay. But his observation made me realize how little I was receiving in return for my many years of training. As I was exploring other careers, a colleague showed me a "great job opportunity." It was one semester, but it was full time and within walking distance of my house. My resolve to move on from academia fizzled.

I was frustrated. The emotional time and energy I had mustered to turn my back on academics might now be wasted. Nevertheless, I submitted my application and hid in an upstairs bedroom during my phone interview to avoid the crashing and banging of three small children below me. I looked for reasons not to take the position and probably sounded demanding, "How many teaching assistants would be available for lab? How many students per lab? How large would the class be? To what extent would I be able to collaborate with others teaching the same course?" I was casting about for reasons to reject the position. Ironically my probing questions probably left my interviewer with the impression that I was knowledgeable and thorough. Twenty years on, I am still in that same position as a contingent faculty member, and still questioning why.

The Good

The rewards of being a non-tenure-track professor, focused primarily on students' education, are easy to point out. Teaching is fun. We engage with enthusiastic young people and, since the field of biology changes so rapidly with new research, teaching gives us an excuse to dive in and keep up with the latest developments, an activity enjoyed by almost anyone who has been to graduate school. Plus, we translate those amazing, constantly evolving discoveries to young people who might not otherwise have encountered science as a creative enterprise.

Since I had been planning to be in this non-tenure-track position for only a year or two before I found a "real job" elsewhere, I came with a "nothing to lose" attitude. Because my undergraduate and graduate experiences as a female in STEM had left me cynical, I leaned toward opportunities that gave me some power to positively affect student outcomes. Of course, saying "yes" was also a way of increasing my chances of being asked back the next year. Taking on responsibilities, especially those that others were not willing to take on, served to illustrate how useful I could be to my department. Like many non-tenure-track faculty, I was reliant on the goodwill of my colleagues.[19] These opportunities shaped the kind of faculty member I became.

After attending to the lack of support for underprepared students in our large introductory biology sections, a colleague asked me to collaborate on a National Science Foundation "Scholarship in STEM" grant that provided support and scholarships for low-income, often first-generation, students in the sciences (NSF S-STEM). I was then able to take on the position of principal investigator on a second NSF S-STEM grant after some thorough checking with NSF that a non-tenure-track faculty member could even accept such a position. I co-taught an interdisciplinary public health course and a summer research course with tenured faculty in statistics and mathematics. I also regularly mentored summer research students, taught Academic Civic Engagement courses, became a Posse mentor, and have facilitated the hosting of about 200 local elementary school students yearly for the past twelve years.[20] Because I did not see myself as a regular faculty member, I took on tasks that many tenure-track faculty avoided because they were not explicitly rewarded by our college's tenure system. Rather than having to tally the number of research articles I published or count the campus-wide committees I served on, I could think more deeply about my teaching and the student experience in my classroom. While the financial risks of coming to the end of a contract mean we live in precarious positions, a point that cannot be overemphasized, there is an unexpected freedom in having less power. We really do not have much to lose.

The Bad

Negative experiences have left me motivated to work toward changes that will make a difference in the experiences of others. The challenges of being a non-tenure-track faculty member are many, with distinct challenges in the sciences. To have any future in the larger academic world, we must continue our research. But a research agenda in the sciences involves equipment, space for that equipment, and, for some of us, travel to field sites. As nontenured faculty, however, we have few if any resources and funds to carry out this work. Research requires time to collect data, analyze results, and write up those results. Non-tenure-track faculty with teaching-intensive positions lack the necessary time and are not paid to focus on research. We might enjoy doing research with students, but we often do not have the means to fund them during the summer. Sometimes NTTs are permitted to apply for internal and external grants, but since we often do not know how long we will remain at an institution, these applications often feel futile. We also keep up with new research by attending academic meetings and conferences to present papers and network, but we often have no regular way of funding attendance at those meetings. Finally, and most importantly, any kind of long-term planning is impossible since many of us are hired on a year-to-year basis. In my field, much of the research is long term. Ecological conditions vary from year to year and data from one year or even several years is not enough to publish sound research. Moreover, much research in the sciences is not only longer term, but also done collaboratively. Our short-term appointments perennially put our ability to collaborate with others at risk, even when colleagues reach out to us. A research project in progress could be thwarted if an NTT contract is not renewed. We can sometimes make connections outside of our institution, but our tenuous situations are all too clear to others.

One might imagine that we could reasonably step back from research for a period of time, put a project on the back burner and focus on teaching or family. However, most scientists understand (and this may be especially true of biology) that what we know changes so quickly that if we step back to take a breath, have a child, or skip a year of attending an academic meeting, we feel an urgent need to catch up. And research in science is competitive. Potential collaborators look for others to work with since the ongoing graduate training system guarantees that there are plenty of others with the skill and ability to commit. We are all replaceable. Once we fall behind on research, we also give up any possibility of qualifying for a tenure-track position, even at a small college. Shifting our focus to teaching, no matter how brief the period, often means there is no going back; it is a one-way path. We are now in the world of short-term, often part-time non-tenure-track teaching.

Biology may differ from other STEM fields. At most institutions, we are big departments with many students, requiring a large faculty. As the number of biology students increases, the number of courses needing teachers increases and introductory classes often balloon in size. But departments may have trouble keeping pace with this growth in terms of tenure-track faculty hiring. While this creates a need for more faculty, such positions tend to be in the courses that are the most challenging to teach. Tenured and tenure-track faculty are typically more enthusiastic about taking on mid- and upper-level courses in their specialty, leaving non-tenure-track faculty to teach the large introductory sections with a greater diversity of students. These classrooms are often filled with students aiming for medical school. Some have taken IB or AP courses at their well-funded high schools and others are first-generation students coming from underfunded rural or inner-city high schools. The complex responsibility of reaching all these students and helping them transition to college learning in large biology classes often rests on the skills of non-tenure-track faculty.

The teaching responsibilities for non-tenure-track faculty are further complicated by the enormous range of courses NTTs accept to teach, as compared to their tenure-track and tenured peers. When I am with other faculty and asked what courses I teach, I often hesitate. I never know where to start, since I have cycled in and out of ten different courses in biology and environmental studies in just the past five years. As different tenured faculty go on sabbatical, we take on their courses out of necessity and sometimes just to illustrate how needed we are in the department. Our choices about courses are not necessarily real choices. Refusing is risky. New course preps, however, take an enormous time commitment, and we never can be certain that this startup investment will pay off in future opportunities to teach that course.

I see the challenges that fit into this "Bad" category as unpleasant and often unnecessary, but mostly manageable. We can improve conditions by providing support for NTT research, encouraging longer-term contracts so that NTTs can plan research projects and collaborations with others, and reevaluating who teaches what courses. In fact, my field of ecology has recently highlighted the need to recognize and legitimize contingent faculty in these and other ways.[21]

The Ugly

Unfortunately, non-tenure-track faculty regularly find themselves in situations that seem particularly dismal and awkward. Addressing these ugly experiences is much more difficult. While we appreciate our institutions and our departments, knowing that they often mean well, colleges and universities are set up to serve students and foster the work of tenure-track and tenured faculty. Our presence as non-tenure-track faculty exposes the cracks. We are not supposed to be there but are essentially a "flexible" workforce upon which these institutions depend. Like all cracks, these tend to widen when the support structures that should be in place are absent. Although institutions depend on us, they prefer that we stay invisible. Establishing support structures for non-tenure-track faculty means acknowledging our existence and the critical role we play in keeping colleges and universities running.[22]

Because of this disconnect, non-tenure-track faculty are frequently confronted with questions from students and colleagues for which good answers are elusive. What do you say when asked why you are called a "visiting professor," despite having been at the institution for ten years? How do you respond to a question about whether you will be teaching a course next year, when you have not yet received your next contract? How do you explain to a student that your institution has hired another person to teach one of your classes in order to ensure that you do not teach full-time for more than six years in a row, because your college follows the letter but not the spirit of AAUP guidelines protecting tenure (see below)? What happens when your child applies to the college where you work to get the discounted tuition and then you lose your teaching position? Three events that began innocuously enough illustrate the deeper bind in which contingent faculty regularly find themselves.

The first event was an invitation to join a book club that was filled with tenured faculty. What a great opportunity to get more involved with my colleagues. I yearned for the collegiality that I observed in other faculty.[23] It would be fun to get to know colleagues outside of our academic buildings, see their houses, and hear their perspectives on topics beyond those we discuss in faculty meetings. Their attention and thoughtfulness to include me seemed to legitimize my position as a faculty member. Maybe they did see me as a real colleague? This wave of enthusiasm was followed quickly by a churning, internal debate that became a growing pit in my stomach. This book club felt awkward and potentially risky on several levels. It would expose me, and my position as a non-tenure-track faculty member. At a more personal level, what would more senior faculty think of me and any comments or perspectives I might share? These are people who regularly (at that point annually) make decisions about my employment. I clearly was not one of them. What would happen if my department decided not to rehire me, or let my contract run out? I decided to stay safely in my own lane and decline politely, pointing out how busy I expected to be in the next year.

The second event was a retirement dinner where I sat at a circular table with several other non-tenure-track faculty, one of whom was particularly outgoing and enthusiastic, along with two more senior tenured men. It was spring, the time when many of us non-tenure-track faculty waited nervously to hear whether we had positions for the coming year. The tenured faculty at the table began to chat about the classes they were teaching in the fall and the other faculty responded, taking turns going from person to person. As we came to the non-tenure-track faculty at the table, my anxiety grew. While I recently had received notice about my teaching assignments, I was unsure of the status of the other nontenured faculty at my table. As I tentatively shared the courses I had been assigned, a boisterous non-tenure-track colleague next in line around the table shot her hand up over her head, gave a whoop, and said, "Give me five, I am going to be here too!" We looked at each other, grinning, sharing a moment of relief with one another. As I turned my head, I remember looking into the faces of the two tenured faculty on the other side of the table. However briefly, they had glimpsed our world and smiled sheepishly.

My mind then wandered as we congratulated the retiree with toasts. Another wave of doubt and uncertainty rose within me. What does retirement look like when you will never be tenured? Would I ever have anyone celebrating my service? How do we honor the work that non-tenure-track faculty do at our institutions? More important are questions about economic survival during retirement, similar to those faced by workers in many other sectors of American society. While some longer-term NTTs have accumulated modest retirement savings in TIAA or other accounts, shorter-term NTTs prospects are often unsustainable, despite working as professionals for institutions that profess humane values.[24]

A final ugly event felt like a slow-moving train wreck. I had been teaching full time and was in my fifth year when it was called to my attention that I was approaching a point where I risked getting entangled in what many call the "6-Year Rule." Institutions seeking to sidestep the AAUP's stated expectation that faculty working full time for six years be automatically tenured regularly make tactical employment decisions based on a narrow reading of this statement. While some institutions terminate non-tenure-track faculty who have reached this stage, my institution required me to step back from full-time employment to reset my clock.[25] I was asked to give up one of my favorite courses. Since the course still needed to be taught, my department hired a fresh new graduate for a single semester. Adding insult to injury, I was asked to meet with that new hire because of my recent experience teaching the course. I shared my teaching materials and guidance as best I could, all while students knocked on my door to ask why I would not be teaching the class I had offered each spring. Unfortunately, these ugly experiences and the cracks they reveal are not easily covered over. Instead, they highlight the contradictory priorities in higher education and place contingent faculty in an untenable position.

All in All

While being a non-tenure-track faculty member is frustrating and tenuous, I have come to appreciate how the experience helps me see the world differently. Insecurity leads to discomfort, but discomfort can help us to see our institutions for what they are. I have felt a sense of urgency to push for change, since I never knew how long I was going to be teaching. As a non-tenure-track faculty member I lived one step at a time, never planned too far ahead, never established long-term career goals, and always questioned my ambitions. I also probably raised my hand far too often, was too flexible, and spread myself thin as I tried to establish my legitimacy. Fortunately, or unfortunately, these were habits I learned as an undergraduate and graduate woman in STEM. As I moved through an academic science and research culture with few women mentors and no clear role models, I felt like an outsider from the beginning of my academic career. Taking on the role of a non-tenure-track faculty member came naturally. At times it was the path that seemed easiest, allowing a degree of flexibility for a working mother. I like to imagine that this path has shifted as more women have joined the STEM academic world but reports from younger female colleagues suggest otherwise. We still ask too much of them. While more women than ever are getting PhDs in biology fields, we know that in STEM fields the academic system continues to lose women at a higher rate at every stage of their careers.[26]

As we consider the effects of climate change, biologists often distinguish between building resistance and resilience. We need to ensure species on the planet have sufficient resources and support both to resist the effects of a changing climate and, in a worst-case scenario, have the resilience to bounce back from the impacts of a changing climate. Preserving species is noble and respectable work, but we should never have allowed our climate system to get to this point. Species should not have to be either resistant or resilient. While the fate of many species on the planet is sealed by the earth's changing climate, the same need not be true of our academic systems. Rather than relying on individual or group resistance and resilience, we have the power to change the academic systems we are a part of. We should not shy away from calling attention to the unique challenges we face as women, as BIPOC faculty, or as non-tenure-track faculty. We all share in the struggle for agency and legitimacy. I hope that all of us continue to question the academic structures we have created and work to build more welcoming environments for all who enter.

Notes

1. Kathryn B. H. Clancy, Robin G. Nelson, Julienne N. Rutherford, and Katie Hinde, "Survey of Academic Field Experiences (SAFE): Trainees Report Harassment and Assault," *PLOS ONE* 9:7 (July 16, 2014): e102172, https://doi.org/10.1371/journal.pone.0102172.

2. Chris Woolston, "Smithsonian Island Outpost Reeling from Sexual-Misconduct Claims," *Nature*, January 14, 2022, https://doi.org/10.1038/d41586–022–00097–4.

3. Linda Nordling, "'It's Not Acceptable.' Conduct Codes Aim to Curb Harassment at Scientific Field Sites," *Science,* October 23, 2019, https://www.sciencemag.org/news/2019/10/it-s-not-acceptable-conduct-codes-aim-curb-harassment-scientific-field-sites; Carolyn Kormann, "Corina Newsome and the Black Birders Movement," *New Yorker*, June 29, 2020, https://www.newyorker.com/magazine/2020/06/29/corina-newsome-and-the-black-birders-movement; Dan Adler, "'How Am I Going to Be Perceived as a Black Man with Binoculars?': J. Drew Lanham on Christian Cooper and Rules for the Black Birdwatcher," *Vanity Fair*, May 5, 2020, https://www.vanityfair.com/style/2020/05/j-drew-lanham-interview.

4. Carolyn J. Mooney, "Uncertainty Is Rampant as Colleges Begin to Brace for Faculty Shortage Expected to Begin in 1990s," *Chronicle of Higher Education*, January 25, 1989.

5. Patricia Roberts Harris Fellowship Program, *Biennial Evaluation Report, FY 93–94* [archived], accessed February 9, 2021, https://www2.ed.gov/pubs/Biennial/521.html.

6. "About," *The Lamphere Case: The Sex Discrimination Lawsuit That Changed Brown*, Pembroke Center, accessed February 15, 2022, http://www.pembrokecenterexhibits.org/about-the-exhibit.

7. National Research Council, *Women in Science and Engineering: Increasing Their Numbers in the 1990s: A Statement on Policy and Strategy* (Washington, DC: National Academies Press, 1991).

8. "How a Famous Academic Job-Market Study Got It All Wrong—and Why It Still Matters," *Chronicle of Higher Education*, September 9, 2018, https://www.chronicle.com/article/how-a-famous-academic-job-market-study-got-it-all-wrong-and-why-it-still-matters/.

9. See also the chapter by Erin Hatton in this volume.

10. Jeremy Fox, "A Data-Based Guide to the North American Ecology Faculty Job Market," *Bulletin of the Ecological Society of America* 101:2 (2020): e01624.

11. Maryam A. Andalib, Navid Ghaffarzadegan, and Richard C. Larson, "The Postdoc Queue: A Labour Force in Waiting," *Systems Research and Behavioral Science* 35:6 (November 2018): 675–686, https://doi.org/10.1002/sres.2510.

12. Erin A. Cech and Mary Blair-Loy, "The Changing Career Trajectories of New Parents in STEM," *Proceedings of the National Academy of Sciences* 116:10 (2019): 4182–4187; KerryAnn O'Meara and Corbin M. Campbell, "Faculty Sense of Agency in Decisions about Work and Family," *Review of Higher Education* 34:3 (2011): 447–476.

13. Tiffany A. Reese, Tamia A. Harris-Tryon, Jennifer G. Gill, and Laura A. Banaszynski, "Supporting Women in Academia during and after a Global Pandemic," *Science Advances* 7:9 (February 26, 2021): eabg9310, https://doi.org/10.1126/sciadv.abg9310.

14. Cech and Blair-Loy, "The Changing Career Trajectories of New Parents in STEM."

15. Catherine White Berheide, Megumi Watanabe, Christina Falci, Elizabeth Borland, Diane C. Bates, and Cay Anderson-Hanley, "Gender, Type of Higher Education Institution, and Faculty Work-Life Integration in the United States," *Community, Work & Family* 25:4 (2022): 444–463.

16. Ibid.

17. Laura Jane Martin, "Where Are the Women in Ecology?," *Frontiers in Ecology and the Environment* 10:4 (2012): 177–178.

18. Stephanie E. Hampton and Stephanie G. Labou, "Careers in Ecology: A Fine-Scale Investigation of National Data from the U.S. Survey of Doctorate Recipients," *Ecosphere* 8:12 (December 2017): e02031, https://doi.org/10.1002/ecs2.2031. See Gwendolyn Alker's essay in this collection.

19. Nathan F. Alleman and Don Haviland, "'I Expect to Be Engaged as an Equal': Collegiality Expectations of Full-Time, Non-Tenure-Track Faculty Members," *Higher Education* 74:3 (2017): 527–542.

20. On Academic Civic Engagement, see https://wp.stolaf.edu/ace/for-faculty/case-for-ace/. On Posse, see https://www.possefoundation.org/about-posse.

21. Ned Fetcher, Mimi E. Lam, Carmen R. Cid, and Teresa Mourad, "Contingent Faculty in Ecology and STEM: An Uneven Landscape of Challenges for Higher Education," *Ecosphere* 10:12 (2019): e02964, https://doi.org/10.1002/ecs2.2964.

22. See also the essays by Claire Raymond and Claire Goldstene in this collection.

23. Alleman and Haviland, "I Expect to Be Engaged as an Equal."

24. TIAA Institute, "Employment Volatility in the Academic Workforce: Implications for Faculty Financial and Retirement Plans," *Research Dialogue* 181 (June 2021).

25. "Serving Time: The 6-Year Rule," *Inside Higher Ed*, June 22, 2005, https://www.insidehighered.com/views/2005/06/22/serving-time-6-year-rule.

26. "Doctorates: PhD Gender Gap," *Nature* 545:7655 (May 2017): 517, https://www.nature.com/articles/nj7655-517a; Junming Huang, Alexander J. Gates, Roberta Sinatra, and Albert-László Barabási, "Historical Comparison of Gender Inequality in Scientific Careers across Countries and Disciplines," *Proceedings of the National Academy of Sciences* 117:9 (2020): 4609–4616.

CHAPTER 10

TALKING BACK AGAINST ABLEISM, AGEISM, AND CONTINGENCY AS A LATINX INSTRUCTOR AND FIRST-GENERATION SCHOLAR

MIGUEL JUÁREZ

Working as a contingent faculty member is challenging. Teaching part-time at two separate institutions with two separate structures presents challenging hardships for me as an older, Latinx scholar with physical disabilities. My experiences at each Hispanic-Serving Institution—identified in this essay as "School A" and "School B"—differ starkly in my semester-to-semester appointments.[1] At School A, I once taught five classes in one semester. During that semester I was considered a full-time employee and received healthcare. But this essential benefit lasted for only one semester; the subsequent semester I shifted back to part-time. At School B before the pandemic, I began teaching a single class and rose to the level of teaching two to three classes per semester, as well as most summers. At both of my institutions, the students that I teach are unaware I am not a tenure-track professor. As Sue Doe and Steven Shulman write in this collection, contingent faculty commuting between multiple campuses often navigate divergent experiences and expectations, while also facing professional isolation.

In School A, contingent faculty have experienced obstacles participating in the faculty senate, and the institution does not usually provide funding for lecturers to attend professional conferences. At School B, more opportunities exist. With roughly eight hundred contingent faculty, the faculty association includes adjunct members, but without voting rights. During a week-long in-service training, all faculty at School B have the choice of dozens of workshops to select from before the new semester begins. While adjuncts at this institution are required to attend only one in-service workshop, I attend as many as I can to update my teaching and technology skills. Contingent faculty at School B also meet in a forum during in-service week and have access to college administrators, who sometimes attend their meetings.

Since both of my institutions are close to the US/Mexican border, these schools attract a large Latinx and international student population. The student bodies at both schools are overwhelmingly Latinx—83 percent at School A and 84 percent at School B—but the tenured faculty members in my discipline are predominantly white. At Institution A, I am one of a handful of first-generation bilingual faculty members in my discipline that students encounter in the classroom. At both institutions, I am the only contingent Latinx faculty member in my discipline with a PhD. In my departments, however, I have little choice about what I teach. I mainly teach core survey courses. Within this limitation, then, I seek ways to innovate and engage students, conveying my love of teaching. I include local history and regional historical events tied to national events, which I find students are eager to learn because they haven't been exposed to it. I have partnered with campus makerspaces and librarians to incorporate new technologies in my classes, such as group-based 3D printing projects, the creation of podcasts, augmented reality projects, or the creation of digital games—all reinforcing topics in the syllabus and giving students opportunities not only to learn history, but also to "create" it.[2]

As a Latinx first-generation scholar my research allows me to see how communities have historically been marginalized, including how highway building has displaced Latinx and other residents and how pollution, rezoning, and gentrification continue to harm communities. I maintain a strong publication record. I also advocate for others in this southern Texas community that I call home, assisting those who are uncomfortable coming forward. Finally, I have built a strong social media and public history presence to engage our communities. As a Latinx scholar and teacher connected to the community in which I research and teach, I seek to be the change that needs to take place and when possible, to speak truth to power.

Teaching in higher education is my second career. Before obtaining my doctoral degree, I worked in academic libraries, appointed at the associate level in my last two positions. This experience enriches my teaching. I also continue to serve in various capacities in library organizations, participating in equity, diversity, and inclusion projects, which bring me great satisfaction and opportunities to connect these different parts of education and scholarship. While in my doctoral program, I coedited a book (with twenty-six contributors) on diversity in libraries. My experience in libraries and now in academe also helps to shape me as a first-generation scholar, understanding how the academic environment is structured and who benefits from it. Unfortunately, educational institutions, in contrast to libraries, tend not to value varied backgrounds and, hence, they often fail to embrace older scholars who enter academe by alternative routes but with additional skills and experience that enhance teaching, service, and scholarship.

Ageism in academe centers on the question of why older scholars with newly granted PhDs are not considered employable in their field and are denied entry to departments filled with associate and full professors who themselves are older. Might it be that most of these entrenched scholars were hired as young freshly minted PhDs, believing both that theirs was the proper path and that they have proven their worth to the academy?[3] Nell Painter, an accomplished African American historian, relates similar challenges in her 2018 memoir *Old in Art School: A Memoir of Starting Over*. Deciding to pursue a BFA after a successful career as a historian, she writes about the skepticism she faced during her first days at Mason Gross School of the Arts at Rutgers, the State University of New Jersey. She was repeatedly asked how old she was.[4] Ageism must not be a deterrent for those who want to forge a new path and pursue a different direction, but American society and its institutions are often not accepting of older workers, especially for tenure-track positions.

How about older scholars with disabilities? How do issues of ableism make the contingent faculty experience even more precarious? During my doctoral studies, in 2012, I took a library position at another institution. One morning, during my early walk on campus, I fell on a runoff of mud and broke my right knee. My first surgery was unsuccessful. Two months later, the hardware that my doctor had placed inside my right knee was separating my knee cap. I left my position and returned home to have a second surgery. The surgery was successful, but given the botched first surgery, my knee fused crooked, which sometimes necessitates the use of a cane.

For others, disabilities range from invisible to visible, from chronic illnesses and health issues to physical conditions that involve persistent pain and require assistive equipment. In their essay "Indivisible Disability, Unacknowledged Diversity," Carla Finesilver, Jennifer Lee, and Nicole Brown state: "In our abled-normative society, there is as yet particularly poor understanding of the existential spaces within and between disabilities and chronic illnesses, with pain conditions notably problematic."[5] The authors make the case that able-bodied persons have little understanding about what constitutes disability, including invisible disabilities. The late scholar and journalist Charles Krauthammer provides an excellent example of how disabled persons should be viewed in this country.[6] We are intellectuals, doers, archivists, historians and able-minded thinkers, journalists, commentators, professors, teachers, and activists. In Krauthammer's case, he was seen as an accomplished writer and thinker, someone beyond his wheelchair. Unfortunately, people often see our disability first and our abilities and experience second. As an older contingent faculty member this combination makes my position in higher education even more tenuous.

As an older Latinx scholar with a visible disability, I may never obtain a full-time job on a single campus, much less a tenure-track position. I share this work status, of course, with a majority of faculty in higher education today. So, how should we advocate for contingent faculty? How should we advocate for older scholars with disabilities who want to continue working in the field, connecting to underserved communities?

As essays in this collection make clear, the label of "contingency" carries a stigma. Just because many of us are employed and defined as part-time faculty or temporary employees does not mean that the scholarly and teaching work we engage in are less important than those of our tenured colleagues. Full-time tenured faculty may frequently choose not to associate with us, using underemployment as a metric of worthiness. As Anne Wiegard observes in this volume: "In academia, intersectionality is further complicated by the politics of academic rank and discipline." Regardless of this marginalization, I and other contingent faculty remain involved in our institutions, communities, and local and national professional associations. At a recent Western History Association (WHA) conference, I collaborated with independent historian Dr. Alida Boorn and Wichita State University historian Dr. Robin Henry to organize one of the first disability history panels. Our efforts helped launch in 2019 the WHA's Subcommittee on Disability.[7]

Contingent faculty lives do not happen in isolation from one another. Contingent faculty associations or committees can advocate for fairer treatment and resources to support teaching and research, as well as engagement with underrepresented communities. We can create and join contingent faculty unions or committees to advance calls for better pay and benefits and to support adjuncts whose classes have been cut. Contingent faculty unions can also develop ties with other unions in their region to press for healthcare and other public goods. Contingent academic laborers should recognize their common cause with other contingent workers—especially in this economy characterized by gig work and precarity.

Contingent faculty, many of whom teach the bulk of core departmental classes, deserve to command the respect of their tenured and full-time colleagues. We need to lobby department chairs for year-long or multiyear contracts, for inclusion in faculty governance, and for better pay and benefits (especially health insurance). At School A, several of us met with the departmental chair over the course of a year to discuss various issues of concern. We managed to secure one-year contracts. After some long-time contingent faculty members retired, the lecturer who organized contingent faculty at School A was offered a full-time position, assuring him a full course load. While an important step, the contingent faculty were told that only a single such position could be offered. The progress is slow, with many impediments to getting better treatment. In School A, an unwritten mandate bars PhD graduates in my discipline from being hired by the institution, even though other departments hire their recent graduates. During my commencement practice, I learned that a fellow doctoral graduate in another field at School A was offered a full-time position in his department after his graduation; evidently, the prohibition against hiring institutional graduates did not apply across the board.

When the pandemic struck in mid-March 2020, I considered myself fortunate because I had the opportunity to teach online. I did not lose my position. But in many respects, teaching from home created a larger course load, although it saved time going from institution to institution. During the pandemic I took time to reflect on what new directions I wanted to pursue and to explore my research interests. I found time to write and even began editing an online publication where I wrote about the lives of artists and writers, commemorated the one-year anniversary of the El Paso Walmart shooting, examined how COVID-19 affected the borderlands, explored questions about communities and gentrification, and recruited writers to produce articles on LGBTQ history. During the shutdown, I also found time to attend online conferences and webinars. I joined with scholars in endeavors such as the Contingent Faculty Committee of the Labor and Working-Class History Association and a campus faculty Social Inequality and COVID-19 Group. Some of this I might not have had time for if I were a full-time faculty member with a full course load, working with numerous graduate students, engaged in various committees, and living in a city far from my family. But, of course, the main story of the pandemic and contingent faculty is one of downsized departments and lost courses, hitting especially those who work with no benefits and no job security.

Being a contingent faculty member forces you to make tradeoffs. It teaches you to innovate when you have time to do so, to learn new skills, to explore what your capabilities can bring, and to reach out to others, often finding yourself in unfamiliar settings. This is important as a teacher, as education is changing constantly and will continue to evolve.

Regardless of my current situation I feel lucky to be where I am. I live in one of the most interesting places in the United States, at the US/Mexico border. I have an opportunity to teach first-generation Latinx, underrepresented, and international students in the community where I was born and grew up. Several years ago, I served on a national editorial board with other Latinx scholars. Many of my colleagues would report seeing maybe one or two Latinx students per semester or per year in their departments. In comparison, I teach survey classes with majorities of Latinx and international students. It gives me great pleasure to teach these students because several decades ago I was one of them!

At the same time, the mismatch between the many Latinx students in my classes and very few Latinx faculty with secure tenure-stream positions is cause for alarm. Lena Palacios, a scholar in gender and sexuality studies, argues: "We must connect the legacy of white settler violence to how the university is currently running on the precarious labor of mostly female adjuncts and adjuncts of color, graduate students, and other casual or contingent workers."[8] As Palacios and many Latinx faculty ask, will the swell of brown bodies in college classrooms and in graduate programs help Latinx contingent faculty secure better employment?

Before the pandemic, I bemoaned that I was not a full-time faculty member at either institution. Since then, I have come to the realization that my contingency allows me to explore ways to engage students in learning history, to have time to be involved in my community, and to use my background and training as an educator, urban historian, and connector. I have embraced my own agency. I am from this community, and I enjoy rich and multifaceted experiences away from both institutions.

In comparison to my late immigrant parents, I have been given a lot and I find ways to go forward despite my contingency. For example, given my background in libraries and research, I was asked by a professor in another department if I would supervise a group of student researchers for a two-year-long community-based project. Funding for the students would be provided by the dean in my department. I would not be paid (unfortunately), but instead I count this project as service that I as an educator offer to the community. I decided to take on this project, because opportunities such as this can open doors and forge previously unimagined paths for students, for the larger community, and for me. While I do not doubt the value of the work that I do as a contingent faculty and community member, we can hope for a time when institutions of higher education will recognize the importance of our work and what it adds to students' lives.

Both schools returned to face-to-face classes in the Fall 2021 semester, but I taught my five classes online. In Spring 2022, we all returned to face-to-face teaching. In our lives, there are constant tradeoffs. But stable work matters; it provides security. As an older, Latinx scholar with physical disabilities, teaching in schools that serve Latinx students, I know that security is not only elusive, but also not sufficient. Dignity, equity, and others' awareness of our struggles as contingent faculty need to accompany our security in our professions.

Notes

1. I refer to my two institutions as "School A" and "School B" to speak generically rather than specifically about each institution.

2. In makerspaces, people with common interests come together to work on projects. In educational settings, students produce projects utilizing 3D printing and game-based and machine technology.

3. Another challenge is hiring committees' overreliance on the prestige of degree-granting institutions. Older graduate students often must consider geography over prestige when choosing programs, because of jobs or other life responsibilities.

4. Nell Irvin Painter, *Old in Art School: A Memoir of Starting Over* (Berkeley, CA: Counterpoint, 2018), 2.

5. Carla Finesilver, Jennifer Lee, and Nicole Brown, "Indivisible Disability, Unacknowledged Diversity," in *Ableism in Academia: Theorising Experiences of Disabilities and Chronic Illnesses in Higher Education*, ed. Nicole Brown and Jennifer Leigh (London: UCL Press, 2020), 145.

6. Sam Roberts, "Charles Krauthammer, Prominent Conservative Voice, Dies at 68," *New York Times*, June 21, 2018, https://www.nytimes.com/2018/06/21/obituaries/charles-krauthammer-prominent-conservative-voice-dies-at-68.html.

7. "Awakenings: Seeking Solutions to Have Diverse Ableism Grow in Academic and History Professions," Western History Association, 59th Annual Conference, October 16–19, 2019, Las Vegas, NV, https://westernhistoryassociation.wildapricot.org/2019-LasVegas.

8. See Palacios in: Louis Mendoza, Nancy Raquel Mirabel, William Yslas Vélez, Yolanda Martínez-San Miguel, and Lena Palacios, "Academia Roundtable: The Underrepresentation of Latinx Faculty and the Future of Higher Education," *Latinx Talk, Research, Commentary, Creativity*, September 19, 2018, https://latinxtalk.org/2018/09/19/the-underrepresentation-of-latinx-faculty-and-the-future-of-higher-education/.

CHAPTER 11

GRADUATE STUDENT LABOR, CONTINGENCY, AND POWER

ERIN HATTON

By any measure, Henry is an academic success story.[1] At the time of our interview, the forty-two-year-old white man was an associate professor of biochemistry at a major research university, as well as his department's director of graduate studies. His career path—through graduate school, a four-year postdoc, and his current job—was generally smooth. In particular, Henry described his experience as a graduate student in positive terms. "It was a very productive and intense time," he recalled. "I was in a large lab, and so there were lots of interactions with a very exciting group of people. . . . I remember it as a very positive experience, but I also remember it as being a time when I put in the longest hours I've ever put in, in my life, and so that was a really intense work experience."

I interviewed Henry and nineteen other former PhD students in the sciences as part of a larger project on different types of legally unprotected workers, including incarcerated workers, student athletes, and graduate student workers.[2] Like Henry, all the former graduate students I interviewed described graduate school as an intense time defined by long work hours, though not all of them described their experience as "very positive." This is likely not surprising to anyone who has attended (or heard of) graduate school. Indeed, PhD work is infamous for its long hours, low pay, and—for some—miserable working conditions. At the very least, as described in the article "9 Things You Should Consider before Embarking on a PhD," graduate school is not a "stereotypical '9-to-5' job."[3] In fact, some of the former graduate students I interviewed recalled their advisors explicitly telling them as much to convey their expectation that students work long hours in the lab, including weekends and holidays. As former graduate student Iris told me, her advisor would say, "'No, this isn't a 9-to-6 job.' So you knew for sure 9:00 to 6:00 wasn't enough," the Hispanic thirty-four-year-old chemistry PhD explained. "But you never know how much was enough."

University officials, faculty members, and graduate students themselves have often justified graduate school's long work hours and sometimes difficult working conditions by describing it (implicitly or explicitly) as a "labor of love" and a "privilege."[4] For example, in the article mentioned above, the graduate student author discusses graduate school's lengthy and irregular work hours. "There are no real breaks," he writes. But then he tempers this would-be complaint by claiming that PhD students "should" have "passion" and "excitement" for their work. "While [such long hours] may seem like a downer, remember that you should have passion for the research you work on (most of the time), so you should be excited to think up new experiments or different ways to consider that data you have collected."[5] In conclusion, the author writes, "A PhD program is quite the commitment and rarely lives up to expectations—but it is well worth the time and effort you will spend for something that truly excites you." Thus, in this construal, if your research "truly excites you"—as it "should"—graduate school's long hours will be worth it. PhD work is a labor of love.

Though the sciences differ from other academic disciplines in many ways, this "labor of love" rhetoric pervades portrayals of PhD work across disciplines. For instance, *Becoming a Historian*, an online manual for history graduate students, follows a similar pattern of seemingly acknowledging but then dismissing the challenges associated with PhD work. Its chapter "Life as a Graduate Student" begins by acknowledging: "New students, who may feel overwhelmed with the financial and emotional stresses of coursework, can barely imagine staying in school for [four, five, or even ten years]."[6] Perhaps it is surprising, then, the manual goes on, that "many professors look back on their time in graduate school with fondness." This is because, the manual claims, graduate school is a "privilege and a unique opportunity for intellectual reflection, stimulation, and community. . . . Think of every stage [of graduate school] as a great adventure, and enjoy your life as a graduate student." Thus, in this (rather patronizing and classist) understanding, being a PhD student is a "great" "opportunity" and "adventure," regardless of its "financial and emotional stresses" and (sometimes decade-long) duration. Graduate students are lucky.

A primary function of this rhetoric is to distinguish graduate student labor from "real" work. It is more than a "stereotypical 9-to-5" job: it is an avocation fueled by "passion" and "intellectual . . . stimulation." It is an "adventure" filled with "something that truly excites you." Such claims are not merely rhetorical. University officials and other stakeholders have repeatedly—and often successfully—used them against graduate students' claims for worker rights, particularly their union organizing efforts (which Jeff Schuhrke examines in this volume).[7]

Yet regardless of such rhetoric, though perhaps underscored by the need for it, graduate student labor is indeed *work*. Although it does not always take place in the context of a legally defined employment relationship (i.e., under a contract, with a boss, and/or for the profit of others), it often does. Many graduate students contractually work as teaching assistants (TAs) and research assistants (RAs) under faculty supervision and for the monetary benefit of universities and other stakeholders.[8]

In some disciplines, moreover, graduate students' education is entirely subsumed under such labor relations. This is particularly the case in the life sciences, in which graduate students' PhD work is generally *designed, directed,* and *owned* by their faculty advisors. PhD students carry out the research their advisor has designed, and they produce results and publications that their advisors own and use for their own purposes, including their grant and patent applications and their own tenure and promotion cases. As several former science PhD students told me, graduate students (along with postdocs) are the "hands" that execute their advisors' research in the lab. This stands in contrast to disciplines such as sociology and history, in which graduate students generally develop their own research agendas, so that their PhD research is distinct from their labor for the university. But in the sciences, as Henry explained, "It is complicated . . . because working in the lab as a job and working in the lab as a student overlap . . . almost 100%." Thus, science graduate students' learning relation is also a labor relation, and so perhaps it is not surprising that many of them call their advisors "boss."

In the remainder of this chapter, I examine graduate student work—as research assistants and teaching assistants—as a form of contingent labor. Yet doing so requires rethinking the meaning of "contingent," at least as typically used in labor research, because PhD students' labor does not fit neatly into this category. As defined by Arne Kalleberg in an early definitive article on this topic, contingent work is any "short-term, unstable employment."[9] As described above, however, graduate student labor—particularly in the sciences—is likely to be long term (though still delimited) and relentless in its grinding hours, though in other disciplines PhD research and teaching assistantships may indeed be unstable. Despite such variation across academic disciplines, however, neither "short-term" nor "unstable" is the defining characteristic of graduate student labor. In general, moreover, graduate student work differs in many ways from the types of work and workers that have been examined in the literature on contingent work, such as temps, day laborers, seasonal workers, gig workers, and academic adjuncts.[10] Through studies of these workers, the meaning of "contingent" is usually defined by its consequences for these workers: instability, insecurity, and (for many) low wages.

Yet another—perhaps more capacious—way of conceptualizing contingent work is through the lens of power.[11] Because, for all traditionally defined contingent workers, the job instability, insecurity, and low wages they experience stem from the outsized power their bosses wield over the terms of their employment. Of course, because many workers in the United States labor under at-will contracts, most employers wield substantial power over the terms of their employment. Yet this power has been mitigated, at least to some degree, by various legal rights and protections, including minimum wage and overtime pay, unemployment insurance, health insurance mandates under the Affordable Care Act, family and medical leave protections, workers' compensation and the right to a safe workplace, protections against discrimination and harassment, and the right to organize and bargain collectively. However, contingent workers are often excluded (either de jure or de facto) from some or all of these already weak protections.[12] For example, Uber drivers and other "gig workers"—the contemporary prototype of contingent work—are not legally covered by any of these employment protections because they are (mis)classified as independent contractors.[13] Meanwhile, in the academy, as several chapters in this volume show, the part-time status of adjuncts often excludes them from many of these workplace protections.

Thus, even more than most workers, contingent workers' labor is shaped by their employers, who have nearly unrestricted power over their wages and benefits, work schedules, and working conditions. Employers such as universities leverage this power over adjuncts through last-minute scheduling and low pay rates, while employers such as Uber do so through opaque wage algorithms and transferring business costs to workers, all of which produce instability, insecurity, and low wages for these contingent workers.

Yet other employers wield this power in different ways with different consequences for workers. This is true of graduate student labor. In the sciences, at least, even though graduate students are not typically concerned about the "short-term, unstable" nature of their work as are many other contingent workers, their work and working conditions are entirely *contingent* on their faculty advisors. In short, much like employers in other contingent jobs, faculty advisors in the sciences have nearly unrestricted power over PhD students and their labor in the lab.

As I show in my book *Coerced: Work under Threat of Punishment*, science faculty wield power over graduate students in at least four key ways. First, they control whether graduate students get and keep funding, and thus whether they remain PhD students and complete this path to high-status employment. One reason for this is that, in the sciences, it is particularly difficult for students to switch advisors and so, if a faculty advisor terminates a student's funding, that student may have to withdraw from graduate school altogether. As former chemistry student Laine said, "If you don't get along with your advisor for whatever reason, they can just walk in, and kick you out." Second, in the sciences, faculty control students' publications, including whether students are listed as first, second, or third author (or as an author at all), which affects students' job prospects and, in some departments, their ability to graduate. For instance, Henry said that his advisor did not include him as an author on a major paper from his lab, even though Henry believed that he had contributed to the project in a "significant, intellectual way." This omission might have derailed his research agenda and job prospects, Henry said, though ultimately it did not. Third, faculty control when PhD students graduate from the program and, thus, obtain this high-status credential and employment in the field. In many cases, former graduate students told me, science faculty delay their students' dissertation defense dates in order to keep them—and, importantly, their labor—in the lab. As Laine explained, "At the very end, your advisor usually doesn't want to graduate you, because they've spent so much time trying to get their lab up and running, and now . . . you're finally a student that produces work for them. So . . . letting you leave is a detriment to their promotion." Finally, through letters of recommendation, faculty wield outsized influence over graduate students' future careers. As Henry said, "Without a doubt, the most profound way an advisor can wield power is in writing a letter of recommendation."[14]

In our interview, former chemistry student Emily pointed to many of these dynamics in describing faculty advisors' power over graduate students. "They have a frightening amount of power," the thirty-year-old white woman explained.

> Because they sort of have unchecked dominion, like, over multiple aspects of your life. I think this is one of the reasons that some groups of graduate students have tried to unionize. Because [advisors] can dictate the hours that you work without any sort of check on that, they can demand any sort of product, whether it's reasonable or not, they can terminate you at will, because they're providing your funding. . . . And, in most cases, they have total discretion over when you can graduate and whether you can graduate. . . . And nobody is going to give you a job unless you have a good letter from your advisor. . . . Your advisor has total power over your life. I mean, *in what job setting is that okay?*

Again and again, Emily emphasized advisors' far-reaching power over PhD students and their labor. They have "a frightening amount of power," she said. They have "unchecked dominion," "total discretion," and "total power" over graduate students' "life," including their education, research agenda, work hours, work products, graduation, accreditation, and future career. They can "dictate" and "demand" any product, any hours—virtually anything—"without any sort of check," she said.

Many of the other former students I interviewed echoed Emily's depiction of faculty-student power dynamics. "In science," former biomedical student Tiffany said, "you're totally dependent on your mentor." Gustavo agreed. Faculty advisors have "absolute and total control" over graduate students in the sciences, the thirty-five-year-old Chicano man said. "They control a lot," former molecular biology student Scott said of faculty advisors. Although one's dissertation committee is supposed to act as a "check and balance against the advisor having absolute power," the thirty-two-year-old white man "didn't see [the committee] having much mitigating effect against the advisor's power. I know how it's supposed to work, I just didn't actually see it working."

To emphasize this point, many former PhD students pointed to universities' lack of robust grievance mechanism for students experiencing difficulties with their advisor, including the absence of HR (human relations) department oversight. As former pharmacology student Sunny said, "There's no HR" department to limit what faculty can do. "Because [graduate student workers are] not really anyone's employee per se. So, there are no repercussions there. The faculty are allowed to really do whatever they want," the forty-one-year-old Hispanic woman said. Both Ron and Henry agreed. "I have never once met a robust HR department in a university," thirty-six-year-old Ron said, and faculty say "things you would *never* get away with working in industry." Even though "there are some industries, especially in the chemical enterprise, that are probably evil," now-professor Ron conceded. "From an HR perspective, you would *never* get away with half the crap you get away with in academia." In the academy, Henry said, "There's not an extensive HR kind of operation. Like, if those conflicts existed in, let's say, 3M [a private company], there would be a clear pathway for how to resolve the problem. [But] there's not nearly as much for graduate students."

Because of all this, former molecular biology student Suzanne said, if a graduate student has a problem with her advisor, "there's not a whole lot you can do." As this forty-two-year-old white woman explained, "I don't even know where you *would* complain. I mean, I think there's usually a person they can go to . . . but it depends. In my case, the graduate student advisors were still acting in the best interest of the university and of the PIs [principal investigators]. . . . The PIs are pretty well protected by the universities. I don't think there's a lot that can be done. I mean, as a graduate student, you're sort of the lowest part of the whole." Sunny agreed. "There's a lot of power that is held there, and graduate students and postdocs are in a position of being very vulnerable." In fact, former biomedical student Rebecca brought up graduate students' "vulnerability" six different times over the course of our interview. Graduate students, she argued, are "vulnerable to being taken advantage of by systemic problems within the structure of the graduate program." Among other things, this forty-year-old white woman maintained, graduate students in the sciences are vulnerable to "professors' power to demand whatever labor they wanted from students."

As Rebecca and the other former PhD students suggested, the very structure of scientific research in the academy is built on vastly uneven power dynamics: faculty advisors' structural power and PhD students' structural vulnerability to that power. Yet, for many in the academy, this power imbalance is simply expected and accepted. Indeed, in many ways, it makes sense. University faculty are experts in their fields and must train graduate students according to the high standards of PhD-level work. Therefore, it seems logical that they have the authority to determine whether students have met such standards, as well as the authority to assess the caliber of students' work for future employers. In specialized fields, in fact, faculty advisors may be among a small handful of people with the expertise necessary to do so. However, it is not just this power differential that renders graduate student labor problematic. It is, in Emily's words, the fact that faculty advisors' power over graduate student workers is largely "unchecked." As my interviews with former graduate students attest, advisors can and do wield this unchecked power over multiple aspects of their lives: their education, their accreditation, and their future careers.

Because unchecked power can easily become abusive power, moreover, the consequences of this extreme power imbalance are too often predictable. Four of the twenty former PhD students I interviewed said that they had experienced harassment, sexual harassment, and/or bullying from faculty advisors (while three others experienced different types of severe workplace problems), and nearly all of them, as Zane said, had "heard horror stories" about other graduate students experiencing abuse and mistreatment in their labs.

Although there are no data on the prevalence of such mistreatment, my research suggests that the power structure of graduate student labor in the sciences facilitates it. Foremost this is because bad behavior—faculty mistreatment of graduate student workers—remains largely unchecked. There is little oversight of faculty as *bosses*—overseers of others' labor. As Henry said, "In academia, it's like, *Who the hell is your supervisor's supervisor?*" Therefore, the students who experienced significant workplace problems felt that they had no recourse. As Suzanne said above, "I don't even know where you *would* complain." Complaining, Laine said, would be "stupid," because it would only endanger graduate students' careers. "You can never burn that bridge," she said. "It's very stupid to do that in this field." In fact, Laine returned to this point several times in our interview. For even though one of the faculty members of her dissertation committee was "mean" and "nasty," Laine said that she "would have never spoken out against him in a million years, *never*, no matter what he did, said, anything." "*And he was really bad*," she emphasized again and again, but "there's nothing he could have said or done that I would have reported. . . . If you don't have clout, and if you're not protected, if you don't have that PhD . . . you're just so vulnerable."

Yet, even in the absence of outright abuse, the structural power of faculty advisors and the structural vulnerability of graduate students in the sciences can produce problematic workplace dynamics. Those I interviewed said that this was particularly true for the graduate students who labor for untenured faculty, who themselves labor under very real pressure. This lopsided labor system allows—and even seems to expect—those faculty members to transfer at least some of their own pressure to the graduate students who are doing the work on which their tenure cases will be built. "Untenured professors," former chemistry student Michelle told me, are often "pretty harsh on their students." As the twenty-nine-year-old white woman went on to explain, "A very big part of the tenure process is that you need to show that you're considered one of the world's best scientists in the field. So you need your students to get really powerful results." Laine agreed. "It's definitely worse for graduate students" who are working for untenured faculty, "but you usually end up being a better scientist after that," she said with a bitter laugh.

For at least some of the graduate student workers I interviewed, these power dynamics had serious consequences for their physical and mental health. "We were all just kind of chronically depressed," Emily said. "A lot of people are just kind of stuck in misery," Sunny said. In graduate school, Laine said that she began experiencing panic attacks, which were severe and frequent enough to require daily medication. But "as soon as I was out of graduate school," she recalled, "I stopped having panic attacks. Like, it all, everything just got better. I gained weight again. Like, it was just—*it was bad*. [Graduate school] was bad." These personal experiences mirror emerging data about the "mental health crisis" among PhD students in the United States, particularly in the sciences, who are reportedly more than six times as likely to experience depression and anxiety than the general population.[15]

My research points to an important explanation for this crisis: a power structure in which graduate student workers' education, research, and careers are entirely dependent on their faculty advisors. Suzanne described this situation as "a bit like the Wild Wild West. It really depends—like, how much you learn and how you're treated—all these things depend a hundred percent on who your advisor is." Not all advisors are bad of course, and many are very good. But because of this power structure, even when faculty bosses are at their best, graduate student labor in the sciences is still predicated on coercion: faculty advisors' ability to wield power over their labor, their education and accreditation, and their future careers. This power does not reside in advisors' disposition but, rather, in their institutionalized capacity to wield expansive power over PhD students, whether or not they choose to do so. Indeed, even when they do not, graduate student workers are acutely aware of their potential ability to wield such power, and this awareness fundamentally shapes graduate student workers' experiences and interpretations of their labor.

Thus, in the sciences, graduate student work is profoundly *contingent* on faculty bosses' power, and it is this contingency that connects them to other contingent workers whose labor and lives are also unduly shaped by their bosses. A more capacious definition of contingent work is therefore one that accounts for the expansive power that bosses can wield over workers, broadly defined, rather than the consequences of such power for only a subset of those workers. By accounting for these power dynamics with this new understanding of "contingent work," we can identify connections between workers that otherwise seem dissimilar. Take, for example, graduate student workers, student athletes, and adjuncts: three groups of workers who labor in seemingly disparate realms of higher education. Yet they all labor under supervisors who wield expansive power over them and their work lives, and therefore these workers might find in each other crucial allies in their efforts to protect themselves against such power. Reframing contingency in this way is, thus, not just an academic enterprise. It is a political one with real-world consequences for contingent workers in the academy and beyond.

Notes

Portions of this article have been published in an alternate form in *Coerced: Work under Threat of Punishment* (Oakland: University of California Press, 2020).

1. "Henry" and all of the names in this chapter are pseudonyms chosen by the informants themselves. Their ethno-racial identities are also self-designated.

2. This project culminated in my book, *Coerced: Work under Threat of Punishment*. The twenty former PhD science students I interviewed for this project were recruited via snowball sampling in 2016 and 2017. They had attended universities across the country, though none of them had attended my own university, and they had studied in a variety of science departments, including chemistry, biology, pharmacology, and neuroscience. For more on my data and methods, see Hatton, *Coerced*, 23–25, 225–226. On the sciences and contingency, see also Diane Angell's essay in this volume.

3. Andy Greenspan, "9 Things You Should Consider before Embarking on a PhD," *Elsevier*, April 13, 2013, https://www.elsevier.com/connect/9-things-you-should-consider-before -embarking-on-a-phd.

4. Sara Matthiesen, "Academic Work Is Labor, Not Romance," *Chronicle of Higher Education*, August 26, 2016, http://www.chronicle.com/article/Academic-Work-Is-Labor-Not/ 237592?cid=rclink; Amy Hungerford, "Why the Yale Hunger Strike Is Misguided," *Chronicle of Higher Education*, May 9, 2017, https://www.chronicle.com/article/Why-the-Yale -Hunger-Strike-Is/240037; Sophie Moullin, "Elite Graduate Student Struggles Are Not Class Struggles," blog, November 21, 2016, https://scholar.princeton.edu/smoullin/blog/ elite-graduate-student-struggles-are-not-class-struggles; Tyce Palmaffy, "Union and Man at Yale: Class Struggle," *New Republic*, June 7, 1999, 18; Rick Perlstein, "Professors to Grad Students: Focus on Studies, Not Wages," *Nation*, December 4, 2013, https://www.thenation .com/article/professors-grad-students-focus-studies-not-wages/; Corey Robin, "When

Professors Oppose Grad Student Unions," *Jacobin*, December 5, 2013, https://www
.jacobinmag.com/2013/12/WHEN-PROFESSORS-OPPOSE-STUDENTS-UNIONS/.

5. Greenspan, "9 Things You Should Consider."

6. "Life as a Graduate Student," *Becoming a Historian*, accessed December 21, 2017, http://
www.chashcacommittees-comitesa.ca/becoming%20a%20historian/chapterfour.shtml.
Also see Jennifer Jordan, "The Privilege of Being a Yale Graduate Student," *Yale Daily News*,
March 24, 2003, http://yaledailynews.com/blog/2003/03/24/the-privilege-of-being-a-yale
-graduate-student/; "Other Students Voice," *Graduate Student Unionization: A Critical Approach*,
accessed December 21, 2017, https://criticalgsu.wordpress.com/other-students-voice/; Jae
Hyun Lee, "Student Union Is No Magic Bullet," *Harvard Crimson*, October 28, 2015, http://
www.thecrimson.com/article/2015/10/28/lee-graduate-student-union/.

7. For examples of university officials using this logic against student worker organizing, see: John Coatsworth, "Provost's Letter on National Labor Relations Board Ruling," *Columbia News*, August 24, 2016, http://news.columbia.edu/content/Provost-Letter
-National-Labor-Relations-Board-Ruling; Jordan, "Privilege of Being"; Matthiesen,
"Academic Work Is Labor"; Preston Cooper, "The Faulty Logic of the NLRB College Student Unionization Ruling," *Forbes*, August 25, 2016, http://www.forbes.com/sites/preston
cooper2/2016/08/25/the-faulty-logic-of-the-nlrb-college-student-unionization-ruling/
#536d086b7d6b; Joseph Ambash, "NLRB's Graduate-Assistant Ruling: Bad News for
Administrators and Students," *Chronicle of Higher Education*, September 7, 2016, http://www
.chronicle.com/article/NLRB-s-Graduate-Assistant/237714; Natasha Baker, "Unmanage-
able Quagmire or Elegant Distinction?," *Inside Higher Ed*, September 8, 2016, https://www.
insidehighered.com/views/2016/09/08/concerns-about-impact-nlrbs-recent-ruling
-grad-student-unionization-essay; Amicus Curiae Brief, National Right to Work Legal
Defense and Education Foundation, *Trustees of Columbia*; NLRB v. Yeshiva University 444
U.S. 672 (1980).

8. Indeed, along with adjuncts and postdocs, graduate students are widely recognized as
"cheap labor" in the academy. See Sheila Slaughter, Teresa Campbell, Margaret Holleman,
and Edward Morgan, "The 'Traffic' in Graduate Students: Graduate Students as Tokens
of Exchange between Academe and Industry," *Science, Technology & Human Values* 27:2
(2002): 285; Richard Freeman, Eric Weinstein, Elizabeth Marincola, Janet Rosenbaum,
and Frank Solomon, "Careers and Rewards in Bio Sciences: The Disconnect between Scientific Progress and Career Progression," *American Society of Cell Biology* (2001), accessed
January 5, 2018, https://depts.washington.edu/envision/resources/CareersBiosciences.
pdf; Viviane Callier and Nathan Vanderford, "Mission Possible: Putting Trainees at the
Center of Academia's Mission," *Nature Biotechnology* 32:6 (June 2014): 593–594; Richard
Freeman, Frank Solomon, Janet Rosenbaum, Elizabeth Marincola, and Eric Weinstein,
"Competition and Careers in Biosciences," *Science* (December 14, 2001), http://www
.sciencemag.org/careers/2001/12/competition-and-careers-biosciences.

9. Arne L. Kalleberg, "Nonstandard Employment Relations: Part-Time, Temporary,
and Contract Work," *Annual Review of Sociology* 26 (2000): 354; also see Arne L. Kalleberg,
Edith Rasell, Naomi Cassirer, Barbara F. Reskin, Ken Hudson, David Webster, Eileen Ap-
pelbaum, and Roberta M. Spalter-Roth, *Nonstandard Work, Substandard Jobs: Flexible Work*

Arrangements in the United States (Washington, DC: Economic Policy Institute, 1997); and Arne L. Kalleberg, Barbara F. Reskin, and Ken Hudson, "Bad Jobs in America: Standard and Nonstandard Employment Relations and Job Quality in the United States," *American Sociological Review* 65:2 (2000): 256–278.

10. E.g., Kalleberg, "Nonstandard Employment Relations"; Erin Hatton, *The Temp Economy: From Kelly Girls to Permatemps in Postwar America* (Philadelphia: Temple University Press, 2011); Gretchen Purser, "The Dignity of Job-Seeking Men: Boundary Work among Immigrant Day Laborers," *Journal of Contemporary Ethnography* 38:1 (2009): 117–139; and the present volume's chapters on adjunct and contingent labor, especially in Part I.

11. In fact, doing so invokes the original meaning of the term. Economist Audrey Freedman coined the term "contingent work" in 1985 to describe work arrangements that were contingent on employers' fluctuating need for labor—or, put another way, employers' desire and power to hire workers intermittently. Audrey Freedman, "Contingent Work and the Role of Labor Market Intermediaries," in *Of Heart and Mind: Social Policy Essays in Honor of Sar A. Levitan*, ed. Garth L. Mangum and Stephen Mangum (Kalamazoo, MI: W. E. Upjohn Institute for Employment Research, 1996), 177.

12. Rebecca Smith, "Legal Protections and Advocacy for Contingent or 'Casual' Workers in the United States: A Case Study in Day Labor," *Social Indicators Research* 88 (2008): 197–213; Nik Theodore, Abel Valenzuela Jr., and Edwin Meléndez, "Worker Centers: Defending Labor Standards for Migrant Workers in the Informal Economy," *International Journal of Manpower* 30:5 (2009): 422–436; Molly Tran and Rosemary Sokas, "The Gig Economy and Contingent Work: An Occupational Health Assessment," *Journal of Occupational and Environmental Medicine* 59:4 (2017): e63–e66.

13. Indeed, their status as such has recently been institutionalized in California with the passage of Proposition 22, which defines app-based workers as independent contractors regardless of whether they fall under legal definitions of "employee."

14. See also Claire Raymond's chapter in this volume.

15. Teresa M. Evans, Lindsay Bira, Jazmin Beltran-Gastelum, L. Todd Weiss, and Nathan Vanderford, "Evidence for a Mental Health Crisis in Graduate Education," *Nature Biotechnology* 36:3 (2018): 282–284.

CHAPTER 12

COMMON GROUND FOR THE COMMON GOOD

What We Mean When We Say
"Faculty Working Conditions
Are Student Learning Conditions"

MARIA MAISTO

"Faculty working conditions are student learning conditions." This saying is ubiquitous in the contingent faculty movement and indeed across all levels of political activism and policymaking in education, appearing on rally and strike placards, punctuating speeches and op-eds, and serving as headlines and report titles. The catchphrase has played an important role in faculty activism since the 1970s. Its exact provenance is unknown but is thought to have originated in a higher ed or K–12 union.[1] The phrase has been a powerful tool, inspiring organizing activity among educators and solidarity with the communities in which they live and work. One could say that it has even led to important, if limited, reforms at institutional and governmental policy levels, thanks to its adoption as a foundational premise by unions, by advocacy groups like New Faculty Majority, and by research centers like the Delphi Project at the University of Southern California.

The motto's breadth of influence is not surprising, given that it communicates with powerful simplicity that the classroom and the campus are literal and figurative shared spaces—common ground—in which students and educators work toward a common good that centers educational quality. As historian and long-time activist Richard Moser observed in 2015, it is "our most insightful and useful motto" because it demonstrates how "rhetorical strategy and organizing strategy are linked."[2]

Despite its success as an organizing tool, however, the motto deserves scrutiny. Contingent academic employment remains today an entrenched component of the gig economy. The very idea of "common ground for the common good" in education, much less in the political economy as a whole, is under assault. Contingent faculty activists ought to closely consider whether weaknesses in the motto might have, even subtly, undermined our objectives. At the same time, does the axiom contain undiscovered strengths that can help us achieve our goals? In this chapter, I explore the achievements, limits, and potential of the motto through rhetorical and historical analysis to examine the notions of faculty work and student learning at its center, the purpose and quality of education that it is meant to advance, and the sense of the common good that it is meant to embody.

2012–2022: Purpose—and Problems

The year 2012 was important in K–16 faculty activism. The success of the historic Chicago Teachers Union (CTU) strike, as Sarah Jaffe reported in *The Nation*, made "the slogan 'Our working conditions are our students' learning conditions' into a mantra for educators around the country."[3] In 2012, the CTU used the slogan as part of an overall strategy that eventually was called Bargaining for the Common Good (BFCG), an approach to organizing, activism, and collective bargaining in which labor activists act in solidarity not just with and for each other, but with the communities they serve and with whom they live. In the BFCG framework, the notion of the common good is expansive; labor and community organizations work together to shape the demands that are brought to the bargaining table. Victory is measured not just by the gains for union members but by the organizing and bargaining gains shared by unions and the community, "challenging the entrenched patterns of wealth and power that limited horizons of possibility on their jobs and in their communities."[4]

Also in 2012, New Faculty Majority (NFM), the national advocacy organization I cofounded, held a national strategy summit in Washington, DC, titled "Reclaiming Academic Democracy: Facing the Consequences of Contingent Employment in Higher Education."[5] The summit explored definitions of, and connections among, faculty work, student learning, and the common good, as a way to jumpstart activism by and for contingent faculty. The day's speakers represented labor, professional associations, higher education administrators, student activists, contingent and tenure-line faculty activists, and community groups, all of whom came to the consensus that shared goals for higher education, from academic rigor to civic engagement and social justice, could not be met on campuses that exploited the majority of their faculty.[6] Out of this summit, NFM launched almost a decade of robust advocacy, consisting in support for organizing, coalition building, media presence, lobbying, and coordination of the biannual Campus Equity Week. By 2017, NFM's policy work had chipped away, however modestly, at Department of Labor, Department of Education, and IRS rules that hurt contingent faculty.

The 2012 summit clarified that the working conditions of contingent faculty, and the challenges to organizing them, were so dire that they required, at minimum, a constant presence in any venue we could find, delivering a message that could succinctly communicate both the problem and the solution. That message was that "faculty working conditions are student learning conditions." We knew the message to be effective strategically for organizing and advocacy. Contingent faculty union organizing had increased exponentially and the public proved sympathetic, understanding better than ever that college teaching was an integral part of the gig economy. Yet in a 2015 reflection on the state of contingent activism, Moser, always prescient, argued that contingent activism would be even more effective if faculty and students would unite around the common experience of higher education debt to demand free college for all.[7] Concurrently, faculty activist Polina Kroik noted that contingent faculty victories were partial and incremental. She called for "an expanded framing of higher education as a common good" in line with the kind of work done within the BFCG framework.[8] In this view, the transformation of higher education itself, which begins by combating the co-optation of higher education into the neoliberal project, becomes the highest order common good, encompassing and addressing the demands of faculty for better working conditions.

Both Moser and Kroik recognize that our most famous motto is a key component of our work toward this goal. But Kroik suggests that "structuring our activism around a vision of a future higher education system that could be truly characterized as a 'common good' does mean engaging in a more radical political project" than the motto has perhaps encouraged.[9] This insight provides the exigence for the following analysis of the motto's politics and implications for both contingent faculty work and activism on behalf of higher education. The motto posits the equal worth of the two sides, but does our activism reflect that understanding? Does the motto encourage a shared commitment by faculty, students, and the wider community to education in the service of the common good?

"Faculty Working Conditions"

As we begin interrogating the motto, the first notable feature of "faculty working conditions" is that it does not distinguish faculty by tenure status, union membership, or academic degrees. Institutions have allowed the inclusivity of the word "faculty" to hide the ugly realities of contingent employment, most notably from students, community members, and even from other campus workers who are not aware of the material implications of academic rank when activists use the word "faculty" without qualifiers. Rhetorically and aspirationally, however, this phrase can unite a diverse faculty, highlighting the damaging effects of the contingent hiring model on the working conditions of *all* faculty, including those apparently most privileged. Using the term "faculty" with intentional inclusivity, as the motto does, thus can sow the seeds of much-needed solidarity and collaboration across faculty ranks.

The phrase "working conditions" emphasizes the structures and systems of faculty work, highlighting institutional support for and impediments to quality teaching, rather than accentuating the personal qualities of individual faculty members, which often diverts debates about education to stories about personal failure or heroism. Research about the impact of contingent faculty on student learning has benefited from activists' attention to this distinction between "faculty" and "faculty working conditions." It is now common for writers and researchers who in the past may have referred to deleterious effects of "exposure" to adjunct faculty to remind readers that negative effects on students are "not because adjuncts are bad teachers but because their working conditions prevent them from being as effective as they could be."[10] Thus, when poverty wages force contingent faculty to work at multiple institutions—making them unavailable to mentor students, engage in professional development that keeps them current in their fields, serve on committees, or expand their pedagogical practices to include effective but time-consuming activities such as service learning and community engagement—audiences that include students, administrators, and the public are more likely to focus on systemic shortcomings rather than blame individual instructors.

Finally, by describing faculty activity *as work* and specifically naming its "conditions," the phrase unambiguously identifies teaching, scholarship, and service—the activities of the professoriate—as *labor*. It makes invisible work visible by elevating the importance of the material conditions that are necessary for it to take place: time, wages, tools, and interactions with other people (i.e., colleagues, students, the public) who depend on that work for their own material and nonmaterial needs.[11] The phrase faculty "working conditions" challenges faculty to self-identify as workers who can be connected to the larger labor movement and invites faculty to reject conflicts between unionism and professionalism. This longstanding disagreement over whether the proper organizing and advocacy model for educators is a union or a professional association has plagued both K–12 and higher education, often interfering with effective organizing.[12]

"Faculty working conditions" thus speaks to shared interests, values, and priorities—a common ground that is critical for effective organizing. However, this opening phrase of the motto also has weaknesses. Significantly, the term "faculty" rarely, at least now, bridges the divide between higher ed and K–12 educators, a division that undermines the effectiveness of some K–16 unions (particularly unfortunate given that there are many K–12 teachers who also work in adjunct faculty positions). The sense of faculty work as labor is also, perhaps, too subtle to encourage solidarity with the full range of campus workers, from custodians to food workers and to administrative/professional staff. These are important limitations, but they also extend beyond the campus grounds. Some contingent faculty, including some activists, take issue with metaphors that refer to them as the "fast food workers of academia"; this often stems from professional blinders that both devalue fast food workers' labor and overlook inspirational labor battles like the "Fight for 15" campaign for a higher minimum wage.

"Student Learning Conditions"

In higher education, to speak of "student learning conditions" is to speak less about "conditions" and much more directly about "students" and "learning." This makes sense given the shift, in a postsecondary context, from a faculty-centered to a student-centered approach to education. Animated by the social movements of the 1960s and 1970s, students took greater ownership—in the best and worst senses of the word—of their education, and colleges and universities followed suit.

The positive dimensions of this cultural transformation in higher education clearly have roots in the late twentieth-century turn to a liberatory pedagogy, memorably developed by Paolo Freire and bell hooks. This educational philosophy is oriented toward transformative political action through the development of critical, engaged learning processes.[13] Such a conception of student learning constitutes the kind of "liberal education" that has been held up as an ideal since the earliest days of higher education in the United States. This type of learning undergirds and fortifies democracy, representing both education for civic responsibility and more radical notions that show "substantial commitment to the core practice of open inquiry in a dialogical community . . . [and] an approach to knowledge that presupposes its connection to lived experience."[14] In this educational orientation one can see a predisposition to activism in support of the common good.

The centering of the student during the rise of neoliberalism, which places market values at the forefront, has also encouraged a consumerist attitude, wherein education is treated as a private good to be purchased for the purpose of advancing personal status and economic gain. Criticism of this neoliberal turn has been a hallmark of contingent faculty activism, but such criticism animates other, sometimes less radical, analyses of higher education. James Keenan, SJ, an ethicist who focuses on the ecosystem of higher education, describes the bewildered response of college leaders to the Obama administration's effort to tie student aid to a college ranking system that quantified graduation rates and other measures such as graduates' incomes, ostensibly to assist students and families in the college search process. This system proudly positioned students and families as consumers. Keenan, grounded in Catholic social teaching, writes: "Many of the colleges that have worked to define the richness of the fabric of our population and its common good are precisely those that stand to lose as market strategies work themselves out in our broadening spectrum of inequity in the United States."[15]

When emphasizing student learning in the context of this double-edged turn toward student-centrism, activists have learned to invoke the "faculty working conditions are student learning conditions" motto with particular care. Measuring learning is famously fraught. Implying that "student learning conditions" are measurable "outcomes," in terms of retention, completion, and transfer rates, can be misleading. Low numbers in these categories are easily misattributed to the shortcomings of individual instructors rather than to the failure of employment structures. Still, assessments of shortcomings in student learning "outcomes" *can* lead to concrete improvements for contingent faculty. For example, research showing that students do better when they can meet with instructors individually has led to contingent faculty being given access to a conference room or office for student meetings. However, such administrative solutions also can quell activism (often by design) and create new burdens, such as expecting faculty to hold unpaid office hours. Unless the activism focused on the "student learning conditions" side of the motto is comprehensive and analytical, it is unlikely to be very effective.

Scholarship on student learning can also be effective activism. Keeping the pressure on higher education reformers, Gary Rhoades has pointed out that the so-called completion agenda, endorsed across the political spectrum, undermines efforts to improve educational quality regardless of the status of instructors teaching within this framework.[16] Neoliberal approaches that aim to raise graduation rates focus myopically on austerity while prioritizing "productivity" and "scale." Such a formula disproportionately hurts disadvantaged students by giving short shrift to the pedagogical practices—including mentorship, intellectual challenge, and time for reflection—that research shows are most closely connected to the deepest forms of learning.[17] Activists interested in supporting faculty through the prism of student learning must be attuned to the nuances and implications of the research on student learning that they invoke. Standards of pedagogical practice that support deep learning cannot be met simply by giving adjuncts keys to conference rooms.

The fact that the phrase "faculty working conditions are student learning conditions" operates in the context of questionable student learning metrics does not mean it cannot be used effectively. The challenge for activists is to transform the terms of the discourse, even while aiming to win smaller-scale victories within the existing one. Activists must be aware that the phrase "student learning conditions" carries sometimes diametrically opposed connotations—on the one hand conveying a notion of education in the service of a "more efficient" faculty and student workforce and on the other seeing the labor of teaching and learning as integral to the common good. As activists we must decide whether and how we can adapt our motto to express and advance the latter version.

On close reading of our long-held motto, we can see that emphasizing "faculty working conditions" draws our attention to opportunities and challenges in organizing faculty, while focusing on "student learning conditions" requires us to accept the challenge of defining and measuring "learning" so that it can be used in advocacy. The motto posits the *equal worth* of the two sides, but does—or can—our activism reflect that understanding in a way that, as Moser suggests, is necessary for progress? Further, does the motto encourage a shared commitment by faculty, students, and the wider community to a clearer conception of higher education's place in the articulation and pursuit of the common good?

The Urgency of the Moment: Education and/as the Common Good

The present moment has a particular urgency, especially with respect to the relationship of education to the common good. The rubble of Trump's American carnage, from which we are only beginning to emerge, includes a pandemic that has exposed and exacerbated deeply rooted structural injustices, particularly in education. Political violence is linked directly to hate, disinformation, and ignorance of both history and civic responsibility—all dangers against which our community of educators can be a frontline defense. It is now a truism that citizens of this country no longer agree, if we ever did, about the definition of the common good.

Where and how does a movement for contingent faculty equity fit into such a context? How do we forge a way forward, particularly when many of us have recognized that the political moment is unreceptive to complaints from a highly educated and relatively privileged profession, no matter how exploited and no matter how much we are committed to exposing and combating the insidious histories animating contemporary socioeconomic and political injustices?

Perhaps, however, the context of the present moment is well suited for the reflective work we recommend. Nowhere was the reality of the material and ethical connection between faculty working conditions and student learning conditions clearer than in the agony of trying to decide whether to reopen schools and colleges during the pandemic. Closely related to this crisis is the epidemic of school shootings that has plagued us for years. These two crises have made the material connection between educators' working spaces and students' learning spaces more urgent and the concerns about teaching and learning more immediate. Such crises, in which students and faculty fear for their health and very lives, may also help people to understand that the classroom itself, as a microcosm of the entire education system, does not simply constitute shared physical space but, indeed, is shared intellectual, social, economic, and political space—space for the active definition and pursuit of a common good.

Yet this also is a time when the concept of "shared space"—especially as a site of education—is fraught. Shared space can be infected with deadly diseases, both physical and political. Tensions between faculty and the public are high as faculty at all levels confront the expectation that they will put their health and lives at risk to serve students, and that they will comply with reactionary state laws attempting to erase histories of racial injustice in this country. Crises like these expose underlying inequities in mottos like ours that seemingly uphold and promote equality and justice. Saying that faculty working conditions are student learning conditions sounds like a claim that faculty and students, and their concerns, are equally important. But rhetorical equivalence does not always translate into equality in *value*. In this neoliberal, pandemic-informed context, the primacy of students over faculty is asserted, framed now as the primacy of consumers over essential workers. The motto actually provides a dangerous justification for a utilitarian exploitation of the ethic of service by implying that if you care about student learning, then you simply need to make sure that those who *serve* students are willing to make sacrifices. As a political tool, the mantra backfires if it communicates that faculty exist only to serve students, if it recasts the demands of the faculty for equitable working conditions as selfish, and if demands for better working conditions can be justified only if they meet *students'* needs.

Students' needs, of course, should not be met at the expense of the faculty. Such an approach belies a distortion of "service" and "care work," both of which are honorable and essential to the common good but are frequently exploited in our society. This devaluation is tied as well to the feminization of academic labor, as many scholars remind us.[18]

Have the last few years revealed that our oldest, most important motto has dangerous, possibly fatal weaknesses? While expanding solidarity among faculty, it subtly impedes solidarity with other campus and community workers. While elevating and empowering students, it seems to encourage an understanding of faculty service as transactional rather than transformational. Can the motto be redeemed to advance a conception of education as truly shared space in which the rights of faculty and students are valued equally? Can the motto make clear that the fair treatment of faculty is integral to students' actual educational interests? I believe that the motto's broader aims can be redeemed by reasserting a common ground and conception of education for the common good. For that, it seems appropriate for faculty to learn from students.

Common Ground for the Common Good:
The Work of Learning from Students

In higher education, the connection between the material reality of faculty working conditions and student learning conditions is usually understood best by students themselves. Witness, for example, this student letter posted on a Facebook page created by Students and Alumni for the CCA (California College of the Arts) Adjunct Union Campaign in September 2014 and supported by over 850 students, alumni, and faculty:

> Many discussions around unionization have focused on student impact. And indeed, we believe strongly in our stake in the conversation: what could be more crucial to the quality of our educations than the employment conditions of our professors? Having openly shared our support for the union across campus, we now wish to reiterate and further clarify our reasoning.
>
> We as students are the reason for CCA's existence, and we have an obvious financial stake in this school, paying a significant amount ($41,592 a year) to attend. . . . As such, we feel that we have a right to greater financial transparency at CCA. If funds are not being used to adequately compensate our instructors' [sic] for their time—which goes beyond the classroom to include outside meetings, planning, grading, committee involvement, etc.—then where is the money going? How do inadequate compensation and job insecurity affect your ability to engage with us as educators? You know the answers better than we do. But it seems to us that these instabilities can only detract from the quality of our educations, and by extension from the quality of CCA as a community. . . .
>
> And not least, we love our adjunct professors! We think you are amazing. You teach us so much every day—not just in technical skill, but in the expertise and wisdom you bring from outside the classroom. Many of you are practicing artists, designers, writers, or scholars in your communities, whose presence at this school breaks down institutional barriers. We believe that a union would further support that flexibility and openness. For those of you who come here to teach out of passion and who value the freedom to step back and focus on other projects as well, the union does not stand in your way. For those who are dedicated to teaching as a long-term endeavor, and who rely on this honorable job as a source of income, a union provides you leverage to negotiate for working conditions that would allow you to be even better teachers to us. More equitable conditions for teaching at CCA would enable the diverse and incredible creative work that adjunct professors are involved with outside our school—not hinder it.
>
> Many of us chose to come to this school because of CCA's core mission, which [emphasizes] the social and political responsibility we as creative people bear. The education we have received here has convinced us that we should be working, always, towards creating a more democratic, compassionate and just society. We believe that those values ought to be paramount not only in the way we engage

with society outside the institution, but in the very structure of the institution that educates us. A union would be a step towards that democratic and compassionate community, because it would give adjunct professors the leverage to better articulate your struggles and represent needs. Not only your own needs, but ours—the needs of the students that you interact with in the classroom every day and understand perhaps better than anyone else in this school.

   As such, we students support an adjunct union without question. We urge you to vote yes—on our behalf as well as your own.[19]

These students' powerful argument reflects an understanding and effective rhetorical use of the two opposed connotations of student-centered learning. The students are aware of the impact of the material conditions of their teachers' work, connecting it directly to their education. They have a deep understanding of the "core mission" of the institution and are savvy enough to invoke what it teaches about "social and political responsibility," ironically and for rhetorical effect. They show an intuitive understanding that the problems they see are structural and that only compassion and solidarity can transform them. Finally, by invoking the price of tuition, they appropriate the consumerism that colleges have embraced. Contingent faculty activists can indeed learn from examples like the CCA students' letter, which exemplifies how the students and their community have internalized the "faculty working conditions are student learning conditions" motto, by identifying a common ground for the common good in the form of specific support for the union and a broader sense of solidarity and social justice.

   Faculty activists can nurture new activists and allies by paying attention to how communities like this one at CCA and others in the BFCG network have understood the relationship among faculty work, student learning, and the common good in their organizing activity. Simply raising the question of contingent faculty as workers begins to activate critical engagement with the labor movement more broadly.

   Service learning and community engagement provide another avenue for strengthening the connections between work, learning, and the role of each in building the common good. These forms of "experiential learning" can embody the shared space for learning, work, and partnership aspired to by the motto. Within most models of such programs, students and faculty function as collaborators and are required to think deeply and critically about their role in and relationship to the community. This activity should include an interrogation of the privilege that higher education bestows on students and faculty; however, as humanities professor Wendy Hesford argues, it is possible to design service-learning projects that engage with labor, community, and social justice organizations, broadening the experiences of students and faculty by reaching well beyond the campus.[20] Such engagement becomes an opportunity to engage, as Kroik argues, in an "expansion" of our struggle and a challenge to think more broadly and deeply about how to define the common good.[21]

Service learning erases the boundaries between learning and work, helping both students and faculty to recognize the connections between faculty work and student learning, as well as the relationship of these to the shared space of academic labor. The idea of faculty and student shared space can be expanded beyond that of the classroom as the physical site of work and learning. "Academic labor" can also be the shared *conceptual* space in which educational work and learning take place.

Conclusion: Academic Labor as Common Ground

For most academics, "academic labor" refers to the work we do in our scholarship and teaching—our engagement with texts and students. It is difficult for many of us to move from that understanding of "academic labor" to one in which we understand ourselves as laborers in the industry of academia. As a final reflection, I propose that we approach this journey just as we begin our work with students—by meeting them (ourselves) where they (we) are. As a former adjunct instructor of composition and comparative studies, I do this using the tools of my disciplinary trade.

The author of our famous motto is unknown, but I am going to bet that the person taught English composition, not least because composition instructors are among the most numerous contingent faculty members in the country and among the most politically active. Many people privileged to attend a college or university, and probably taught at some point by an adjunct instructor, will recognize that the source of our motto's rhetorical power lies in the figure of speech that it exemplifies: antithesis. In writing and speech, antithesis is the device used to present "a seeming contradiction of ideas, words, clauses, or sentences within a balanced [usually parallel] grammatical structure."[22] Famous examples include uses by the novelist Charles Dickens ("It was the best of times, it was the worst of times") and the boxer Muhammad Ali ("float like a butterfly, sting like a bee").

In these examples of antithesis, the contrasts being exploited are obvious: best/worst; float/sting; and butterfly/bee. They are inserted into poetic paradoxes that define a new reality: a time that can be simultaneously wonderful and horrible, a strength that is both soft and sharp. Reading or hearing "faculty working conditions are student learning conditions," an audience experiences that same kind of simultaneous dissonance followed by understanding—but not because two things that are obviously opposite are shown to be equivalent. Instead, the revelatory shock that turns the sentence into a powerful political statement is that the two things presented as opposites in the sentence—faculty work and student learning—are *not* antithetical even though they are regularly posed that way.

This is a meta-level realization (for many, perhaps, unconscious); it explains why the slogan is not merely utilitarian but in fact exhortatory. Invoking it becomes a demand to correct the erroneous and insulting assumptions that faculty and students are adversaries or that working and learning are opposites. The motto works politically because it describes the context of teaching and learning that we too often take for granted, while also provoking judgment and a call to action. It works because it puts students and faculty on common ground—both rhetorically, by placing them side by side in a sentence, and conceptually, by linking their identities, their needs, and their fates. In that rhetorical and conceptual common ground may lie a better understanding of the common good that is a too-often unspoken or unexamined goal of the work of teaching and learning.

Notes

1. Joe Berry, *Reclaiming the Ivory Tower: Organizing Adjuncts to Change Higher Education* (New York: Monthly Review Press, 2005), 15; and Joe Berry, e-mail message to author, February 10, 2021.

2. Richard Moser, "A Shot at Strategy," *Working USA* 18:3 (2015): 461–467.

3. Sarah Jaffe, "The Chicago Teachers Strike Was a Lesson in 21st-Century Organizing," *Nation*, November 16, 2019, accessed February 13, 2021, https://www.thenation.com/article/archive/chicago-ctu-strike-win/.

4. Joseph McCartin and Merrie Najimy, "The Origins and Urgency of Bargaining for the Common Good," *Forge*, March 31, 2020, accessed February 15, 2022, https://forgeorganizing.org/article/origins-and-urgency-bargaining-common-good.

5. NFM was founded in 2009 by a group of contingent faculty activists who met online through the Coalition on Contingent Academic Labor (COCAL), a grassroots coalition of union-affiliated activists chiefly known for holding an important biannual, trinational conference and for promoting Campus Equity Week. NFM was meant to complement COCAL's grassroots character by functioning as a stable advocacy organization, independent from but allied with labor unions, that would focus exclusively on the goal of ending exploitative contingent faculty working conditions.

6. Maria Maisto and Steve Street, "Confronting Contingency: Liberal Education and the Goals of Academic Democracy," *Liberal Education* 97:1 (Winter 2011): 6–13.

7. Moser, "A Shot at Strategy."

8. Polina Kroik, "Expanding Our Struggle: Higher Education as a Common Good," *Working USA* 18:3 (2015): 457–460.

9. Ibid., 459.

10. Colleen Flaherty, "New Study Shows Employment of Part-Time Faculty Doesn't Impact Student Success Positively or Negatively at Community Colleges, while Institution Size and Location Do," *Inside Higher Ed*, November 15, 2013, accessed February 13, 2021, https://www.insidehighered.com/news/2013/11/15/study-finds-no-impact-student-success-having-adjunct-instructors.

11. For a discussion of what is involved in the shift from manual to knowledge work and the invisibility of the latter, see Fred Nickols, "The Shift from Manual Work to Knowledge Work," 2012, accessed February 20, 2021, https://www.nickols.us/shift_to_KW.htm

12. For helpful discussions of the professionalism/unionism divide, see Kevin Mattson, "The Academic Labor Movement: Understanding Its Origins and Current Challenges," *Social Policy* 30 (2000): 4–10; and Adam Mertz, "A Century of Teacher Organizing: What

Can We Learn?," in *The Teachers Initiative Project*, Labor and Working-Class History Association, n.d., accessed February 14, 2021, https://www.lawcha.org/century-teaching-organizing/.

13. bell hooks, *Teaching to Transgress: Education as the Practice of Freedom* (New York: Routledge, 1994); Paolo Freire, *Pedagogy of the Oppressed*, trans. Myra Bergman Ramos, intro. Donaldo P. Macedo, 30th anniversary ed. (New York: Bloomsbury, 2012).

14. Stephen C. Rowe, "Liberal Education: Cornerstone of Democracy," *American Journal of Economics and Sociology* 76:3 (May 2017): 579–617.

15. James F. Keenan, *University Ethics: How Colleges Can Build and Benefit from a Culture of Ethics* (Lanham, MD: Rowman & Littlefield, 2015), 190.

16. Gary Rhoades, "The Incomplete Completion Agenda: Implications for Academe and the Academy," *Liberal Education* 98:1 (2012).

17. See, for example, Patrick Terenzini "Six Characteristics That Promote Student Learning," *Inside Higher Ed*, July 29, 2020, accessed February 23, 2021, https://www.insidehighered.com/advice/2020/07/29/six-characteristics-promote-student-learning-opinion.

18. Eileen E. Schell, *Gypsy Academics and Mother-Teachers: Gender, Contingent Labor, and Writing Instruction* (Portsmouth, NH: Boynton/Cook Publishers, 1998); Tamara Hammond, Marie Burns, and Rachelann Lopp, *The Female Precariat: Gender and Contingency in the Professional Work Force* (Montreal: Universitas Press, 2019); and Gwendolyn Alker's essay in this collection.

19. Students and Alumni Activists for the CCA Adjunct Union, "LETTER: STUDENT PERSPECTIVES ON UNIONIZING Sent to Adjunct Faculty Today," Facebook, September 27, 2014, accessed February 22, 2021. https://www.facebook.com/CCAStudentsAndAlumniForAdjunctUnion. See also Josh Carmony, "Ground Operations," *Contingent Magazine*, March 22, 2021, https://contingentmagazine.org/2021/03/22/ground-operations/.

20. Wendy S. Hesford, "Global/Local Labor Politics and the Promise of Service Learning," in *Radical Relevance: Essays Toward a Scholarship of the "Whole Left,"* ed. Steven Rosendale and Laura Gray-Rosendale (Albany: SUNY Press, 2005), 183–202. Hesford warns that service learning "has been uncritically positioned in recent national educational reform as a herald for democracy, diversity, and civic responsibility." R. Eugene Rice, John Saltmarsh, and William W. Plater issue a similar warning, with attention to impact of contingent faculty working conditions on the credibility of higher education's involvement in defining the public good; see "Reflections on the Public Good and Academic Professionalism," in *Faculty Work and the Public Good*, ed. Genevieve G. Shaker (New York: Teachers College Press, 2015), 251–265.

21. Kroik, "Expanding Our Struggle."

22. S.v. "Antithesis," *The Columbia Encyclopedia*, 8th ed. (New York: Columbia University Press, 2018).

CHALLENGING PRECARITY
AND CONTINGENCY
IN HIGHER EDUCATION

CHAPTER 13

FRAMING PART III

"To Move Things Forward"

ANNE WIEGARD

When I became an adjunct faculty member, I slowly recognized that the marginalized "shadow world" of shifting identity and "official invisibility" I inhabited originated in the employment practices I was subjected to, not in any professional inadequacy on my part.[1] I suspected that my peers felt the same "disillusion and alienation," and that we all felt profoundly exploited, disrespected, and disempowered in our lonely silos.[2] Although the grievances of the majority of faculty closely resemble those of other low-paid and precarious laborers with far less formal education, ironically, our diverse higher education workforce is more difficult to organize, partly because our "mixed consciousness" prevents us from truly identifying as "workers."[3] Despite an increasing inclination to leave the profession, I persevered in adjunct positions at various institutions for eleven years until finally securing a full-time non-tenure-track (NTT) position in upstate New York. Winning a delegate seat in 2005 in United University Professions (UUP)—the union that represents about 35,000 State University of New York (SUNY) faculty and professional staff—validated the authority of my voice within a genuinely democratic wall-to-wall local, affording opportunities to eventually effect positive change.

I followed the same activist trajectory of countless others. At first, naïvely certain that those in power would correct the status quo once they understood the realities of the "adjunctification" rapidly consuming academia, a likeminded colleague and I searched for labor leaders and lawmakers who would embrace our objectives. We were greeted with sympathetic, patient explanations of why what we sought to change could not be changed. We listened, learned, and kept coming at the problem of inequity from any angle we thought promising, determined "to make a way out of no way."[4] We recruited allies and learned by doing the seemingly impossible work of the "academic labor movement's vanguard."[5] We volunteered for projects and ran for office until we had the power to accomplish some of what we had urged others to achieve for us. In effect, we became the leaders we'd been hoping to find.

Because "the problem of adjunct labor reaches far beyond any individual adjunct's capacity to stand up for herself," building a political base must be prioritized.[6] Despite their avowed ethos of equality, union politics too often reflect larger cultural systems of racial, gender, and class privilege. In academia, intersectionality is further complicated by one's assigned academic status and the perceived market value of one's discipline. My hierarchal position was lowly; although I was white, earned a terminal degree, and secured a full-time position, I was a mid-career-change female consigned to the NTT academic rank in the humanities. Trying to cultivate a shared agenda with both those who have less and those who have more privilege than I have has been a diplomatic balancing act fraught with challenges. Over time, I expanded our base by instinctively using the tool of engagement essential to effective organizing—one-on-one, story-sharing conversations designed to establish bonds with coworkers that authenticate leadership.

As I endeavored to learn the union ropes, I was concurrently cofounding New Faculty Majority (NFM), a national nonprofit organization of contingent activists. NFM argues that the sustainable university should be reconceived to advocate professional equity for faculty through conversations with all stakeholders. Making common cause with activists from all over the country, some not represented by unions, shaped my understanding of the specific vision we needed to articulate if it were to resonate broadly in the movement for equity.

In 2009, just after NFM formed, I was appointed to the UUP Task Force on Contingent Employees and elected its chair. As well as writing its lengthy 2010 report, whose key recommendations resulted in constitutional changes that more fully enfranchised contingent members in union governance, I wrote the ensuing 2015 "UUP Position Statement on Contingent Employment." These publications brought buy-in for reform across the union's very diverse constituencies and led to my appointments to the Negotiations Teams for the 2011—2016 and 2016–2022 contracts. No venue offers more opportunity to move things forward than the bargaining table.

By 2013 I had learned enough to win a seat on UUP's statewide executive board, and to facilitate spontaneous nominations of fellow contingent faculty delegates from the floor for two other open seats, thereby amplifying the NTT voice in statewide governance. More importantly, I had reimagined my community and understood the connections shared among *all* workers (see Anne McLeer's essay in this volume) and helped others do the same. I could not expect colleagues to support my initiatives unless I truly understood the workplace issues affecting other interest groups in a wall-to-wall union. I not only supported candidates who were invested in improving contingent employment practices, but I also consistently acted in solidarity, participating fully in every union battle, doing my best to earn a reputation for being diligent and trustworthy, thereby banking political capital.

I became fully assimilated into a union that often required me to temper specific demands for change, but I continually both infiltrated and confronted the body politic[7] of labor institutions in line with the national contingent equity movement's goals. Outreach from my foothold in UUP to a wider network of veteran activists led to being part of a cross-pollination of ideas and the honing of a more unified advocacy agenda across union affiliates—New York State United Teachers (NYSUT), American Federation of Teachers (AFT), and National Education Association (NEA)—and disciplinary organizations, coalitions, campaigns, and the New Faculty Majority, where I served on the board of directors. I functioned as a conduit for outside groups to exert pressure on UUP's agenda and, conversely, to exert pressure from inside UUP to influence the agendas of outside organizations.

The effectiveness of labor's "inside/outside" strategy in leveraging power is evident in a recent multiyear national campaign to improve access to unemployment compensation for contingent faculty. Local agencies routinely denied benefits based on US Department of Labor (DOL) unemployment regulations' assumption that academics working in temporary positions have "reasonable assurance of future employment." NFM's president Maria Maisto conceived a way to improve interpretation of these regulations by updating DOL guidance. Fellow NFM officer Judy Olson and I coordinated passage of resolutions through the NEA and the AFT, which obliged them to work with us and other organizations to develop a US Department of Labor policy guidance letter. Our project came to fruition when the DOL issued "Unemployment Insurance Program Letter No. 05-17" to clarify the application of the long problematic "reasonable assurance" clause so that faculty would more readily be eligible for unemployment benefits.[8]

This prolonged struggle often threatened to overwhelm me. I persisted because other leaders shared their knowledge and power with me. During her keynote address at the United Association for Labor Education's Northeast Summer School for Union Women in 2013, American Federation of State, County, and Municipal Employees (AFSCME) Secretary-Treasurer Laura Reyes memorably offered a counterintuitive insight: "Sharing your power will bring you more power." A resilient web of power-sharing collaboration weaves through the contingent equity movement from the grassroots to union presidents. Thanks to numerous supportive allies, I've been able play a part in achievements such as influencing national unemployment policy and negotiating the first statewide salary minima for SUNY's thousands of adjunct faculty.

When I embarked on what I thought was a strictly transactional course of action, I could not foresee the titanic legal, economic, and political barriers all union leaders grapple with, nor the ways that the struggle would transform and enrich my life. In the face of frequent setbacks, I took heart from the camaraderie of those whose perseverance inspires me, principled altruists who show up to do the often tedious, unseen, thankless work, and who uplift others as they climb. Like the poet and activist Marge Piercy,

> I love people who harness themselves, an ox to a heavy cart
> who pull like water buffalo, with massive patience,
> who strain in the mud and muck to move things forward,
> who do what has to be done, again and again.[9]

Contrary to the consolatory cliché "no one is irreplaceable," every single soul who harnesses themselves to our Sisyphean cart is indispensable to our beloved community's progress. To move things forward, we must do whatever we can to sustain all those who strain alongside us with massive patience.

Notes

1. See Claire Raymond's and Elizabeth Hohl's essays in this volume.

2. See Aimee Loiselle's essay in this volume.

3. Joe Berry, *Reclaiming the Ivory Tower* (New York: Monthly Review Press, 2005), 18.

4. John Lewis (@repjohnlewis), "We must work together to make a way out of no way. #goodtrouble," Twitter, posted January 29, 2017, 7:16 p.m., accessed July 30, 2020, https://twitter.com/repjohnlewis/status/973929038954844162.

5. See Gary Rhoades's essay in this volume.

6. See Raymond's essay in this volume.

7. Jo Freeman, "Crises and Conflict in Social Movement Organizations," *Chrysalis: A Magazine of Women's Culture*, no. 5 (1978): para. 38, accessed August 3, 2015, https://www.jofreeman.com/socialmovements/crisis.htm.

8. See also Rhoades's essay in this volume.

9. Marge Piercy, "To Be of Use," in *The Impossible Will Take a Little While*, ed. Paul Rogat Loeb (New York: Basic Books, 2014), 206.

CHAPTER 14

SO MANY ROADS, SO MUCH AT STAKE

The Composition of Faculty Bargaining Units

WILLIAM A. HERBERT AND
JOSEPH VAN DER NAALD

A central issue when higher education faculty unionize is bargaining unit composition—the specific personnel and job titles that will be represented in collective bargaining. The critical importance of this issue cannot be overstated. It reflects organizing strategies, expresses values and interests, determines who can vote in a representation election, affects the topics negotiated and prioritized, and helps establish the working and learning conditions at an institution.[1] Fundamentally, bargaining unit composition determines whether ranks of faculty negotiate separately, bargain as a combined group, or bargain together with a broader range of campus workers.

This chapter examines the historical, practical, and legal factors that have resulted in faculty being organized based on the model of professional craft unionism rather than as part of a broad wall-to-wall organizing strategy. A clear historical trend toward separate bargaining units for contingent faculty has persisted into the twenty-first century. We argue that this trend stems directly from the hegemony of "professionalism," which divides faculty based on rank and status and separates faculty from other campus workers.[2] The ethos of professionalism hinders solidarity on campus necessary to meet the myriad challenges facing higher education today.

To demonstrate the tendency toward faculty bargaining unit separation, we analyze two unique datasets that include the composition of faculty units drawn from studies by the National Center for the Study of Collective Bargaining in Higher Education and the Professions. The first dataset comes from a 2012 report based on survey data, which identified the composition of units recognized from 1963 to 2012.[3] The second dataset is drawn from a 2020 study of all new faculty units between 2013 and 2019.[4] The 2020 dataset was gathered from primary sources, including union certifications, administrative agency decisions, and other available documents.

A note about terminology: we use the phrase contingent faculty to indicate both full-time (FT) and part-time (PT) non-tenure-eligible, or non-tenure-track (NTT) faculty; the acronym TTT refers to tenured and tenure-track faculty; the phrase "combined bargaining unit" describes units that include contingent faculty, TTT faculty, and sometimes other professional employees. We use the phrase "wall-to-wall" to denote both an organizing strategy and a form of unit composition encompassing a broad spectrum of campus workers, including faculty, other instructional and non-instructional professionals, and nonprofessionals.

Professional Craft Unionism or Wall-to-Wall Unionism?

There have always been different approaches to organizing on campus. In the early twentieth century before collective bargaining in higher education, the American Federation of Teachers (AFT) organized college locals to advocate for faculty, lecturers, and graduate assistants through campus and citywide locals, the latter being an antecedent of today's metro-strategy.[5] The American Association of University Professors (AAUP) formed in the same era to advocate for academic freedom and tenure but eschewed the union label.[6] The National Education Association (NEA), which prided itself as a non-union professional organization of educators and administrators, had a lighter footprint in higher education at that time.[7] The pervasiveness of the construct of professionalism delayed these organizations from adopting collective bargaining as a goal.[8]

When the Congress of Industrial Organizations (CIO) formed in the late 1930s, it adopted industrial unionism that included organizing wall-to-wall bargaining units in education.[9] The CIO's State, County, and Municipal Workers of America (SCMWA) emphasized that in "the public sector, where there are so many types and classifications of employees, industrial unionism is perhaps even more vital and necessary than in the field of private employment."[10]

However, the CIO's initial approach to industrial unionism in the public sector differed from the one it pursued in the private sector. In July 1937, CIO leader John L. Lewis made this clear when he announced SCMWA's formation: "The use of strikes and picketing shall be deemed a violation of the principles of this organization."[11] The SCMWA policy came five months after the end of the Flint sit-down strike, which resulted in General Motors recognizing the CIO's United Auto Workers.[12] Even more significantly, the policy was announced within days of President Franklin D. Roosevelt's press conference where he stated his opposition to government worker strikes. His position against strikes and other militant tactics was later memorialized in his better-known August 1937 letter to a federal employee leader on public sector collective bargaining.[13]

In 1938, the SCMWA negotiated a closed shop wall-to-wall agreement intended for all employees of a West Virginia school district, including custodial employees and teachers.[14] Five years later, a New Jersey SCMWA local bargained a contract for a school district unit of janitors, secretaries, and teachers.[15]

Amid the fight against fascism during World War II, union leader Charles Hendley, in successfully advocating for the New York Teachers Union (NYTU) and the College Teachers Union (CTU) to affiliate with the SCMWA, emphasized that "teachers cannot survive as a *privileged* class of workers and must align with labor" at a time when "organized attacks upon education surpasses anything we have witnessed in America. This is inevitable for the schools are the very heart of our democratic system."[16] Hendley insisted that labor solidarity required educators to "slough off some of their bourgeois snobbery" and "recognize themselves as honest-to-good workers rather than hoity-toity professionals."[17]

After World War II, the CIO's United Public Workers of America (UPW) extended wall-to-wall unionism to higher education when it organized bargaining units at Howard University and the Hampton Institute with teachers, librarians, and nonprofessional staff.[18] One of these contracts, however, excluded part-timers.[19] During the postwar years, the CIO's organizing reached other institutions and resulted in the earliest known contract for a distinct contingent faculty bargaining unit. The 1948 UPW-New School of Social Research agreement covered FT and PT contingent drama and art faculty who taught at least two hours a week.[20]

The CIO's organizing strategy for higher education lapsed with its expulsion of the UPW, along with other left-led unions, during the domestic Cold War. Only recently have campaigns to organize all campus workers regardless of professional status been reembraced[21] by advocates of all-campus worker solidarity.[22] One such example is a coalition at Rutgers University, which comprises over a dozen unions representing a wide array of faculty, professional, and nonprofessional employees.[23]

The recent renewal of a wall-to-wall campus strategy for higher education represents an important break from the original approach adopted by the AFT, NEA, and AAUP in the years after higher education collective bargaining began to be legally recognized in the 1960s.[24] Consistent with their historical orientations, the three traditional education unions, along with most faculty, viewed campus organizing through the ideological lens of professional exceptionalism, which is at variance with industrial unionism's egalitarian ethos.[25] Under the precept of professionalism, faculty are internally divided by rank and status, and are deemed to have fundamentally different interests and goals than others working on campus. The result has been a history of professional craft bargaining, where the primary unit composition question centers on whether faculty subgroups should be in separate or combined units.[26]

Practical Factors in Bargaining Unit Composition

In general, a union seeks to represent a bargaining unit with demonstrable support that will result in certification and a first contract. This judgment is assessed through a dialogue between the organizing committee and union organizers, which will lead to a tactical decision about the breadth of the unit sought. The ultimate decision will be premised on the perceived depth of solidarity among TTT faculty, contingent faculty, and other campus workers.

There are strategic arguments in favor of seeking a combined bargaining unit or a more inclusive wall-to-wall unit. From an organizing perspective, contingent faculty are more likely to support unionization and they can be the margin of victory. Contingent faculty can also inform the campaign and negotiations with information about policies and practices at other institutions where they work.[27] Unity among TTT and contingent faculty can lead to greater workplace power with TTT faculty providing key support and messaging on contingent faculty issues, which can result in better contractual terms.[28]

The inclusion of postdoctoral scholars, graduate assistants, nonteaching professionals, and nonprofessionals in the bargaining unit can also help win an election, expand campus worker power, foster greater communication among worker groups, aid in tackling systemic campus issues, and increase the likelihood for social unionism, which connects union demands with broader community concerns.[29]

However, there are also arguments against more inclusive bargaining units. Generally, occupation-specific bargaining units elicit greater internal solidarity among represented employees.[30] In higher education, broader units require overcoming entrenched attitudes related to professionalism, hierarchy, and privilege. Known differences and rivalries among employees can dissuade unions from seeking to organize combined or heterodox units, particularly at large institutions.[31]

Overlapping fault lines can cause intrafaculty tensions: tenure status or eligibility, FT or PT status, degrees and disciplines, length of appointment, age, ideology, and compensation and benefits.[32] Differences exist even among PT faculty who have diverse backgrounds and needs.[33] The history of disrespect by TTT faculty, including ignoring their contingent colleagues, along with privileges sustained through faculty bifurcation, can exacerbate these tensions.[34] Similar practical obstacles to the inclusion of nonprofessionals in a combined bargaining unit may exist due to prior mistreatment or to distinctions premised on educational or class background.

These factors may lead contingent faculty to prefer separate bargaining units as the best means to ensure prioritization of their bargaining demands. Similarly, TTT faculty may desire separate units, viewing inclusion of contingent faculty and others as undermining their status, benefits, and privileges.[35] Related elements of disunity can exist between FT and PT faculty[36] and, as Gary Rhoades has shown, the interests of PT faculty can be sacrificed in combined FT-PT units.[37]

Countervailing factors also lead to separate bargaining units. Contingent faculty are less identifiable and reachable on campus, although they frequently outnumber TTT faculty.[38] Additionally, internal union differences that reflect disparities in working conditions can undermine effective negotiations and lead to claims of inadequate union representation. Lastly, an existing faculty bargaining unit on campus, affiliated with the same or a different union, can derail efforts at attaining a wall-to-wall unit.

Another key factor is the respective positions of unions and institutions concerning unit composition. Disputes over a proposed bargaining unit can center on the inclusion or exclusion of employees based on perceived support or opposition to union representation.[39] Both sides understand that unit composition can affect election results and subsequent negotiations. Unresolved objections to a proposed unit can lead to protracted litigation and delays in holding the representation election, which can undermine an organizing campaign. With rare exceptions, however, unions and institutions are at liberty to stipulate to the composition of a bargaining unit with compromises over inclusion of job titles and personnel.

Legal Standards for Bargaining Unit Composition

Another key factor in unit composition is the law. Legal standards shape and sometimes trump other considerations, including employer, union, and employee preferences. Well-established precedent can lead parties to stipulate to unit composition to avoid litigation and proceed to a relatively quick representation election. The general legal standard in unit composition is whether a community of interest exists between employees to warrant a combined unit or whether conflicting interests require separate units.[40] The application of that legal standard has never been consistent and can vary depending on facts, preferences, and precedent.

The outcomes of two contingent faculty organizing campaigns exemplify how the same legal standard can lead to inconsistent results. In 2015, the Pennsylvania Labor Relations Board ordered contingent faculty placed into a preexisting FT unit, while in New York contingent faculty at two community colleges were ordered into separate units from FT faculty already represented by the same union.[41]

Some state laws restrict the composition of higher education bargaining units,[42] others define the units but permit modifications,[43] and still others exclude PT and contingent faculty from the right to unionize entirely.[44] In contrast, the University of Michigan and Michigan State University have formal policies requiring acceptance of proposed bargaining units deemed "reasonable," and have agreed to participate in mediation and arbitration over unit composition disputes.[45]

In the private sector, federal labor law establishes a procedural barrier to a combined bargaining unit of professionals and nonprofessionals through a statutory requirement that professionals vote in favor of including nonprofessionals in the same unit before the National Labor Relations Board (NLRB) will certify a combined unit.[46] This procedure reinforces a presumption favoring exclusive professional units, which separates different groups of workers and undermines a wall-to-wall organizing strategy.

The Application of Practical and Legal Factors in Bargaining Unit Composition

Labor organizing strategies, along with faculty preferences, institutional responses, and the applicable law, substantially impact whether faculty unionize in separate or combined units. However, these factors are not themselves a guarantor of a specific composition.

When the earliest community college faculty bargaining units were established in Wisconsin and Michigan between 1963 and 1969, a majority were limited to TTT faculty, a few were combined units, and two were separate contingent faculty units.[47] In the same period, ten faculty units formed in Illinois, with only two that included contingent faculty. It took four decades before contingent faculty at the City Colleges of Chicago and Joliet Community College were unionized into their own separate bargaining units.[48]

In 1966, the AFT sought a single unit of faculty, professionals, and instructional support staff at the Fashion Institute of Technology to the exclusion of other employees. A municipal labor relations agency rejected the proposed unit. Instead, the AFT was certified to represent two units: one for faculty and professionals and another for instructional support personnel.[49]

Two years later, separate faculty units based on rank were ordered by a New York labor relations agency at the City University of New York (CUNY). The decision found a conflict of interests between groups of faculty due to disparities in job security, benefits, governance responsibilities, professional loyalty, and the substantial size of the contingent faculty workforce.[50] The following year, a combined unit of all faculty and non-academic professional employees was certified at the State University of New York (SUNY), despite the applicability of the same state law in the CUNY case.[51]

The two CUNY faculty units were permitted to merge after a supervised election in 1972, and as Luke Elliott-Negri has shown, it took decades before the union began to embrace and prioritize contingent faculty interests, following changes in leadership and the adoption of internal organizing strategies to enfranchise faculty with precarious appointments.[52] Similarly, at SUNY, a genuine union concern for contingent faculty issues took years to develop, as chapters without PT officers persisted until 2002.[53]

In the early 1970s, contingent faculty in Michigan were included in a combined unit at one public university, while they were excluded at another pursuant to an agreement between the union and institution.[54] After passage of California's Educational Employment Relations Act of 1976,[55] a state labor relations agency ruled that FT and PT community college faculty belonged in the same unit.[56] Despite that ruling, faculty at California's Coast Community College were split into separate units in 1979, while some community college units were limited to FT-TTT faculty.[57] At California State University, contingent faculty were included in a combined faculty unit established in 1981.[58] However, like the history at CUNY, it took new statewide leadership and internal organizing before that union became dedicated to more fully representing contingent faculty interests.[59]

In the private sector, the original legal rule applied by the NLRB determined that faculty belonged in a single bargaining unit with other professionals.[60] The agency changed that rule in 1975, at the AAUP's urging, to find that PT faculty should be excluded from a FT faculty unit that included other professionals.[61] The AAUP successfully argued that separate units were required because "part-time faculty had a limited attachment to the university, did not participate in university governance, and did not carry out research" as part of their job responsibilities.[62]

In 1980, the issue of contingent faculty inclusion in combined units at private nonprofit institutions became largely moot after the Supreme Court's *Yeshiva University* ruling, which found that TTT faculty involved in shared governance were managerial.[63] However, the *Yeshiva* decision did not prohibit continued recognition of combined or separate faculty units. By 2012, there were eighty-six private sector bargaining units in higher education: thirty-six separate contingent, twenty-six separate TTT, twenty-two combined, and two undefined units.[64] While *Yeshiva* continues to discourage unions from organizing TTT faculty for purposes of collective bargaining due to the costs associated with litigating managerial status issues, it has had less impact on contingent faculty organizing.[65]

Composition of New Units with Contingent Faculty, 1963–2012

The following two sections examine composition data concerning the frequency of contingent faculty unionization into separate or combined bargaining units, the first from 1963 to 2012 and the second from 2013 to 2019.[66] Figure 14.1 demonstrates that each year prior to 1981, growth in combined units outpaced that in separate units. The spike in combined units in the mid-1970s seen in figure 14.1 reflects, in part, successful organizing in California under legal precedent requiring a single unit for community college faculty.[67]

New combined unit growth nationally began to slow in 1981, with fewer than five new units per year over the next four decades. Starting in 1985, growth in separate units increased, a trend that continued into the twenty-first century. An important driver for this increase was the growth in contingent faculty appointments.

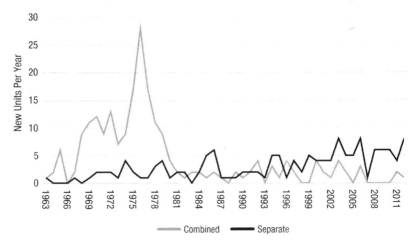

Figure 14.1. Newly Recognized Units with Contingent Faculty per Annum, 1963–2012
Sources: Berry and Savarese, *Directory of U.S. Faculty Contracts and Bargaining Agents in Institutions of Higher Education*; Herbert, Apkarian, and van der Naald, *2020 Supplementary Directory of New Bargaining Agents and Contracts in Institutions of Higher Education, 2013–2019.*

Table 14.1. Total Separate and Combined Units with Contingent Faculty by Sector, 2012

	Public Sector	Private Sector	Total
Combined	194	22	**216**
Separate	114	36	**150**

Sources: Berry and Savarese, *Directory of U.S. Faculty Contracts and Bargaining Agents in Institutions of Higher Education*; Herbert, Apkarian, and van der Naald, *2020 Supplementary Directory of New Bargaining Agents and Contracts in Institutions of Higher Education, 2013–2019.*

In 1969, contingent faculty represented only 21.7 percent of all faculty, yet by 2011 that percentage had increased to 70.8 percent, with over 60 percent working on a part-time basis.[68]

As table 14.1 shows, combined units with contingent faculty were more prevalent in 2012 at public institutions than at private institutions, which is reflective of distinct legal landscapes.

Composition of New Units with Contingent Faculty, 2013–2019

Data from the study of all new faculty units in 2013–2019 reveals that separate units of contingent faculty continued to grow, a reflection of the fragmented structure of higher education collective bargaining.[69] The data also shows professional craft unionism remains central to faculty organizing, despite the emergence of nontraditional unions in faculty representation.[70]

Over 75 percent of new faculty units formed between 2013 and 2019 contain only contingent faculty. The scope of these units, and the existence of multiple new units on some campuses, reflect the practical and legal factors associated with higher education organizing. The surge in unionization was an outgrowth of concerted nationwide contingent faculty activism and campaigns by the Service Employees International Union (SEIU), AFT, NEA, and AAUP.[71] The strategy was aimed at seeking relatively quick representation elections by avoiding litigated disputes based on *Yeshiva* and other legal arguments. Therefore, none of the new units replicated the wall-to-wall model pioneered by the CIO in the late 1940s, nor were such units even sought. Contingent faculty and graduate assistants did not seek combined bargaining units during the 2013–2019 period,[72] although each group

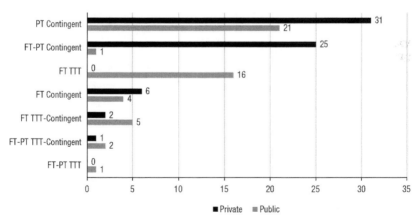

Figure 14.2. New Faculty Units by Sector, 2013–2019
Source: Herbert, Apkarian, and van der Naald, *2020 Supplementary Directory of New Bargaining Agents and Contracts in Institutions of Higher Education, 2013–2019.*

constituted precarious academic workers, as Eric Fure-Slocum acknowledges in the introduction to this volume.[73]

Figure 14.2 provides a breakdown of the composition of all new units with contingent faculty in 2013–2019.[74] Of the sixty-five new faculty units at private nonprofit institutions, 47.7 percent (31) were limited to PT contingent faculty, 38.5 percent (25) had PT and FT contingent faculty, and 9.2 percent (6) were made up of FT contingent faculty. Only three units were combined units of contingent and TTT faculty.[75]

Litigation over unit composition at private institutions was relatively rare during the period. There were only a handful of litigated disputes based on *Yeshiva*,[76] and no employer legal objections to three new combined faculty units.[77]

At Notre Dame de Namur University, a combined faculty organizing committee made the tactical decision to seek two distinct units to limit the potential of a *Yeshiva* defense by the university, which did not materialize.[78] The result was two bargaining units: one PT contingent faculty unit and one combined FT unit with contingent faculty and TTT faculty.[79] An essay about this organizing drive by Kim Tolley and her colleagues reveals that from the outset the campaign was limited to faculty unionization to the exclusion of other campus workers.[80]

At the Minnesota College of Art and Design, the institution objected to SEIU's proposed FT-PT faculty unit, arguing that FT faculty were managerial, and FT and PT faculty belonged in separate units. The NLRB rejected the managerial argument but ordered separate FT and PT bargaining units, finding that the two groups lacked a community of interest, relying on NLRB precedent dating back to the mid-1970s.[81]

Of the fifty new public-sector faculty units in figure 14.2, thirty-three contained contingent faculty, with twenty-six of these limited to contingent faculty only: 42 percent (21) PT faculty; 8 percent (4) FT faculty; and 2 percent (1) FT-PT faculty. Contingent faculty were also included in seven combined faculty units. The remaining 34 percent (17) were separate units of TTT faculty.[82]

Even when broader units were sought at three universities, they were limited to professional titles. An organizing drive at the University of Illinois–Chicago for a combined faculty bargaining unit was thwarted by a court ruling finding that state law mandated separate faculty units.[83] While this led to separate negotiations, it did not deter a two-day joint faculty strike in support of contingent faculty's salary demands.[84] At the University of Oregon, an agreement was reached for a combined faculty unit that also included librarians and postdoctoral scholars. A different outcome occurred at the University of New Mexico. There, the university objected to a proposed combined faculty unit, which led to the parties stipulating to separate contingent and TTT faculty bargaining units.

Additional evidence of professional craft unionism is the general lack of nonfaculty employees in new bargaining units with contingent faculty. As figure 14.3

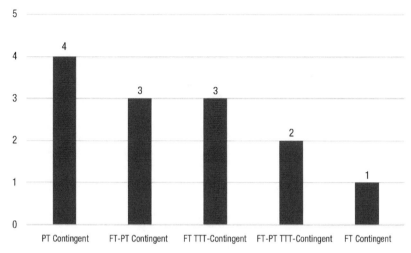

Figure 14.3. New Units with Contingent Faculty, Other Professional Titles, and Postdocs, 2013–2019
Source: Herbert, Apkarian, and van der Naald, *2020 Supplementary Directory of New Bargaining Agents and Contracts in Institutions of Higher Education, 2013–2019.*

demonstrates, only thirteen of the ninety-eight new public and private nonprofit bargaining units (13.3 percent) with contingent faculty in figure 14.2 included other professional titles and postdoctoral scholars.

Finally, separate faculty bargaining units did not preclude faculty from collaborating in negotiations or creating bargaining coalitions with unions representing other campus workers. The two faculty units at Notre Dame de Namur University negotiated together and reached a single contract with the university applicable to both units.[85] Similarly, single contracts were negotiated for separate contingent faculty units at Boston University and Northeastern University.[86]

Conclusion

In 1943, Charles Hendley successfully argued that teachers needed to affiliate with the CIO's SCMWA as part of the battle against fascism. Hendley emphasized that labor strength required teachers to reject their self-imposed isolation premised on professionalism.[87] Following the affiliation, the CIO organized the first wall-to-wall university bargaining units and the first contingent faculty bargaining unit. While the CIO's industrial union model for education was cut short during the domestic Cold War, it has been revived recently on some university campuses across the country.

Today, higher education is under fierce partisan, ideological, and anti-intellectual attack, fueled by the growth of a domestic fascist movement. At the same time, it is subject to multiple interrelated crises related to finances, job security, student debt, and COVID-19. The profound scope of these crises should be a catalyst for unions and larger percentages of faculty to modify their tactics and preferences to seek broad inclusive campus organizing rather than separate or combined faculty units. Wall-to-wall union organizing is a much stronger labor vehicle than professional craft unionism for responding to the campus-wide ramifications of these crises. Nevertheless, obstacles to campus solidarity in organizing and bargaining are real and cannot be wished away, including the inability or unwillingness of tenure-track faculty to recognize the disparate working conditions of contingent faculty. Overcoming those obstacles requires principled leadership with an investment in labor education, internal organizing, and intergroup dialogue during and following an organizing campaign.

The first necessary step toward wall-to-wall unionism requires cross-rank faculty solidarity described by Naomi R Williams and Jiyoon Park in this volume. As Julie Greene has argued, tenure-track faculty's role in perpetuating its class status and privilege has impeded broad campus worker alliances necessary for a more egalitarian academy.[88] To achieve wall-to-wall unionism, faculty, regardless of rank, status, or political persuasion, must drop the pretense of superiority and strive to end the pervasive academic culture of elitism and arrogance. To do so will require the reeducation of the academy and an end to treating contingent faculty, graduate assistants, and non-professionals as inferior, if not invisible.

Notes

1. Gary Rhoades, *Managed Professionals: Unionized Faculty and Restructuring Academic Labor* (Albany: State University of New York Press, 1998), 131–171.

2. Ladd and Lipset attributed faculty resistance to trade unionism to professional autonomy that is inconsistent with labor's emphasis on interdependence among workers, "collectivism and accompanying egalitarian norms." See, Everett Carll Ladd and Seymour Martin Lipset, *The Divided Academy: Professors and Politics* (New York: McGraw-Hill, 1975), 244–245.

3. Joe Berry and Michelle Savarese, *Directory of U.S. Faculty Contracts and Bargaining Agents in Institutions of Higher Education* (New York: National Center for the Study of Collective Bargaining in Higher Education and the Professions, 2012).

4. William A. Herbert, Jacob Apkarian, and Joseph van der Naald, *2020 Supplementary Directory of New Bargaining Agents and Contracts in Institutions of Higher Education, 2013–2019* (New York: National Center for the Study of Collective Bargaining in Higher Education and the Professions, 2020).

5. Timothy Reese Cain, "Long History of Activism and Organizing: Contingent Faculty, Graduate Students, and Unionization," in *Professors in the Gig Economy: Unionizing Adjunct Faculty in America,* ed. Kim Tolley (Baltimore, MD: Johns Hopkins Press, 2018), 47–51; William A. Herbert, "The History Books Tell It? Collective Bargaining in Higher

Education in the 1940s," *Journal of Collective Bargaining in the Academy* 9, art. 3 (2017): 19–20.

6. William A. Herbert and Jacob Apkarian, "You've Been with the Professors: An Examination of Higher Education Work Stoppage Data, Past and Present," *Employee Rights and Employment Policy Journal* 13:2 (2019): 253–254.

7. William E. Chancellor, "College Professors and the N.E.A.," *Journal of Education* 85:18 (1917): 481–483.

8. Herbert, "The History Books Tell It?," 23n138.

9. Robert H. Ziegler, *The CIO, 1935–1955* (Chapel Hill: University of North Carolina Press, 1995); William A. Herbert and Jacob Apkarian, "Everything Passes, Everything Changes: Unionization and Collective Bargaining in Higher Education," *Perspectives on Work* 21 (2017): 30–35.

10. "C.I.O.: A Modern Union for Public Employees," *The State, County, and Municipal Employee* 1:2 (1937): 7–8.

11. Statement of John L. Lewis, Chairman of the Committee for Industrial Organization, 13 July 1937, box 11, CIO Files of John L. Lewis, Pt. I: Correspondence with CIO Unions on Microfilm, Collection 5830 mf, Catherwood Library, Kheel Center for Labor-Management Documentation and Archives, Cornell University. SCMWA's original national constitution included a no-strike provision. Constitution of the State, County, and Municipal Workers of America, art. II, sec. 2 (1939).

12. Ziegler, *The CIO, 1935–1955*, 50–52. The SCMWA no-strike position was like the longstanding AFT policy. Herbert and Apkarian, "You've Been with the Professors," 254.

13. Roosevelt to Luther C. Steward, "Letter on the Resolution of Federation of Federal Employees against Strikes in Federal Service," 16 August 1937, American Presidency Project, University of California, Santa Barbara, https://www.presidency.ucsb.edu/node/208681.

14. "School Employees Win Closed Shop: Teachers Join after Foiling AFL Attack," and "Agreement between Logan County Board of Education of Logan County, West Virginia, and SCMWA Local Industrial Union No. 23 (Jan. 13, 1938)," reprinted in *The State, County, & Municipal Employee* (March 1938): 6. The Logan County contract and two similar SCMWA agreements were declared unlawful by West Virginia Attorney General Meadows. Herbert, "The History Books Tell It?," 21n124.

15. Agreement between Board of Education of Gloucester City and SCMWA, CIO, Local 410, 1 July 1943, Art. 1, BLS Collective Bargaining Agreements, collection 6178–022, reel 157, Catherwood Library, Kheel Center for Labor-Management Documentation and Archives, Cornell University. Later, New Jersey Attorney General Wilentz found that the state and its political subdivisions were precluded from entering into labor contracts without explicit statutory authorization. David T. Wilentz to David L. Cole, 12 January 1944, reprinted in Charles S. Rhyne, *Labor Unions and Municipal Employee Law* (Washington, DC: National Institute of Municipal Law Officers, 1946), 279–280, https://hdl.handle.net/2027/uc1.$b583514.

16. Emphasis in original. Handwritten speech by Charles James Hendley, undated, TAM. 109, box 3, folder 27, Charles James Hendley Papers, Tamiment Library and Robert F.

Wagner Labor Archives, New York University. The SCMWA affiliation occurred after NYTU and CTU were expelled from the AFT over ideological differences. See Andrew Feffer, *Bad Faith: Teachers, Liberalism, and the Origins of McCarthyism* (New York: Fordham University Press, 2019), 234–335.

17. Ibid.

18. UPW was formed in 1946 through the merger of SCMWA and the CIO's United Federal Workers of America. Herbert, "History Books Tell It?," 18–19.

19. Ibid., 27–30.

20. Agreement between the New School for Social Research and the Faculty Association of the Dramatic Workshop, 30 September 1948, collection No. 5015, box 39, folder 639f13, Teachers Union of the City of New York Records, 1916–1965, Kheel Center for Labor-Management Documentation and Archives, Cornell University Library.

21. Herbert, "History Books Tell It?," 10. The United Campus Workers has adopted a wall-to-wall strategy in Arizona and eleven other states. See Elin Johnson and Vimal Patel, "How Covid-19 United the Higher-Ed Work Force," *Chronicle of Higher Education*, August 19, 2020, https://www.chronicle.com/article/how-covid-19-united-the-higher -ed-work-force. See also, President and Trustees of Bates College, NLRB Case No. 01-RC -284384, Decision and Direction of Election (2021), https://apps.nlrb.gov/link/document .aspx/09031d458362182e.

22. Adrianna Kezar, Tom DePaola, and Daniel T. Scott, *The Gig Academy: Mapping Labor in the Neoliberal University* (Baltimore: Johns Hopkins University Press, 2019), 132–135, 153–154; Daniel Scott and Adrianna J. Kezar, "Intergroup Solidarity and Collaboration in Higher Education Organizing and Bargaining in the United States," *Academic Labor: Research and Artistry* 3 (2020), https://digitalcommons.humboldt.edu/alra/vol3/iss1/10.

23. AAUP-AFT Rutgers, "Who We Are: Coalition of Rutgers Trade Unions," November 11, 2020, https://www.rutgersaaup.org/who-we-are-coalition-of-rutgers-trade-unions/#.

24. Timothy Reese Cain, *Campus Unions: Organized Faculty and Graduate Students in U.S. Higher Education* (Malden, MA: ASHE Higher Education Report, 2017), 30–32.

25. Ladd and Lipset, *The Divided Academy*, 260–261; Herbert and Apkarian, "You've Been with the Professors," 256.

26. Daniel J. Julius, "Making Collective Bargaining Work," in *Academic Collective Bargaining,* ed. Ernst Benjamin and Michael Mauer (New York, and Washington, DC: Modern Language Association and the American Association of University Professors, 2006), 204–206.

27. Kim Tolley, Marianne Delaporte, and Lorenzo Giachetti, "Unionizing Adjunct and Tenure-Track Faculty at Notre Dame de Namur University," in *Professors in the Gig Economy*, ed. Tolley, 113.

28. Peter Feuille and James Blandin, "Faculty Job Satisfaction and Bargaining Sentiments: A Case Study," *Academy of Management Journal* 17:4 (1974): 678–692; Richard Mosher, "Organizing the New Faculty Majority: The Struggle to Achieve Equality, Revive Our Unions, and Democratize Higher Education," in *Equality for Contingent Faculty: Overcoming the Two-Tier System*, ed. Keith Hoeller (Nashville, TN: Vanderbilt University Press, 2014), 89.

29. Kezar, DePaola, and Scott, *The Gig Academy*, 153–154.

30. William A. Herbert, "Public Workers," in *City of Workers, City of Struggle: How Labor Movements Changed New York*, ed. Joshua B. Freeman (New York: Columbia University Press, 2019), 142.

31. Edwin D. Duryea, *Faculty Unions and Collective Bargaining* (London: Jossey-Bass, 1973), 30–31.

32. Ladd and Lipset, *The Divided Academy*, 290–298.

33. Adrianna Kezar and Tom DePaola, "Understanding the Need for Unions: Contingent Faculty Working Conditions and the Relationship to Student Learning," in *Professors in the Gig Economy*, ed. Tolley, 30.

34. See Elizabeth Hohl's and Claire Goldstene's essays in this volume.

35. Tolley, Delaporte, and Giachetti, "Unionizing Adjunct and Tenure-Track Faculty at Notre Dame de Namur University," 104.

36. Keith Hoeller, "Preface," in *Equality for Contingent Faculty*, ed. Hoeller, 4.

37. Rhoades, *Managed Professionals*, 131–171.

38. Feuille and Blandin, "Faculty Job Satisfaction and Bargaining Sentiments," 678–692.

39. Matthew W. Finkin, Robert A. Goldstein, and Woodley B. Osborne, *A Primer on Collective Bargaining for College and University Faculty* (Washington, DC: American Association of University Professors, 1975), 17.

40. Duryea, *Faculty Unions and Collective Bargaining*, 29–33.

41. Herbert and Apkarian, "Everything Passes, Everything Changes," 34.

42. Ill. Compiled Statutes, 115 ILCS, Art. 5, § 7(a); Rev. Code of Wash., § 41.76.005(11); Minn. Statutes, § 179A.11(1); SEIU v. Univ. of Minn., Unit 8, 902 N.W.2d 54 (Minn. Ct. App. 2017).

43. Me. Rev. Statutes, 26 M.R.S.A. § 1024-A.

44. Ohio Rev. Code § 4117.01(C)(14), http://codes.ohio.gov/orc/4117.01; Nevada System of Higher Education, Title 4–Codification of Board Policy Statements, chap. 4, §2(13), https://nshe.nevada.edu/wp-content/uploads/file/BoardOfRegents/Handbook/title4//T4-CH04%20Professional%20Staff%20Collective%20Bargaining%20Regulations.pdf.

45. University of Michigan Board of Regents, Board Resolution Regarding Employer Neutrality, Cooperative Determination and Recognition of Bargaining Units, and Notification of Agreements (25 June 2020), https://regents.umich.edu/files/meetings/07-20/2020-07-I-1.pdf; Michigan State University Board of Trustees, Collective Bargaining Resolution (17 December 2021), https://trustees.msu.edu/AA1%20Collective%20Bargaining.pdf.

46. 29 U.S.C § 159(b).

47. Berry and Savarese, *Directory of U.S. Faculty Contracts and Bargaining Agents*, 42–43. Separate NTT units were located at the Milwaukee Area and Chippewa Valley Technical Colleges, with the former being a PT NTT unit and the latter a FT-PT NTT.

48. Berry and Savarese, *Directory of U.S. Faculty Contracts and Bargaining Agents*, 15.

49. Fashion Inst. of Tech., NYCDOL No. R-111–66 (6 June 1966), Bd. of Higher Ed. of the City Univ. of N.Y., 27 February 1968, NYPERB Case File No. C-0008 (174892–08), box 56, New York State Archives.

50. Bd. of Higher Ed. of the City Univ. of N.Y., 2 NYPERB ¶ 3056 (N.Y. Pub. Empl. Rel. Bd. 1968).

51. Robert K. Carr and Daniel K. Van Eyck, *Collective Bargaining Comes to the Campus* (Washington, DC: American Council on Education, 1973), 82. Nevertheless, the stand-alone principle was applied in 2015 when NTT faculty unionized at a New York community college. See Cnty. of Cayuga, 49 PERB ¶ 3007 (N.Y. Pub Empl. Rel. Bd. 2016).

52. Luke Elliott-Negri, "Wall to Wall: Industrial Unionism at the City University of New York, 1972–2017," in *Professors in the Gig Economy*, ed. Tolley, 153–171.

53. Nuala McGann Drescher, William E. Scheuerman, and Ivan D. Steen, *United University Professions: Pioneering in Higher Education Unionism* (Albany: State University of New York Press, 2019), 132, 197, 214.

54. Carr and Van Eyck, *Collective Bargaining Comes to the Campus*, 83–85.

55. Cal. Gov't Code, §§ 3540–3549.3.

56. Los Rios Comm. Coll. Dist., 1 PERC ¶ 01850 (Cal. Pub Empl. Rel Bd 1977); Hartnell Comm. Coll. Dist., 3 PERC ¶ 10016 (Cal. Pub. Empl. Rel. Bd. 1979).

57. Berry and Savarese, *Directory of U.S. Faculty Contracts and Bargaining Agents*, 10.

58. Cal. State Univ., 5 PERC ¶ 12152 (Cal. Empl. Rel. Bd. 1981).

59. Elizabeth Hoffman and John Hess, "Organizing for Equality within the Two-Tier System," in *Equality for Contingent Faculty*, ed. Hoeller, 9–27.

60. C. W. Post, 198 NLRB 453 (1971); Long Island Univ., 189 NLRB 909 (1971); Adelphi Univ., 195 NLRB 639 (1972).

61. N.Y. Univ., 221 NLRB 1148 (1975).

62. Finkin, Goldstein, and Osborne, *A Primer on Collective Bargaining for College and University Faculty*, 22.

63. NLRB v. Yeshiva Univ., 444 U.S. 672 (1980).

64. Herbert, Apkarian, and van der Naald, *2020 Supplementary Directory*; Berry and Savarese, *Directory of U.S. Faculty Contracts and Bargaining Agents*.

65. Tolley, Delaporte, and Giachetti, "Unionizing Adjunct and Tenure-Track Faculty at Notre Dame de Namur University," 111–112.

66. We use data derived from Herbert, Apkarian, and van der Naald, *2020 Supplementary Directory* and Berry and Savarese, *Directory of U.S. Faculty Contracts and Bargaining Agents*, table 2, to determine the number of new units with contingent faculty per year and whether they are in a separate or combined unit. We have excluded new units limited to TTT faculty.

67. Of the seventeen new combined units established in 1977, one year after enactment of the Educational Employment Relations Act, 88.2 percent (15) were community college units. Berry and Savarese, *Directory of U.S. Faculty Contracts and Bargaining Agents*, table 2.

68. Kezar and DePaola, "Understanding the Need for Unions," 30; Scott and Kezar, "Intergroup Solidarity and Collaboration in Higher Education Organizing and Bargaining in the United States," 108.

69. Kezar, DePaola, and Scott, *The Gig Academy*; Scott and Kezar, "Intergroup Solidarity and Collaboration in Higher Education Organizing and Bargaining in the United States."

70. Herbert, Apkarian, and van der Naald, *2020 Supplementary Directory*, 16–18.

71. William A. Herbert, "The Winds of Changes Shift: An Analysis of Recent Growth in Bargaining Units and Representation Efforts in Higher Education," *Journal of Collective Bargaining in the Academy* 8, art. 1 (2006): 6.

72. William A. Herbert and Joseph van der Naald, "Graduate Student Employee Unionization in the Second Gilded Age," in *Revaluing Work(ers): Toward a Democratic and Sustainable Future*, ed. Tobias Schulze-Cleven and Todd E. Vachon (Ithaca, NY: Cornell University Press, 2021), 238.

73. See also the essay by Jeff Schuhrke in this volume.

74. These figures exclude three new for-profit units established between 2013 and 2019.

75. Herbert, Apkarian, and van der Naald, *2020 Supplementary Directory*.

76. Ibid., 15–16.

77. Ibid., 16.

78. Tolley, Delaporte, and Giachetti, "Unionizing Adjunct and Tenure-Track Faculty at Notre Dame de Namur University," 115–116.

79. Herbert, Apkarian, and van der Naald, *2020 Supplementary Directory*, 36.

80. Tolley, Delaporte, and Giachetti, "Unionizing Adjunct and Tenure-Track Faculty at Notre Dame de Namur University," 110-111.

81. Minn. Coll. of Art and Design, NLRB No. 18-RC-182546, Decision and Direction of Election, 18 (2016), https://apps.nlrb.gov/link/document.aspx/09031d458220f39f.

82. Herbert, Apkarian, and van der Naald, *2020 Supplementary Directory*, 17.

83. Bd. of Trustees of the Univ. of Illinois v. Ill. Ed. Labor Rel. Bd., 966 N.E.2d 1239 (App. Ct, 4th Dist. 2012).

84. Colleen Flaherty, "U. of Illinois at Chicago Faculty Strike for First Contract," *Inside Higher Ed*, February 14, 2014, https://www.insidehighered.com/quicktakes/2014/02/19/u-illinois-chicago-faculty-strike-first-contract.

85. Tolley, Delaporte, and Giachetti, "Unionizing Adjunct and Tenure-Track Faculty at Notre Dame de Namur University," 117–118; Herbert, Apkarian, and van der Naald, *2020 Supplementary Directory*, 39.

86. Herbert, Apkarian, and van der Naald, *2020 Supplementary Directory*, 85.

87. Hendley, handwritten speech, Charles James Hendley Papers.

88. Julie Greene, "Rethinking the Boundaries of Class: Labor History and Theories of Class and Capitalism," *Labor: Studies in Working-Class History* 18:2 (2021): 106–107.

CHAPTER 15

GRADUATE WORKER ORGANIZING AND THE CHALLENGES OF PRECARITY IN HIGHER EDUCATION

JEFF SCHUHRKE

As universities model themselves on corporations—prioritizing revenue maximation over their fundamental teaching and research mission—they have become increasingly dependent on the labor of low-paid and badly treated graduate student workers. Often paid poverty wages, but disinclined to quit before they have completed their degree, they find themselves in a precarious employment situation. The exploitation of graduate workers is often excused by an academic culture that implicitly tells them they somehow deserve to be miserable because graduate school is a hazing ritual of sorts they voluntarily choose. Since 2016, however, more and more graduate workers around the United States have been fighting back in defense of their rights and economic wellbeing by exercising their collective power. Although media headlines in recent years frame graduate unions as a novel concept, asking questions like, "Should Graduate Students Unionize?" and "Are Grad Students Employees?" there is nothing new about graduate workers forming unions and engaging in collective bargaining.[1] For over half a century, unionized graduate teaching and research assistants in the United States have been winning improved pay, benefits, and workplace rights. But, facing hostile university administrations that often refuse to recognize student labor as "real" work, and dealing with the logistical challenges of trying to organize precarious academic employees across hundreds of departments on sprawling university campuses, graduate unions often struggle to simply exist, yet alone to thrive.

Being a Graduate Worker

University administrators and people outside of academia often imagine graduate workers as privileged youngsters free from any grown-up responsibilities. Graduate school has traditionally been characterized as a pause from "real life" and a refuge from the "real world," where students can simply focus on their studies, get a doctorate, then ease into a cushy and well-paid tenure-track job. The reality, of course, is nothing like this. According to data gathered by the US Department of Education, 61 percent of PhD students are thirty years old or older, while 33 percent have dependents. And, obviously, even twenty-something graduate workers without dependents have real-life, adult responsibilities, like paying bills and feeding themselves, which do not go away simply because they enroll in graduate school. Meanwhile, 52 percent of PhD students are women, 42 percent are people of color, a quarter are non-US citizens, and 12 percent have a disability—hardly the profile of a socially or economically privileged group.[2]

Far from spending their days simply taking classes and completing homework assignments, graduate workers devote a considerable amount of their time—typically twenty or more hours per week—to performing vital labor for their university. They work as course instructors, teaching assistants, research assistants, and clerical workers. In STEM fields, graduate assistants sometimes spend sixty or more hours per week doing lab work. As Erin Hatton argues in this volume, graduate workers in these fields face a particular form of "status coercion" through their relationships with their faculty advisors. With the erosion of stable, tenure-track jobs, universities are becoming more reliant on graduate labor. Between 2005 and 2015, for example, the number of graduate workers employed by universities increased by 16.7 percent, while the number of tenured and tenure-track faculty rose by only 4.8 percent in the same period.[3] According to the Economic Policy Institute, the average US graduate assistant is paid only $13,969 per year.[4] Universities frequently justify this low pay by weaponizing the common misperceptions about graduate school as a break from reality for privileged kids on their way to lucrative careers, or else by exploiting notions of scholarship and teaching as vocations where lower pay is simply to be expected. Further, universities often frame tuition waivers for graduate workers as a generous form of compensation. But without tuition waivers, far fewer people would enroll in PhD programs in the first place. The waivers are less a form of generous aid and more a necessity for universities wishing to maintain doctoral programs and a steady supply of graduate labor.

In addition to their paid work as university employees, graduate assistants have other responsibilities and stressors. They are busily trying to complete their degree requirements, conduct research, travel to and present at conferences, get published in scholarly journals, and line up permanent jobs by the time they graduate. Their labor as teaching and research assistants or as course instructors is usually their only means of remaining financially afloat. Their supervisors at work tend to also be their academic advisors, individuals with whom they must remain on good terms if they are to have any of hope of pursuing a career in academia (see Erin Hatton's essay in this volume). Twenty-one percent of PhD students report being bullied in their programs, and 48 percent of those say the bully is their supervisor. Another 21 percent say they have been sexually harassed or discriminated against on the basis of gender, race, age, religion, disability, or sexual orientation.[5] One in ten women graduate workers say they have been sexually harassed by a faculty member—someone with professional and economic power over them—though the real number is likely far higher as students often do not report because of a justified expectation that nothing will be done or out of fear of retaliation. Of those who do come forward, over half say a professor sexually assaulted, groped, or physically abused them, and over half also say these were not one-time incidents, but serial harassment on the part of the faculty member.[6]

Managing all of this, while simultaneously trying to get by on poverty wages and being disinclined to quit after years of effort and sacrifice spent pursuing their degree, puts graduate workers in an extremely precarious position. Not surprisingly, living with this precarity causes intense psychological distress. Numerous studies in recent years have uncovered what is often referred to as a mental health crisis in graduate school. These studies reveal that 39 percent of graduate workers experience moderate to severe depression, compared to 6 percent of the general population. In fact, PhD students are at a higher risk of developing a psychiatric condition than people working in defense and emergency services. A staggering 57 percent of transgender or gender-nonconforming graduate workers suffer from depression, while 41 percent of cis women and 35 percent of cis men in graduate school are depressed. One in two PhD students experiences some form of psychological distress, and over 7 percent have suicidal thoughts. The work context is found to be a significant predictor of graduate assistants' mental health.[7]

It would seem a major cause of this mental health crisis among graduate workers is their powerlessness and precarity. Like other academic workers, graduate assistants are forced to function within a cult of careerism and extreme individualism, thus internalizing their suffering, accommodating themselves to exploitation, and believing the problems they face result from their own shortcomings. Unions serve as a collective corrective to the hyper-individualized culture fostered by the corporate university model, allowing graduate workers to see that they are not alone in their struggles, that the precarity they face is due to the unjust structure of higher education, and that they can gain more stability and dignity through their collective strength. It is no wonder that graduate workers in the United States have been organizing unions for over fifty years.

A Brief History of Graduate Unions

Although administrators at private universities and many media outlets in recent years have presented graduate unionization as a new, experimental concept, many graduate workers have had recognized unions for over half a century. The oldest existing graduate union in the United States is the Teaching Assistants' Association (TAA) at the University of Wisconsin–Madison. Formed in 1966 by graduate workers opposed to the Vietnam War, in 1969, the TAA signed up 1,900 members and won recognition following a failed attempt by the Wisconsin legislature to raise out-of-state tuition. As negotiations on a first contract dragged on into 1970, the teaching assistants held a month-long strike before winning a historic collective bargaining agreement, which included funding guarantees, a healthcare plan, workload limits, and a grievance procedure. In 1974, the TAA affiliated with the American Federation of Teachers (AFT), becoming a progressive force within the state and national labor movement.[8]

Throughout the 1970s, graduate workers at public universities in New Jersey, Michigan, Oregon, and Florida followed the TAA's lead, forming unions, winning recognition, securing first contracts, and affiliating with the AFT. The next significant wave of graduate unionization came in the 1990s and 2000s, including at large public university systems such as the University of California, University of Massachusetts, State University of New York, and University of Illinois, as well as at urban universities like Temple and Wayne State. With union density in manufacturing plummeting thanks to deindustrialization and offshoring, national unions in addition to the AFT—most significantly, the United Auto Workers (UAW)—began organizing graduate workers in this period, in part to keep up their membership levels. At virtually every public university where graduate workers organized, campus administrators fought against union recognition by arguing that they were more "students" than "employees" and therefore ineligible for collective bargaining rights, only to be overruled by state lawmakers, state labor boards, or state courts. Once recognized, graduate unions at public institutions repeatedly won higher wages, better healthcare, tuition and fee waivers, grievance procedures, protections against discrimination, and many other rights and protections. Today, approximately 66,000 graduate workers at over thirty public universities have union representation and are covered by a collective bargaining agreement.[9]

Since labor relations at private universities fall under the jurisdiction of the federal National Labor Relations Board (NLRB), graduate workers there have faced legal obstacles to unionization distinct from those of their peers at public institutions. Between 2000 and 2016, the NLRB continuously tacked back and forth on the question of whether graduate workers at private universities have collective bargaining rights. During this time, the UAW-affiliated Graduate Students Organizing Committee (GSOC) at New York University waged a remarkable seventeen-year

battle (1998–2015) that saw it become the first graduate union at a private university to win legal recognition and a contract, only to be stripped of recognition and
denied the right to negotiate a second contract, then to win voluntary recognition,
and then, finally, to see a second contract a decade after the first one had expired.

The GSOC victory was followed by a 2016 NLRB decision granting collective
bargaining rights to graduate workers at private universities, which opened the
floodgates to an unprecedented wave of graduate unionization across the country.
But the election of Donald Trump that same year, and the consequent appointment
of anti-union Republicans to the NLRB, meant that graduate organizing at private
institutions would continue to face legal barriers for another four years. Though
the Trump-appointed NLRB majority had signaled its intention to overturn the
2016 decision on graduate workers' collective bargaining rights, by the time Joe
Biden took office in 2021, the decision remained in place and the plan to overturn
it was quickly scrapped.[10] As they fight for recognition and fair contracts amid the
shifting politics at the NLRB, graduate unions at private institutions like Harvard,
Columbia, Georgetown, NYU, and Brown have gained widespread national attention in recent years.

Despite the many challenges they encounter, graduate unions—whether recognized or unrecognized, whether at public or private universities—have repeatedly
proven to be effective vehicles for advancing the rights of graduate student workers
over the past five decades. One of many recent examples of this is the 2019 graduate worker strike at the University of Illinois at Chicago (UIC).

UIC Strike

In the spring of 2019, graduate workers at UIC—myself included—went on strike
for nearly three weeks to win a new collective bargaining agreement, as well as to
assert our dignity and affirm the value of our labor. We organized the work stoppage through our union, the Graduate Employees Organization (GEO), AFT Local
6297, which represents over 1,500 graduate workers at UIC. GEO won recognition
in 2004 and secured a first contract in 2006. Because it is entirely sustained by the
voluntary dues of poorly paid, part-time employees, GEO is—by necessity—an
intensely democratic, member-run union local. The local has only one paid staff
person, and all of its elected officers, who serve one-year terms, volunteer their
time for the union while simultaneously fulfilling all the regular obligations associated with being a graduate worker.

Most GEO members at UIC work as teaching assistants or course instructors.
With over 30,000 students, UIC is Chicago's largest university. The majority of
undergraduates are from working-class or immigrant backgrounds who typically
commute to campus and have to balance school with part-time jobs. A growing

number are international students struggling to break through cultural and linguistic barriers. As dedicated teachers, graduate workers provide the understanding and direct attention undergraduates need for academic success. GEO members offer students one-on-one tutoring, do the vast majority of grading, and often serve as primary course instructors.

Despite the value of our work, when our fourth contract expired in 2018, we were paid a minimum salary of $18,000 while being required to pay fees of up to $2,000 to the university, leaving only $16,000 to live on in a major city. Nearly half of the employees represented by GEO are international graduate workers, whose visa status does not allow them to supplement their income with off-campus jobs and who are typically ineligible for financial aid. They were required to pay an additional, $260-per-year "international student fee," which had been instituted four years earlier. A rapid community health assessment conducted in spring 2019 by Radical Public Health, an advocacy organization at UIC's School of Public Health, found that 77 percent of UIC graduate workers could not afford all their basic living expenses, with 57 percent saying they had skipped meals due to lack of money for food. Further, a staggering 70 to 80 percent reported experiencing anxiety and depression due in part to living under constant financial stress in their precarious graduate positions.[11]

Meanwhile, for UIC administrators, it was a boom time. Each year between 2016 and 2018, the university president received a $100,000 bonus on top of his $600,000 salary. In 2016 and 2017, the chancellor got a $75,000 bonus in addition to his $400,000 salary. Enrollments reached an all-time high and continued to grow after 2017, and UIC acquired the John Marshall Law School in 2018. Using the fees taken from students, the university began several multimillion-dollar construction projects, building a $100 million academic and residential complex and a $43 million engineering building between 2017 and 2019, while also making plans for a $95 million performing arts center. Bigger yet, at the start of 2019, the administration announced an ambitious plan to spend $1 billion on campus infrastructure renovations over the next decade.[12] For UIC graduate workers struggling to get by, seeing top administrators throw enormous sums of money at real estate developments while rewarding themselves with exorbitant bonuses was intolerable. With GEO's old contract expiring and a new round of negotiations beginning in 2018, the union was determined to fight for significant gains.

Negotiations began on March 1, 2018, with the existing contract set to expire that August. One of the union's top priorities was winning fee relief in addition to wage raises. In our previous four contracts, GEO had won raises only to see them clawed back later through fee increases. Further, we sought more transparency and consistency about how departments make reappointment decisions. Graduate workers often do not know whether they will still have a teaching appointment from one semester to the next. When departments are not required to follow any standards about how they make such hiring decisions, they leave the door open to favoritism, discrimination, and retaliation. GEO activists recognized that the union's greatest leverage in negotiations comes from its strength in numbers and, given the university's anti-union record, we knew there was a decent chance we would ultimately have to strike to get the contract we deserved. Indeed, our fellow graduate workers at the University of Illinois's flagship campus in Urbana-Champaign had been forced to go on strike in early 2018 to preserve the guarantee of tuition waivers.[13]

To prepare for withholding our labor and risking losing pay—an enormous gamble for workers living paycheck to paycheck—we organized a long-term contract campaign in conjunction with the negotiations to build a sense of unity and solidarity among members. This was crucial because graduate workers, like others who labor in academia, are often siloed in their own departments or focused on their own individual research, remaining isolated and divided. Promoting union democracy and transparency in leadership was a key component of our effort to build unity. As part of the contract campaign, rank-and-file members were encouraged to attend every bargaining session. When administration negotiators would temporarily leave the room so both sides could engage in private caucuses, union members would share their ideas and pose questions to their fellow members on the bargaining team, allowing for an open and democratic process. At some sessions, rank-and-file members were invited by the union bargaining team to offer personal testimonials about how they were affected by issues like discrimination, opaque appointment procedures, low wages, and high fees. Though the testimonials did not convince the administration negotiators to alter their position, hearing them allowed other union members in the room to see that they were not alone in their various struggles and helped to forge a concrete sense of solidarity.

Following each negotiating session, the GEO bargaining team quickly wrote a summary of what had happened and sent it out to the membership via email listserv and social media. Social media was also used to make our campaign and our members more visible. In the fall of 2018, dozens of GEO members had their individual photos taken holding a small sign that read, "We need GEO because . . . " followed by the individual member's own handwritten message stating why the union and contract mattered to them. Examples included "Grad workers deserve a living wage and we shouldn't have to pay to work here," "GEO makes my voice heard while the university only pretends to listen," and "I am a worker and my work matters." Every day for about two months, at least two of these photos were posted on the union's Facebook and Twitter accounts, along with the first name and department of the individual GEO member in each photo. Seeing fellow union members visually convey the importance of the contract campaign further helped establish a sense of camaraderie and shared struggle among graduate workers.

Importantly, the contract campaign included a series of escalating protest actions. As the administration persistently rejected union proposals with virtually no constructive feedback, dragging the negotiations out for months, these protests became increasingly militant. Our first action was a "work-in," where GEO members packed the lobby of one of the main administrative buildings on campus and did our normal work of grading and advising students there for several hours, thereby making our labor more visible. A later action involved going to a panel discussion on campus, hosted by the provost, on the topic of students' mental health. There, a small group of GEO members handed out flyers laying out the shocking statistics about the mental health crisis in graduate school, how it is linked to graduate students' status as precarious workers, and calling on the UIC administration to settle a fair contract. A few months later, our union staged an informational picket in front of one of the campus's main entrances, which had the look and feel of a strike without being one. This allowed union members the chance to imagine, in real terms, what a strike might be like, as well as to begin making creative, handmade picket signs. By February 2019, with the administration still dismissing GEO concerns at the bargaining table, members voted overwhelmingly—99.5 percent in favor—to authorize an indefinite strike. The vote was only successful because members were well informed, involved, and ready to act.

Despite further bargaining sessions following the strike authorization vote, the administration refused to cede ground. The strike began on March 19, 2019, more than thirteen months after the first bargaining session had been held. We chose that date because it was only a few days after our monthly paycheck, allowing the maximum amount of time we could stay out before potentially having our pay docked, which the administration was threatening to do. Hundreds of classes were cancelled, and normal operations at UIC were brought to a standstill.[14] It was a genuine work stoppage, not a symbolic protest. The campus community overwhelmingly supported us. In the run-up to the strike, GEO had sought the support of faculty and undergraduates, knowing the administration would attempt to divide us. The union had given members employed as teaching assistants and instructors a handout to share with their undergraduate students, as well as some talking points, to explain the stakes of the contract campaign and the necessity of going on strike. GEO had also been coordinating closely with UIC United Faculty, the union of tenured/tenure-track and non-tenure-track faculty, which was going through a contentious round of contract negotiations of its own.[15] We informed the faculty union that the best ways to support us during the strike would be to not take on any of our regular labor and to try to either cancel their classes or move them off-campus if possible.

Throughout GEO's work stoppage, faculty refused to be strikebreakers, despite the administration's pleas. Undergraduates not only joined us on the picket lines, but also chose not to attend classes when administrators in a couple of departments tried teaching in our place. The administration was unwittingly helpful by sending out flat-footed anti-union emails to the entire campus community. One message made the preposterous claim that UIC grad workers make "akin to $62,375" every year, prompting some GEO members to respond that since they only took home $18,000 the previous year, UIC owed them $44,000. The administration's messaging, which was openly mocked by undergrads on a meme page they created, built support for our strike. Further, the administration's attempts to have faculty perform graduate labor and thus become scabs did not go over well with many professors. In department after department, faculty collectively issued letters to top administrators expressing full support for their graduate colleagues. When the semester resumed after spring break and the work stoppage still had no end in sight, the provost and chancellor reportedly held a meeting with department chairs to strategize about how to break the strike. But the department chairs pushed back and demanded the administration reach an amicable settlement.

In addition, we had the backing of the wider community. The graduate union from the University of Illinois at Urbana-Champaign not only joined our picket lines, but also loaned us megaphones and buckets for drumming from their strike the year before. Dozens of other unions and over 600 individuals donated to our strike fund. UPS drivers with Teamsters Local 705 honored the picket line by refusing to make deliveries on campus. The Chicago Symphony Orchestra, which was also on strike for seven weeks in early 2019, joined our pickets with trumpeter John Hagstrom giving a moving solidarity performance. Local and state elected officials likewise joined our picket lines, and Senator Bernie Sanders tweeted out a message of support.[16] As the strike neared the three-week mark, the administration could no longer hold out. The chancellor and provost heard from dozens of organizations and constituencies on campus, including alumni, urging them to reach a fair settlement. For the first time in over a year of negotiations, the provost showed up to a bargaining session, ready to grant concessions. Demands the administration had repeatedly told us were impossible to meet suddenly became possible, leading to an agreement that ended the strike on April 5. The agreement included a provision that allowed us a month to make up lost work hours before potentially having any pay docked. In the end, only a few graduate workers lost pay, and GEO was able to fully compensate them thanks to the strike fund.

Because of the successful strike, GEO won its strongest contract to that point. Scheduled fee increases would be offset by matching wage increases, future fees would be automatically waived, and the discriminatory "international student fee" would be cut in half. While the administration initially wanted to give us only a 7 percent raise over five years, which would not have even kept up with inflation, we instead negotiated a 14 percent raise over three years—twice as much money in almost half as much time, and our biggest raise to that point. We also won a stipulation requiring departments to implement transparent appointment and reappointment guidelines by fall 2020, a step toward eliminating employment precarity. We reduced healthcare costs and the university agreed to cover a portion of dependent-care coverage for the first time. We also added new nondiscrimination protections around immigration/citizenship status and arrest record, an important victory allowing graduate workers to feel a little safer in the age of Trump. Further, we refused to accept a five-year or four-year contract that would have only benefited the administration, instead winning a three-year contract. The shorter contract length meant GEO returned to the bargaining table only two years later to fight for more wage increases, fee reductions, and other protections—which they secured following a second strike in spring 2022. This is especially significant given the natural turnover in graduate unions as veteran members complete their degrees and newer members take on leadership roles, which often makes it difficult to maintain the institutional memory needed to avoid being outfoxed by the administration at the bargaining table.

Conclusion

GEO members at UIC came away from the 2019 strike feeling empowered, learning that when graduate workers fight collectively for the respect and dignity they deserve, they can win. This was an especially important lesson for international graduate workers, who are traditionally the most hesitant to get involved in union activism due to cultural barriers and fears of visa complications.[17] Riding this momentum, the union won several concessions from the university in the early days of the COVID-19 pandemic, including expanded paid sick leave and healthcare coverage, more summer funding opportunities, and free summer housing for international students left stranded in the United States because of pandemic-related travel restrictions.[18]

The UIC strike served as a reminder that while graduate school is supposed to be challenging, it need not be exploitative. In the past five years, graduate unions at numerous universities—including Columbia, Harvard, University of California, University of Michigan, Temple, and Indiana University—have staged work stoppages demanding and winning improved pay and conditions. Meanwhile, graduate workers are organizing new unions at a rapid pace, winning recognition at institutions like MIT, Northwestern, Yale, Johns Hopkins, Boston University, and the University of New Mexico. Despite graduate workers' precarious and exploited position within the corporate university structure, the graduate union movement continues to build momentum and flex its muscles.

Notes

1. Yuki Noguchi, "Are Grad Students Employees? Labor Board to Again Weigh In," *All Things Considered*, NPR, April 7, 2016; Amruta Byatnal, "Should Graduate Students Unionize?," *Pacific Standard*, May 24, 2017.

2. National Center for Education Statistics, "Profile and Financial Aid Estimates of Graduate Students 2015–16," US Department of Labor, January 2019, 7–8.

3. Teresa Kroeger, Celine McNicholas, Marni von Wilpert, and Julia Wolfe, "The State of Graduate Student Employee Unions," Economic Policy Institute, January 2018.

4. Margaret Poydock, Celine McNicholas, and Julia Wolfe, "EPI Comments on NLRB's Proposed Rule Regarding Nonemployee Status of Students at Private Institutions," Economic Policy Institute, January 15, 2020, https://www.epi.org/publication/epi-comments-nlrb-rule-student-employee-status/.

5. Chris Woolston, "PhDs: The Tortuous Truth," *Nature*, November 13, 2019.

6. Nancy Chi Cantalupo and William Kidder, "A Systematic Look at a Serial Problem: Sexual Harassment of Students by University Faculty," *Utah Law Review* 3:2 (2018): 671–786.

7. Teresa M. Evans, Lindsay Bira, Jazmin Beltran Gastelum, L. Todd Weiss, and Nathan L. Vanderford, "Evidence for a Mental Health Crisis in Graduate Education," *Nature Biotechnology* 36 (March 2018): 282–284; Katia Levecque, Frederik Anseel, Alain De Beuckelaer, Johan Van der Heyden, and Lydia Gisel, "Work Organization and Mental Health Problems in PhD Students," *Research Policy* 46:4 (May 2017): 868–879; Jyllian Kemsley, "Grappling with Graduate Student Mental Health and Suicide," *Chemical and Engineering News* 95:32 (August 2017): 28–33; Academics Anonymous, "Academia Is Built on Exploitation. We Must Break This Vicious Circle," *The Guardian*, May 18, 2018.

8. Peter B. Levy, *The New Left and Labor in the 1960s* (Urbana: University of Illinois Press, 1994), 158–160.

9. Colleen Flaherty, "Ruling Out Grad Unions," *Inside Higher Ed*, September 23, 2019.

10. Dawn Tefft and Jeff Schuhrke, "A Ph.D. in Organizing," *Labor Notes*, December 19, 2016; Jeff Schuhrke, "Graduate Workers Will Fight Like Hell to Stop the Trump Labor Board's New Rule," *In These Times*, September 25, 2019; Cara J. Chang and Meimei Xu, "Grad Student Unions, Experts Expect Friendlier Climate for Labor under Biden," *Harvard Crimson*, January 20, 2021; Danielle Douglas-Gabriel, "Labor Board Withdraws Rule to Quash Graduate Students' Right to Organize," *Washington Post*, March 12, 2021.

11. Jeff Schuhrke, "How UIC Grad Workers Fought the Neoliberal University Model— And Won," *Jacobin*, May 1, 2019.

12. Dawn Rhodes, "University of Illinois at Chicago Flourishes Amid Struggles at State's Public Universities," *Chicago Tribune*, October 10, 2018; "$100K Bonus Approved for U of I President," *Associated Press*, November 15, 2018; Dawn Rhodes, "U. of I. President, UIC Chancellor Receive $175K in Bonuses for Second Straight Year," *Chicago Tribune*, November 16, 2017; Dawn Rhodes, "UIC Approves Merger with John Marshall Law School," *Chicago Tribune*, July 19, 2018; Dawn Rhodes, "UIC Pursues $100m Residence Hall and Academic Complex," *Chicago Tribune*, September 19, 2017; "UIC's New Engineering Innovation

Building Supports Nano- to Mega-Scale Research and Dramatic Growth in Engineering Student Enrollment," *UIC Today*, July 22, 2019; Jason Koziarz, "UIC Announces Three Finalists Teams to Design $95M Performing Arts Center," *Curbed Chicago*, April 9, 2019; Ravi Baichwal, "UIC Unveils $1B Campus Renovation Plan," *ABC7 Chicago*, January 2, 2019.

13. Graduate workers at Urbana had previously struck for two days in 2009, a successful action that transformed the labor and political climate on campus.

14. Dawn Rhodes, "Tentative Deal Reached to End UIC Strike that Caused Hundreds of Classes to Be Cancelled," *Chicago Tribune*, April 5, 2019.

15. Dawn Rhodes, "University of Illinois at Chicago Avoids 2nd Strike This Spring as Faculty Reach Tentative Contract Deal," *Chicago Tribune*, April 23, 2019.

16. Alexandra Arriaga, "Bernie Sanders Tweets Support for UIC Graduate Workers Strike," *Chicago Sun-Times*, March 25, 2019.

17. Zukhra Kasimova, "International Student Workers Key to Chicago Grad Strike Victory," *Labor Notes*, April 22, 2019.

18. Zukhra Kasimova and Dawn Tefft, "Chicago Grad Workers First to Win COVID-19 Demands," *Labor Notes*, April 28, 2020.

CHAPTER 16

FROM COMMUNITY OF INTEREST TO IMAGINED COMMUNITIES

Organizing Academic Labor
in the Washington, DC, Area

ANNE MCLEER

In the late spring of 2002, with thirteen weeks left to finish my PhD dissertation, I started volunteering on an organizing campaign to unionize 1,500 adjunct faculty and graduate students at George Washington University (GW) in Washington, DC. The adjuncts who began the campaign had affiliated with the United Auto Workers, which at that time also represented adjunct faculty at New York University (NYU), though they ultimately affiliated with Service Employees International Union (SEIU) Local 500. While I should have been spending time writing my history of the nanny in American popular culture, the working conditions I faced as a recently hired adjunct faculty member spurred me to spend part of my days persuading other adjuncts and graduate students to sign union cards. I had been told that once I received the PhD my salary would increase from $2,500 per class to $2,700.

In my previous position at GW as an administrative assistant, I had received retirement contributions and had access to health and other benefits from my employer, all of which disappeared when I started teaching as a part-time faculty member, that is, as an adjunct. In 2008, when we signed the first collective bargaining agreement for part-time faculty at GW, my rate per course increased to $3,800. I got a $200 bump in pay for the seven and a half years it took to get a PhD, but $1,100 for forming my union!

This became an object lesson about the power of collective action and the difference collective bargaining makes, which also explains why institutions spend so much money fighting unionization. The contrast between the culture of unionism and the culture of graduate school could not have been starker. Graduate school is an intensely competitive arena of individualistic striving, where hundreds of hopeful scholars in every field battle for a handful of careers. One's future is in the grip of faculty members (advisors) whose own careers and livelihoods exist in a competitive hierarchy. Engaging in collective bargaining illuminated the opera-tion of power relations in the academic workforce. There was a significant contrast between how my employer valued my degree and my teaching when that employer viewed me as an isolated individual and operated as the unilateral decision-maker and when that employer was compelled to bargain collectively with all adjunct fac-ulty in a bilateral negotiation. Collective bargaining revealed that what we got paid and that decisions about our working conditions were based not on our individual skill as teachers or any perception of the value of our scholarship but, rather, on cold market forces. By coming together collectively to unionize we had accessed the only means to successfully push back against institutional power.

This essay is a personal reflection on the origins of contingent faculty unioniza-tion and mobilization in Washington, DC, and Maryland. I explore how organizing contingent faculty in the area began twenty-one years ago, along with how we learned to break most of the rules of organizing when doing so among academic laborers. I will examine evolving and enduring successes of, as well as the chal-lenges to, creating solidarity and an "imagined community" for contingent faculty.

From Community of Interest to Imagined Communities

In *Imagined Communities,* historian and political scientist Benedict Anderson shows how the rise of print media allowed people and groups who never met or directly communicated to perceive themselves as part of a community—such as a nation. In collective bargaining law, unions are allowed to petition for a bargaining unit of workers who share a "community of interest," often defined as craft, workplace, or industry. In organizing more broadly, this community of interest could be a group of workers who come together on the factory floor, at a union hall, or in an office lunchroom. However, the American workplace has changed dramatically since 1935 when the National Labor Relations Act was passed and the subsequent era of postwar prosperity, moving from predominantly full-time, permanent jobs to part-time, temporary, precarious positions in a "gig economy." When organizing and mobilizing contingent or precarious workers, including marginalized contin-gent faculty, a community of interest is almost always an imagined community.

In most colleges and universities, the adjunct faculty (who are often greater in number than full-time faculty and teach up to half the courses in a semester), fre-quently do not know one another and have few opportunities to meet. An adjunct faculty member could be teaching in a university with 600 other adjunct faculty and not encounter a single one of these colleagues over a semester. Many come to campus only once or twice a week, teach their class, and leave. Many do not have office space to meet with students or prepare classes; where office space is provided it is often underused, as adjuncts regularly rush from a teaching gig on one campus to another teaching gig at a different campus or from campus to another job. Adjuncts generally do not meet in institution-wide forums, such as faculty senates, in the ways that full-time faculty do, nor attend departmental meetings. Many universities do not have in-person orientations for new adjunct faculty employees and, if they do, only a small number of adjuncts can attend. They are not only unaware of who the other adjunct faculty are, they are unaware of how many of the instructional faculty are adjuncts. That is, until they organize a union.

Anderson points out that all communities larger than a small village are, in fact, imagined. An American, in Anderson's example, will never meet nor know *every* other American, and has no idea what they are all doing at any given time. Nevertheless, each one of us "has complete confidence in their steady, anonymous, simultaneous activity."[1] An imagined community is socially constructed and can be created, destroyed, or manipulated for political and economic reasons. As such, imagined communities constantly change and evolve. Anderson shows how the rise of print-capitalism and newspaper reading from the eighteenth century "made it possible for rapidly growing numbers of people to think about themselves, and to relate to others, in profoundly new ways."[2] He uses the example of "men" simultaneously reading the morning newspaper and being "well aware that the ceremony he performs is being replicated simultaneously by thousands (or millions) of others of whose existence he is confident, yet of whose identity he has not the slightest notion."[3]

Contingent academic workers do not have a coffee pot around which they can gather to build their community and their union. This is not the reality for adjunct faculty, nor a reality of twenty-first-century urban life. In this essay, I show how an imagined community of academic workers unionized with SEIU Local 500 grew and changed in a constantly evolving effort to gain collective power and contest the exploitative structures of their industry. Organizing and building a strong member-led union among the most marginalized and disconnected faculty in academia demanded the creation of an imagined community. However, constructing that community presented a fundamental challenge. In building an imagined community of adjunct faculty, we needed to make our colleagues aware of their exploited position; however, to succeed as a union, our imagined community had to be empowered to fight for change. We asked people simultaneously to fully imagine the extent of their disempowerment in the university system while also convincing them that they could wield effective power—through collective action.

In most other workplaces outside the academy, reluctance to unionize comes largely from a place of fear—fear of losing your job or losing perks you may have (or perceive yourself to have) over others in the workplace. Adjunct and contingent faculty often refuse to acknowledge the very circumstances of exploitation that lead to a unionization effort in the first place. I believe that much of the hesitation among adjuncts to support unionization in our initial efforts came from the cognitive dissonance that arose from simultaneously embodying conflicting social statuses—the high status of holding a PhD or other higher educational degree and the low status of being a low-waged worker. One adjunct teaching late at night burst into tears when she told us she could not afford a taxi home if she missed the bus. The code of meritocracy in academia shames contingent faculty into feeling that they are just not good enough to have made it. So, being unable to afford a taxi home becomes internalized as a sign of personal failure. This is a crucial falsehood in the dominant ideology of the academic industry, and one our reimagined community must constantly challenge and debunk.[4] Viewing teaching in a prestigious university as work, not a marker of status, was essential to moving people beyond their hesitation to act. From the earliest days of organizing at GW, we knew that we should organize all the adjunct faculty in the city into one union. We called ourselves the "Coalition of Academic Labor," deliberately using the term "labor" to emphasize teaching as work, not a position of prestige.

At George Washington University we insisted on calling ourselves "part-time faculty," rather than adjuncts.[5] The term allowed us to forefront both the *equity* of the work we did with that of "full-time" faculty and the *inequity* of our compensation and working conditions. There is a pay and job disparity between faculty who teach "full-time" and faculty who teach "part-time." But students pay the same tuition to take a course regardless of who teaches it, while the cost of hiring part-time faculty to teach a course can be one-fourth or less than the cost to hire a full-time faculty member to teach that same course. That we were "adjunct" or an addendum to the curriculum and the mission of the university was an outdated assumption. "Part-time faculty" also implied that the difference between us and the full-time faculty was one of degree (we taught fewer courses, did not receive support for our research and scholarship, and had no benefits) rather than one of kind. "Part-time faculty" suggested that the value of our teaching was equal to that of the full-time faculty and that, by extension, we should be equally compensated for our teaching.

The disparity between part-time and full-time faculty is only one of the inequities that exist in the higher education teaching world. Scholar and activist Pablo Eisenberg wrote that "the caste system in higher education is alive and well."[6] The professoriate is a stratified system of academic labor with multiple layers of decreasing value—from tenured faculty, the highest paid and highest status faculty, through layers of non-tenured full-time faculty (with contracts of varied lengths), through regular part-time faculty, to part-time faculty paid by the course. Adjuncts sit at the bottom of the higher education teaching ladder, although "ladder" may be a faulty metaphor since most adjunct faculty find it impossible to climb. Additionally, institutions themselves are stratified in terms of academic labor—private and public universities, four-year colleges, community colleges, and for-profit colleges, with the last paying their part-time faculty the least.

The existence of these hierarchies within academia meant that any successful organizing had to take them into account. Thus, different challenges and opportunities emerged among various contingent groups within the same institution as well as at different types of institutions. Fairly consistent through these varied efforts, however, and especially during the earliest unionization campaigns, was a general lack of support from tenured/tenure-track faculty, a result of their own lack of labor organization as well as pressure from university leaders and administrators. Organizing among community college adjuncts (Montgomery College in Maryland, and ongoing organizing at the Community College of Baltimore County, Anne Arundel Community College, Prince George's Community College, and Howard Community College) began with a stronger sense of community, as these academic workers were more likely to know or encounter each other than adjuncts at four-year universities. Adjuncts at Montgomery College are permitted to teach more courses per semester than those at four-year universities and they spend more time on campus since they are invited to and attend faculty meetings and often live in the same neighborhoods. Campus layout also provides opportunities for adjunct faculty in community colleges to meet each other. A faculty dining room at Montgomery College is open to adjuncts, where they can bring a sandwich and meet other faculty. At GW and Georgetown, faculty-only dining occurs at a university or faculty club where you must purchase a pricey meal.

In the first few years of organizing adjunct faculty in DC, we tried to create an imagined community among adjuncts that built on their common experience as exploited labor but that was also empowering. We did this partly by raising awareness and knowledge about the structural and economic circumstances in which we found ourselves. To construct an imagined community of adjunct faculty we had to connect to each other around the specifics of our exploitation and, for many of us, around how the system that trained and produced us had perpetrated a bait and switch. This meant shifting many adjuncts away from a self-conception that they were part of one imagined community—"The Faculty" in a meritocratic academia—and toward another—the bottom layer of a stratified profession where employers control both the labor supply and the demand for that labor.

To encourage such a transformation among adjunct faculty we had to develop new organizing tactics. The traditional organizing conversation involves "agitating on the issues." That is, talking to a person about the working conditions they are unhappy with, then moving them from individual anger to collective action through unionization in order to change those conditions. Organizing connects the personal to the structural through solidarity with others, which in traditional organizing begins by reaching someone chiefly on an emotional level. Early in the GW campaign, however, we found that this approach backfired among some adjunct faculty who became angry and defensive if we raised the subject of low wages, marginalization, and lack of respect. The very subjects that traditional organizing depended on to spur people to collective action caused some adjuncts to oppose unionization. Others continued to embrace the myth of meritocracy, claiming that they were on the brink of getting a full-time position. Others considered leaving the profession altogether to pursue a career elsewhere. These adjuncts saw themselves as part of an imagined community that did not, in fact, include them. In the imagined community of the Meritocratic Professoriate, low pay, insecurity, and lack of respect were indicative of individual failure. To build support for unionization we had to reimagine a community where adjuncts could accept and then challenge their exploitation as structural, not personal.

We began constructing an imagined community of contingent faculty around research on the structural changes within academia and the move, since the 1970s, toward an overreliance on contingent faculty. The use of "big picture" research helped those adjunct faculty reluctant to acknowledge their own positioning in an exploitative system to embrace unionization and reimagine themselves as part of a community that was coming together to challenge that system. We produced materials that laid out the facts of academic employment in individual institutions, as well as in higher education nationally. These fact sheets presented information about the university budget, executive salaries, and number of adjunct faculty teaching in a given semester, along with national figures on the use of contingent faculty. Very few adjunct faculty knew how little of the university's budget went toward paying them, or indeed how heavily the university relied on contingent academic labor. We showed that in the DC area the cost of employing adjunct faculty constituted around 4 percent of the budget for instruction and 1.5 percent of the revenue generated from tuition and fees, while adjuncts taught anywhere from 30 to 50 percent of the classes. In one university, we calculated that the annual salaries of the 13 highest paid executives equaled those of 650 adjuncts.

We also used data to show that institutions of higher education controlled both the supply and the demand of labor in their industry. As universities cut full-time faculty lines and reduced the number of tenure-track positions, they also produced the PhD and MA degree recipients that filled the adjunct labor pool. In the DC area, with such a high concentration of universities and such a rich source of potential adjunct faculty, institutions had little incentive to offer better pay—until unionization came along. An administrator from one prominent university told us in a bargaining session when we were arguing for higher rates per course, "if you don't want to teach for those rates, there are nine people standing behind you who will and who we are happy to hire." Instead, an imagined community of adjuncts organized and applied pressure on the administration, so that now the minimum pay rate for a 3-credit course in that institution is 65 percent higher than it was before unionization! We don't control how many PhDs and MAs are produced, nor what decisions are made regarding whether teaching positions are full-time, part-time, or tenure-track. However, the imagined community of unionized adjunct faculty is, in the long-term, having a "reverse snowball effect" on academic labor practices. As union contracts raise compensation and increase employment stability, the "pool" of underemployed adjuncts becomes less cheap and less disposable, and institutions of higher education have less of a disincentive to create full-time regular positions.

We also faced the "bandwagon effect" at the beginning of each campaign—adjuncts preferred to see what others in their departments wanted to do before they would act. But, when asked if they knew other adjuncts or spent time with other adjuncts, the answer was often "no." The building block of union organizing is the one-on-one, colleague-to-colleague conversation, which is extremely difficult to facilitate among adjuncts. Our challenge was to replicate the power of this one-on-one connection by constructing an imagined community in the pre–social media era. At GW, we did this by creating a large full-color union authorization card with photographs of activists in the campaign and quotes about why we wanted our union. We also spoke up in the student newspaper and at rallies on campus. This tactic contravened a traditional "stealth campaign" used for instance by the United Auto Workers when they trained adjunct organizers. (At GW, we spent the 2002–03 academic year organizing with UAW, before affiliating with SEIU in fall 2003.) The "stealth campaign" emphasized constructing a network of behind-the-scenes person-to-person contacts until the majority of workers supported the union. In contrast, an imagined community needs a public face so that members can be aware of what Anderson calls the "steady, anonymous, simultaneous activity" of their peers.[7]

Support from student groups on campus helped adjuncts form their imagined community, even though students themselves were not part of that community. Student support was an important element in many of our successful campaigns. Progressive student groups at GW, American University, Georgetown, Goucher College, and McDaniel College supported our campaigns in the form of events, petitions, flash mobs, videos, and more. These became visible reminders for adjuncts of the existence of their imagined community. Student labor groups initially worried that increased pay and benefits for adjunct faculty would prompt tuition increases at already expensive private universities. Our research about how administrators spent their tuition dollars, though, helped alleviate these concerns. Information on executive salaries, revenues, and spending clarified that adjunct and other faculty salaries were not the cause of rising tuition.

Support from student groups helped us move understandably reluctant adjuncts—the most precarious faculty on campus—to get involved, sign a union authorization card, or publicly support a union. Visible and active student support also pressured administrators to not fight unionization, though many did use tuition revenue to pay union-busting law firms. When the adjuncts chose unionization, the universities hired more labor-friendly law firms. Georgetown University was unique in issuing a letter of neutrality to their campus community when adjuncts embarked on an effort to organize a union, a decision compelled by their Just Employment Policy, itself a result of earlier student activism (including a week-long hunger strike in 2005). As Nicholas Wertsch and Joseph McCartin point out, Georgetown University was also unique at the time in not contesting the NLRB's jurisdiction over a religious institution of higher education.[8] Nevertheless, organizing adjunct faculty at Georgetown was more like organizing other institutions than it was different. Adjuncts at Georgetown told us they felt marginalized, disconnected, underappreciated, and lacking in community, just as we heard from adjuncts in other institutions. Wertsch and McCartin point out that it was unusual for a union to target "the highest paying employer early in a multiemployer organizing campaign, for that employer can most easily dismiss union demands by arguing that it is already paying above market rate."[9] However, the research we shared with the adjuncts at Georgetown showed that the budget and allocation of resources at Georgetown University mirrored those of other universities—pay for adjuncts constituted a small percentage of spending on instruction even though they comprised a large percentage of the faculty. Adjuncts at Georgetown, as in every other institution we have organized, also fundamentally rejected the idea that their compensation be judged on market rates. Rather, they understood that the value of their teaching and scholarship should be measured against other faculty teaching at Georgetown and not against that of adjunct faculty in other institutions.

Employer Responses and the Anti-Union Playbook

In the first few organizing campaigns, especially at GW, the university did not take us too seriously and, I believe, underestimated the animus with which many adjuncts viewed the administration. The assumption that adjunct faculty feel privileged to teach at prestigious universities and "get a line on their CV" was already outdated in 2002, but undergirded the employer response in our early campaigns. As we constructed an imagined community of academic workers increasingly aware of and fighting against their low-level position in an oppressive hierarchy, university administrations remained mired in the myth of meritocracy. This worked to our advantage.

In 2012, I heard a dean from the University of Maryland comment on National Public Radio that adjunct faculty should be happy to teach for free. Before adjuncts started organizing in large numbers in the 2000s, before the higher ed press began taking an interest in the burgeoning movement, and before social media exploded with contingent faculty issues, university administrations rested on decades-old assumptions about "spousal hires," "white glove academics," and adjunct faculty as professional practitioners from outside academia. We heard often from administrations in the first few rounds of contract negotiations that the majority of adjunct faculty have other jobs and do not depend on the income they earn from teaching. No institution, however, could provide evidence to support this assumption. Our internal estimates suggested that more than half of the adjunct faculty we represented were "full-time part-timers" who would accept a full-time academic job if it was available. Yet we also found strong support from among the adjunct faculty who did not depend on teaching as their primary source of income. Many of these "avocationalists" keenly felt a lack of respect and exclusion from the institutions in which they taught. They also shared with the "vocational" adjuncts a concern about job security and a desire to have more certainty around regular teaching appointments. What united vocationalists and avocationalists was a love of teaching and a desire to shape young minds.

I consider this love of teaching both a blessing and a curse when organizing academic unions. On the one hand, you have a group of workers already committed to social change through critical thinking and their teaching. On the other hand, you have workers who so love their work (though not the working conditions) that they fear rocking the boat and potentially jeopardizing that work.[10]

In the early days of our organizing, the institutions, ironically, often underestimated the ability of their own faculty to decode the thinly veiled anti-union messages coming from their employers. Administrators and their anti-union law firms seemed to forget that faculty contextualize and deconstruct texts for a living. In one institution, the employer directed department chairs to send an email to adjunct faculty discouraging them from unionization. However, because the department chairs all used the same language in their email, adjuncts felt insulted by the transparent "boilerplate" anti-union message.

Employers inclined to launch an anti-union campaign against adjunct faculty faced similar changes to those union organizers confronted—a dispersed, marginalized workforce who did not know each other and who had few or no opportunities to meet one another, or other faculty or staff. Thus, traditional methods of fighting unionization—such as holding "captive audience" meetings—were not possible.

Instead, in most instances they resorted, often with assistance from an anti-union law firm, to a rhetorical campaign designed to dissuade support for the union.

The "playbook" used by university-hired anti-union law firms, such as Krupin O'Brien, Epstein Becker Green, and Jackson Lewis, cautiously tried to dissuade the faculty from unionization while avoiding the appearance that the administration was violating either the law or academic freedom and free speech. The playbook included multiple elements: (1) maintain the appearance of consistency with the university's liberal values by saying that it is not anti-union but simply asking the adjunct faculty to consider whether *this* union really is the right fit; (2) appeal to professional snobbery by emphasizing how SEIU, a union founded by janitors, cannot possibly represent academics; (3) portray "the union" as an interfering third party and interloper on campus that knows nothing about higher education and will, specifically, undermine the faculty/student relationship and faculty-to-faculty collegiality; (4) imply that the university is surprised and mildly offended that the adjuncts did not come to the administration directly to address their concerns; (5) make a "give us a chance to address your issues" pitch; and (6) claim that unionization will cause the university massive financial distress and result in fewer courses for adjuncts to teach.

In addition, administrators painted organizers as harassing or threating adjuncts. Adopting a stance as protectors of faculty and academic values, administrators issued statements that adjuncts did not have to talk to organizers and that they were free to complain if they felt harassed. Because it was difficult for administrators on self-proclaimed "liberal" campuses to take a stance against employee "free speech" rights, they focused, instead, on the right *not* to speak to organizers.

Much of this anti-union messaging failed because it exposed the hypocrisy and ironies at the heart of academic labor.[11] Through education about university budgets, adjuncts knew that their teaching was a small part of the overall budget, so claiming that unionization would result in fewer classes made no logical sense. Also, someone had to teach the increasing number of students as enrollments grew. And since universities did not offer cut-rate tuition for courses taught by adjunct faculty, adjuncts understood that their labor remained cost effective for the institutions.[12] Further, implying that "the union" would interfere with the student/faculty relationship did not resonate with adjuncts who felt marginalized from and unsupported in their teaching by departments and the institution as a whole.

The Evolving Vision of the Metro-Strategy

Adjunct faculty at universities in the DC area are now perhaps the most densely organized contingent faculty in any city in the country. From the beginning we debated the opportunities that such density could bring. We have imagined creating citywide contract standards, a hiring hall, professional development support, curriculum commons, peer-to-peer evaluation, and engaging with a nationwide network of contingent faculty.

However, as we continue to struggle to push institutions of higher education to redistribute resources to their contingent faculty (resources the faculty themselves produce in tuition-reliant institutions), to offer pay equitable to that earned by full-time faculty, to extend benefits, job stability, and career advancement, there is still much work to do. To use Joe Berry's *Reclaiming the Ivory Tower* as a mirror, looking back we concentrated our considerable energies and limited resources on an "outside strategy"—creating imagined communities of contingent faculty pushing for change through their unions.[13] We need a more intentional galvanized "outside strategy" as well as a stronger "inside strategy" built on solidarity among all campus employees and supportive student groups. Uniting all adjunct faculty under a citywide contract is less pressing than uniting all workers on campus. We must reclaim the definition of academic labor to include everyone who exchanges their labor for wages on a university or college campus. The inside groups—faculty senate, student government, graduate student associations, various progressive student groups (which I consider "inside/outside" groups)—must work in tandem with unionized and non-unionized workers on campus to raise the standards of working conditions for all. Joining the dots that are adjunct faculty is just the first imagined community we need to create. There is much more power to leverage by creating unified coalitions of the "outside" groups—labor unions, community allies, not-yet-unionized worker associations, and so forth, with the "inside" groups.[14]

While we need a national network, more importantly, we need a coalition on each campus (if campus is not itself an outdated concept or a new type of imagined community). These campus coalitions must be grassroots efforts, connecting actual workers with students and allies. The universities and colleges in the DC area where SEIU Local 500 represents contingent academic workers contain other progressive (imagined) communities—food service and custodial worker unions, staff associations, full-time faculty associations, faculty governance groups, student governance groups, student political groups, and so forth. I envisage these groups campaigning together for just working conditions on campus, and for social and racial justice in the community. I envisage a citywide University Labor Council that engages in legislative and policy advocacy and public education on behalf of the campus coalitions that would comprise it, as a counterpart to the existing employer advocacy association—The Consortium of Universities of the Washington Metropolitan Area.

"Striketober," the nationwide wave of strikes and concerted action in late 2021, showed that American workers are willing to be more militant than they have been in decades, a willingness to take action I have also seen intensify among academic laborers. Students, both undergraduate and graduate, having nothing to lose except a lifetime of debt, are also much more engaged. The campus quad (real or imagined) is now fertile ground for the kind of coalition building and strategic solidarity that can create systemic change.

Notes

1. Benedict Anderson, *Imagined Communities: Reflections on the Origin and Spread of Nationalism* (New York: Verso, 1983), 26.

2. Ibid., 38.

3. Ibid., 35.

4. About five years ago I attended the annual meeting of the American Anthropological Association. It became clear to me that many of the newly minted PhDs in the field had no idea what the job prospects were for tenure-track positions. I went to a workshop where graduates on the academic job market were raising concerns about discrimination in hiring without being aware that 75 percent of the teaching positions in higher education were contingent, non-tenure-track positions (52 percent of those part-time/adjunct positions).

5. Despite our practice at GW, I have used the term "adjunct" throughout this essay, a word frequently used to designate part-time contingent faculty and better understood than "part-time faculty."

6. Pablo Eisenberg, "The Caste System in Higher Education," *HuffPost,* September 4, 2012, https://www.huffpost.com/entry/caste-system-higher-education_b_1853917.

7. Anderson, *Imagined Communities*, 26.

8. Nicholas M. Wertsch and Joseph A. McCartin, "A Just Employment Approach to Adjunct Unionization: The Georgetown Model," in *Professors in the Gig Economy: Unionizing Adjunct Faculty in America*, ed. Kim Tolley (Baltimore: Johns Hopkins University Press, 2018), 87–103.

9. Ibid.

10. See also Maria Maisto's essay in this collection.

11. The firm Jackson Lewis wrote a playbook on how to prevent unionization: Jackson Lewis, *Winning NLRB Elections: Avoiding Unionization through Preventive Employee Relations Programs* (Chicago: CCH: 1997).

12. We used to tell student activists that they should be demanding their "adjunct discount."

13. Joe Berry, *Reclaiming the Ivory Tower: Organizing Adjuncts to Change Higher Education* (New York: Monthly Review Press, 2005).

14. An example (unfortunately, stymied by the global pandemic of 2020 and 2021) was an effort at GW, driven by the Progressive Student Union and supported by a burgeoning coalition of labor unions and non-organized faculty and staff associations, to demand a $20 per hour minimum wage for all campus workers.

CHAPTER 17

THE "ARMY OF TEMPS" IN THE HOUSE OF LABOR

How California's Public Sector Labor Unions Struggle
to Resist the Deprofessionalization of College Teachers

TREVOR GRIFFEY

While the gig economy is partly a result of decades of neoliberal union-busting and the disciplining and demoralization of the working class, contingent workers aren't just found in the world outside of labor unions—they are increasingly found within labor unions as well. In higher education, the house of labor in the United States represents what the American Federation of Teachers (AFT) has called an "army of temps."[1] According to data from the National Center for the Study of Collective Bargaining in Higher Education and the Professions, 57 percent of all instructional faculty represented by labor unions in 2012 (roughly 159,000 college teachers) were ineligible for tenure.[2] And for too many of these temporary workers, union representation alone has been insufficient to turn poverty wages into living wages or to turn casual gigs into professional full-time jobs.

Studying the experience of temporary instructors in California's public colleges and universities can help explain why faculty labor organizing has so far produced limited and often unsatisfying results for its non-tenure-track members. Nearly all of California's public higher education faculty are represented by labor unions, yet most of its undergraduate courses are still taught by contingent instructors. Their failure to effectively resist deprofessionalization is structural. It reflects the variability and insufficiency of public funding for higher education, which limits the ability of public sector unions to bargain for salary and benefits parity between temporary and permanent teachers. And it reflects the insufficient solidarity between faculty who are eligible for tenure and those who are not, which limits all faculty's power to resist their own deprofessionalization and exploitation. My analysis, which recognizes structural constraints on faculty labor union power, is meant to improve and support contemporary faculty labor organizing, which is currently experiencing a resurgence following the Supreme Court decision in *Janus v. AFSCME* in 2018.

Faculty Contingency and Higher Education Underfunding in California

Because the state of California manages the largest public higher education system in the United States, it provides an important site for evaluating the organizing challenges faced by faculty labor unions. California is famous for its higher education "Master Plan," which formally organized the state's colleges and universities into three tiers in the early 1960s: community colleges, teaching colleges (the California State University [CSU] system), and research universities (the University

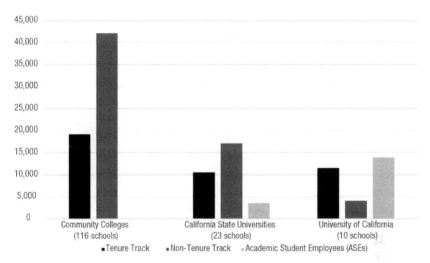

Figure 17.1. Instructional Faculty and Academic Student Employees in California Public Higher Education by Headcount, Fall 2019
Note: ASE data from UCs is from 2017, not 2019—the last publicly available.
Sources: On community college faculty, see California Community College Chancellor's Office, "Faculty & Staff Demographics Report," Management Information Systems Data Mart, accessed May 5, 2020, https://datamart.cccco.edu/Faculty-Staff/Staff_Demo.aspx. On CSU faculty, see "Employee Profile: Previous Years' Reports," California State University, accessed May 5, 2020, https://www2 .calstate.edu/csu-system/faculty-staff/employee-profile/Pages/past-reports.aspx. On UC faculty, see University of California Infocenter, "UC Employee Headcount," University of California, accessed May 5, 2020, https://www.universityofcalifornia.edu/infocenter/uc-employee-headcount. On the number of ASEs in the UC system, see UCNet: Union Represented Employees, "About the Academic Student Employees Unit," University of California, accessed January 2, 2021, https://ucnet.universityof california.edu/labor/bargaining-units/bx/about.html.

of California [UC] system). This plan, with its embrace of the concept of a "multi-versity," became a model for the development of complex, public higher education systems around world.[3] In the fall of 2019, California's 149 public higher education schools employed over 100,000 instructors and academic student employees who teach, grade, or tutor over 2.5 million students per year (figure 17.1). About two thirds of these instructors and academic student employees are temps who are ineligible for tenure.

Although California's reliance upon temporary college instructors is not unique, the severity of its laws that limit state and local government tax authority, and the expansive growth of its carceral state, help explain how a state so well known for, and proud of, its public higher education system became increasingly reliant upon low-wage temps for college instructors, graders, and tutors. Anti-tax Republicans controlled the California governor's office for thirty-one of the forty-four years between 1966 (when Ronald Reagan was first elected) and 2010 (when Arnold Schwarzenegger left office). To safeguard against democratic governance during years when they were not in power, anti-tax activists used the passage of Proposition 13 in 1978 to make substantially raising taxes or creating new taxes in California almost impossible. Proposition 13 is most well known for capping annual property tax increases at 2 percent per year and 1 percent of a property's assessed value. But it also amended the state constitution to require a two-thirds vote of the California state legislature to pass a budget or to increase taxes, and a two-thirds vote of the electorate to pass new taxes by ballot initiative. To this day, even with the Republican party having fallen into near-irrelevancy at the statewide level in the past decade, the California legislature cannot pass a tax increase without a two-thirds vote of both chambers. The only way for California voters to approve a tax increase with a simple majority vote is to amend the state constitution to pass taxes that expire after a certain number of years.

As California voters severely limited the ability of their state government to spend more money, they massively expanded its policing functions. "Tough on crime" laws enacted between the 1970s and 1990s established high mandatory minimum sentences for a wide range of consensual, nonviolent offenses, especially related to the "war on drugs." The creation and enforcement of these laws focused policing on disproportionately nonwhite communities with high structural unemployment that were experiencing the brunt of economic downturns in the 1970s and 1980s—communities that Proposition 13 effectively blocked from receiving additional social services and economic support. One result was that California became a pioneer in the development of mass incarceration, as its prison population grew from 21,300 in 1978 to 161,500 in 2000.[4] At the same time, Proposition 13's limitation on new taxes all but ensured that funding for the mass incarceration of people arrested in California as part of the war on drugs during this time would come at the expense of the state's other services.

Pitting the development of the carceral state against the maintenance of the California master plan for education meant that even during years when the state government experienced budget windfalls, demands for new revenue for law enforcement and corrections limited politicians' ability to increase funding for schools. Between 1976 and 2008, California politicians reduced funding for the CSUs and UCs from 18 percent to 11.1 percent of the general fund, while increasing the state's corrections and rehabilitation spending from 3 percent to 10.7 percent (see figures 17.2a and 17.2b).[5] So even as full-time equivalent student enrollment increased by 53 percent in the UCs and 93 percent in the CSUs between 1980 and 2014, funding for these systems declined by 13 percent.[6]

The growing cost of healthcare in the United States, combined with state governments' ambitious attempts to extend health insurance to residents who otherwise might not be able to afford it, have also constrained the resources available for spending on public higher education. In her book *Degrees of Inequality*, the sociologist Suzanne Mettler estimates that per capita state government spending on Medicare grew by 400 percent between 1980 and 2010 in real dollars, while higher education spending remained relatively constant and sometimes declined.[7] Similar trends occurred in California, where healthcare spending grew from 10.6 percent of the state budget in 2000 to 19 percent in 2017.[8] As Mettler points out, this spending, though laudable, is often considered mandatory in a way that can constrain higher education spending and make it more susceptible to cuts during recessions.

Although higher education proponents had long bemoaned the effects of the state's austerity politics on California's Master Plan, the severity of budget cuts and corresponding tuition increases in 2008–2011 finally provoked more mainstream awareness of the problem. This discussion took the form of journalistic exposés and academic reports that declared the famed California Master Plan all but dead, with titles including "The Dream Is Over," "From Chaos to Order and Back Again?," "From Master Plan to No Plan," and "From Master Plan to Mediocrity."[9] The California Faculty Association has also rightly pointed out that the per-capita defunding of public higher education has coincided with California's student body becoming more diverse, thus making the need for more funding a racial justice issue.[10]

There is a direct and clear connection between the systematic underfunding of public higher education and school administrators' growing reliance upon temporary and low-wage staff and faculty. Inflexible state tax systems, without offsets from federal deficit spending to cover revenue shortfalls, bring capitalism's boom-bust cycles straight into government's provision of services, including education. Budget cuts encourage higher education administrators to raise new revenue through tuition, fees, and services (such as housing, food, parking, and athletic facilities), making them more dependent upon enrollment to cover costs. This unpredictability in long-term budgeting provides an economic incentive for

Percent Change in Enrollment and Direct General Fund Spending Since 1981–82

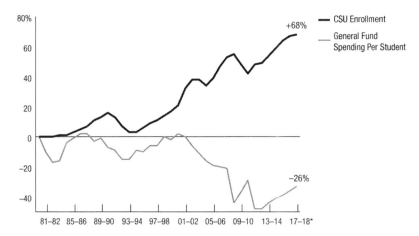

Figure 17.2a. Even as CSU Enrollment Has Increased, State General Fund Support Has Declined
* Estimated.
Note: Figures reflect "full-time equivalent" enrollment, which accounts for credits taken by each student relative to a full-time course load. Expenditures are inflation-adjusted and exclude indirect state funding for the CSU attributable to Cal Grant tuition and fee payments.
Source: California State University and Department of Finance

administrators to hire "just-in-time professors" who can be hired or fired at the last minute to accommodate changes in enrollment or government funding, whether or not they are paid less or receive fewer health or retirement benefits.[11]

Just about every campaign to reform Proposition 13 in California has been led by or strongly supported by teachers' unions. Their years of activism led to the passage of Proposition 98 in 1988, which established minimum funding levels for K–12 and community colleges based on student enrollment. They led the campaign to pass Proposition 38 in 2000, which reduced the threshold for passage of local school bonds (for K–12 and community colleges) from 67 to 55 percent. Teachers' unions supported Proposition 25 in 2010, which reduced the vote required for the state legislature to pass a budget from two thirds to a simple majority. They were also leaders in the creation and passage of Proposition 30 in 2012, which increased taxes to fund K–12 and community college schools and healthcare after the devastating cuts during the previous four years, and whose taxes were renewed in 2016. And they ran the campaign for Proposition 15 in 2020, which would have eliminated Proposition 13's cap on commercial real estate taxes, but which was unfortunately rejected by voters.

Largely unable to roll back Proposition 13, and having not significantly organized against the carceral state or for federally funded universal healthcare, California's

Percent Change in Enrollment and Direct General Fund Spending Since 1981–82

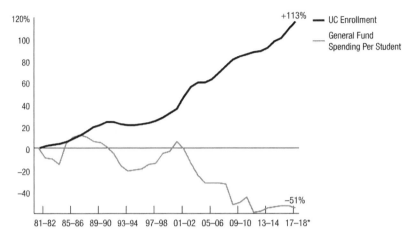

Figure 17.2b. Even as UC Enrollment Has Increased, State General Fund Support Has Declined
* Estimated.
Note: Figures reflect "full-time equivalent" enrollment, which accounts for credits taken by each student relative to a full-time course load. Expenditures are inflation-adjusted and exclude indirect state funding for the UC attributable to Cal Grant tuition and fee payments.
Source: Department of Finance and the University of California
Sources: Amy Rose, "Data Hit: Even as CSU Enrollment Has Increased, State General Fund Support Has Declined," and "Data Hit: Even as UC Enrollment Has Increased, State General Fund Support Has Declined," California Budget & Policy Center (blog), May 2018, accessed January 3, 2021, https:// calbudgetcenter.org/wp-content/uploads/Data-Hit_Even-as-CSU-Enrollment-Has-Increased-State -General-Fund-Support-Has-Declined.pdf; https://calbudgetcenter.org/app/uploads/Data-Hit_Even -as-UC-Enrollment-Has-Increased-State-General-Fund-Support-Has-Declined.pdf.

faculty unions have been at a fundamental disadvantage when trying to use collective bargaining to resist or ameliorate the state's reliance upon low-wage, temporary college teachers.

Faculty Unions: Modest Reforms in a Degraded Environment

Of California's more than 100,000 public college and university instructors and academic student employees, only the UC's roughly 11,000 tenure-track faculty are not represented by a labor union. In 2012, 27 percent of all instructional faculty in the United States represented by labor unions worked in California's public colleges and universities.[12] In fall of 2019, most college faculty teaching at public colleges and universities in California were temps: roughly 40,000 part-time lecturers teaching at 115 community colleges located in 72 districts, over 14,000 part-time and 2,500 full-time lecturers teaching at 23 different CSU campuses, and well over 4,000 non-senate faculty teaching in the 10 UC schools (see figure 17.1). The unions that represent these faculty have primarily been affiliated with the NEA or AFT, though a small number in the community colleges are independent or affiliated with other unions like UPTE-CWA. These unions in general, and the California Faculty Association (CFA) and University Council–American Federation of Teachers (UC-AFT) in particular, have pioneered reforms to create job stability and career pathways for non-tenure-track instructors. Their main accomplishments so far relate to the creation of seniority systems and pay scales for some longtime non-tenure-track faculty, without fundamentally altering the high turnover and low wages that define the experience of the majority of faculty.

Each of California's three public higher education systems has a unique history of faculty resistance to and accommodation of the decline of tenure, based on differences in faculty organization and funding for their schools. Throughout the system, the normalization of inequality between faculty tiers has undermined the organizing necessary for faculty to resist financial austerity and instability.

COMMUNITY COLLEGE PART-TIME FACULTY

The lowest paid and most precarious teachers in the California system are part-time faculty in community colleges. They are ineligible for tenure and teach at least 45 percent of all classes in these institutions. Except for a few wealthy school districts like Santa Monica College and the College of Marin, California's community colleges provide most of what administrators call "temporary academic" employees with starting salaries between $2,000 and $3,500 per sixteen-week course. Since 2008, their workload has been capped by state law at three courses per campus per term, which compels a large minority of instructors to teach at multiple campuses to make ends meet. Paid an hourly wage for time in the classroom, many California community college faculty are not paid to hold office hours and may not even be provided with shared office space. Like their CSU colleagues (and some teach at both), it is common for non-tenure-track instructors in the California community college system to teach 200–300 students per term. But unlike CSU faculty, those community college faculty who earn a living as "freeway fliers" are more likely to teach closer to eight, nine, or even ten classes per term and still may have to pay for their health insurance out-of-pocket. A report by UPTE-CWA Local 9119 in 2012 estimated that only about 17 percent of non-tenure-track faculty in California's community college system had health benefits provided by their employer, and that their average annual salary per campus was $14,381.[13]

The experience of the roughly 19,000 tenure-track faculty in California's community college system could not be more different than that of their more than 40,000 non-tenure-track colleagues. Since 1961, state law has required that "50 percent of the district's current expense of education" must go toward "payment of salaries of classroom instructors."[14] But most unions representing community college faculty are dominated by tenure-track faculty and have not used spending increases to bargain for substantially increased tenure density or to reduce the wage gap between part-time and full-time faculty. Instead, in good times and bad, the lion's share of government spending on instructor salaries and benefits goes to the 30 percent of faculty with full-time status. In 2012, the average tenure-track community college instructor earned about $85,897 per year, which was substantially higher than the $73,367 that tenure-track instructors in the CSU earned.[15] This is between double and triple what their non-tenure-track colleagues earn per course, often to teach the very same classes. And it does not include the "overload" of summer teaching through which tenure-track instructors can earn an additional $10,000 or more, which can push many full-time community college faculty salaries above $100,000 per year.

State legislators have passed laws to prevent extreme exploitation and inequality among college faculty, but community colleges have subverted these legislative efforts and union contracts have codified this subversion. In 1988, community college instructors successfully convinced the California State Legislature to both affirm the policy that "at least 75 percent of the hours of credit instruction in the California Community Colleges, as a system, should be taught by full-time instructors" and provide funding to assist California's community college school districts with meeting that goal. However, this goal has never been met.[16]

The few bright spots for part-time faculty teaching in California's community college system have been achieved through union activism. In 1989, activists with AFT Local 2121 in the San Francisco Community College system secured a state court victory that made non-tenure-track instructors throughout California eligible for unemployment benefits between terms.[17] Until recently, this made California one of only two states in the United States that provided unemployment benefits to lecturers without multiyear teaching contracts. For those lecturers who know about this ruling and take advantage of it, unemployment insurance serves as an important supplement to income, making the poverty wages they earn during the school year slightly more manageable. And in 2016, faculty unions successfully lobbied the California State Legislature to require that all community college districts bargain "re-employment preferences for part-time, temporary faculty," though it has taken years to create these various forms of seniority for each school district and many are still inadequate.[18]

The appeal of using legislation to resist and reverse the deprofessionalization of community college teachers is that doing so in California would avoid the need to negotiate contracts for all 116 schools in 73 different districts on different timelines, which could take at least a decade. But bypassing the collective bargaining process to raise the floor for all part-time faculty at once still requires overcoming substantial resistance. Though lobbying can provide a shortcut to organizing at the district level, higher education administrators tend to oppose bills that could raise the cost of providing an education or reduce their discretionary power as employers. For example, in 2021 the California Community College Chancellor's Office opposed a bill co-sponsored by the CFT that would require all community colleges to move toward pay equity between full-time and part-time faculty, warning that the bill would undermine "local control and locally negotiated collective bargaining agreements." It also complained that "closing the pay equity gap between part- and full-time faculty alone could cost between $300 and $900 million. These are dollars that could be better dedicated to hiring more full-time faculty and developing institutional capacity to support our faculty and staff diversity initiatives."[19] Less than a month later, the Association of Chief Business Officers of the California Community Colleges (which technically lobbies separately from the chancellor's office) revealed the hollowness of administrators' gestures toward increasing tenure density, and lobbied state legislators *against* increasing community college funding by $170 million to hire 2,000 new full-time faculty. Community college administrators, they argued, should not be required to increase faculty tenure density, which they argued could exacerbate "fiscal crises" and result in "reductions in classified staffing or other reductions that may be harmful to student success."[20] California community college administrators also successfully convinced the governor of California to veto a bill in 2021 that would have allowed community college part-time faculty to teach four courses per term instead of three—ostensibly because it might have required that schools provide health benefits to some close-to-full-time instructors.[21]

CALIFORNIA STATE UNIVERSITY LECTURERS

In 2001, following a years-long rank-and-file movement of lecturers in the California Faculty Association to both address the decline of faculty tenure and increase the representation of lecturers in the union, the California State Legislature passed a resolution that encouraged the CSUs to "raise the percentage of tenured and tenure-track faculty to at least 75 percent."[22] At the time, about 43.5 percent of all faculty in the CSUs were on the tenure track.[23] The next year, the CFA signed an historic agreement that provided all full- and part-time lecturers with job security provisions unlike almost anything available to non-tenure-track faculty anywhere in the United States: an "entitlement" to teach the average of the same number of courses taught the previous year; priority hiring before new lecturers are hired; three-year renewable contracts after six years of satisfactory teaching; health benefits if one teaches a minimum of two courses in a semester; salary scales and regular opportunities to move up those scales after a certain number of years teaching; and more. This created what adjunct activist and Central Connecticut

State University instructor Donald W. Rogers called the "gold standard" for non-tenure-track faculty contracts.[24]

The CFA's contract with the CSU has even inspired longtime adjunct activists Joe Berry and Helena Worthen to write *Power Despite Precarity*, which celebrates the CFA and its contract as models for others around the country to aspire to.[25] But what Berry and Worthen don't address in their book is that CSU administrators have undermined faculty union victories by growing on the cheap, which has stymied CFA's attempt to increase tenure density and create parity between tenure track and non-tenure-track faculty.

Although the CSUs substantially boosted tenure-track hiring in the 2000s, that hiring did not significantly increase tenure density because it was offset by growing student enrollment and faculty retirements, departures, and deaths. The 2008 recession halted attempts to raise tenure density. Further, the lecturer salary scale the CFA bargained for was made meaningless by eight years of wage freezes between 2008 and 2016. When the state government began to restore funding to the CSUs, following the passage of Proposition 30 in 2012, CSU administrators aggressively expanded enrollment and non-tenure-track faculty hiring to maximize tuition and fee revenue and to minimize teaching costs.[26] The system saw a net increase of over 4,000 new part-time lecturers and over 1,000 new full-time lecturers, but only 709 new tenure-track instructors, between 2010 and 2017.[27] For the first time in CSU history, the percentage of its faculty on the tenure track dropped below 40 percent in 2014 and has remained there ever since. And because non-tenure-track faculty teach a higher percentage of courses at CSUs, many CSU campuses have even worse tenure densities measured by full-time equivalent (FTE) status than the state's community colleges.

CSU administrators have relied on tenure-track faculty fatalism and demoralization during years of budget austerity to get them to oversee the destruction of their own profession within their very own departments. Departments are promised that by enrolling a greater number of students, they might someday receive authorization to hire a new tenure-track faculty member. To increase the number of students a department teaches, deans encourage department chairs to hire less expensive non-tenure-track faculty to demonstrate demand for a department's courses. The courses that enroll the most students satisfy graduation requirements, so every department is encouraged to maximize enrollment in general education and introductory courses, using lecturers as instructors, and to maximize the class size of those courses. The commitment to eventually phase out non-tenure-track with tenure-track instructors is informal, however, and administrators never grant departments sufficient positions to meet student demand solely with tenure-track instructors. So, in the end, faculty complicity in hiring temp teachers mainly goes unrewarded. At the same time, tenure-track instructors who are expected to teach four courses per semester while managing an army of temps find themselves buried by an avalanche of department and campus service, because there are fewer tenure-track colleagues to participate in shared governance.

Despite the important job security victories secured almost two decades ago, the lived experience of most non-tenure-track faculty in the CSUs is unenviable. Introductory courses and lower-division general education courses (other than writing, languages, and sometimes math) tend to be capped at sixty students per course (up from forty to forty-five two decades ago). Upper-level courses tend to be capped at forty-five students, but sometimes can also be extended to sixty students for general education courses. Because in 2020 lecturers without a PhD earned roughly $4,200 per fifteen-week course, and those with a PhD earned $5,000, the non-tenure-track majority of teachers in the CSUs have to choose between excessive workload or poverty wages, if they are given a choice at all. It is common for both part-time and full-time lecturers to teach four to six courses at a time (five 3-credit courses is considered full-time, six is the maximum allowed), and to teach between 200 and 300 students per term, just so they can earn over $40,000 per year. Some CSU lecturers also teach at local community colleges to supplement their income, pushing their total workload above 120 percent time. This overload in the number of students and courses taught, made necessary by inadequate pay per course and the high cost of living in California, provides lecturers with an incentive to cut corners on course rigor and reduce individualized attention to students to make grading manageable. Faculty poverty and insecurity also provides lecturers with an incentive to accept teaching assignments for which they are minimally or not at all qualified.

Compared to community college part-time faculty, CSU lecturers who survive this systemic exploitation have higher wages, better job security, and more consistent access to healthcare benefits. But these protections secure their participation in a system in which they remain second-class citizens (because they are excluded from most service) and receive unequal pay for unequal work (compared to their tenure-track colleagues).

UNIVERSITY OF CALIFORNIA NON-SENATE FACULTY

The only time that non-senate faculty have made significant gains at the bargaining table with the University of California is when they have gone on strike or threatened to do so. In fall 2002, the University Council–American Federation of Teachers organized a short strike at multiple campuses, which compelled the UC system to prohibit the dismissal and replacement of lecturers without cause prior to their seventh year of teaching. This change disallowed the widespread practice of what the union calls "churning" through temporary lecturers by laying them off prior to their becoming eligible for multiyear "continuing" contracts.[28] Those who make it to continuing status with full-time or close-to-full-time appointments enjoy salaries over $50,000 per year, reasonable workloads, job security, quality health benefits, pensions, and can move up salary scales—effectively turning a precarious gig into a stable career. Continuing status for longtime lecturers has especially benefited those who teach in UC departments that most depend upon non-tenure-track instructors: composition, English language learning, language instruction, math, and some professional schools such as Business, Law, and Education.

The problem with this system, however, is that most lecturers never received the chance to achieve continuing status in the UCs. Department chairs often resist the culture change required to treat lecturers as professionals deserving of respect after having treated them as the teaching equivalent of day laborers. So the practice of laying off faculty before they can achieve some level of job security—while technically a contract violation—remains more common than it should be, including in departments whose chairs consider themselves labor or social justice activists. Even if there were no "churning" of faculty, enduring six years of term-to-term teaching contracts as essentially at-will employees, sometimes without appointments sufficient to qualify for health benefits, has been too torturous a road for most lecturers to endure when there is little certainty that one will eventually receive a continuing appointment. Although lecturers teach 32 percent of all undergraduate credit hours at the UCs, turnover is high.[29] Some of this turnover is natural and uncontroversial, as some departments continue to use lecturers to temporarily replace tenure-track faculty on leave. Some of it is an effect of patronage, as prominent faculty secure temporary, ad hoc, unadvertised appointments for some of their graduate students after they receive their doctoral degrees. But much, if not most, lecturer turnover in the UCs is an effect of their systematic demoralization by their insecure and insufficient appointments.

UC lecturers' wages, though higher per course than those for community college and CSU contingent faculty, are still abysmal given the substantial resources possessed by the institutions where they teach. In 2020, UC lecturer salaries started at a little over $6,000 per ten-week term, with two or three courses considered full-time, and courses often capped at forty to forty-five students (or provided with teaching assistants or graders if higher). But because most UC lecturers do not have full-time appointments, their average salary is less than $20,000 per year, which then pushes them to teach at other campuses to supplement their income. Many lecturers earn less than UC academic student employees per course, a humiliating difference when they are assigned to supervise teaching assistants or graders. In addition, a decades-old clause in the UC-AFT contract still allows the UC to replace even the most senior lecturer with a graduate student instructor at any time, for any reason—though rarely invoked, it indicates how little the UC values teaching experience, and how much it values having a disposable teaching workforce.

Post-*Janus* Organizing

Contrary to many people's expectations, the Supreme Court decision in *Janus v. AFSCME* in 2018 seems to have helped more than hurt public sector labor unions, at least for higher education labor unions in California. The Court's ruling prohibited the collection of service fees from nonmembers, which reduced unions' budgets. But the change was not accompanied by large numbers of union members choosing to cancel their memberships en masse. This ongoing support prevented a feared collapse of union capacity to effectively bargain or enforce contracts. In addition, greater dependence on voluntary dues and less reliance upon involuntary fees has created a financial incentive for public sector unions to pay greater attention to the concerns of their members. Unions that want to maintain their membership levels need to commit to internal organizing, become more transparent (ideally with open bargaining), and create contract campaigns that address the outsourcing, misclassification, and deprofessionalization that all employers use to turn union jobs into non-union gigs.

In California, the need to organize or die has been accompanied by a growing number of activists from the anti–budget austerity campaigns of 2008–2015, led by UAW 2865 (which represents academic student employees in the University of California), completing their graduate programs, finding work as contingent faculty, and becoming leaders of their faculty unions. Two bargaining campaigns in CFT seem to reflect this new militancy on behalf of contingent faculty. First, inspired by the CFA's example in the CSUs, UC-AFT successfully organized a contract campaign from 2019 to 2021 for greater job security for UC lecturers in their first six years of teaching. Two strike authorization votes in 2021 indicated that a supermajority of union members would be willing to strike if UC continued to reject union demands for raises and job security. A two-day strike was called off just hours before it was set to begin on November 17, 2021, after UC met most of UC-AFT's core demands. The new contract provides lecturers with a "1–2–3" contract system in which, after their first year, lecturers will receive a two-year contract, and after that a three-year contract. Each reappointment comes with a 3 percent raise. And, similar to what the CFA bargained for twenty years ago, UC Unit 18 non-senate faculty now must be given priority consideration for teaching new courses before those courses are offered to new hires. Making the victory even sweeter, UC-AFT also bargained for up to 30 percent raises over the next five years.[30] Second, following a ten-year campaign to increase membership and develop solidarity between full-time and part-time faculty, the CFT at Peralta Community College organized a contract campaign that successfully won 100 percent salary parity between part-time and full-time faculty in 2020.[31]

Drawing from the excitement generated by both of these successful campaigns, in 2022 the CFT launched what it has billed as "one of the most robust legislative campaigns ever on behalf of part-time contingent faculty" in California's community colleges.[32] This includes using contract campaign organizing strategies to lobby the State Legislature to require salary parity between part-time and full-time instructors as well as provide health insurance and increased job security for part-time faculty. But even these bills continue the longstanding practice of setting guidelines for bargaining at the district level rather than establishing a higher floor for all. Even if the legislation passes, faculty unions must still invest heavily in contract campaign organizing to prevent money allocated for healthcare from going unused and to prevent districts from defining salary "parity" for part-time faculty as far less than 100 percent of what full-time faculty earn. Consolidating the seventy-three different community college bargaining units or aligning contracts to all expire at the same time could assist with this organizing but would take years to accomplish—years that most adjunct activists simply don't have.

Professional Teaching Standards Require a New Political Economy

Ten years after the Great Recession delegitimized and accelerated the commercialization of higher education, and with schools only recently emerging from the recession produced by public health responses to the COVID-19 pandemic, the need for a new mechanism for stable, robust public funding for higher education in the United States has never been clearer. Teachers' unions in California have been at the front lines of trying to develop such a system. But the undemocratic nature of the region's political economy has made it extremely difficult for unions to overcome the financial pressures that lead school administrators to reduce the quality of public schools, especially those that cater to the state's majority nonwhite, poor, and working-class student body. Collective bargaining in this context has provided reforms that offer short-term improvements to the status quo, but whose long-term effects do not address and sometimes even accelerate the decline of the teaching profession. Collective bargaining agreements operating under the constraints of austerity budgeting have institutionalized inequality between faculty by formalizing their different ranks, while largely failing to provide living wages, job security, or reasonable workloads for most college instructors (especially in the community colleges) who find themselves ineligible for tenure or full-time status. In California, lobbying and legislative advocacy have produced incremental improvements, but these are easily undermined unless protected by collective bargaining power.

Following *Janus v. AFSCME*, faculty union leaders and their staff have a financial as well as political incentive to embrace rank-and-file organizing and "striking for the common good," as a growing number of their affiliates in K–12 teachers' unions have done in the past decade.[33] Increased teacher militancy also seems to be inspiring new kinds of political action that could transform the lives of tens of thousands of college instructors in California, and serve as a model for other states and even federal legislation. For such organizing to be successful, however, whether working toward faculty parity or the end of the two-tier system in its entirety, faculty labor unions need to move beyond collective bargaining to also work toward the development of a more equitable and democratic economy that can sustain such demands.

Notes

1. American Federation of Teachers, "An Army of Temps: AFT 2020 Adjunct Faculty Quality of Work/Life Report," 1, accessed November 20, 2020, https://www.aft.org/sites/default/files/adjuncts_qualityworklife2020.pdf.

2. From "Dataset: Faculty & (Some) Professional Staff," shared with author via email on August 31, 2020; Joe Berry and Michelle Savarese, "Directory of U.S. Faculty Contracts and Bargaining Agents in Institutions of Higher Education," National Center for the Study of Collective Bargaining in Higher Education and the Professions, September 2012.

3. Simon Margison, *The Dream Is Over: The Crisis of Clark Kerr's California Idea of Higher Education* (Oakland: University of California Press, 2016), 51–120.

4. Ruth Wilson Gilmore, *Golden Gulag: Prisons, Surplus, Crisis, and Opposition in Globalizing California* (Oakland: University of California Press, 2007), 73–74.

5. Sonya Tafoya and Sarah Bohn, "Spending on Corrections and Higher Education," Public Policy Institute of California (blog), University of California, August 4, 2016, accessed January 3, 2021, https://www.ppic.org/blog/spending-on-corrections-and-higher-education/.

6. California Budget Project, "From State to Student: How State Divestment Has Shifted Higher Education Costs to Students and Families," Budget Brief, May 6, 2014, accessed January 4, 2021, https://calbudgetcenter.org/wp-content/uploads/140506_From_State_to_Student_BB.pdf.

7. Suzanne Mettler, *Degrees of Inequality: How the Politics of Higher Education Sabotaged the American Dream* (New York: Basic Books, 2014), 126.

8. "Fiscal 50: State Trends and Analysis," Pew Charitable Trusts, November 27, 2013 (updated November 15, 2021), accessed December 8, 2021, https://www.pewtrusts.org/en/research-and-analysis/data-visualizations/2014/fiscal-50#ind7.

9. Margison, *The Dream Is Over*; John Aubrey Douglass, "From Chaos to Order and Back? A Revisionist Reflection on the California Master Plan for Higher Education@50 and Thoughts About Its Future," Research & Occasional Paper Series, UC Berkeley, Center for the Study of Higher Education, May 1, 2010, accessed November 29, 2020, https://escholarship.org/uc/item/6q49t0hj; Aaron Bady and Mike Konczal, "From Master Plan to No Plan: The Slow Death of Public Higher Education," *Dissent* (Fall 2012), accessed November 29, 2020, www.dissentmagazine.org/article/from-master-plan-to-no-plan-the-slow-death-of-public-higher-education; Joni E. Finney, Christina

Riso, Kata Orosz, and William Casey Boland, "From Master Plan to Mediocrity: Higher Education Performance and Policy in California," Institute for Research on Higher Education, University of Pennsylvania Graduate School of Education, 2014, accessed November 29, 2020, https://www.gse.upenn.edu/pdf/irhe/California_Report.pdf.

10. California Faculty Association, "Equity Interrupted: How California Is Cheating Its Future," accessed April 18, 2022, https://www.calfac.org/wp-content/uploads/2021/10/equity_interrupted_1.12.2017.pdf.

11. House Committee on Education and the Workforce Democratic Staff, "The Just-in-Time Professor: A Staff Report Summarizing eForum Responses on the Working Conditions of Contingent Faculty in Higher Education," January 2014, accessed March 22, 2021, https://edlabor.house.gov/imo/media/doc/1.24.14-AdjunctEforumReport.pdf.

12. National Center for the Study of Collective Bargaining in Higher Education and the Professions, "Dataset: Faculty & (Some) Professional Staff," September 2012.

13. Sara R. Smith, "Supporting California's Community College Teaching Faculty: Improving Working Conditions, Compensation, and the Quality of Undergraduate Education," UPTE-CWA 9119, 2012, 5, accessed January 5, 2021, http://www.upte.org/cc/supportingfaculty.pdf.

14. Findlaw, "California Code, Education Code—EDC § 84362," accessed January 5, 2021, https://codes.findlaw.com/ca/education-code/edc-sect-84362.html.

15. Smith, "Supporting California's Community College Teaching Faculty."

16. Academic Senate of the California Community Colleges (ASCCC), "Assembly Bill 1725," accessed April 18, 2022, https://www.asccc.org/sites/default/files/1988%20AB%201725%20Community%20College%20Reform%20Act%20(Vasconcellos).pdf.

17. California Federation of Teachers, "Landmark Cervisi Decision Turns 25: Part-Time Faculty Won Unemployment Benefits," May 1, 2014, accessed January 5, 2021, https://www.cft.org/california-teacher/landmark-cervisi-decision-turns-25-part-time-faculty-won-unemployment-benefits.

18. California Federation of Teachers, "New Law Brings Reemployment Rights for Part-Time Faculty: Successful CFT-sponsored Legislation Calls for Districts to Negotiate," December 1, 2016, accessed March 3, 2021, https://www.cft.org/california-teacher/new-law-brings-reemployment-rights-part-time-faculty.

19. David O'Brien, Vice Chancellor of Government Relations, California Community Colleges, Letter to Honorable Lorena Gonzalez, "RE: AB 1269 (C. Garcia): Community colleges: part-time faculty—OPPOSE," May 13, 2021, accessed June 13, 2021, https://calmatters.org/wp-content/uploads/2021/06/AB-1269-CCCCO-Oppose-Letter-Assembly-Appropriations.pdf.

20. Aaron Brown, President Elect of the Association of Chief Business Officers, Letter to State Senator Nancy Skinner and Assembly Member Phil Ting, "RE: Full-Time Faculty Hiring and FON," June 1, 2021, accessed June 13, 2021, https://calmatters.org/wp-content/uploads/2021/06/Legislative-Budget-Committees-Community-College-Full-Time-Faculty-Hiring-Budget-Proposal-06.01.2021.pdf.

21. CFT, "Governor Signs Three CFT-Sponsored Bills, Vetoes AB 375 to Increase Part-time Faculty Workload," October 11, 2021, accessed December 8, 2021, https://www.cft.org/

article/governor-signs-three-cft-sponsored-bills-vetoes-ab-375-increase-part-time
-faculty-workload.

22. On the lecturer activist movement in the CFA, see Elizabeth Hoffman and John Hess, "Organizing for Equality within the Two-Tier System: The Experience of the California Faculty Association," in *Equality for Contingent Faculty: Overcoming the Two-Tier System*, ed. Keith Hoeller (Nashville, TN: Vanderbilt University Press, 2014); California Legislative Information, "Assembly Concurrent Resolution No. 73," 2001, accessed January 5, 2021, https://leginfo.legislature.ca.gov/faces/billTextClient.xhtml?bill_id=200120020ACR73.

23. California State University, "Employee Profile: Previous Years' Reports," accessed March 15, 2023, https://www.calstate.edu/csu-system/faculty-staff/employee-profile/Pages/past-reports.aspx.

24. Donald W. Rogers, "A New Deal for Contingent Historians? The Current State of Contingent Faculty Labor Organizing," *Process: A Blog for American History*, December 3, 2015, accessed January 5, 2021, http://www.processhistory.org/a-new-deal-for-contingent-historians-the-current-state-of-contingent-faculty-labor-organizing/.

25. Joe Berry and Helena Worthen, *Power Despite Precarity: Strategies for the Contingent Faculty Movement in Higher Education* (London: Pluto Press, 2021).

26. Trevor Griffey, "Can Faculty Labor Unions Stop the Decline of Tenure?," *Process: A Blog for American History*, July 5, 2016, accessed January 5, 2021, http://www.processhistory.org/unions-tenure/.

27. California State University, "Employee Profile: Previous Years' Reports."

28. *UC-AFT Perspective* 6:1 (Fall 2002), accessed January 5, 2021, https://ucaft.org/sites/default/files/main/PerspectiveF03.pdf.

29. University of California, "Accountability Report 2020," chapter 8, accessed January 5, 2021, https://accountability.universityofcalifornia.edu/2020/chapters/chapter-8.html; Mikhail Zinshteyn, "UC Workforce Churn: Why a Quarter of Lecturers Don't Return Each Year," *Calmatters.org*, October 5, 2021, accessed April 18, 2022, https://calmatters.org/education/higher-education/2021/10/uc-workforce-lecturers/.

30. UC-AFT, "2021–2026 Teaching Faculty Contract Summary," November 29, 2021, accessed April 29, 2022, https://ucaft.org/content/2021–2026-teaching-faculty-contract-summary.

31. CFT, "Peralta Reaches 100 Percent Pay Parity; Locals Win Distance Education Support," October 20, 2020, accessed April 18, 2022, https://www.cft.org/article/peralta-reaches-100-percent-pay-parity-locals-win-distance-education-support.

32. CFT, "A 'Red Letter Year' for CFT Legislation in Support of Contingent Faculty," April 14, 2022, accessed April 18, 2022, https://www.cft.org/article/red-letter-year-cft-legislation-support-contingent-faculty.

33. Rebecca Kolins Givan and Amy Schrager Lang, *Strike for the Common Good: Fighting for the Future of Public Education* (Ann Arbor: University of Michigan Press, 2020).

CHAPTER 18

CASUALIZATION IN THE UNITED KINGDOM

Causes, Scale, and Resistance

STEVEN PARFITT

Where there are academics, there is contingent academic labor. Rest your finger on any part of the globe where a university exists and you will find academics who teach and conduct research unsure if they will have a job in a year's time, or even a month's time. This chapter concerns contingent academic labor in a country whose university system is closer to the American one than virtually all others: the United Kingdom. Like US universities, UK universities are (by world standards) lavishly funded and expensive. UK universities also follow the American model when it comes to contingent academic labor. Figures remain imprecise, but at least 75,000 academics in the United Kingdom—something like a quarter of the academic labor force—work on a contingent basis. While the proportion of the contingent workforce is lower in the UK than in the US, the trend is the same. The word in the UK that expresses that trend is casualization, the process by which secure work is made insecure.

The story of casualization at UK universities—how it happened, its nature and scale, and how it has been resisted—stretches from the years of Margaret Thatcher's premiership in the 1980s to the austerity years of the 2010s. It involves the making of markets in higher education, transforming universities into businesses, by direct government action. One of the key consequences of these changes was the great expansion of a casual academic labor force at UK universities and the extension of job insecurity to academics who were previously considered secure.

Activists from that casual academic labor force have for some time resisted casualization and tried to reverse it. The UK story is bound up with the development of the University and College Union (UCU), formed in 2006 as a merger between two higher and further education unions. The UCU is the largest tertiary education union in the world, with somewhere between 100,000 and 120,000 members, and, since its inception has remained committed to organizing all academic staff regardless of employment status. (Unless explicitly described otherwise, "staff" refers here to academics whose main task is teaching and/or research.) Yet the UCU has always had a complicated relationship with casualization as an issue, and with casual academics themselves. An implied comparison with the United States lurks behind that relationship, and a question: why, given that contingent academics in the United Kingdom can join a relatively powerful union, where their American counterparts cannot, has resistance to casualization proved similarly ineffective on both sides of the Atlantic?

This essay addresses that question, first by exploring the nature and scale of the problem and its causes. Secondly, it charts the growth of "anticasualization" activism within and without the UCU, and the roles played by steady organizing work, strikes, and austerity in shaping that activism. The picture that emerges is complicated. It is, in part, a slow accumulation of small victories. In the twenty-first century, contingent faculty gradually forced the UCU to take them seriously, to create structures that allowed casual faculty to agitate more effectively, and to adopt their demands. They made casualization a major issue within the UCU during a 2018 national strike that began over pensions, and they encouraged the UCU to push for an end to casualization in subsequent national strikes in 2019 and 2020. Yet this is also a story of promise unfulfilled. Despite some victories and hopeful moments, contingent faculty and the UCU have not yet managed to halt the process of casualization, let alone reverse it. That failure points to the limits of the UCU as a vehicle to represent the interests of contingent faculty, especially if they are to remain a permanent minority of the union's membership. The question of how to overcome those limits will preoccupy contingent faculty for years to come.

Casualization in the United Kingdom: What It Is and Where It Comes From

The origins of widespread contingent academic labor in the United Kingdom rest on the word that most commentators use to explain changes at UK universities (and other parts of the public sector) in the past forty years: marketization. Put simply, this refers to the transformation of universities from public bodies, however inefficiently run, to organizations that resemble for-profit business in virtually every respect, except that they do not formally strive for a profit—though they do plan, where possible, for an operating "surplus." All governments since Margaret Thatcher's 1979–1991 administration have extended private capital and business methods into the public sector, from the privatization of the rail system to the creation of internal markets in the National Health Service (NHS).[1]

In higher education, UK governments have created markets and made businesses of public bodies. They encouraged universities to compete for scarce research funding through the Research Assessment Exercise, introduced in 1986 and now named the Research Excellence Framework, which allocates research funding to departments by evaluating the quantity and quality of the published work of its members. Governments expanded the number of universities, especially since 1992 when polytechnics, technical colleges similar, in status at least, to community colleges in the United States, could now brand themselves as universities and award recognized university degrees. They moved the cost burden of tuition from the state to the student, introducing tuition fees—though not in Scotland, where the devolved Scottish government kept tuition free—and withdrawing state funding per student. Tony Blair's Labour government introduced a £1,000 annual fee cap in 1998, tripled to £3,000 in 2004, which the Conservative/Liberal Coalition tripled again to £9,000 in 2010.[2] Finally, the Conservative/Liberal Coalition encouraged universities to compete with one another for students by removing the limits on student enrollment that previously existed for each institution: the expectation was that competition would encourage students to flow to the "good" institutions and force the "bad" ones to lower their fees to remain in business.

These reforms have radically reshaped UK universities, and especially the composition of their employees. Universities now employ more administrators than academics in order to respond to government regulations and maximize tuition and research income, while the numbers of middle- and upper-level managers have rocketed upward.[3] Those managers have borrowed recklessly to invest in new buildings, while the people who do the research and teaching, and keep campuses safe and clean, have seen their incomes squeezed.[4] Essential support workers, from security guards to cleaners, are often outsourced, and they have engaged in the most militant—and effective—trade union action on campus. The Independent Workers of Great Britain at the University of London, the United Voices of the World at the London School of Economics, and Unison at the School of African and Oriental Studies (SOAS) have all waged long and at least partly successful struggles in the last decade. In short, except for those at the top, downward pressures on wages and conditions have hit all those who work at the university. This includes academic staff.

Since 2009, salaries for academic staff fell further behind inflation, even as their workloads increased and staffing levels stagnated. At the same time, the use of casual and temporary academic labor has exploded. Casual academic staff are cheaper than permanent staff and allow managers to fine-tune staff numbers each semester to meet student demand: a just-in-time system of employment, where people are employed as close to the start of semester as possible so that less money is "wasted" on hiring permanent staff to teach courses that fail to meet expected student enrollment numbers. The rapid expansion of PhD programs in the past several decades created a pool of surplus academic labor to meet this demand, accommodating administrators' desire for "flexibility." By these means, most UK universities managed to grow and build, even as they remain saddled with high levels of debt.

This is the context in which casualization, the greater use of contingent academic labor, emerged at universities in the United Kingdom. The term itself remains difficult to define. Until recently, the Higher Education Statistical Agency (HESA) labeled any academic who did not fall into "permanent full-time" and "permanent part-time" as "atypical." HESA now distinguishes casual contracts from other forms of employment and places those on fixed-term contracts—those who work on a full salary for a certain period of time, usually from nine months to two years—outside the "atypical" category.[5] In 2018–2019, HESA estimated that 34 percent of academic staff worked on fixed-term contracts.[6] The UCU, on the other hand, sees fixed-term contracts as part of the "casual" or "atypical" grouping. This chapter adopts the UCU definition, as it more fully encapsulates what is meant by casualization—academic labor performed by people without job security and unable to plan for the long term in their careers or their personal lives.

The numerical dimension of casualization tells a clear story. In 1999, UK universities employed 131,136 academic staff; by 2016, they employed 270,000. In 1999, 15 percent of the workforce were listed as permanent part-time, and none as atypical. By 2016, the proportion of full-time permanent staff fell below 50 percent, with 75,000 atypical staff added and a near quadrupling of permanent part-time staff, from 18,000 to 66,000.[7] Naturally, these numbers fail to reflect that casual work, especially the use of PhD students as part-time teachers, existed before 1999 and did not simply spring into existence afterward. Some of the rise in part-time work, and even in casual work, may also reflect universities' accommodations for staff with caring and childcare responsibilities. But they do show a dramatic expansion in the use of casual staff. What was once marginal and atypical is now mainstream and typical. And the scale of the problem seems greatest at the most prestigious institutions, especially those in the so-called Russell Group, which represents twenty-four research-intensive universities. According to UCU studies, the proportion of academics teaching on insecure contracts at these universities reaches as high as 70 percent, with most around 60 percent. According to an investigation by the *Guardian* in 2016, 70 percent of teaching staff at the University of Birmingham, and 68 percent at Warwick University, worked on insecure contracts.[8] The UCU further estimates that at many universities, casual staff assume 25–30 percent of the total teaching load.[9] They might only form one quarter of the academic workforce, but it is clear from these numbers that casual staff remain indispensable for the operation of most UK universities.

Casual contracts exist on a spectrum, both in terms of (relative) job security and pay and conditions.[10] At one end are so-called fixed-term contracts, for a year or longer, with the pay and benefits of junior permanent staff. These contracts provide temporary relief from immediate financial problems. Yet even they can vary wildly. Some are full-time, yet many are not: the ubiquitous ".5" contract, which pays half a full-time salary yet generally comes with the expectation of full-time work, is a common feature at universities across the United Kingdom.

At the other end of the spectrum are a range of contracts with little to no job security and low pay. The best of them are fixed-term contracts that run for merely nine months, six months, or even three months or less, but may come with a proper salary. The worst are hourly-paid contracts, in which academics work by the hour, usually teaching seminars and sometimes giving lectures. The sheer variety of this category defies easy generalization. Many hourly-paid teachers are PhD students, but many others already have their PhD in hand and teach on a casual basis as their main income. The number of hours worked on these contracts ranges from an hour per week to a teaching load equivalent to that of a full-time member of staff. Wages and paid work fluctuate wildly among universities, even between departments within the same university: some pay for lectures, others do not, and many different calculations are used for preparation and grading time. What holds hourly paid teachers together as a group is their complete lack of job security. They have, at least, one advantage over adjuncts in the United States, namely access to free healthcare through the National Health System, and to a range of other social security benefits—although these have been cut back and restricted in the austerity years between 2010 and 2020.

Casualization also affects those academics usually labeled as "permanent." There is a clear correlation between the rise of casualization and the stagnation of pay and conditions for permanent staff over the past twenty years: the emergence of a large layer of casual staff, qualified and able to replace their more secure colleagues, naturally exerts a downward pressure on salaries. At the same time, the job security of permanent staff has declined. Since the Thatcher government's 1988 Education Reform Act, tenure as previously understood in the UK no longer exists: before then, removing an academic on a permanent contract required "good cause," narrowly defined as being unable to perform one's duties or gross misconduct. After the act, any desire to move resources from one field to another or the perception of financial problems could be invoked to give rise to redundancy (severance) procedures.[11] Universities also require new junior permanent staff to undergo probation schemes, where they must meet several conditions related to teaching and research before they are considered permanently employed—though here again, "permanency" always remains subject to financial pressures and the whims of management in ways that the old understanding of tenure did not.

Casualization means the extension of job insecurity throughout the whole academic labor force. To borrow terms from the economist Guy Standing, a growing academic precariat (casual staff) brushes up against a stagnating academic salariat (permanent staff), with contradictory results.[12] The distinction between the two groups is made clear whenever budgets are squeezed: casual staff can be laid off without a legally mandated redundancy process. Yet the distinction narrows in other ways, as the insecurity faced by casual staff extends over time to permanent staff. Such are the consequences of a university system based on market values and where the need of universities to compete, to seize income, to build, and to save on their staffing cost has led to the present stratification of the academic labor force. Over time, however, that casualized labor force has fought back.

Resistance to Casualization

For some time, casualization at UK universities has attracted interest from the media, and, of course, from casual workers themselves. A subgenre of literature details the experiences of casual academics in the United Kingdom, from individual posts and blogs to occasional exposés in newspapers such as the *Guardian* or the *Times Higher Education* and reminiscences in the *Guardian*'s "Higher Education" section. These writings cover the full panoply of problems and indignities suffered by casual academics: the stress involved in holding down multiple jobs, the strains on personal and family life, and the financial devastation caused by insufficient hours and pay.[13] They generate short-term outrage among parts of the wider public and have alerted many senior academics, for some reason oblivious to the great shifts operating beneath them, to the nature and scale of the problem. Most importantly, they are the literary expression of a growing resistance to casualization by casual academics themselves.

In the 2000s and early 2010s, that resistance took the form of informal associations at the level of individual institutions or even individual departments. Some, like Fractionals for Fair Play at the School of African and Oriental Studies, or Warwick Anti-Casualisation (at Warwick University), have survived since the first half of the 2010s. Most of them, however, came and went in quick succession and failed to even leave much of a digital imprint. Their failures reflect the organizing difficulties for casual workers in any industry and especially the high and continual turnover of staff. As soon as leading figures move on, or are not rehired, or lose enthusiasm for the project, the group usually soon collapses. With these constraints, casual academics in the United Kingdom have been drawn further toward working with and within the UK's national higher education union, the UCU.

The membership of the UCU is divided along several lines. The first is between its membership in higher education, that is, universities, and further education, which covers a range of technical colleges, prison programs, and other forms of postsecondary education. That division is the product of the UCU's own origin story, as a merger in June 2006 between two unions, the Association of University Teachers and the National Association of Teachers in Further and Higher Education. The second is between academics and a range of white-collar support workers, from librarians to research center staff, with the latter often rendered invisible by the public perception that the UCU is a lecturers' or professors' union. The third division is between staff on permanent contracts and those on casual ones. This fact is crucial because the UCU claims jurisdiction over all academic and academic-related staff, regardless of their contractual situation. Casual academics in the United Kingdom thus try to improve their lot with what seems like a powerful ally, one that can bargain directly with university managers and their sector-wide representatives and has financial, legal, and other resources otherwise unavailable to them. Their activism in that union is simultaneously one of slow accretions of influence and one of sharp breaks that have brought casualization to much greater prominence within the UCU.

These slow accretions of influence were the product of a small number of active casual UCU members. At successive UCU Congresses (national conventions), they introduced and passed resolutions that formally committed the UCU to reversing the casualization of academic work and recruitment of casual staff. A national UCU committee on casual labor was formed in 2007 to coordinate the work of activists across the country, along with an annual conference where anticasualization activists could meet, discuss, and plan their strategy for the year ahead, as well as agree on resolutions guaranteed to be introduced and debated at the UCU's wider annual Congress. These activists also ensured that the coordinating committee of each local branch would have a dedicated anticasualization officer so that casual staff would be directly represented in local negotiations, as well as in national ones. In 2017, they won an important concession when PhD students were offered free membership as an inducement to become a part of the union at the earliest possible stage in their careers.

By these means the UCU developed a national infrastructure for casual staff. At the same time, relationships between the UCU and casual staff were transformed by the consequences of austerity, along with the stagnating pay and conditions for permanent staff described earlier. That stagnation amounted to somewhere between a 12–20 percent pay loss in real terms between 2009 and 2019, depending on the inflation index used. It not only accelerated the use by universities of casual contracts but also led to a contradictory response from the UCU and its membership: a desire to reverse the real pay cuts alongside a widespread feeling that little could be achieved when academic jobs were in short supply and a swelling army of casual staff stood ready to replace them. These tensions led the UCU to declare strikes over pay in 2013 and 2016 and also ensured that turnout on picket lines and enthusiasm for the strikes remained low.[14] Between 2010 and 2017, UCU membership declined by as much as 20,000 under the impact of these failures.[15] University managers were further emboldened to make new inroads into pay and benefits, and were drawn to make savings as they coped with the mounting debt incurred as universities built in order to grow and capture a greater fraction of domestic and, especially, international students. The issue they chose was pensions.

The Universities Superannuation Scheme (USS), the pension plan for academic staff at universities founded before 1992, had long been a target for university managers who wished to keep down long-term costs. In 2011, the USS underwent several major rule changes, with various benefits capped for new members; further caps were introduced in 2016. Yet the plan remained a defined-benefit scheme, rather than a defined-contribution one: that is, the USS continued to offer its members a specific set of payments on retirement, rather than simply pay out the combined total of contributions plus any gains from the investments of the USS fund. In 2017, the employer representatives on the USS board and the managers of the USS fund overruled the UCU representatives on the board and insisted that the scheme was in financial trouble. To survive, they said, it had to be changed from a defined-benefit to a defined-contribution scheme. The UCU disagreed, and balloted members for an unprecedented fourteen days of strike action in February and March 2018 to reverse the USS decision.

Sixty-one universities met the stringent conditions placed on strike ballots by UK law: a majority vote for strike action *and* a minimum 50 percent turnout by affected members. The turnout on picket lines was not only higher than expected, but also younger, given that the ostensible issue at hand was the pension plan, which many casual staff saw as a remote problem compared with their immediate financial problems and insecurity. But the strike exposed a wider disenchantment with academic work, and the struggles of casual academic staff became a common topic of conversation on picket lines and social media. This was a sharp break in the history of resistance to casualization at UK universities. When UCU members resisted the first offer from employers, which left open the possibility that the USS would still become a defined-contribution scheme after a three-year transitional period, casual staff and younger academics were particularly vocal in demanding what became known on Twitter as #nocapitulation.[16] By the time the strike ended after fourteen days, with a deal that did not completely reverse all of the original planned changes but did keep the USS as a defined-benefit scheme, casual staff had asserted themselves as an important bloc within the UCU. Casualization ascended much higher on the list of the union's priorities from then on.[17]

The second sharp break in the story of anticasualization activism came in 2019, when the union's long-serving general secretary, Sally Hunt, stood down for health reasons. The union's two main factions, the Independent Broad Left and UCU Left, each stood a candidate. Yet it was a third, independent candidate, Jo Grady—who had become a minor celebrity among UCU strikers in 2018 for her social media presence during the dispute and who talked regularly about casualization—who captured the enthusiasm of most voting UCU members and was elected general secretary. Veteran anticasualization activists such as Vicky Blake, who won election as an independent for vice president, also shifted the ground at the top of the union in favor of more attention to casual staff. They and other casual academic staff ensured that the UCU would now push beyond the mere reversal of existing cuts to pensions, pay, and working conditions and articulate positive demands of its own.

In 2019, the UCU called a strike ballot for two disputes: the first was for renewed action to defend the USS, and the second was in support of the "Four Fights," which called for a pay rise of 3 percent above inflation; real action on gender, racial, and disability pay gaps; pushing back against rapidly increasing work pressures; and, finally, addressing casualization. This was the first time that casualization rated a mention as a key demand in a national strike in UK higher education.

Yet the eight-day strike from November 25 to December 4, 2019, failed to match the enthusiasm and numbers of the 2018 action. It was overshadowed by the impending General Election on December 12, 2019. Turnout on the picket lines was much lower than in 2018, and university managers refused to concede ground as they had in the first strike. To force concessions, the UCU declared a further fourteen days of strikes in February and March 2020. This strike proved even less effective than the one in 2019. Turnout on picket lines—and, despite the difficulty of measuring this, response to the strike action altogether—continued to drop at most of the seventy-four affected universities.[18] Strike fatigue and the prospect of losing significant pay for little perceived gain undoubtedly played a part in declining support for the action. Just as the strike neared its end, moreover, the COVID-19 pandemic made its appearance in the United Kingdom.

Since then, the focus of UCU activity shifted for some time from offensive to defensive action. Rather than advancing the Four Fights platform, the UCU tried to limit the destruction of jobs. In 2020, tens of thousands of casual staff were let go and others told they would not be rehired while a long list of universities announced redundancy programs for academic staff. There was a bitter irony in all this. For the first time in decades, the growth of casual academic labor temporarily reversed. Yet that reversal did not mean enhanced job security across UK universities. It meant, instead, the mass unemployment of casual staff and the imposition of their duties on increasingly insecure "permanent" staff, who faced the threat of layoffs and the reality of increased work pressures.

University managers will need to negotiate for some time between two employment models. The first is the previous one, based on the expansion of casual work and a just-in-time employment system; the second relies on less casual labor and much more on the greater exploitation of permanent academic staff: increasing their teaching loads, temporarily removing—as has already happened across the UK—independent research time from their contracts, and, in effect, adding that work previously carried out by casual staff to their own. Financial pressures led to an abandonment of the first model during the pandemic, while the second is probably unsustainable in the long run because of the amplified risk of burnout among permanent academic staff and a possible exodus of those staff from the sector. Already, in 2022, there are signs that university managers will return to the old reliance on casual labor as soon as possible. After all, the costs of casual work remain lower and the fears of many universities that student numbers would severely decline, especially among international students, have not come to pass.

Nor have the problems afflicting higher education been solved in the meantime. The strikes for the Four Fights that began in 2019 and continued in 2020 resumed in 2022, with casualization still one of the four key areas under dispute. As in the strikes before COVID, the ones in 2022 do not seem likely to result in victory for either side. Academic staff, casual or otherwise, will not easily accept yet more erosion of their pay, job security, and working conditions; university managers will not easily cease trying to eke out an operating surplus at the expense of their employees. The grounds for conflict remain the same, and so conflict continues.

Resistance to casualization, meanwhile, remains at an impasse. On the one hand, casual academic staff have forced the union to take the issue seriously. This is evident in the establishment of anticasualization officers, the annual national anticasualization conference, and the inclusion of casualization as a key demand at local and national levels. The election of Jo Grady owed much to casual staff energized during the 2018 strike. On the other hand, the importance of casual staff within the union remains uncertain and diffuse. Most UCU members in higher education remain full time and permanent, and their interests have not always aligned with their contingent colleagues. The 2019, 2020, and 2022 strikes have failed to make good on the upsurge of interest in casualization among UCU members at large. And the pandemic has forced many anticasualization activists from their jobs, and in some cases from academia altogether.

For the foreseeable future, the task for contingent faculty will be to rebuild and prepare for better times. At least they do not have to start from scratch. The existing infrastructure of anticasualization officers, national casualization conferences, and other structures within the UCU, built by the last generation of activists, remains. People with personal experience of casual work now hold leading positions in the union. While the promise of the strikes of 2018–2020 has not been realized, the slow accretion of influence by casual staff in the UCU persists. When the pandemic ends, and the demand for contingent faculty rises again, the next generation of anticasualization activists will not need to construct something new but, instead, can build on past experience. How they fare will be up to them.

Conclusion

This is not a story that can be summed up easily by simple words such as "success" or "failure." If we return to the comparison between the United States and United Kingdom, we see that for all the advantages enjoyed by contingent faculty on the British side of the Atlantic the results have not been dramatically different. Along with an accelerating process of casualization and deepening job insecurity, the novel coronavirus did more in several months to reduce the number of casual academic staff than the efforts of UCU activists over ten years. The strikes of 2019, 2020, and 2022 exposed the great weakness of the UCU as a vehicle for remedying the struggles of contingent faculty. As a permanent minority in a union comprised mainly of permanent staff the interests of casual academic staff always risk being subordinated to the interests of the majority. Many permanent academic staff sympathize with the plight of those on insecure contracts—but that is different from being willing to make sacrifices, in the form of strike action and lost pay. The small, much weaker organizations created by contingent faculty in the United States, on the other hand, do not suffer from this problem.[19]

That is not to say, however, that the disadvantages of belonging to an industrial union like the UCU outweigh its advantages, or that resource-poor organizations of contingent faculty in the US are paradoxically in a better position to fight casualization than their colleagues in the UK.[20] Neither statement is true. But the record of the past ten years, in the UK at least, suggests that an active minority of contingent faculty in a national union is not sufficient to reverse the casualization of academic work. To achieve this end, more activism outside formal union structures might prove necessary, perhaps following the successful struggles by cleaners, security guards, and other campus workers in small, independent unions such as the Independent Workers of Great Britain and United Voices of the World. In these initiatives, outsourced and casualized staff won improvements to their position through sustained direct action.[21] Successful anticasualization activism will also almost certainly require greater support from permanent academic staff, who must be convinced that unless they also take real action their own job security will come under threat. In short, if contingent faculty in the UK are to make the most of their membership in a large national, industrial union where they will remain a minority, they must make the permanent majority of that union take them and their concerns more seriously. That, along with rebuilding an activist base after so many casual staff have been pushed out of academia by the COVID-19 pandemic will occupy the UCU for years to come.

And when it comes to questions of self-organization, anticasualization activists in the United Kingdom can learn much from their counterparts in the United States. American activists have much to teach their UK counterparts about building independent sources of strength at the local level in a way that could magnify the voices and influence of casual staff within the UCU. UK activists can likewise teach their American comrades about building national campaigns and can encourage the UCU to aid their struggles more directly. Put simply, there is no reason why contingent faculty in the US and UK should not form their own version of the famous "special relationship." During the 2018 pensions strike, UCU members on snow-laden picket lines were heartened by images of striking teachers in West Virginia with banners supporting the UCU. A real relationship between contingent faculty in the US and UK would do much more than boost morale and warm frostbitten hearts. It would make future victories more likely, sharing lessons of defeats and successful strategies more widely. We have allies at home and abroad. Let's not spurn them.

Notes

1. For a fuller treatment of marketization and its effects, see, among others: Mike Molesworth, Richard Scullion, and Elizabeth Nixon, eds., *The Marketisation of Higher Education and the Student as Consumer* (Abingdon: Routledge, 2011); Peter John and Joelle Fanghanel, eds., *Dimensions of Marketisation in Higher Education* (Abingdon: Routledge, 2015); Roger Brown and Helen Carasso, *Everything for Sale? The Marketisation of UK Higher Education* (Abingdon: Routledge, 2013). Also, see chapters 1–3 of this volume.

2. As of March 15, 2022, £1,000 is equivalent to $1,300; £3,000 to $3,900; £9,000 to $11,700.

3. See, for instance, "The Borrowers: Will Universities' Debts Pay Off?," *Times Higher Education*, April 5, 2018.

4. Lee Jones, "The Seven Deadly Sins of Marketisation in British Higher Education," *Bella Caledonia*, December 4, 2019.

5. "Definitions: Staff," Higher Education Statistics Agency, accessed December 12, 2020, https://www.hesa.ac.uk/support/definitions/staff.

6. "What Are Their Employment Conditions?," Higher Education Statistics Agency, accessed December 12, 2020, https://www.hesa.ac.uk/data-and-analysis/staff/employment-conditions.

7. Steven Parfitt, "Academic Casualisation in the UK," *International Labor and Working-Class History* 93 (2018): 223.

8. "Universities Accused of Importing Sports Direct Model for Lecturers' Pay," *Guardian*, November 16, 2016.

9. University and College Union, "Counting the Costs of Casualisation in Higher Education," June 2019, 3; accessed December 10, 2020, https://www.ucu.org.uk/media/10336/Counting-the-costs-of-casualisation-in-higher-education-Jun-19/pdf/ucu_casualisation_in_HE_survey_report_Jun19.pdf.

10. See Sue Doe and Steven Shulman's chapter in this volume.

11. See Stephen Court, "Academic Tenure and Employment in the UK," *Sociological Perspectives* 41:4 (1998): 767–774. For a shorter version: Michael Otsuka, "Is There Academic Tenure in the UK?," *Medium*, August 5, 2019, accessed December 8, 2020, https://medium.com/@mikeotsuka/is-there-academic-tenure-in-the-uk-93aecc388616.

12. Guy Standing, *The Precariat: The New Dangerous Class* (London: Bloomsbury, 2011).

13. Some examples: "Universities Accused of Importing Sports Direct Model for Lecturers' Pay"; "Don't Get Comfortable: The Rise of the Precarious Academy," *Times Higher Education*, August 3, 2018; Anonymous Academic, "Casual Contracts Are Ruining Universities for Staff and Students," *Guardian*, February 12, 2016.

14. For a fuller analysis of this period see Jamie Woodcock and Sai Englert, "Looking Back in Anger: The UCU Strikes," *Notes from Below*, August 30, 2018, accessed December 12, 2020, https://notesfrombelow.org/article/looking-back-anger-ucu-strikes.

15. "Level of Membership in University and College Union (UCU) in the United Kingdom (UK) from 2006/07 to 2017/18," *Statista*, accessed December 12, 2020, https://www.statista.com/statistics/286147/university-and-college-union-ucu-membership-in-the-united-kingdom-uk/.

16. Ed Rooksby, "No Capitulation," *Jacobin*, March 13, 2018.

17. Steven Parfitt, "Turning the War in Our Favour," *Jacobin*, April 20, 2018; Mark Bergman, "'Do You Believe in Life after Work?': The University and College Union Strike in Britain," *Transfer: European Review of Labour and Research* 24:2 (2018): 233–236.

18. Leon Rocha and Claire Marris, "Learning the Lessons from the UCU Strikes," *Tribune*, May 20, 2020.

19. See chapters by William A. Herbert and Joseph van der Naald, Anne McLeer, and especially Jeff Schuhrke in this volume.

20. See chapter by Naomi R Williams and Jiyoon Park in this volume.

21. See, for instance, Steven Parfitt, "A New Unionism for the Twenty-first Century," *Monthly Review Online*, April 4, 2019.

PATHS FORWARD FOR ACADEMIC LABOR AND HIGHER EDUCATION

CHAPTER 19

BUILDING LABOR SOLIDARITY ACROSS TENURE LINES

NAOMI R WILLIAMS AND JIYOON PARK

Efforts to save the democratic function of higher education demand faculty solidarity. As the cultural critic and educational reformer Henry A. Giroux points out in *The University in Chains*, universities should "educate [people] to contest workplace inequalities, imagine democratically organized forms of work, and identify and challenge those injustices that contradict and undercut the most fundamental principles of freedom, equality, and respect for all people who constitute the global public sphere."[1] Yet, the decades-long neoliberal restructuring of higher education has replaced the public-good function of universities with corporate profit strategies. These corporatization strategies (market-based practices, criteria, and norms) implemented by administrators have led to worsening working conditions for all faculty, regardless of access to tenure, while also reducing students to consumers and commodifying nearly all aspects of higher education. This undermining of the public work of higher education extends to the US political system itself and, as the historian Max Krochmal argues, it "does not reflect the democratic will of the majority."[2]

Faculty organizing should be central to reversing the almost forty-year trend of job insecurity or "adjunctification" at public colleges and universities. As scholars have pointed out in this collection, unionization and collective bargaining are important tools to counter the neoliberal university and expand democracy, and especially to challenge the increasing precarity of academic work. Institutions have been replacing tenure-stream faculty lines with full- and part-time contract faculty in a process described as the "casualization" of academic labor in several previous chapters.[3] These contingent faculty hires have less job security, lower salaries, and fewer opportunities to participate in shared governance. As a result, the work environments in higher education are deteriorating. This situation strains academic freedom, raises questions about the ownership of course materials, lowers wages, makes all faculty positions less secure, and reduces teaching standards. As contingency has exploded over the last decades, more and more faculty have been organizing.[4] Yet, a class divide persists within higher education as the two-tier system of tenure-stream and contingent faculty has flipped since the 1970s, with contingent faculty now the majority at public colleges and universities.[5]

If faculty remain divided, they will have limited success in maintaining the values of a public higher education system. Public universities should be sites of debate and discourse, critical engagement, and development of civic responsibility. Strong alliances among faculty will help create egalitarian, equitable workplaces, and stop the corporatization of higher education. Contingent faculty are organizing themselves, joining unions at increasing rates, working within professional organizations, and demanding dignity at work. Yet, they are unlikely to be successful if they act in isolation. Contingent faculty need powerful allies to support these efforts.

While the numbers of tenure-stream faculty continue to decline, they have the most power when bargaining with administrations and state governments. Tenure brings a greater degree of job security, respect, and a voice in curriculum and administration issues on many campuses. While it may make some tenure-stream faculty uncomfortable, these benefits come at the expense of contingent faculty and suggest that tenure-stream faculty should play a key role in building solidarity to increase job security for all faculty, maintain rigorous standards in the classroom, and protect academic freedom. Yet, many contingent faculty feel that tenure-stream faculty offer only minimal support and, in some instances, oppose improving working conditions for contingent faculty. When asked about their experiences with organizing and bargaining, contingent faculty who volunteer with their unions pointed to the perception that "[tenure-stream faculty] are not there when the rubber meets the road," or cited the "lack of transparency" concerning bargaining around their particular job concerns, which increases insecurity.[6]

Tenure-stream faculty should recognize the urgency of building alliances with contingent faculty to maintain the public good of universities: educating autonomous, self-reflective, social-justice-oriented citizens capable of fostering human dignity and a democratic public rule. This chapter outlines the need for cross-rank solidarity and examines how tenure-stream and contingent faculty can build solidarity to increase their collective power to resist the neoliberal university. It outlines what contingent faculty have been doing to improve their working conditions and the role of unionization and collective bargaining in these efforts. The final section offers ways that tenure-stream faculty can and should demonstrate solidarity with contingent faculty to reverse troubling trends in higher education.

The Case for Cross-Rank Solidarity

The corporatization of higher education has dramatically altered the public university and has reinforced historical harms regarding access to education and workplace inequities. This has led to increased workloads and the loss of academic freedoms for all faculty. It has also diminished shared governance across colleges and universities and led to skyrocketing tuition costs.[7] Administrative growth, reflecting corporatized practices, means smaller portions of universities' budgets go to faculty salaries. Over the last forty years, colleges and universities have replaced tenure-stream job lines with contract faculty, full- or part-time. This puts an undue burden on precarious workers, who too often are disconnected from the intellectual life of the institutions where they work. Whether tenure-stream or not, most faculty positions, as essays by Elizabeth Tandy Shermer and Aimee Loiselle have illustrated in this collection, come with less pay, fewer benefits, constricted academic freedom, and little to no role in university governance.[8] These changes strain the ability of all faculty members to conduct research. They have also disrupted the relationship among faculty, staff, and students. In the market-based approach, students are treated as consumers. Combined with precarious employment, this creates a culture of entitlement among students who lobby for grades, increases the emotional labor of faculty and staff, and lowers standards when faculty are judged on student evaluations.[9]

Without cooperative efforts, faculty have limited means to reverse these trends. In the past, faculty power rested in the security of tenure. Most faculty were on the tenure stream and could collectively confront threats to the democratic functions of the university without fear of termination. But by 2015, 75 percent of college faculty were underpaid contract workers.[10] That most educators work without job security and academic freedom and receive unlivable wages far below their training and experience is antithetical to the democratic mission of public colleges and universities.[11] The adjunctification of faculty employment through contract labor lessens the job security and power of all faculty members. Rigorous intellectual work is put at risk with increased class sizes, little or no time or pay devoted to research, and the loss of academic freedom that comes with the commodification of undergraduate education. All faculty face increased demands, leaving them less time to prepare for teaching, conduct research, and engage in governance work. Tenure-stream faculty need their contingent colleagues to help lighten their own increased service responsibilities. As David Kociemba has argued, tenure should be understood as the privileges granted in a timely fashion to *all* competent teachers, providing "job security, a living wage, training, respect in the workplace, and a voice in curriculum issues," not to just a select few.[12] On the latter points alone, the increased use of contract labor also diminishes the power of faculty governance, as fewer faculty meet the criteria for voting rights.[13]

The increase in contract labor within higher education also reinforces the marginalization of historically excluded groups, including women, and especially people of color. Structural racism and sexism already place people of color and women across racial lines in the most precarious positions in the academy.[14] As the adjunctification of higher education continues, they are overrepresented in precarious employment in the academy. Increased contingent faculty labor also reinforces already existing disparities within departments, as any new positions are likely to come without the benefits of tenure, ensuring their continued exclusions from positions of power.

As the American Federation of Teachers (AFT) discovered in its 2010 report on faculty diversity, racially underrepresented professors held only 10.4 percent of faculty positions in 2007, and 73 percent of those positions were contingent.[15] Women are overrepresented in part-time positions and, as discovered in a 1993 American Association of University Professors (AAUP) analysis, the proportion of Black faculty in non-tenure-track positions was more than 50 percent greater than white faculty.[16] Black faculty made up only 4.7 percent of full-time faculty in 1993, and by 2007, that number had only increased to 5.4 percent. In 2007, Black faculty held only 1.4 percent of tenured or tenure-track positions; most of the increase in job placement happened in contingent positions.[17] This lack of growth illustrates the ways Black scholars have been excluded from the benefits of tenure, and when hired, held in the most precarious job positions. As studies have shown, the continued underrepresentation of Black women at colleges and universities (outside of historically Black colleges and universities) and the low-status positions they hold demonstrates that tenure and promotion are geared toward white, male faculty. It leads to discrimination and stereotyping, and an "unbreakable glass ceiling."[18] As Chaumtoli Huq argues, this situation is due to the long history of structural racism in the United States.[19]

Even when in supposedly secure, tenure-stream positions, Black faculty face more job precarity than their colleagues.[20] They suffer disproportionately from the growing precarity of academic labor and, too often, women of color are pushed out of tenure-stream positions due to the extreme racism, discriminatory practices, and hostile environments that exist within the academy. For example, in an analysis of diversity efforts by twenty-seven institutions, the Association of American Colleges and Universities discovered that despite success in hiring, the turnover rate was 50 percent, demonstrating a lack of retention of underrepresented faculty.[21] While tenure provides a procedural and institutional framework for faculty job security and academic freedom, it also is a political process that plays out in the context of colleges and universities as racialized and gendered spaces. Tenure decisions continue to benefit white, male professors and limit access to marginalized groups, particularly Black scholars. The myth of meritocracy tied to the tenure system suggests that those outside the tenure stream are less capable and somehow less qualified or experienced than their colleagues, which increases the class, race, and ethnic divides within faculty ranks.[22]

The marginalization of underrepresented faculty has intensified with the corporatization and adjunctification of public higher education, as essays by Diane Angell and Miguel Juárez in this collection make clear. Tenure-stream faculty need to recognize their common interest with contingent faculty, including resisting the artificial divisions along intersecting lines of race, class, gender, as well as rank distinctions created by the neoliberal university. The increasing attacks on public education and educators is a symptom of the current crisis of democracy and demands urgent, collective action to defend the democratic nature of public higher education. Colleges and universities can fulfill the principles of fairness and equal pay for equal work and gain support from a public that recognizes the value of an educated, engaged citizenry. To effectively organize and defend public education, educators need to combine resources and build alliances across divides within the academy.

Contingent Faculty Activism

As Anne Wiegard and others have discussed in this collection, contingent faculty have been working increasingly over the last few decades to call attention to their precarious working conditions and diminishing academic freedom. The Coalition of Contingent Academic Labor (COCAL) formed in December 1996 as "a network of North American activists working to improve higher education through the collective achievement of job reliability, livable wages, academic freedom, and time and resources . . . for contingent academic laborers."[23] In 2012, at the COCAL X conference, members signed a political declaration urging solidarity among all faculty "to work . . . toward a common goal: the expansion of social and democratic rights in education and in welfare for all humans, within and beyond our national borders."[24]

Likewise, the New Faculty Majority (NFM) was founded in 2009 by a group of faculty members seeking ways to advocate for contingent faculty. NFM has hosted campus equity weeks that draw attention to the working conditions of contingent faculty and lobbies legislatures to improve these conditions. They have also conducted research on women working as contingent faculty and their work experiences.[25] The Faculty Forward movement, organized by the Service Employees International Union (SEIU), brings faculty, graduate students, and communities together to fight against the corporatization of higher education, unfair working conditions, and rising tuition, which limits access to education and increases poverty among campus workers as incoming tuition funds are allocated not to wages and salaries for faculty but, instead, to administrative bloat. Over 50,000 faculty and graduate student workers have formed unions with Faculty Forward to provide key benefits for contingent faculty nationwide, mostly at private schools.[26] Some studies suggest that growing activism within organizations like COCAL and others have led to increased unionization efforts among all faculty.[27]

Union Contract Advances

Unionization and collective bargaining efforts have produced key protections for full- and part-time contingent faculty at public colleges and universities. For example, 73.3 percent of faculty and graduate students voted to unionize in certification elections in 2016.[28] Examining union contract advances highlights the results of these collaborations. Using a selection of recent contracts from the AAUP database,[29] we selected sixty-three collective bargaining agreements at sixty institutions for analysis of faculty rights and working conditions. These institutions vary in terms of type (i.e., four-year/two-year; public/private), size, location, and bargaining unit composition (see table 19.1 for a list of these institutions). These contracts and institutions offer a basic contour of recent advances in union contracts in higher education. Among sixty institutions reviewed, only 25 percent had a collective bargaining agreement based on solidarity between full-time and part-time faculty.

Despite some key gains, a review of these contracts demonstrates that collective bargaining has yet to produce stability and livable wages for contingent faculty, especially adjuncts. Part-time faculty have negotiated pay scales, raises, payment for nonteaching duties, grievance rights, evaluation procedures, criteria for promotion, and some fringe benefits with various levels of job security. Aspects of many of these agreements provide added security in terms of reappointments, especially when combined with length of service. However, most of the contracts revealed that part-time lecturers work under a tiered system of employment based on semesters of service, which effectively divides faculty. Faculty with seniority receive higher pay rates per course and priority in reappointment. For example, Emerson College–LA has a four-step pay clause based on seniority and credits taught.[30] Likewise, Rutgers University has a three-step clause where a total of twelve (cumulative) semesters of teaching qualifies a faculty member to move up to the next tier, based on performance criteria. Interviews with faculty in these types of bargaining units reveal that while these contracts provide some security and pay increases, the various tiers limit solidarity among faculty.[31] Those at the lowest levels receive the smallest pay increases. Importantly, part-time faculty have failed to secure significant across-the-board wage increases in their bargaining agreements to support the lowest-paid faculty.[32] In many cases, reappointments

Table 19.1. Selected Sample of Contracts and Institutions

Bargaining Unit	University
Combined full-time/part-time bargaining unit	Adelphi University (2016–2021); Bard College (2017); Bloomfield College (2018–2021); Connecticut State University (2016–2021); Curry College (2015); Hofstra University (2016–2021); New York Institute of Technology (2017–2022); Oakland University (2015–2020); Rider University (2017–2020); St. John's University (2017–2019); University of Connecticut (2017–2021); University of Delaware (2016–2021); University of Oregon (2015–2020); Wayne State University (2013–2021); UUP contract for the State University of New York system (2016–2022)
Combined tenure-track/non-tenure-track faculty bargaining unit	Bowling Green State University (2016); California State University—California Faculty Association (2020); Central State University (2017–2020); Cincinnati State Technical and Community College (2018–2020); Cleveland State University (2017–2020); D'Youville College (2017–2021); Delaware State University (2016–2021); Delaware Valley University (2017–2020); Eastern Michigan University (2019–2021); Emerson College (2006–2011); Fort Hays State University (2018–2019); Indian River State College (2019–2020); Kalamazoo Valley Community College (2018–2022); Monmouth University (2018–2021); Montgomery College (2019); New Jersey Institute of Technology (2015–2019); North Central State Faculty Association (2017–2020); Raritan Valley Community College (2015–2019); Santa Fe College Community College (2019–2020); Union County College (2015–2018); University of Akron (2015); University of Alaska (2017–2019); University of Cincinnati (2019–2022); University of Nebraska at Omaha (2018–2021); University of Rhode Island (2018–2021); University of Scranton (2015–2018); University of Vermont (2018–2020); Utica College (2015–2020); Western Michigan University (2017–2020)
Part-time faculty bargaining unit	Emerson College (2019–2024); Emerson College–LA (2016–2020); Raritan Valley Community College (2017–2019); Rutgers University (2018–2022); Suffolk University (2015–2018); University of Alaska (2017–2020); University of Rhode Island (2017–2020); University of Vermont (2018–2021); Wright State University (2019–2023)
Tenure-track bargaining unit	Cuyahoga Community College (2019–2022); Kent State University (2019–2022); Plymouth State University (2018–2021); University of Illinois at Chicago (2018–2022); University of New Hampshire (2016–2020); University of Toledo (2018–2022)
Non-tenure-track faculty bargaining unit	Kent State University (2013–2016); University of Illinois at Chicago (2018–2022); University of Illinois at Urbana-Champaign (2019–2024); University of Toledo (2018–2022)

Note: Contract effective duration in parentheses.

Sources: Data from American Association of University Professors, *Contract Database*, accessed March 18, 2020, https://www.aaup.org/chapter-resources/contract-database; The State of New York and United University Professions (UUP), Collective Bargaining Agreement, July 2, 2016 through July 1, 2022, https://uupinfo.org/contract/pdf/20162022NYSUUPAgreement.pdf; and RVCC Faculty Federation, accessed March 18, 2020, "Adjunct Faculty Contract": Agreement between Raritan Valley Community College Board of Trustees and Raritan Valley Community College Adjunct Faculty, July 1, 2019 through June 30, 2022, adjunct-faculty-contract-2019-2022.pdf (wordpress.com).

are based on management discretion and only a few agreements allow grievances for failure to reappoint.

Part-time faculty members in combined bargaining units with full-time faculty have some additional job security, although they also have inherent tensions. Some part-time faculty in these units have access to multiyear contracts, as opposed to semester-by-semester or one-year terms. For instance, Hofstra University's agreement with faculty includes five-year contracts for those with ten or more years of service.[33] Oakland University offers regular part-time faculty who teach sixteen or more credits in a calendar year a one-year contract; after four years of service, contracts extend to two-year terms, renewable indefinitely.[34] Items of note in these combined units include clauses that limit the number of adjunct faculty or their course load. The University of Connecticut and Rider University both limit part-time faculty to 20 percent of full-time faculty. Such provisions guarantee job protections for full-time faculty and maintain existing full-time job lines, though they can also limit opportunities for part-time employees.

Some adjunct faculty in combined units also have access to base salaries. For example, in 2016, the United University Professions (UUP) ratified an agreement with the State University of New York to provide a system-wide minimum salary for part-time faculty compensated on a per-course basis.[35] Connecticut State University and St. John's University also have minimum salary rates for part-time faculty.[36] Performance evaluations in combined units reflect similar patterns to those in part-time-only bargaining units. These evaluation procedures are often less formal than those for full-time faculty.

Unionized full-time contingent faculty members generally have more security and better compensation than part-time faculty. Full-time, non-tenure-stream faculty often have many of the same job rights as their tenure-track colleagues, with increased teaching loads. Commonly, the teaching load for full-time employees is three or four courses each semester, and minimum annual compensation in 2020 was about $60,000. Rider University sets the base salary for full-time contingent faculty at 92 percent of tenure-track faculty.[37] Non-tenure positions also come without compensation for scholarly research or other professional endeavors. As such, scholarship and service receive less weight in criteria for non-tenure-track positions, regardless of scholarly activity. While access to health insurance and other fringe benefits varies widely across institutions for part-time faculty, full-time contract faculty have a wider range of benefits than their part-time colleagues at most institutions.

This short review of faculty bargaining agreements reveals that unionization and contract negotiation provide some job stability for contingent faculty. Yet too many contingent faculty remain unrepresented, and unionization still leaves many in precarious situations. While tensions exist across faculty lines, cross-rank solidarity against artificial divisions created by the neoliberal university offer the best path forward to improve working conditions and job security. By forming alliances with all their colleagues and exercising their collective power, those in the tenure-stream ranks can improve the working and learning conditions at colleges and universities.

What Tenure-Stream Faculty Can Do

In testimonials and trade publications, contingent faculty have consistently suggested areas where tenure-stream faculty can step up. Contingent faculty members want the same things others want at work: dignity and respect. Like tenure-stream faculty, they deserve job security, fair wages, and decent working conditions. The reality that contingent faculty are just as qualified and work just as hard as their tenure-stream colleagues explodes the myth of meritocracy related to tenure positions as well as the artificial divides created by the corporatization of the university. Most of the demands and advice contingent faculty have for their tenured (and to-be-tenured) colleagues revolve around issues of respect and solidarity. These recommendations will go a long way toward improving both structural issues and toxic cultures within the academy; they will strengthen faculty power on campuses and provide better learning conditions for students and fair working conditions for faculty and staff. Too often, department leadership feel as if their hands are tied when addressing the exploitation of contingent faculty. Yet by taking proactive steps throughout the employment contract, tenure-stream faculty can provide many no- or low-cost resources for contingent faculty.

The following list of actions is intended to address the corporatization of higher education that has led to many cost-saving and profit-generating initiatives that force departments to limit faculty hires, depend more on part-time faculty, and reduce job security. We have assembled these actions through an analysis of the bargaining agreements in table 19.1, from interviews with faculty and union organizers, previous research, and faculty organizing campaigns. They offer ways to stop the erosion of the working and learning environment of all faculty, students, and the communities that public institutions are supposed to serve.

Tenure-stream faculty should know who works on contract in their departments and under what conditions they work. Many contingent faculty members, as Claire Goldstene and Elizabeth Hohl describe in this collection, feel invisible. Some of this reflects structural barriers to inclusion—adjuncts often work for different institutions and must commute back and forth throughout the week. Despite these logistical challenges, full-time faculty should take the time to meet their part-time colleagues. One interviewee, who also volunteers as an organizer for their union, stressed how disparities across departments lead to inadequate solidarity across faculty lines.

For example, at their West Coast institution, some departments provide research funds based on teaching loads while other departments treat contingent faculty like "cashiers at McDonald's."[38] One part-time faculty member who has worked at a large public institution for seven years still has limited contact with other faculty members. While their department provides protections unavailable to other contingent faculty within the university system, they continue to be excluded. Department culture maintains the boundaries. When asked what tenure-stream faculty could do, they responded that part-time faculty need to be valued.[39] Tenure-stream faculty should know the teaching loads of contingent faculty and whether they have adequate office space and access to sufficient administrative support. They should make the effort to get to know their full- and part-time colleagues.

Contingent faculty are so diverse that building solidarity requires understanding the different circumstances of those who fill these positions and why. Some are part-time, semi-retired professionals; some have decided to work as educators after retiring from other professional careers; some are recent PhDs hoping to make a living; and some are teaching professionals who prefer to focus on teaching excellence without the responsibility of ongoing research. Getting to know the faculty within departments means that these varying circumstances are considered. For example, a new PhD discovered that a one-year gig teaching four classes one semester and three in the other also came with the responsibility of overseeing honor requirements for some students. While the tenure-stream faculty in this department were supportive, it did not occur to them that hiring a replacement for someone on sabbatical might mean shifting responsibility for honors advising. This extra workload made teaching and applying for jobs for the following year challenging.[40] Knowing the colleagues who fill these positions, and their specific situations, demonstrates respect and leads to a greater appreciation for their valuable contributions.

Tenure-stream faculty should actively build inclusive departments. "Othering" describes how group-based identities can be used to exclude some and create an "us" versus "them" mentality. john a. powell and Stephen Menendian offer methods to create a sense of belonging through inclusive practices that help end marginalization and inequality. All faculty should feel they belong, that their work, experience, and training are valued and their input welcome.[41] Contingent faculty often observe that tenure-stream members treat them as if they are teaching automatons rather than fellow scholars and researchers. Many are exploited for their labor and contend that their contributions to the equally important work of active research and engagement with their broader fields are ignored. To counter this, tenure-stream faculty should invite contingent faculty to participate in research symposiums. Part-time faculty felt most included where they were invited to department functions, colleagues knew their names, and they had opportunities to receive staff support. As

Patrick Iber pointed out in a 2014 article, a simple way to start building inclusion is welcoming contingent faculty when they arrive. A lunch or dinner meeting with the chair and some interested faculty and staff can help new faculty feel connected and open lines of communication. Inclusion also means invitations to department events like receptions, graduations, and convocations.[42] While many of these invitations cannot be accepted due to time restraints or other barriers, invitations without expectations or consequences for refusal go a long way toward building inclusive environments.

Inclusion also involves connecting incoming and current contingent faculty to existing resources and opportunities. Departments can solve many issues by simply offering short orientations that introduce new contingent faculty to staff and what they do. A brief orientation will further help incoming part- and full-time contingent faculty feel connected to the department and understand whom to ask for what resources. Creating access to administrative support and to office equipment for evening and weekend classes is also essential. In addition, departments can communicate opportunities to participate in professional development trainings. One faculty member at a small four-year comprehensive college remembered being surprised that they were eligible for professional development opportunities; they accidently overheard they were eligible to apply. Another part-time faculty member received professional development information from their union but did not know how to take advantage of the programs through their department.[43] Informal mentoring programs provide opportunities to build connections within departments.[44] Open communication and attention to these types of details help create a sense of shared purpose.

In turn, because contingent faculty are in the classroom and regularly advise students, they can often provide vital information or missing perspectives. Contingent faculty input should be sought, and they should be compensated for their labor. Administrative roles like program directors can open the door for more stable employment for some contingent faculty members. Yet, these positions should not just be offered as a stopgap for the department's needs without full disclosure of working conditions and timelines. And faculty should not be penalized if they turn down these positions.

Contingent faculty have commented on what these scenarios look like in practice. As one interviewee noted, despite having a one-year contract filling the position of a tenured-faculty member on sabbatical, the department members welcomed them as a full-fledged member. Several department members offered career advice and mentoring, and three wrote letters for job applications. In a blog post, Annemarie Pérez describes moving from contingent faculty to tenure track as "lottery-level lucky." She explained that the chair of the first department that hired her asked about career goals and then promised to help Pérez find a permanent position. The chair followed through with tangible actions.[45] Another interviewee detailed the ways their current department welcomed them and immediately included them in department events. As a full-time contract faculty member, they were regularly included with the tenure-stream junior faculty in both professional and social opportunities. However, when a new chair took over department leadership, suddenly the contract faculty members were excluded from department events.[46] This example illustrates the need for institutionalized, normalized policies that lead to inclusive work environments. It also shows how individual behavior can be powerful in offering support to contingent faculty members, even within institutional constraints.

Tenure-stream faculty should respect the work and the time of contingent faculty. Importantly, consider contingent faculty for open tenure-stream positions within departments.[47] When tenure lines become available, qualified contingent faculty should be encouraged to apply. Too often, departments go in search of candidates when faculty within the department fit the criteria for open positions. By actively encouraging applications from these internal candidates, department leadership can demonstrate not only labor solidarity, but also respect for the work contingent faculty are already doing.

Among part-time contingent faculty, a huge area of stress revolves around contract renewal and course assignments. Often, departments wait until the last minute to offer faculty contracts for the next term. Even when faculty receive contracts, delays in course assignments add to uncertainty. Late course assignments give faculty limited time to prepare and could cause the course to be dropped because of low enrollment. While many of these issues depend on student enrollment and faculty schedules, every effort should be made to ensure timely contracts and course assignments for part-time faculty. Delays limit any sense of job security and could mean the loss of alternative job opportunities or unemployment compensation. The COVID-19 pandemic reinforced these concerns, during which the first response at many institutions was to lay off the most vulnerable employees or withhold contracts while awaiting budget decisions.[48] At the end of each term, and especially when faculty contracts are not renewed, departments can offer appreciation and acknowledgment of the work of contingent faculty.[49]

Tenure-stream faculty should expand access to faculty governance at all levels. Tenure-stream faculty should work to change systemic elements that reinforce the class divide within higher education. Part of this should involve reevaluating bylaws and practices for departments, faculty senates, or other governing bodies, to incorporate contingent faculty more fully in decision-making at all levels. Such changes create a culture of collective endeavor in fulfilling the teaching and service mission of departments and schools. Full-time non-tenure-track faculty are well positioned to serve on teaching committees, to mentor new faculty, and engage in other service opportunities focused on curriculum development and student retention, with proper compensation. This approach also elevates the value of teaching within departments. Even when structural barriers to participation exist, contingent faculty can be consulted on teaching-related initiatives and paid for their labor to perform this service.

Tenure-stream faculty should support unionization efforts on campus. It is vital that tenure-track faculty support contingent faculty organizing. Tenure-stream faculty have more power and resources to support organizing campaigns. While evidence suggests that wall-to-wall faculty unions offer slightly more stability, even if in separate bargaining units or where tenure-stream faculty are not organizing, tenure-stream faculty should support contingent faculty organizing campaigns and bargaining efforts. Implementing the strategies described above will allow tenure-stream faculty to know contingent faculty and understand their working conditions so they can advocate for greater protections for their colleagues. Tenure-stream faculty can show support by wearing union attire and educating students and administrators about contingent faculty working conditions and the benefits of greater stability and just working conditions. This also reasserts the democratic function of public colleges and universities and provides a challenge to the neoliberal university. Where faculty are in separate bargaining units, plentiful opportunities exist for collaborative efforts in negotiations. As contingent union activists and staffers suggest, tenure-stream faculty unions need to demonstrate solidarity "when the rubber meets the road."[50]

Too often, administrators create wedges between faculty by offering incentives to tenure-stream faculty bargaining units at the expense of contingent faculty. In these cases, tenure-stream faculty unions must center the needs of their most vulnerable colleagues. Unions with separate bargaining units can also offer financial assistance to support organizing part-time units that often have fewer resources by, for example, sharing the cost of paid organizers. Regardless of bargaining unit makeup, faculty must build solidarity, remove artificial barriers between themselves, and operate under the motto: "an injury to one is an injury to all."

Strong, social justice–focused unions can alleviate faculty poverty, loss of academic freedom, and deteriorating working conditions. Social justice unionism recognizes that economic and political struggles must go beyond the shop floor. It eschews the business unionism that arose with the emergence of collective bargaining as the main focus of labor law in the United States and encourages members to become involved in community-wide campaigns for economic and political justice.[51]

In the aftermath of the *Janus* decision, where the Supreme Court ruled that non-union members did not have to pay agency fees, many activists worried that public sector union membership would decline to private sector union levels. That has not proven to be the case, in part, because of the public sector unions' effective revival of social justice unionism. For example, the #RedforEd mobilizations among K–12 educators have demonstrated the results of successful social justice unionism through the tool Bargaining for the Common Good. In Chicago, Los Angeles, and other cities, teachers built organizing demands around community needs. They expanded bargaining terms beyond workplace bread-and-butter issues to address the demands of parents and students in the broader community. To address the attacks on the most vulnerable workers on Rutgers's campuses across New Jersey, nineteen unions came together and formed the Coalition of Rutgers Unions. By joining forces with all workers and some community groups across the state, the faculty union was able to work with others to protect part-time lecturers, food ser-vice workers, and other low-wage workers in the state. These types of broad-based mobilizations by public sector unions have reshaped local and national politics. They also provide the basis for increased organizing and mobilizing on college campuses to ensure the protection of the US political system by educating engaged citizens who value the democratic mission of higher education.[52]

Tenure-stream faculty should train PhD students to remove stigmas associated with contingent faculty positions. Tenure-stream faculty have important responsibilities for training PhD students. Despite the decades-long decrease in the number of tenure-stream positions across higher education and the increasing precarity of academic employment, only recently have faculty acknowledged this in the recruiting and training of graduate students. Too many graduate programs enroll more students even as job placement numbers decline. Despite these realities, however, advisors continue to view contingent faculty positions—and contin-gent faculty members—as inferior. This is evident in the ways contingent faculty are treated as second-class members (at best) in departments, as well as in the failure to prepare students for this reality. Many contingent faculty, especially part-time lecturers, internalize a sense of failure. They often feel shunned at professional conferences and struggle to build networks that will advance their research and publishing goals. Again, tenured faculty at universities with gradu-ate programs shape the culture of professional conferences since they popu-late the boards of most professional organizations. These tenured faculty have a responsibility to help reshape professional cultures and to inform graduate students about hiring trends in their fields, foremost the limited availability of tenure-stream placements. Advisors must be open when communicating about the precarity of adjunct and non-tenure-track positions without stigmatizing these positions. And tenure-stream faculty must be aware of the working condi-tions of contingent faculty, fighting to improve job security, pay, and the academic freedom rights of all faculty, present and future.[53]

Conclusion

The COVID-19 public health crisis and related economic turmoil have accentuated threats to economic and civic democracy in the United States. Colleges and universities have used these crises to further corporatize their institutions as austerity measures are implemented across the country. Yet, faculty are in key positions to struggle against these efforts. By building solidarity across ranks, by creating inclusive workplaces, by organizing broad-based unions, and by supporting the public-good role of the academy, faculty can strengthen workers' collective power to reverse these trends. Collective worker power is the answer to the assault on democracy that has continued to reinforce inequality and to leave millions in poverty. Tenure-stream faculty must work with their contingent colleagues to reassert their traditional roles in the academy, without re-creating old harms.

Notes

1. Henry A. Giroux, *The University in Chains: Confronting the Military-Industrial-Academic Complex* (Boulder, CO: Paradigm Publishers, 2007), 104.

2. Max Krochmal, "Race, Democracy, and Civic Engagement in U.S. History," *Take Care*, December 6, 2018, accessed December 26, 2020, https://takecareblog.com/blog/race-democracy -and-civic-engagement-in-u-s-history; Nancy MacLean, *Democracy in Chains: The Deep History of the Radical Right's Stealth Plan for America* (New York: Viking, 2017).

3. See Part I in this collection, especially the essay by Joe Berry and Helena Worthen, and William A. Herbert and Joseph van der Naald's essay in Part III.

4. William A. Herbert, "The Winds of Changes Shift: An Analysis of Recent Growth in Bargaining Units and Representation Efforts in Higher Education," *Journal of Collective Bargaining in the Academy* 8:1 (December 2016): art. 1.

5. By contingent faculty, we mean all full- and part-time faculty who work on short- or long-term contracts, with no opportunity for tenure. In fact, all faculty are somewhat contingent based on the corporatization of higher education, with the response to budget crises due to the COVID pandemic as an extreme case.

6. All interviews were confidential; the names of interviewees are withheld by mutual agreement. Interviews with contingent faculty members, August 13, 17, 25, 2020, and September 13, 2020.

7. Stephanie Ross, Larry Savage, and James Watson, "University Teachers and Resistance in the Neoliberal University," *Labor Studies Journal* 45:3 (September 2020): 227–249.

8. Ibid., 231–232.

9. Ibid., 232. See also Maria Maisto's essay herein.

10. For more data on these trends, see Sue Doe and Steven Shulman's essay in this collection.

11. David Kociemba, "Overcoming the Challenges of Contingent Faculty Organizing," *Academe* 100:5 (September-October 2014): 10–17.

12. Ibid.

13. Giroux, *University in Chains*, 188–121; Annelise Orleck, *"We Are All Fast-Food Workers Now": The Global Uprising against Poverty Wages* (Boston: Beacon Press, 2018), 66–67; Jack Longmate and Frank Cosco, "A Program for Change: Real Transformation over Two Decades, Revision: August 2016," Vancouver Community College Faculty Association, http://vccfa.ca/wp-content/uploads/2021/01/ProgramForChange.pdf.

14. See Gwendolyn Alker's essay in this collection for more detail on the feminization of contingency in the academy.

15. American Federation of Teachers (AFT), *Promoting Racial and Ethnic Diversity in the Faculty: What Higher Education Unions Can Do*, 2010, https://www.aft.org/sites/default/files/facultydiversity0310.pdf.

16. Tressie McMillan Cottom, "The New Old Labor Crisis," *Slate,* January 24, 2014, https://slate.com/human-interest/2014/01/adjunct-crisis-in-higher-ed-an-all-too-familiar-story-for-black-faculty.html; AAUP, "The Status of Non-Tenure-Track Faculty," 1993, https://www.aaup.org/AAUP/comm/rep/nontenuretrack.htm-2.

17. "The Snail-Like Progress of Blacks in Faculty Ranks of Higher Education," *News & Views* (Blog), *Journal of Blacks in Higher Education*, accessed December 24, 2020, https://www.jbhe.com/news_views/62_blackfaculty.html; AFT, "Promoting Racial and Ethnic Diversity in the Faculty."

18. Sherri L. Wallace, Sharon E. Moore, Linda L. Wilson, and Brenda G. Hart, "African American Women in the Academy: Quelling the Myth of Presumed Incompetence," in *Presumed Incompetent: The Intersections of Race and Class for Women in Academia*, ed. Gabriella Gutierrez y Muhs, Yolanda Flores Niemann, Carmen G. Gonzalez, and Angela P. Harris (Boulder, CO: University Press of Colorado, 2012), 421–438. See also Nancy MacLean, *Freedom Is Not Enough: The Opening of the American Workplace* (New York: Russell Sage Foundation, 2006), 187–192.

19. Chaumtoli Huq, "Women of Color and the Precarity of Their Intellectual Labor," *Women's Studies Quarterly* 45:3/4 (Fall/Winter 2017): 353–358.

20. Ibid.

21. Interview with full-time contingent faculty member, December 15, 2020. AFT, "Promoting Racial and Ethnic Diversity in the Faculty"; see also Gutierrez y Muhs et al., *Presumed Incompetent.*

22. Cottom, "The New Old Labor Crisis"; "The Snail-Like Progress of Blacks in Faculty Ranks of Higher Education."

23. COCAL, "About COCAL," accessed October 29, 2020, www.cocalinternational.org/aboutus.html. See essays by Anne Wiegard, Herbert and Van der Naald, and Jeff Schuhrke in this collection.

24. COCAL, "Political Declaration of COCAL X Coalition of Contingent Academic Labor, Mexico City, August 9–12, 2012," accessed November 3, 2020, https://www.cocalinternational.org/declaration.html.

25. New Faculty Majority, "History," and "NFM's 7 Goals," accessed October 29, 2020, www.newfacultymajority.info; see also Wiegard's essay in this collection.

26. SEIU Faculty Forward, "United to Transform Higher Education," accessed November 3, 2020, http://seiufacultyforward.org/about/; see also Anne McLeer's essay in this collection.

27. Herbert, "The Winds of Changes Shift"; Ross, Savage, and Watson, "University Teachers and Resistance in the Neoliberal University"; See also Herbert and van der Naald's essay in this collection.

28. Herbert, "The Winds of Changes Shift." For a more detailed discussion of faculty unionization, see also Herbert and van der Naald's essay in this collection.

29. American Association of University Professors, *Contract Database*, accessed March 18, 2020, https://www.aaup.org/chapter-resources/contract-database.

30. Collective Bargaining Agreement between Emerson Los Angeles chapter of the American Association of University Professors (ELA-AAUP) and Emerson College, September 1, 2016 through June 30, 2020, https://emerson.app.box.com/s/v6d4aq0y86u00 zvy5nfpv830uscpn7fm.

31. Agreement between Rutgers, the State University of New Jersey and PTLFC-AAUP-AFT and July 1, 2018 through June 30, 2022, https://rutgersaaup.org/wp-content/ uploads/2020/03/PTL-Final-Agreement-2018–2022.pdf.

32. Interview with part-time lecturers, August 25, 2020 and September 13, 2020.

33. Collective Bargaining Agreement, by and between Hofstra University and the Hofstra Chapter of the American Association of University Professors, September 1, 2016 through August 31, 2021, https://aaup-hofstra.org/wp-content/uploads/2016/11/Final-2016 -2021-AAUP-Collective-Bargaining-Agreement.pdf.

34. Collective Bargaining Agreement, Board of Trustees of Oakland University, Rochester, Michigan, and the Oakland University Chapter of the American Association of University Professors, September 1, 2015, through August 14, 2020, http://oaklandaaup.org/ res/2015–20agreement.pdf.

35. Agreement between the State of New York and United University Professions, July 2, 2016, through July 1, 2022, https://uupinfo.org/contract/pdf/20162022 NYSUUPAgreement.pdf.

36. Collective Bargaining Agreement between Connecticut State University American Association of University Professors and Board of Trustees for Connecticut State University System, August 26, 2016, through August 26, 2021, https://www.ct.edu/files/ pdfs/2016–2021%20AAUP%20Contract.pdf; Collective Bargaining Agreement Administration of St. John's University, New York, and the St. John's Chapter of the American Association of University Professors (AAUP-FA), July 1, 2017, through June 30, 2019, https://www.stjohns.edu/sites/default/files/uploads/cba_final_2017-2019.pdf.

37. Collective Bargaining Agreement, Rider University and the Rider Chapter of the American Association of University Professors (AAUP), September 1, 2017, through August 31, 2020, https://www.rider.edu/sites/default/files/files/aaup_agreement_2017-20_rev -Oct2018.pdf.

38. Interview with full-time lecturer, August 23, 2020; see also the essays by Claire Goldstene and Claire Raymond in this collection.

39. Interview with part-time faculty member, August 17, 2020.

40. Interview with full-time faculty member, September 11, 2020.

41. john a. powell and Stephen Menendian, "The Problem of Othering: Towards Inclusiveness and Belonging," *Othering and Belonging* 1 (Summer 2016), http://www.othering andbelonging.org/issue-1/.

42. Patrick Iber, "How to Treat Adjuncts," *Inside Higher Ed*, October 24, 2014, https://www .insidehighered.com/advice/2014/10/24/essay-how-tenure-track-faculty-members -should-treat-adjuncts.

43. Interviews with contingent faculty members, August 17, 2020, and September 13, 2020.

44. Iber, "How to Treat Adjuncts."

45. Interview with contingent faculty member, September 11, 2020; Annemarie Pérez, "A Radical Idea about Adjuncting: Written for Those with Tenure (or on the Tenure Track)," *Cited at the Crossroads*, accessed August 2020, https://citedatthecrossroads.net/ blog/2018/04/01/a-radical-idea-about-adjuncting-written-for-those-with-tenure-or -on-the-tenure-track/.

46. Interview with full-time contingent faculty member, December 15, 2020. See also Aimee Loiselle essay herein.

47. See Loiselle essay.

48. Interviews with contingent faculty members, August 17, 2020, and August 23, 2020.

49. Iber, "How to Treat Adjuncts."

50. Interview with part-time lecturers, August 25, 2020, and September 13, 2020.

51. For a detailed discussion of business unionism see Trevor Griffey's essay in this collection; see also Gary Rhoades's essay on social justice unionism, as well as the essay by Herbert and van der Naald in this collection.

52. Joseph A. McCartin, Marilyn Sneiderman, and Maurice BP-Weeks, "Combustible Convergence: Bargaining for the Common Good and the #RedforEd Uprisings of 2018," *Labor Studies Journal* 45:1 (2020): 97–113; Rutgers AAUP-AFT, "Who We Are: Coalition of Rutgers Unions," accessed December 26, 2020, https://www.rutgersaaup.org/who-we-are -coalition-of-rutgers-trade-unions/.

53. Rick Baum, "The Exploitation of Part-Time Teachers in Higher Education," *New Politics*, February 7, 2019, accessed September 15, 2020, https://newpol.org/the-exploitation -of-part-time-teachers-in-higher-education/.

CHAPTER 20

HOW THE ISOLATION OF CONTINGENCY UNDERMINES THE PUBLIC GOOD OF EDUCATION

CLAIRE GOLDSTENE

Ideas are indeed the most dangerous weapons in the world.
—William O. Douglas

A myth persists that universities are isolated from the "real world." In that story of higher education, faculty and students exist in a sheltered enclave where the consideration of abstract ideas has little relevance to the seemingly mundane concerns—such as preparing to make a living—so central to the lives of most people. Despite this imagined idyll, however, and no less than any other essential sector of American society, postsecondary education is deeply enmeshed in and affected by real-world political economy.

Over the last forty years, higher education has undergone a series of wide-ranging transformations. These include a dramatic increase in the number of students and their greater diversity, a change that has been accompanied by deep cuts in state funding to public universities; the privatization of costs through rapidly rising tuition at public and private colleges and correspondingly crushing student debt; a growing number of for-profit colleges; a renewed enthusiasm for managing universities as businesses; and a burgeoning number of highly paid administrators.[1] An essential part of this remaking of college life has been a remaking of the faculty. Since 2010, upward of 75 percent of those teaching in higher education are contingent faculty, or off the tenure-track, while only 25 percent are tenure-track/tenured. This transformation in higher education is, of course, part of a trend in other economic sectors with downward pressures on working conditions and pay amid a greater reliance on gig workers.[2]

Broadly, "contingent faculty" encompasses a multitude of part-time and full-time employment arrangements, all of which feature some measure of uncertainty. Among these are: adjuncts hired semester-to-semester and generally paid per course, faculty on one-year or multiyear contracts, visiting professors, graduate student workers, and post-docs.[3] In the 1970s, however, the ratios were flipped: 75 percent of faculty were tenure-track/tenured and 25 percent contingent. At that time, adjuncts mostly worked full-time outside of academe and taught an occasional course in their area of expertise. Today, though, increasing numbers of contingent faculty, many more of whom hold PhDs than in the past, struggle to support themselves and their families in a field that shares many features with other precarious work—low wages (notoriously difficult to determine, most contingent faculty report making less than $25,000 annually and less than $3,500 per course), generally no health or retirement benefits, few opportunities for upward advancement, and little-to-no job security.[4] The explanation for this decline in the working conditions for a majority of higher education faculty is as much political as it is economic.

Escalating inequities among faculty mirror the vast inequalities of wealth that currently plague the country—a small number of highly paid academic superstars at elite institutions, a growing majority of insecurely employed low-paid contingent faculty who do the majority of teaching, and a shrinking middle of fewer and fewer tenure-track job holders. The intensification of economic disparities in the United States has been dated to the 1980s and the implementation of policies that consolidated corporate power, deregulated major industries, launched a successful political and legal assault against workers and unions, and enacted tax policies that redistributed wealth upward, all of which resulted in greater wealth for the few and declining or stagnant wages for the many. So too, the growing reliance on contingent faculty can be traced to the Reagan era.

Certainly the 2008 recession and more recent economic contractions, along with cuts to state budgets, accelerated the swelling numbers of temporarily employed faculty. But it is a transition with a longer history. Over the past four decades, universities have increasingly embraced a corporate and market-driven model of management and what William Deresiewicz calls a "commercial relationship" with students.[5] This manifests itself in an understanding of the mission of universities to be less about the public good of a quality education and more about branding, perceived prestige, institutional growth, and enhanced fundraising, all in pursuit of higher national rankings. At the same time, the decline in working conditions for faculty over the last few decades has corresponded with an increase in demand for academic labor. Thus, there is not an overproduction of PhDs but, rather, a shortage of tenure-track jobs. And, while money for faculty wages has declined, overall expenditures have not, as financial resources are redirected to hire more professional staff, to pay administrative salaries, and to build and renovate.[6] The move to a contingent majority has been accompanied by a decline in the standards of faculty employment, with particular implications for the meaning and experience of education. Campuses are not isolated from the "real world" of political and historical developments.

In spring 2020, COVID-19 disrupted the personal and work lives of millions of people who were suddenly subject to stay-at-home orders. In many ways, the changes compelled by COVID extended to others the social isolation and economic uncertainty that so profoundly inform the experience of being contingent faculty. Those deemed nonessential workers scrambled to work from home, homeschool their children, and protect family members considered high risk. Millions more lost their jobs and faced acute and immediate financial hardship. People were instructed to engage in "social distancing" and found themselves isolated from family, friends, and colleagues. These adjustments to COVID parallel how the itinerant and precarious working conditions of contingent faculty, and the structures that maintain them, breed a profound sense of personal and professional isolation. Despite technological innovations that helped to connect people remotely during the pandemic, anxiety, depression, and alienation spiked amid a renewed appreciation for the inherent sociability of humans and the emotional toll of isolation.

The Body

The physical segregation of contingent from tenured faculty on campuses both epitomizes and symbolizes their subordinate status. Those contingent faculty afforded a workspace frequently find that it is temporary, if they are camped out in someone else's office; generally not private, if they are sharing a desk in a room with other contingent faculty and graduate students; and almost always geographically distant from tenured faculty offices. Too often, however, the trunk of a car serves as an office to store papers, books, and other teaching material. A corporeal reminder of their subservient standing, this physical isolation makes teaching difficult. Frequently, contingent faculty must meet students in cafes, lounges, hallways, or on public benches to discuss confidential matters and retreat to the library to find a place to prepare for class. Further, these arrangements isolate contingent faculty from the collegial life of a department, as this separation often extends to departmental social gatherings, departmental meetings, and other department-sponsored activities. All of this limits the chances of serendipitous encounters while marking the gap, both real and metaphorical, between tenured and contingent faculty. In some cases, contingent faculty are explicitly excluded; in others they are simply not thought about enough to be invited.

The embodiment of this physical isolation is exacerbated by the conditions of contingent labor. In order to cobble together some sort of living, adjuncts often travel from campus to campus to teach. This itinerant and ephemeral existence extends to the hiring and firing of contingents. Long-term adjuncts may be re-tained, new adjuncts hired, and other contingent faculty simply "disappeared" from a department days before a term ends or begins and without due process or announcement to others in the department. Contingent faculty are quite literally not seen by their tenured colleagues. Some have likened the experience of contin-gency to being "untouchable."[7]

The Mind

Contingent faculty are generally not considered full intellectual members of their departments. Despite often doing the majority of teaching—whether measured by the number of classes or the number of students taught—contingent faculty are generally not part of discussions related to curriculum and program development. Though presumed to be short-term hires and, hence, less invested in departmental concerns than tenured faculty, many contingents work for years or even decades in the same department, despite not knowing, from one year to the next, or even one semester to the next, if they will return. Existing at the periphery constrains opportunities to share pedagogical strategies or scholarly interests or to discuss pertinent departmental or campus issues. All of this conspires to intensify intel-lectual isolation. The implicit message to students is that, while these faculty *are not* sufficiently qualified to enjoy full membership in the campus community, they *are* sufficiently qualified to teach you.

The cumulative effect of intellectual isolation, and the constraints that result from teaching a large number of classes and students, prioritizes efficiency in in-struction. This creates structural impediments that contingent faculty continually struggle against. Overworked contingents often have little time to identify new reading assignments, refresh syllabi, or incorporate new interpretative develop-ments into their courses. Thus, teaching can begin to resemble an assembly line—and like an assembly line, there is little time or space for originality to flourish. These difficulties can be compounded when contingent faculty, especially those in the most precarious positions, might self-censor or reduce the rigor of courses for fear of critical student evaluations that could jeopardize already uncertain em-ployment or develop course material with administrators rather than students in mind. Higher education should expose students to controversial material, push them to question what they previously took for granted, and allow teachers time to think about the material they present. This all requires that faculty take risks in the classroom. However, in the twenty-first-century iteration of higher education the working conditions of contingent faculty contrive to preclude such an education. Despite often being among the strongest educators on campus, the obstacles that contingents confront cheat students out of experiencing the best versions of those who teach them.[8]

Further, that contingent faculty are assigned primarily introductory survey courses implies that they lack the capacity to teach more advanced classes, serving as yet another reminder of their presumed inferiority.[9] Ironically, though, introductory teaching is among the most important on a college campus. It is also the most difficult, with the heaviest workload and the greatest challenges. These classes reach the largest number of students and offer a chance to recruit new majors into a department. Sadly, however, students drawn to a field of study through a survey taught by contingent faculty often have little opportunity to take another course with those teachers, since they are generally consigned to teach only introductory classes. In the long run, this strategy often lowers enrollment in departmental programs, since students take teachers, not courses. All of this exposes the hypocrisy of the frequently invoked claim about the symbiotic relationship between teaching and scholarship—not because there is no truth to it but, rather, because too often "scholars," under enormous pressure to endlessly publish, teach very little.

The challenges encountered by those contingent faculty interested in participating more fully in their respective scholarly communities exacerbate this intellectual isolation. Often, they have neither the time nor the money to do so. As permanently temporary faculty, contingents are generally ineligible for departmental or university-wide funding to support research and writing or attendance at professional conferences; with no course releases or sabbaticals, any extended time away from teaching to pursue a research agenda necessitates a drop in an already uncertain and low income. The myriad ways that contingent faculty working conditions make professional participation difficult further fortifies the perception that they are not the intellectual peers of tenured faculty. Thus, an enthusiasm about their field that they would hope to share with students is diminished. That some contingent faculty manage to engage in scholarly work is testament to their commitment, not a reflection of welcome or encouragement. Consequently, and despite claims about the importance of teaching, in an academic environment that affords greater prestige to research and publishing the circumstances under which contingents labor act as barriers to scholarly pursuits which, in turn, reaffirms their lower status within the profession.

The physical and intellectual isolation that typify academic contingency are manifestations of the institutional structures through which contingent faculty must navigate their careers. But more than this, such isolation reinforces and reproduces these same structures, imbuing them with a kind of inevitability.

The Spirit

Many assume that opportunities exist within the academy, that the talented are recognized and rewarded, and that the status of contingent faculty reflects merely their professional inadequacies. Such a view is embedded in the deeply American notion of equal opportunity and its accompanying claims to meritocracy, effectively placing responsibility for the outcomes of underlying conditions on the shoulders of individuals. Historically in America, the ideology of equal opportunity has functioned to place the onus for one's economic and social status on character and effort as opposed to larger systemic causes, which functions to perpetuate inequities and the structures that sustain them.[10] Thus, a social phenomenon is reshaped and experienced as personal failure. In the meantime, 75 percent of advertised faculty positions are non-tenure-track.[11]

For those who experience the attendant physical and intellectual isolation of contingency, attachment to the ideological tradition of equal opportunity expresses itself as political isolation in the form of self-blame: "If I was a better teacher, I'd have a tenure-track job"; "If I was a better scholar, I'd have a tenure-track job"; "If I'd published more as a graduate student, I'd have a tenure-track job." And there is a deep sense that these judgments are shared by others in the university. As long-term adjunct Herb Childress remarked, "the presumption of others' unworthiness and the ability to keep them out of sight have always been powerful potions that soothe the conscience of the comfortable."[12]

One antidote to the self-blame engendered by the deleterious working conditions of contingent teaching, and the sense of powerlessness that often accompanies it, is collective action.[13] A united response helps break down the walls that facilitate the physical, intellectual, and political isolation that too often characterize contingency. Building on a shared experience among contingent faculty, as well as other low-paid temporary workers in an economy where the casualization of labor is becoming the norm, union and worker organizing among contingent faculty has blossomed across the country over the last ten years in community colleges, private four-year colleges, and large public universities. At a time of historically low union density, and despite near unanimous resistance from administrators as well as, in many cases, tenured colleagues, union growth among contingent faculty has been on the rise. Demands have centered not only on pay and benefits but, equally, on job security and employment due process.

Central to many organizing campaigns have been efforts to situate the altered working conditions for college and university faculty within a context of changes in higher education management that are themselves a manifestation of national political and social forces; in other words, to respond to the political isolation of contingency with political engagement. This begins with redirecting a critical gaze away from individual "failure" and toward, instead, the institutional structures that breed and benefit from a growing contingent faculty workforce. In turn, this compels consideration of the role of the university in the public sphere, the larger consequences for higher education at play in the shift to a majority contingent faculty, and how the intersection of these two factors both reflects and affects broader political conditions. Thus, what happens on college and university campuses is deeply enmeshed in the struggles of the communities of which they are a part.

The Soul

As part of the public sphere, universities are political spaces. And, within them classrooms are contested terrains. Education provides necessary skills and knowledge to fulfill the needs of prospective employers while it simultaneously contains a disruptive potential as, especially through the liberal arts, it prepares students for greater engagement in civic life. This is seen, for example, in frequent and heated debates about how US history is taught. Is it a triumphant story of expanding rights? Is it a story infused by oppression? Is it a story of great men and their accomplishments? Is it a story of marginalized people struggling to exercise agency? Is it a simple story or a complex and multifaceted one? That so many people remain so deeply invested in how that story is told speaks to the power of education generally, and to the power of historical narrative particularly. And, while the arc of the story may change, there is wide agreement that curriculum is a matter for public discussion and debate.

At various times in the twentieth century universities acted as important sites for the elaboration of ideas essential to progressive politics. This tendency was vividly displayed early in that century as the Wisconsin Idea informed the emergence of Progressivism; in the middle of the century with the student protests of the 1960s; and, more recently, in the influence of multiculturalism on American political and public life, which in numerous ways grew out of that earlier activism. While many celebrated these developments, for others they clearly demonstrated the threat that education could pose to the status quo when, rather than focusing on job training for emerging industry, it led students to question social norms and, most alarmingly, encouraged them to imagine altering those norms.

In 1962, students at the University of Michigan drafted the Port Huron Statement, a foundational document for Students for a Democratic Society, as well as student protests throughout that decade. A reflection of deep dissatisfaction, the statement famously begins by proclaiming, "We are people of this generation, bred in at least modest comfort, housed now in universities, looking uncomfortably to the world we inherit."[14] Secure in their expectation of a continued middle-class existence after graduation, these SDS members critically assessed society with a certain confidence. Reflecting a mood among students at universities across the country and building on the civil rights protests of the 1950s, what ensued were demands for civil rights, calls for student rights and free speech on campuses, protests against the US war in Vietnam, a questioning of the economic system, and an insistence on a more diverse faculty, student body, and educational curriculum.

But this democratization and opening of higher education did not go unchallenged. By 1971, the US Chamber of Commerce commissioned future Supreme Court Justice Lewis Powell to draft a plan on behalf of the Chamber's Education Committee to counter what they considered, as proclaimed in the memo's title, an "Attack on American Free Enterprise System."[15] The memo identified college campuses as the place where "much of the criticism emanates," especially among social science faculty. To counter this, Powell recommended a well-funded nationally coordinated response that included identifying scholars and speakers sympathetic to free enterprise who could also evaluate the content of assigned course readings, demanding "political balance" among faculty, and extending this influence to all elements of the media.[16] While not formally adopted by the Chamber, the memo provided a blueprint for much conservative activism that followed.

In the late 2010s, the conservative youth organization Turning Point USA created a "Professor Watchlist," publishing the "names of professors that advance a radical agenda in lecture halls." Additionally, various state legislatures have proposed laws to, among other things, use political party affiliation to determine faculty appointments (Iowa in 2017) and require faculty members to "reflect the ideological balance of the citizens of the state" (North Carolina in 2017). Although both of these bills failed, they would have compelled faculty to reveal their political preferences as part of the hiring process.[17] In 2021 and early 2022, efforts to ban or restrict the teaching of "critical race theory"—misrepresented and ill-defined—in secondary and, in some cases, postsecondary public schools gained traction in thirty-seven state houses across the country.[18] By early 2023, Florida considered legislation that sought both to weaken tenure by allowing political appointees to review the tenure status of any faculty member and to control the content of teaching by eliminating majors/minors in "Critical Race Theory, Gender Studies, and Intersectionality," while also prescribing content favoring "western civilization."[19]

These legislative efforts are overt in their attempt to control the content of education. The isolation that attends teaching as a contingent faculty member, however, functions covertly to constrict the content of education. Such endeavors, whether in the open or embedded in institutional structures, are precisely what academic freedom is intended to deflect. Academic freedom shields teachers against reprisals from administrators, donors, students, politicians, and others for the articulation of controversial or unpopular views that are essential to innovative intellectual work, which promotes the public good through the unfettered advancement of knowledge.[20] In turn, this is protected by the economic security and due process provisions of tenure. And, as academic freedom comes under attack, so too does tenure.

In 2021, lawmakers in Iowa, Georgia, and South Carolina proposed legislation that would have prevented any public university or college from extending tenure to faculty.[21] In the meantime, tenure in other states, notably in the University of Wisconsin system, has been substantially weakened.[22]

As various legislative efforts to diminish academic freedom wend their way through the political process, the same outcome is achieved by creating a majority of temporarily employed faculty often laboring in isolation and who, by definition, are excluded from the protections of academic freedom and tenure. As former Secretary of Education Betsy DeVos made clear when she warned college students that "the faculty, from adjunct professors to deans, tell you what to do, what to say, and more ominously what to think," the political stakes of education's public purpose center on what happens inside the classroom.[23] Those on the political right have long recognized the importance of the educational arena in their efforts to roll back the social and economic changes that resulted from the activism of the 1960s. This work has, at least in part, animated the decades-long increase in the numbers of contingent faculty as part of a larger offensive against tenure and, with it, academic freedom.

Academic freedom is rooted in an understanding of education derived from a liberal arts tradition that challenges assertions of fixed truths and of claims that greater knowledge inheres in some people by virtue of birth or position. This version of education promotes a mode of inquiry that requires the continual reconsideration of scientific and social phenomena through a commitment to perpetual and expanded collective learning as advancing the public good. As such, it disdains the seeming permanence of orthodoxy and celebrates questioning what was previously thought inviolate. Born out of a rejection of historic claims to special knowledge among, for example, religious and political leaders, academic freedom is yoked to efforts intended to expand access to learning and knowledge to greater numbers of people and, in so doing, extending to them greater power. In these ways, an education that asks critical questions about existing power arrangements is inherently progressive, regardless of partisan affiliation. One way to erode an education grounded in this liberal arts tradition is to create a large caste of economically insecure teachers and, thus, foster intellectual isolation and timidity rather than intellectual collaboration and courage.

The most potent element of education is an approach to knowledge. Hence, the politics of education are not about political parties or even prescriptive policies but, instead, about ways of thinking. Academic freedom ultimately protects collective inquiry that challenges conventional wisdom and encourages the reconsideration of seemingly established and settled truths. This informs both the sciences and the humanities. The philosopher Robert Paul Wolff described universities as "the only major viable institutional centers of opposition to the dominant values and politics of the society," a role that "flows from its very nature as a center of free inquiry."[24] As information expands and debates about what constitutes evidence evolve, knowledge and understanding shift. Hence, there is no "end of history," only a perpetual seeking that builds on prior knowledge.

However, the financial precariousness, intense isolation, and marginalization of contingent faculty profoundly undermine a model of education centered on critical thinking and the free exchange of ideas so crucial to open inquiry. The working conditions of those who do the most college teaching affect the substantive content of curricula—what is taught and how it is taught. Given the circumstances under which contingents struggle, teachers can too easily become interchangeable parts whose influence is diluted as they deliver a set of data points lacking nuance, creativity, or independent thought. A large pool of low-paid economically insecure faculty teaching from a position of fear are less likely to take intellectual risks, which reduces the possibility of rigorous classroom discussion that questions the status quo. Students then experience a commensurate education, as they themselves, facing an uncertain financial future and the prospect of entering postcollege life deeply in debt, are encouraged to view college as merely an investment in job training. As a result, the vision of an alternative future—one that looks different from the present—is unlikely to emerge from universities, which further diminishes their social relevance. This fundamentally alters the role of the university in the public sphere. The rise of contingency is, finally, about who controls teaching and the very purpose of an education. As a consequence, the educational experience for students is narrowed at precisely the moment it should be broadened.

Importantly, the distribution of these competing models of education is not equitable. Rates of contingency are highest at community colleges, which serve a greater percentage of first-generation students, often from working-class backgrounds, and students of color. Thus, while the "value" of education for these students is calculated in terms of job training imparted by an overworked and underpaid faculty, students at elite universities continue to enjoy an education more firmly grounded in the liberal arts that prioritizes intellectual and social exploration, with an expectation that they will graduate to fulfill more influential and often lucrative occupations. In part, then, the response to the expansion of access to higher education for previously excluded groups has been to further institutionalize a tiered system that is hardened by the shift to a majority contingent faculty.

We arrive at a place, then, that involves more than frustration about minimal access to the institutional support necessary to teach well. We arrive at a place where the physical, intellectual, and political isolation that characterize contingent teaching embody the imposition of obstacles that actually *impede* the capacity of the majority of higher education faculty to teach. That contingent faculty teach as well as they do illustrates their determination to navigate the many barriers that, cumulatively, reduce their influence inside their own classrooms and among their students. Essential to any response to this alarming circumstance is for those laboring in isolation and under the burdens of the contingent teaching regime to reclaim both their personal and political power as part of efforts to ensure the realization of education as a public good, while also connecting their efforts to other precarious workers' struggles to overcome isolation and secure stable employment.

Notes

1. See Elizabeth Tandy Shermer's and Gary Rhoades's essays in this volume.

2. These changes are dramatically illustrated in the California State University System. Between 1990 and 2017, full-time enrollment increased by 51.6 percent, while fulltime faculty, many of whom were also contingent, increased by only 23 percent during that same time, and as the number of tenure-track faculty *decreased* by 4.7 percent. At the same time, between 1993 and 2016, there was an 88.5 percent increase in the number of administrators and senior staff. Henry Reichman, *The Future of Academic Freedom* (Baltimore: Johns Hopkins University Press, 2019), 139. See also Trevor Griffey's essay in this volume.

3. The language of contingency can be problematic. Labels such as "non-tenure-track" define someone by what they are not, rather than what they are, while "contingent" implies something that is nonessential and peripheral. However, it is also important to highlight the marginalized status and precarious employment of academic workers who lack the political and economic protections available to their tenured colleagues. Also, problematically, other labels can obscure the contingent nature of employment. For a list of contingent faculty job titles, see Joe Berry, *Reclaiming the Ivory Tower: Organizing Adjuncts to Change Higher Education* (New York: Monthly Review Press, 2005), xi.

4. Colleen Flaherty, "Barely Getting By," *Inside Higher Ed,* April 20, 2020, accessed April 15, 2022, https://www.insidehighered.com/news/2020/04/20/new-report-says-many-adjuncts-make-less-3500-course-and-25000-year.

5. William Deresiewicz, *Excellent Sheep: The Miseducation of the American Elite and the Way to a Meaningful Life* (New York: Free Press, 2014), 69.

6. Adrianna Kezar, Tom DePaola, and Daniel T. Scott, *The Gig Academy: Mapping Labor in the Neoliberal University* (Baltimore: Johns Hopkins University Press, 2019), 63, 70.

7. See Claire Raymond's essay in this volume.

8. See Claire Goldstene, "Designed to Fail: Adjunct Faculty and the Fight for Education," *Working USA: The Journal of Labor & Society* 18 (September 2015): 367–375.

9. The History Department at Oberlin has enacted a policy that, as part of meeting the requirements of the major, students must take "at least 5 full courses taught by faculty regularly appointed in the History Department." The implication being that courses taught by those temporarily appointed are not adequate. See https://catalog.oberlin.edu/preview_program.php?catoid=40&poid=5737&returnto=1448.

10. For a discussion of the origins of the ideology of equal opportunity see Claire Goldstene, *The Struggle for America's Promise: Equal Opportunity at the Dawn of Corporate Capital* (Jackson: University Press of Mississippi, 2014), 3–20.

11. Kezar, DePaola, and Scott, *The Gig Academy,* 44.

12. Herb Childress, *The Adjunct Underclass: How America's Colleges Betrayed Their Faculty, Their Students, and Their Mission* (Chicago: University of Chicago Press, 2019), 113.

13. See Part III of this volume for examples of such collective action.

14. Students for a Democratic Society (US), "The Port Huron Statement (1962)," accessed July 12, 2020, http://www.progressivefox.com/misc_documents/PortHuronStatement.pdf.

15. Lewis F. Powell Jr., "Attack on American Free Enterprise System," August 23, 1971, accessed September 15, 2012, https://www.greenpeace.org/usa/democracy/the-lewis-powell-memo-a-corporate-blueprint-to-dominate-democracy/. Among the remedies suggested in the Trilateral Commission's 1975 report on student unrest was to temper those demanding progressive change by reinserting a measure of economic anxiety into the economy. See Paul N. Goldstene, *Revolution, American Style: The Nineteen-Sixties and Beyond* (Novato, CA: Chandler & Sharp, 1997), 65–67.

16. The memo also identified other areas of American political life where similar programs could be implemented. See Nancy MacLean, *Democracy in Chains: The Deep History of the Radical Right's Stealth Plan for America* (New York: Viking, 2017), 125–126; and Kim Phillips-Fein, *Invisible Hands: The Making of the Conservative Movement from the New Deal to Reagan* (New York: W. W. Norton, 2009), 156–165.

17. Reichman, *The Future of Academic Freedom*, 263.

18. "Map: Where Critical Race Theory Is Under Attack," *Education Week,* June 11, 2021, updated February 3, 2022, accessed February 5, 2022, https://www.edweek.org/policy-politics/map-where-critical-race-theory-is-under-attack/2021/06.

19. "An Act Relating to Public Postsecondary Educational Institutions," Florida House of Representatives, 2023, HB 999, 13, 22–23, accessed March 11, 2023, https://www.flsenate.gov/Session/Bill/2023/999/BillText/Filed/PDF.

20. As Joan Scott and others have noted, the dependence of academic freedom on peer review, or "communal self-regulation," can lead to a circumstance where, in the name of professional standards, an academic discipline becomes "necessarily exclusionary" and that, consequently, "scholarly critique could be threatened from within." Joan Wallach Scott, *Knowledge, Power, and Academic Freedom* (New York: Columbia University Press, 2019), 23.

21. Vanessa Miller, "Iowa Lawmaker Wants Public University Employees Polled about Their Political Affiliation," *Gazette,* February 10, 2021, accessed February 5, 2022, https://www.thegazette.com/education/iowa-lawmaker-wants-public-university-employees-polled-about-their-political-affiliation/; and Mark J. Drozdowski, "Tenure Under Attack Nationwide," *Best Colleges,* December 8, 2021, accessed February 5, 2022, https://www.bestcolleges.com/news/analysis/2021/12/07/tenure-under-attack-nationwide/.

22. Reichman, *The Future of Academic Freedom*, 263. Among other changes, post-tenure dismissal is allowed on the "sole initiative of an administrator," and it is easier to eliminate program areas and their associated faculty.

23. Quoted in Scott, *Knowledge, Power, and Academic Freedom*, 113.

24. Quoted in Reichman, *The Future of Academic Freedom,* 206.

Contributors

GWENDOLYN ALKER, PhD, is the director of Theatre Studies and an associate arts professor (contract faculty) in the Drama Department at Tisch School of the Arts, New York University, where she teaches classes on gender and Latinx performance. She has published in *Theatre Journal*, *Drama Therapy Review*, *TDR*, and *Dance Research Journal,* and is the former editor of *Theatre Topics* and former managing editor of *Women & Performance: A Journal of Feminist Theory*.

DIANE ANGELL has taught as a non-tenure-track faculty member at St. Olaf College for the last twenty years, teaching both biology and environmental studies. She has taught approximately eight to ten different courses in the last six years. She has a PhD from Brown University in ecology and evolutionary biology and frequently works in the field of conservation biology.

JOE BERRY is a retired contingent labor educator and organizer and author of *Reclaiming the Ivory Tower: Organizing Adjuncts to Change Higher Education*. He edits the Coalition of Contingent Academic Labor (COCAL) Updates. With Helena Worthen, he coauthored *Power Despite Precarity: Strategies for the Contingent Faculty Movement in Higher Education*. He serves on the board of New Faculty Majority, the International Advisory Committee of COCAL, and is a delegate to Higher Education Labor United from COCAL and to AFT Local 2121.

SUE DOE, a professor of English, teaches composition, autoethnographic theory and method, reading and writing connections, research methods, and graduate teaching assistant preparation for writing instruction. She taught off the tenure track for the first twenty-plus years of her career, recently served as chair of the Colorado State University Faculty Council, and directs the university's Institute for Learning and Teaching. She does research in three areas—academic labor and the faculty career, writing across the curriculum, and student-veteran transition in the post-9/11 era.

ERIC FURE-SLOCUM, a long-term contingent faculty member at St. Olaf College, authored *Contesting the Postwar City: Working-Class and Growth Politics in 1940s Milwaukee* and coedited *Civic Labors: Scholar Activism and Working-Class Studies* (University of Illinois Press, 2016). He taught as a Fulbright scholar in Norway and Romania, served as a Posse mentor, cofounded the Labor and Working-Class History Association's contingent faculty committee, and serves on the Organization of American Historians' executive board.

CLAIRE GOLDSTENE taught as contingent faculty at the University of Maryland, the University of North Florida, and American University. She has published extensively on contingent faculty issues and served on the board of New Faculty Majority Foundation. She is also the author of *The Struggle for America's Promise: Equal Opportunity at the Dawn of Corporate Capital* and is currently working on a book about free speech in the early twentieth-century United States.

TREVOR GRIFFEY, PhD, is a lecturer in labor studies at UCLA and in US history at UC Irvine. He coedited *Black Power at Work: Community Control, Affirmative Action, and the Construction Industry* and cofounded the Seattle Civil Rights and Labor History Project (https://depts.washington.edu/civilr). He serves as vice president of legislation for the University Council–American Federation of Teachers (UC-AFT), AFT Local 1474.

ERIN HATTON is a professor of sociology at the University at Buffalo (SUNY). Her research is centered in the sociology of work, while also extending into the fields of gender, race, culture, law, and social policy. Her recent book, *Coerced: Work Under Threat of Punishment*, compares four very different groups of workers—incarcerated, workfare, college athlete, and graduate student—to identify control over status as a form of labor coercion.

WILLIAM A. HERBERT is executive director, National Center for the Study of Collective Bargaining in Higher Education and the Professions at Hunter College. His areas of scholarship include labor law and history. He coauthored the *2020 Supplementary Directory of New Bargaining Agents and Contracts in Institutions of Higher*

Education, 2013–2019 and authored "Public Workers" in *City of Workers, City of Struggle: How Labor Movements Changed New York,* edited by Joshua B. Freeman.

ELIZABETH HOHL, an adjunct professor for over twenty years, is currently a full-time non-tenure-track assistant professor of the practice, History Department, at Fairfield University. She is part of the Black Studies Program and cofounder of the Women, Gender, and Sexuality Studies Program. From 2016 to 2020, she co-chaired with Amy Essington the Organization of American Historians' Committee on Part-Time, Adjunct, and Contingent Employment. Her research focuses on African American women activists in the Jim Crow–Progressive Era.

MIGUEL JUÁREZ, PhD, is a writer and faculty/lecturer in history, humanities, and women's and gender studies at two Hispanic-serving institutions in west Texas. He was an associate librarian/archivist from 1999 to 2013 at five tier 1 institutions. His books include *Where Are All the Librarians of Color: The Experiences of People of Color in Academia*, coedited with Rebecca L. Hankins, and *Colors on Desert Walls: The Murals of El Paso*, with photographs by Cynthia Weber Farah.

AIMEE LOISELLE is an assistant professor of history at Central Connecticut State University. She studies the modern United States with a focus on women workers, gender, and race in relation to transnational labor and capital. Her book, *Beyond Norma Rae: How Puerto Rican and Southern White Women Fought for a Place in the American Working Class*, examines how commercial cultural production marginalizes alternative narratives. Loiselle taught as an adjunct professor while completing her award-winning dissertation.

MARIA MAISTO taught English composition as a contingent faculty member for over fifteen years in Maryland and Ohio and has published and spoken widely on the topic of contingent faculty equity, organizing, and coalition building. In 2009, she cofounded New Faculty Majority: The National Coalition for Adjunct and Contingent Equity, a 501(c)(6) membership and advocacy organization, and serves as its president. She has undergraduate and graduate degrees from Georgetown University in Washington, DC.

ANNE MCLEER is the director of Higher Education and Strategic Planning at SEIU Local 500 in the Washington, DC/Maryland area where she oversees the higher education work of the union. She earned a PhD in human sciences from George Washington University in 2002 and has taught in American studies, English, and women's studies as a part-time faculty member at George Washington University. She also served on the board of New Faculty Majority Foundation.

STEVEN PARFITT currently teaches history at a UK secondary school. He has written numerous books and articles on labor history, including *Knights across the Atlantic: The Knights of Labor in Britain and Ireland*, as well as many articles in magazines and newspapers from *The Guardian* to *Jacobin* on historical and contemporary issues, especially casual labor and recent UK university strikes. He has previously served as an anticasualisation officer for the University and College Union.

JIYOON PARK, a PhD candidate in the School of Management and Labor Relations at Rutgers University, researches precarious work/workers, labor institutions, and the future of work. She is particularly interested in new forms of organized labor to protect precarious workers' rights.

CLAIRE RAYMOND taught as a non-tenure-track lecturer at the University of Virginia from 2007 to 2020. Now a visiting collaborative researcher at Princeton University and a visiting assistant professor at Bates College, she is the author of nine books of critical theory, including *Photography and Resistance: Anticolonialist Photography in the Americas*. As Claire Millikin, she is a poet, and recipient of the Maine Literary Award. She lives with her family in rural, coastal Maine.

GARY RHOADES is professor, Center for the Study of Higher Education at the University of Arizona. His research addresses restructuring of academic institutions/occupations/professions, as in *Managed Professionals: Unionized Faculty and Restructuring Academic Labor* and (with Sheila Slaughter) *Academic Capitalism and the New Economy*. A former AAUP general secretary and New Faculty Majority Foundation board member, Rhoades works with various national/local unions and is a UCWAZ, Local 7065 of CWA member.

JEFF SCHUHRKE is an assistant professor at SUNY Empire State University's Harry Van Arsdale Jr. School of Labor Studies in New York City. He earned his PhD in history at the University of Illinois at Chicago (UIC), where he was copresident of the UIC Graduate Employees Organization, American Federation of Teachers Local 6297, from April 2018 to May 2019. He is the author of *Blue-Collar Empire: The AFL-CIO and the Global Cold War*.

ELIZABETH TANDY SHERMER finished her PhD at the University of California, Santa Barbara, where she was a member of the TA union (UAW Local 2865). She is now a professor of history at Loyola University of Chicago. Her most recent book is *Indentured Students: How Government-Guaranteed Loans Left Generations Drowning in College Debt*. She is currently finishing a book on the complex financing of higher education entitled *The Business of Education*.

STEVEN SHULMAN, a professor of economics at Colorado State University since 1984, is director of research for the Center for the Study of Academic Labor. His current research is on academic labor markets and the economics of higher education.

JOSEPH VAN DER NAALD is a PhD candidate in the Program in Sociology at the Graduate Center of the City University of New York, and a researcher at the National Center for the Study of Collective Bargaining in Higher Education and the Professions at Hunter College. His dissertation examines the emergence of public-sector unionization in the US Midwest. Van der Naald has taught as contingent faculty at the CUNY School of Labor and Urban Studies since 2021.

ANNE WIEGARD taught various English courses at many institutions in California and New York in adjunct positions before securing a full-time, non-tenure-track job at SUNY Cortland. She chaired the New Faculty Majority Foundation board of directors from 2011 to 2016. She served on two contract negotiations teams and the statewide executive board for United University Professions (AFT Local 2190). She was appointed to the American Federation of Teachers Higher Education Program and Policy Council, 2017–2020.

NAOMI R WILLIAMS, assistant professor of labor history at Rutgers University, researches working-class urban politics in the late twentieth century. After earning a PhD from University of Wisconsin–Madison in 2014, Williams worked as a full-time contingent faculty member for three years, teaching US labor and Black history. They volunteer with Higher Ed Labor United to help build a wall-to-wall, coast-to-coast, higher education labor movement. Their current book project examines the transformation of class politics in the late twentieth-century United States.

HELENA WORTHEN became active in her union while working as contingent faculty in California. Her book, *What Did You Learn at Work Today? The Forbidden Lessons of Labor Education*, won the Best Book award from the United Association for Labor Education (UALE) in 2014. She and Joe Berry coauthored *Power Despite Precarity: Strategies for the Contingent Faculty Movement in Higher Education*. She is also a delegate to Higher Education Labor United from the National Writers Union.

Index

Morrill, Justin, 41
Morrill Act (1862), 41, 42
Moser, Richard, 63–64, 156, 158, 162

Nation, The, 157
National Bureau of Economic Research, 99
National Center for the Study of Collective
  Bargaining in Higher Education and the
  Professions, 176, 216
National Defense Education Act (NDEA)
  (1958), 48
National Education Association (NEA), 7,
  23, 173, 176
National Health Service (NHS), 235
National Labor Relations Act (NLRA)
  (1935), 7, 8, 25, 45, 47, 62, 76
National Labor Relations Board (NLRB), 7,
  76, 180, 181; Graduate Students Organizing Committee (GSOC), New York University and, 196; graduate unionization
  and, 195
National Public Radio, 212
National Science Foundation (NSF), 130–131
National Study of Postsecondary Faculty, 83
National Youth Administration (NYA), 46
neoliberal higher education, 4, 10, 18, 38–39,
  75, 160–161, 249; contraction, 58–65;
  declining funding and, 59–60; diversity,
  inclusion, and austerity and, 64–65; fac-
  ulty solidarity and, 62–64; just-in-time
  student body and, 60–62; what's next for,
  65–66
neo-racism, 22
New Deal, 45–46, 71
New Deal for Higher Education, 7
New Faculty Majority (NFM), 7, 25, 27, 156,
  157–158, 172–173, 253
New Jersey, 177, 195, 262
New Mexico, 26
New School for Social Research, 177
New Yorker, The, 8
New York, 47, 172, 180
New York State United Teachers (NYSUT),
  173
New York Teachers Union (NYTU), 177
New York University, 195–196, 204
Nixon, Richard, 58
NLRB v. Catholic Bishop of Chicago, 7
NLRB v. Yeshiva University, 7, 62, 76, 181, 183,
  184
non né, 112, 114

non-senate faculty, University of California,
  226–227
nonteaching duties, 178, 254
non-tenure-track (NTT) faculty, 4–5, 6,
  92, 171; disenfranchisement from shared
  governance, 96; inadequate compensation of, 92–93; women in the sciences as,
  125–126. *See also* contingent faculty
nontraditional students, 60–62
North Carolina, 41, 62, 274
North Dakota, 126
Northeastern University, 185
Northwestern University, 201
Notre Dame de Namur University, 184, 185

Oakland University, 256
Ohio, 26
Old in Art School: A Memoir of Starting Over, 140
Olsen, Tillie, 74
Olson, Judy, 173
onboarding, 100
online teaching, 27
Oregon, 26, 195
Organization of American Historians
  (OAH), 6, 35–37; *Standards for Part-Time,
  Adjunct, and Contingent Faculty,* 36
organizing by contingent faculty. *See* collec-
  tive bargaining and organizing
othering, 258
O'Toole, James, 78–79
outsourcing, 9, 228

Pacific Lutheran University, 7, 25, 76
Paine, Thomas, 17
Painter, Nell, 140
Palacios, Lena, 142–143
Park, Jiyoon, 186
Pasadena City College, 98
Patterson, Orlando, 112, 114, 115
pay rates. *See* compensation
Pennsylvania Labor Relations Board, 179–
  180
philanthropy, 39, 43, 45, 47, 51, 56
Piercy, Marge, 174
podcasts, 139
Polishook, Irwin, 23
political base, 172
political capital, 173
political economy, 9, 10
Poo, Ai-Jen, 71
postdoctoral workers, 18, 20

THE WORKING CLASS IN AMERICAN HISTORY

The University of Illinois Press
is a founding member of the
Association of University Presses.

_____

University of Illinois Press
1325 South Oak Street
Champaign, IL 61820-6903
www.press.uillinois.edu